PRAISE FOR *ACT NATURALLY*

"A terrific read that puts the Fabs' films into an insightful and fact-filled context with a fresh perspective on just how important the movies were to their lasting legacy." —**Dennis Elsas**, legendary WNEW FM and WFUV New York disc jockey and co-host of Fab Fourum on Sirius XM

"With *Act Naturally: The Beatles on Film*, Steve Matteo provides readers with the definitive, go-to book for understanding the group's cinematic forays. Chock full of new information, *Act Naturally* is rife with stories about the Fabs' filmic excursions, key aspects of their unparalleled contribution to music and celebrity culture." —**Kenneth Womack**, author of *John Lennon 1980* and *Fandom and the Beatles*

"Steve Matteo is the perfect companion and tour guide in navigating the Beatles' fascinating dalliance with film, from the British New Wave of Richard Lester's *A Hard Day's Night* to the atmospheric verité of Michael Lindsay-Hogg's *Let It Be*. This is a most welcome—and long overdue—exploration of an important but often overlooked facet of the Beatles' saga." —**Mark Rozzo**, author of *Everybody Thought We Were Crazy* and a founding member of Bambi Kino

"Fans of the films of the Beatles have not been given a book to revel in for many years. Steve Matteo has provided one; a deep dive look at the Beatles, their soundtrack music, and films. The Beatles remain the epitome of what a band can be. All-time greats. Matteo's history swiftly and clearly follows their path, transporting the reader to swinging 1960s London and beyond. This book is every Beatles fan's ticket to ride." —**Noah Charney**, author of *The Devil in the Gallery: How Scandal, Shock, and Rivalry Shaped the Art World*

"The Beatles are a gift that keeps on giving. Steve Matteo's book is a gift in itself. For those of us who will always love The Beatles, Matteo's book renews and expands this love of the songs and the four guys we thought we knew." —**David Yaffe**, author of *Reckless Daughter: A Portrait of Joni Mitchell*

T0267278

THE BEATLES ON FILM

AcT NaTuRaLLy

STEVE MATTEO

Backbeat
Books

Backbeat Books

An imprint of Globe Pequot, the trade division of
The Rowman & Littlefield Publishing Group, Inc
4501 Forbes Boulevard, Suite 200, Lanham, Maryland 20706
www.rowman.com

Distributed by NATIONAL BOOK NETWORK

British Library Cataloguing in Publication Information Available

Library of Congress Cataloging-in-Publication Data

Names: Matteo, Stephen, author.
Title: Act naturally : the Beatles on film / Steve Matteo.
Identifiers: LCCN 2022044274 (print) | LCCN 2022044275 (ebook) | ISBN
  9781493059010 (paperback) | ISBN 9781493059027 (ebook)
Subjects: LCSH: Beatles—In motion pictures. | Rock musicians in motion
  pictures. | Motion pictures and rock music. | Rock
  music—1961-1970—History and criticism.
Classification: LCC ML421.B4 M194 2023 (print) | LCC ML421.B4 (ebook) |
  DDC 782.42166092/2—dc23/eng/20221123
LC record available at https://lccn.loc.gov/2022044274
LC ebook record available at https://lccn.loc.gov/2022044275

∞™ The paper used in this publication meets the minimum requirements of American National Standard for Information Sciences—Permanence of Paper for Printed Library Materials, ANSI/NISO Z39.48-1992.

Contents

InTRoducTion and AcKnowLedGmenTs

Some people might wonder why the world needs yet another book on the Beatles. While I can't say for sure the book you are about to read will add greatly to the Beatles book canon, I believe the time is right for just such a book. While there have been some wonderful books that focus on the movies of the Beatles and, in some cases, individual movies starring the group or individual members of the group, there hasn't been a general trade book on the subject for fans of the group and the casual reader alike in many years. There is also now available a treasure trove of material that has come to light, through the reissues of the group's films on DVD and Blu-ray and in some cases, soundtrack albums, that fleshes out the story of the making of these movies and the accompanying soundtrack music. While there is still more out there yet to be released or discovered, as of this writing, all of the group's five major films have been released on DVD and Blu-ray, except for *Let It Be*, with Peter Jackson's *Get Back* series, a fulsome complement to the *Let It Be* film project and temporary stand-in for Michael Lindsay-Hogg's *Let It Be* film. All of these film reissues have also provided a depth of information on the people who worked on these movies. One thing the Beatles always did was surround themselves with great people—whether they were people just getting started in their field or veterans of their craft that helped the Beatles bring their art to the marketplace. One of the aims of this book is to try, even in some small way, to acknowledge the talented people who were integral to the success and creativity of the group's films. Taking that notion one step further, this book also seeks to elucidate the enormous impact the British films and film industry of the 1960s had on the overall history of the medium. The lasting power of many of these films resonate today and new audiences are continuing to discover these extraordinary motion picture achievements. It's also amazing how the Beatles were inextricably tied in with many of the legends, both known and unsung, of the era's British films. This book is as much a celebration of the films of the Beatles, as it is a championing of the British films of the 1960s in general.

While I have spent most of my adult life writing books and articles on music and worked in various capacities related to music, I don't profess to be a film scholar. However, my love and affection for British films of the 1960s, especially the actors of the era, like Sean Connery, Michael Caine, Peter Sellers, and Julie Christie, to name four, inspired me to dig deep into the history of the 1960's British film era for this book. I also wanted to explore how the Beatles didn't simply just create their films by themselves in some sort of vacuum. There is a sense, especially with *A Hard Day's Night* and to a lesser degree with *Help!*, that Richard Lester and the Beatles were the sole reason for the success of these films. Although I will make it abundantly clear what a major force Lester was as a film director in general, and a wildly underrated one at that, there were many other people and forces at work that assured the success of their early films.

There are certain topics that will be touched on in this book that relate to the films of the Beatles, but lengthy detail on these particular subjects will not occur. The story of Apple Corps in itself would require a book, and many excellent books have been written on the company. Books, articles and websites on bootlegs or unreleased music and even film of the Beatles, particularly from the *Get Back/Let It Be* period, are abundant. Instead of diving too deep into the bootlegs or recorded music and audio of this period, I tried to focus instead, as much as possible, on the *Let It Be* film and the *Get Back* series. To delve into the entire history of recorded material related to *Get Back/Let It Be* would have been too far off the subject and would have at least doubled the word count of that section. There are many great books, articles, and websites that delve deep into the bootleg history of the group. This book is also not a deep critical analysis of the group's films or music, filled with personal analysis and my opinions. I will not try to untangle the endless thorny web of "who broke up the Beatles." Again, many of these topics will be touched on when looking at the group's films but only to add context when appropriate.

I first broached the idea of writing this book with John Cerullo, on a beautiful afternoon late in May as we were both leaving the 2019 BookExpo at the Javits Center in New York City, but it's a book that in some ways I have been working on for years. The films of the Beatles are so central to their musical careers. Four of their 12 official British albums were soundtrack albums, and when adding the full-length US *Magical Mystery Tour*, that constitutes a large percentage of their album output, although to be fair *Yellow Submarine* included only four new songs.

In tackling a project like this, any author is indebted to the extraordinary and voluminous scholarship that already exists on the Beatles. When I first started this project, I began researching using the nearly 180 books I already owned on the group.

Reaching the conclusion of writing this book now brings the number of books closer to 250. Of course, no one can write a book on the Beatles without first consulting the books of Mark Lewisohn. His book, *The Complete Beatles Recording Sessions*, is not only the baseline history book on the recordings of the Beatles, but it also offers much more on the group's time together. That book, combined with his books, *The Beatles Day By Day* and *The Complete Beatles Chronicle*, is the most accurate record and diary of the group. I consulted these books on a nearly hourly basis when writing my book to fact-check dates, places, people, time lines, and activities. I could not have written this account of the movies of the Beatles without those books. I did not consult *Tune In*, Lewisohn's first volume of his narrative biographical trilogy on the group because my book begins well after that first volume concludes. I also used many other books to establish the time line of events, but the various editions of *The Beatles Diary* by Barry Miles was also a go-to book for establishing time lines and fact-checking, while also providing an insider's perspective from someone who was there. I also relied heavily on two books that John C. Winn wrote, *Way Beyond Compare: The Beatles' Recorded Legacy, Volume 1, 1957–1965*,and *That Magic Feeling: The Beatles' Recorded Legacy, Volume 2, 1966–1970*, for time lines, fact-checking, and myriad details that bring together history, discography, information on unreleased material, and invaluable raw data. Of course, Bruce Spizer, like Mark Lewisohn, has written books that are the definitive texts on the group. His books on the various recording labels that issued the music of the Beatles are comprehensive, and I referred to them repeatedly. His later books that focus on individual albums were also filled with so much useful information for my research, particularly the books on *Magical Mystery Tour*, *Yellow Submarine*, and *Let It Be*. Jerry Hammack's five-part *Recording Reference Manual* books are invaluable additions to the history of the recordings of the Beatles. *The Unreleased Beatles* by Richie Unterberger is also, like the Winn books, invaluable in time lines, fact-checking, discography, filmography, and particularly unreleased material and the group's history in general. *Beatles Gear* by Andy Babiuk and *Recording Reference Manuals* by Jerry Hammack were the primary sources for which instruments and equipment the Beatles used on the recordings that I cover. *The Beatles as Musicians*, the two-volume critical evaluation of the music of the Beatles by Walter Everett, is another indispensable and erudite addition to the vast canon of important books on the Beatles.

There were a core group of books that were invaluable in writing this book that have been published on the movies of the Beatles. They accounted for the foundation of the research on the making of the movies and the analysis and historical, social, and cultural contexts of the films. They range from beautifully illustrated books to scholarly dissertations on the films or an individual film. All of these books are must-have books for the fan of the group's movies and include *The Beatles A Hard Day's Night: A Private Archive* by Mark Lewisohn, *A Hard Day's Night: Music on Film*

Series by Ray Morton, *A Hard Day's Night* by Stephen Glynn, *Beatles at the Movies: Stories and Photographs from Behind the Scenes at All Five Films* by Roy Carr, *The Beatles Movies (Cassell Film Studies)* by Bob Neaverson, *A Hard Day's Night* by Phillip J. Di Franco, *Beatlemania: The History of the Beatles on Film, Vol. 4 (Beatles Series)* by Bill Harry, *A Hard Day's Night: The Ultimate Film Guide* by Lorraine Rolston, *The Beatles on Film* by Roland Reiter, and *Fab Films of the Beatles* by Ed Gross. Two books on film were indispensable to the narrative thread that ties the Beatles films to British films of the 1960s in general and the United Artists (UA) film company during the period: *Hollywood, England* by Alexander Walker and *United Artists: The Company that Changed the Film Industry* by Tino Balio. The films of the Beatles is a fascinating topic, and I am sure new books will come out on the subject; I hope my book, like the books listed here, will also become a staple of the canon of the group's films.

The Beatles London by Piet Schreuders, Mark Lewisohn, and Adam Smith was the primary book used to pinpoint and identify the group's life and work geographically in London. Other books that were invaluable for geographical context are *The Beatles England* by David Bacon and Norman Maslov, *The Beatles Fab Four Cities* by David Bedford, Richard Porter, Susan Ryan, and Simon Weitzman, and *The Beatles in Liverpool, Hamburg, London: People Venues Events That Shaped Their Music* by Tony Broadbent, covering the group, beyond London. *In the City* by Paul Du Noyer, *Swinging London* by Mark Worden and Alfredo Marziano, *The New London Spy* edited by Hunter Davies, and *London Calling* by Barry Miles, looks at London and its music and culture way beyond just the music of the Beatles.

A Hard Day's Write by Steve Turner, *Beatlesongs* by William J. Dowlding, *The Beatles Lyrics* by Hunter Davies, *I Me Mine* by George Harrison, and *The Lyrics: 1956 to the Present* by Paul McCartney were my main sources on the songwriting of the Beatles. There are a lot of books on the *Get Back/Let It Be/Abbey Road* period that also concurrently examined Apple Corps, the breakup of the Beatles, and the beginning of the solo careers of the Beatles including *Solid State: The Story of Abbey Road and the End of the Beatles* by Kenneth Womack, *Those Were the Days* by Stefan Granados, *And in the End: The Last Days of the Beatles* by Ken McNab, *The Roof: The Beatles' Final Concert* by Ken Mansfield, *The Beatles on the Roof* by Tony Barrell, *Get Back* by Doug Sulpy, *You Never Give Me Your Money* by Pete Doggett, and *Apple to the Core* by Peter McCabe and Robert D. Schonfeld.

Of course, the books I have mentioned so far, are merely reflective of the books I seemed to refer to again and again or which were invaluable to specific aspects of the group's movies. A complete and detailed bibliography appears at end this book and includes the works cited.

There were many people who were extremely helpful during the nearly three years it took to conceive, research, write, and prepare this book for publication. John Cerullo and I have threatened for years to work together and finally did. When I first told him about my idea to write a book on the movies of the Beatles, he was immediately excited. At Rowman & Littlefield, final work on the editing and publication preparation of the manuscript was done by Chris Chappell, Laurel Myers, and Della Vache. The book's art, photography, and so much more was handled by Barbara Claire.

Writing a book on film was made easier by having several esteemed film directors take time for me to interview them. Cameron Crowe was one of the first directors I contacted because I knew he would provide context about music and film that few could muster. Also, thanks to Greg Marioti at Vinyl Films for all his help. Ralph Bakshi was one of the early innovators of feature-length, adult animation for the rock generation, and he provided a rare perspective on the chapter on *Yellow Submarine*. Ryan White took time from a hectic film production schedule and offered me a fresh take on making movies these days with a Beatles angle, through his work directing *Good Ol' Freda*. Eammon Bowles, the president of Magnolia Pictures, has always been a joy to talk to about film and music, and he was helpful in connecting me with Ryan White. Finally, I couldn't have written the section on *Get Back/Let It Be* without the gracious assistance of Michael Lindsay-Hogg. I've been fortunate over the years to interview him on several occasions and even spend some time with him just hanging out. He is a gentleman, a true Renaissance man, and a peerless film director. I also spoke to others who worked on *Let It Be*, including director of photography Anthony Richmond. Richmond also worked on the Rolling Stones *Rock and Roll Circus* with Lindsay-Hogg, and throughout his long and still flourishing career, he has worked with Nicolas Roeg, Jean-Luc Godard, Basil Dearden, Michael Apted, and Blake Edwards, among many other legendary film directors. His insights were invaluable. Les Parrott, camera operator on *Let It Be*, provided vivid accounts on the *Let It Be* shoot. Dave Harries, who worked on sound for the film, also was invaluable in his help. I was lucky to speak with four of the animators who worked on *Yellow Submarine*: Malcolm Draper, Lucy Elvin, Campbell Ford, and Norman Drew. Michael Seresin was one of the camera operators on *Magical Mystery Tour*, and he embraced the creative chaos of the film and was a joy to interview.

There have been a handful of people instrumental in preserving the legacy of the films of the Beatles. Martha Karsh and her husband Bruce A. Karsh, along with the Beatles, share in the rights to *Help!*, and she and her husband are the sole steadfast curators of the legacy and ownership of the film and archive of *A Hard Day's Night*. Martha was kind enough to answer questions about the time and money she and her husband have put into preserving the critical legacy of the film and the vast archive that goes along with it. I would also like to thank Beth Clark for facilitating the interview with Martha. Kim Hendrickson with the Criterion Collection was also helpful in answering questions about the continued efforts to preserve and present *A Hard Day's Night*.

I was lucky to get to interview various people who worked for NEMS and Apple Corps or assisted the Beatles. John Kosh, better known simply as Kosh, has designed some of the most iconic album covers in rock history and, in two separate interviews, detailed his work on the *Let It Be* album and *Abbey Road* album covers, along with the design for the picture sleeves for the singles "The Ballad of John and Yoko," "Give Peace a Chance," and "Cold Turkey." Thanks to Bob Catania for coordinating the interviews with Kosh. Kevin Harrington also offered his recollections working on the *Get Back/Let It Be* project. Along with Kevin and those mentioned, Chris O'Dell was also on the roof of Apple Corps the day of the famous rooftop concert and fondly recalled that cold, historic January day in London. Fiona Andreanelli was working for Apple Corps when the company celebrated the 30th anniversary of the release of *Yellow Submarine* and was responsible for all the artistic design of the reissues and the picture book that was published. Tony Bramwell recalled his work on various visual projects the Beatles worked on in the 1960s.

I've been lucky enough to get to know Billy J. Kramer over the years, and he regaled me with tales of various film premieres of the movies of the Beatles. Klaus Voormann is another person who was part of the group's inner circle who I have been able to spend time with and interview on several occasions. He was kind enough to provide his insights on the "Instant Karma" sessions and the introduction of Phil Spector to the working world of the Beatles. It was enlightening interviewing Hunter Davies, one of the first authors to offer a lengthy biography of the Beatles and a patron saint of sorts for those of us who still are trying to find new ways to write about the group. Marijke Koger of The Fool Collective answered questions about her time as part of the Beatles psychedelic period. Thanks also to Donald Dunham and Marianne Dunham. I referred back to previous interviews I had done with Ethan Russell and Kevin Howlett. I also referred to interviews I did with Billy Preston, Robert Freeman, Alistair Taylor, Geoff Emerick, and Tony Barrow for this book and value the time when I interviewed these men when they were still with us.

Others I interviewed for this book include David Thomson, Gered Mankowitz, David Hurn, Guy Massey, John Illes, Debbie Greenberg, Neil Sinyard, Tom Lisanti, Debra Supnik, and Wayne Massey.

Thanks to Jon Meyers of *The Vinyl District*. My articles on the *Get Back* Disney series and *Let It Be* album reissue and companion book were the basis for my writing on those specific projects for this book.

There were a number of people who read all or parts of the manuscript. Gillian Gaar was the editor of the manuscript. Her razor-sharp editing skills and indefatigable knowledge of the subject matter were invaluable in dealing with and shaping a long, dense, and complex manuscript. Joe Fallon read the entire manuscript after Gillian first edited the book. He was helpful in looking at the Beatles story and the underlying film story of this book. Kenneth Womack also had the entire manuscript to read after Gillian and Joe. Several people read various sections of the book. British film scholar Melanie Williams read the first section of this book on the British film industry. Her fact-checks and help with clarifying British film history were invaluable. British film historian and author John White also read chapter 1, and his suggestions were also invaluable. Al Sussman read the *A Hard Day's Night* part of the book, one of the longest sections of the book. His knowledge of the Beatles is peerless, and he greatly added to my writing on this key movie in the filmography of the Beatles. Mitchell Axelrod, Laura Cortner, and Dr. Robert Hieronimus read the section on *Yellow Submarine*. Laura and Robert are unquestionably the sole experts on the *Yellow Submarine* film. Axelrod's background on the cartoons of the Beatles and those involved with the cartoons and *Yellow Submarine* further helped flesh out one of the more challenging sections of the book. Walter J. Podrazik read the section on *Magical Mystery Tour* and brought multiple perspectives to this section of the book. Tom Hunyady read the section on *Help!*, which came in the 11th hour, and I am grateful for his assistance so late in the game. Bruce Spizer read a tricky part of the *Magical Mystery Tour* section. Chip Madinger helped clarify the time line when Allen Klein was first getting involved in the business of the Beatles.

Fred Migliore, Al Boccio, Tom Ryan, and Steve Lombardo, along with many others, have shared my obsessive passion for music and the Beatles in particular and have offered inspiration, help, and tea and sympathy when needed, even if sometimes they didn't know it was the case. Bob Kranes and John Weston were there (and are still fellow travelers and brothers in arms) when I first tried to start my creative musical mystery tour of a career.

Over the years I have been lucky enough to interview writers and authors from the music world and, separate from my music journalism, who have been a true inspiration, especially Gay Talese, Lawrence Ferlinghetti, and Ben Fong-Torres. On several occasions I interviewed and spent time with Pete Hamill. His long career as an editor, journalist, and author is as inspiring as his self-effacing warmth and generosity when gently offering insights into the writing game with the many writers who have sought him out over the years.

Thanks to all the Beatles people who helped in various ways in making this book happen. Mark Lewisohn, Joe Johnson, Darren DeVivo, Jerry Hammack, Ken Michaels, Scott "Belmo" Belmer, Bill King, Simon Weitzman, Mark Rozzo, Allan Kozinn, Patricia Gallo-Stenman, David Leaf, Robert Rodriquez, Richard Porter, Jason Kruppa, Tony Traguardo, Joe Wisbey, and Kit O'Toole.

Additional thanks to Joe Hagan, Maura Spiegel, Adrian Winter, Martine Montgomery, Abe Brooks, Eleanor Sax, Steve Chibnall, Susan King, Kevin Donnelly, Elizabeth Goldstein, Duncan Petrie, Peter Watts, Nick Barney, Adrian Crane, Robert Edgar, and Rowland Wymer.

During and previous to this project, various record company and independent publicists have assisted in my writings on the Beatles and related subjects including Bob Merlis, Steve Martin, Ken Weinstein, Jennifer Ballantyne, and Tim Plumley.

This book is dedicated with much love and a heavy heart to Henry Matteo, Jenny Matteo, Annabelle Murphey, Tony Mohr, Michael Lombardo, Kenny Ostraco, John Kudla, Pete Fornatale, Kevin Kelly, Carey Koleda, Mark Biggs, Roni Ashton, Ray White, Rita Houston, John McWhinnie, and Pam Long.

Finally, I need to thank my sister Gina. There are things I could never have made it through without her. Also, my son Christopher has made being father a breeze. Maybe someday I will grow up and be as smart as him. There is no one in my life who has been as supportive of my work and obsession with music as my wife Jayne. She is beautiful, sweet, and smart, and the longer we are together, the more I love her.

1

A Hard Day's Night in London

The Beatles saved the world from boredom.

—George Harrison

OPENING CREDITS

On Monday, July 6, 1964, Shaftesbury Avenue in London's West End was a scene of pandemonium the likes of which London hadn't witnessed since the day the Second World War ended. On this hot summer night, an invasion that had been percolating in the north of England for years finally came to a full boil. The Beatles' debut film was having its world premiere at the London Pavilion, replacing *Tom Jones*, the film that heralded the critical and even more importantly commercial arrival of the new British cinema explosion. The Beatles—John Lennon, Paul McCartney, George Harrison, and Ringo Starr—had burst onto the international pop music scene. Only a few short years ago, they were scruffy young lads from Liverpool, the industrial port city of the north of England, in love with rock 'n' roll, with faint dreams of stardom. The current lineup began with John Lennon asking Paul McCartney to join his group the Quarrymen, McCartney bringing in Harrison, with Lennon's art-school friend Stuart Sutcliffe joining, and Pete Best settling in as their drummer, after many held that position in the group. Sutcliffe eventually dropped out to stay in Hamburg and pursue a career in art. When the group finally signed to Parlophone Records, Best was sacked, and Starr took his place. From their earliest days as the Quarrymen, various lineups that included Lennon, McCartney, and Harrison slowly ascended in Liverpool and most importantly honed their sound in the unforgiving club circuit

The Beatles enjoying the pleasures of tea. Courtesy Photofest.

in Hamburg, Germany. They were approached by the scion of a wealthy Liverpool family—Brian Epstein, who ran one of the family's NEMS record stores—to manage them. He helped them sharpen their image, provided much-needed organization and direction, and most importantly secured them a recording contract. Starring in a motion picture and being the biggest pop music phenomenon in the world followed two number one albums, three UK number one singles, and raucous concerts, defined by hordes of young screaming fans (mostly girls) caught up in the hysteria of what came to be defined as Beatlemania.

It was the London Pavilion Theatre where, eight years previously, *Rock Around the Clock* premiered as perhaps the first successful rock 'n' roll teen exploitation movie. The venerable old theater had opened in 1885, began presenting musicals in 1912, and first started screening movies on September 5, 1934, with Alexander Korda's *The Private Life of Don Juan*. Two years later, it became almost exclusively the showcase cinema for films from UA, the same company releasing *A Hard Day's Night*. In October 1962, it hosted the debut of another UA film, and another significant British film of the 1960s, *Dr. No*, the first James Bond movie. The Pavilion would host the premieres of all the Beatles' theatrical films, except *Magical Mystery Tour* (which debuted on television), as well as premiere Richard Lester's (the director of *A Hard Day's Night*) *How I Won the War*, costarring John Lennon.

The four lads from Liverpool had taken the world by storm by 1964, solidifying their position with a landmark appearance on *The Ed Sullivan Show* in New York the previous February. Their newfound importance to Britain was confirmed by making their film debut a prestigious Royal World Premiere charity event, hosted by Her Royal Highness Princess Margaret, and her husband Antony Armstrong-Jones, the Earl of Snowdon, sponsored by The Variety Club of Great Britain to aid the Dockland Settlements and the Variety Club Heart Fund.

Although nearly 35 years old, the princess fit right in with the young Beatles and the rebellious, youthful spirit of the times. The same was the case for Lord Snowdon, who ran with the fast London set and didn't let his marriage to the queen's sister interfere with his extracurricular activity. While the Beatles, especially Paul McCartney, were clearly nervous at their London film premiere, the Armstrong-Joneses were clearly thrilled to have escaped the prison of Kensington Palace for the evening.

The huge neon billboard above the theater lit up the night with cartoon caricatures of the Beatles. The billboard blazed with hype, the name of the film, and proclaimed "The Beatles in Their First Full Length, Hilarious, Action-Packed Film and 12 Smash Song Hits." The nearly 12,000 fans who jammed the street and didn't have one of the tickets that cost nearly £16 had to be content to catch a glimpse of a Beatle or two as they arrived. The four were impeccably dressed in elegant black formal wear: matching tuxedos with velvet collars, crisp white shirts with cufflinks, bow ties, black satin stripes down the leg, and their trademark Cuban-heeled Beatle boots. Choruses of "Happy Birthday" wafted through the frenzied crowd aimed at Ringo Starr, whose birthday was the following day. July 6 was actually Paul's father's 62nd birthday, marked by Paul giving his father a painting of the racehorse he'd bought for him, named Drake's Drum.

Upon entry, the Beatles, along with their manager Brian Epstein, who sartorially matched his famous clients, and Wilfred Brambell, who played Paul's grandfather in the film, easily mixed and mingled with the royal couple in the foyer of the theater. The evening began with the Metropolitan Police Band playing "God Save the Queen," in honor of the princess and Lord Snowdon, followed by a short travelogue film about New Zealand. Then the main event: The screening of *A Hard Day's Night* was official. This was the second time the group would see the finished film, having already seen a preview on July 4.

Following an after-party at the Dorchester Hotel in Park Lane, the Beatles headed to London's swinging Ad-Club with Keith Richards, Brian Jones, and Bill Wyman from the Rolling Stones, who hadn't been invited to the after-party but attended anyway. The Ad-Lib was one of the clubs the Beatles and the Rolling Stones could be found at and was perhaps the one club the Beatles most frequented at the time. Located above the Prince Charles Theatre on the fourth floor, the short-lived club (which was open from 1963 to 1966) was where Ringo would propose to his future wife Maureen early in 1965. Shaking off the stuffy old clubby atmosphere of its past, American R&B and soul provided music to dance to all night. With the Beatles set to appear on *Top of the Pops* the next day, Paul bailed early, but Ringo stayed until after 4 a.m. John knocked back scotch and Cokes with the Stones until dawn.

A HARD DAY'S NIGHT IN LIVERPOOL

If the London premiere of *A Hard Day's Night* was not enough, the Liverpool charity "Northern Premiere" of the film on July 10 was an emotional roller coaster and exceeded any expectations the Beatles had about how their hometown would react to such a prestigious entertainment milestone.

It's not surprising that the Beatles were unsure about how Liverpool would treat them upon such a lofty return. The group was not unaware that once their international stardom hit, and their business drew them away from Liverpool, many of their fans and friends in Liverpool who claimed them as their own felt sadness, resentment, and a sense of abandonment. But for the most part, Liverpool, a city of about 750,000 inhabitants at that time—the city where they grew up and that formed the basis of the cheeky personas that the world was falling in love with seemingly overnight—treated them as conquering heroes, returning to the place that, for the most part, had made them. The people of Liverpool, whose influence had waned since its nineteenth-century heyday, could now bathe in the glow of the success and what was fast becoming the most important popular cultural phenomena of the age.

From the moment the group's British Eagle Britannia plane touched down amid bright sunshine late in the afternoon, just after a quarter past five at Liverpool Airport in Speke, Liverpool's unique version of Beatlemania was fully unleashed. After disembarking, an impromptu press conference had journalists firing off questions at the four, and their replies were in line with the cheeky answers they normally offered to the befuddled old-guard reporters. One reporter asked about future ambitions, and John answered, "Don't know. I'd like to make more films, I think. We'd all like to do that, 'cos it's good fun, you know. It's hard work, but you can have a good laugh in films." After Ringo, Paul, and George also weighed in on making movies and how good *A Hard Day's Night* was, John added, "Not as good as James Bond though, is it?" "Oh no, not as good as James Bond," Paul concurred. When a reporter challenged them by saying, "You fancy yourselves as actors then, do you?" George said, "No, definitely not. We enjoyed making the film, and especially the director was great, you see, and it made it much easier for us. None of us rate ourselves as actors, but, as you know, it's a good laugh and we enjoy doing it. So we'd like to make a couple more."

While estimates of the numbers who greeted the group during the long day and night vary widely, most news accounts of the day reported between 1,500 and 3,000 screaming fans were waiting for their plane to touch down at Liverpool Airport. From there, eight police motorcycles and cars led the 10-mile trek to Liverpool Town Hall, with estimates of hundreds of thousands of fans lining the roads, some breaking through throngs of police, forcing the cavalcade to occasionally stop.

It was near 7 p.m. when the Beatles and their entourage arrived at Liverpool Town Hall, in the city center, met by the screaming of 20,000 fans packed into the plaza. The magnificent eighteenth-century Georgian edifice was built in 1754, rebuilt in 1802, and restored after World War II, due to being bombed during the Blitz of 1940–1941. Further restoration was done in the mid-1990s, and as recently as 2015, additional restoration related to the Blitz was done, with a cleaning of centuries of pollution carried out at the same time.

The Beatles were met by a host of Liverpool dignitaries during that early evening, including the Bishop of Liverpool and Lord and Lady Derby, and Liverpool's member of Parliament (MP) Elizabeth Braddock, better known as Bessie and a member of the Cavern Club, which she made clear to all that day by proudly wearing her Cavern Club membership pin. The Cavern Club, on Mathew Street in Liverpool, where the Beatles and Mersey-beat sound exploded, still held a special place in the story of the Beatles, even at this time of their international fame. A letter was delivered to the four from Queen Elizabeth, bearing a request to autograph six souvenir programs; later, a congratulatory telegram from Prince Philip was read.

After a break for dinner, the group stepped out onto the Town Hall balcony facing Castle Street and waved to fans below while the Liverpool City Police Band played "Can't Buy Me Love." Moving to the large ballroom inside Town Hall, the Lord Mayor of Liverpool, Alderman Louis Caplan, accompanied by the Lady Mayoress, Mrs. Fanny Bodeker, spoke to the assembled multitude of more than 700. The Beatles, surrounded by many of their family members (especially from John and Ringo's families), were presented with keys to the city.

The Beatles were next presented with an oblong cake featuring a map of the world and the inscription: "The City of Liverpool Honours The Beatles." They donated the cake to the Alder Hey Children's Hospital in West Derby. The hospital is where Paul's late mother Mary started her nursing career.

After nearly two hours of festivities, the Beatles headed to the Odeon Cinema in an Austin Princess limousine for the *A Hard Day's Night* premiere. The Odeon was not too far away from the River Mersey, close to Lime Street railway station at the corner of London Road and Hotham Street and almost next door to the Empire Theatre, where the pre-Beatles group the Quarrymen played their first-ever gig, as did another early iteration of the band, Johnny and the Moondogs. Until Buddy Holly and the Crickets played at the Liverpool Philharmonic Hall in March 1958, the Empire was the first time a rock 'n' roll show had happened in Liverpool. The Beatles themselves played the Empire, making their first appearance there on October 28, 1962; fittingly, it was also the site of their last-ever Liverpool concert on December 5, 1965.

At the Odeon, the Liverpool Police Band continued the brass band serenading of Beatles music, as well as the theme from the British television police show *Z Cars*, which was set in Liverpool. David Jacobs, DJ and host of the BBC's *Juke Box Jury*, was on hand to introduce the group at their prescreening press conference.

After all the hometown excitement, the group departed in the rain and would not return to the city in any official capacity again until November 8, for another appearance at the Empire.

A Hard Day's Night would open in the US on August 11, at only 18 theaters, with the US premiere held at the Beacon Theatre in Manhattan. On August 12, the film would be shown in the US in 500 theaters. Debbie Gendler Supnik, a television producer, was a teenager from New Jersey who attended the Beacon Theatre premiere. "When it was time for *A Hard Day's Night* to be released, I received a large pink colored ticket to the 2:30 p.m. preview screening at the Beacon Theatre on Broadway on July 14th. Seeing the Beatles that large on a movie screen was overwhelming! I remember the closeups and thinking this was unreal! I hadn't heard any of the music before and the energy of the film got all of us bouncing in our seats."

ENGLAND AFTER THE WAR

The deal with UA to make the Beatles' screen debut, and the expansion of Beatlemania first beyond Liverpool and then England, did not occur in a vacuum and must be understood amid the backdrop of the political, social, and historical contexts of postwar England. While some of the historical context may not have directly influenced the Beatles' music and rise to fame, their prominence as 1963 turned into 1964 cannot be fully understood without a brief look at some of the key events in England and the general mood of the country after the Second World War.

Although England played a key part in the Allied victory, the religious, royal, and ruling class of the country had been experiencing a steady decline for decades. While this decline caused traumatic reverberations for the upper and ruling classes, and a general sense of apprehension, uneasiness, doubt, and confusion, it was ultimately the catalyst for the seismic changes that relaunched Britain from a global empire to the world center of popular culture for a brief time in the 1960s.

Two seemingly unrelated events created an enormous and profound change in the British people. The first came when ITV, England's first commercial television network, went on the air on September 22, 1955, thus curtailing the government monopoly the BBC had on the country since its inception in 1922. Perhaps an even more profound event occurred several months later in 1956 when the country was gripped by the Suez Crisis, when Britain, along with France and Israel, invaded Egypt to recover control of the Suez Canal. International pressure put on the invading countries to withdraw was successful, but the British people, weakened by the outcome, questioned their relevance as a military superpower, and the event was seen by many as a failure that signaled the beginning of the end of Britain as the world's most dominant empire.

The launch of commercial television ushered in seismic changes in media and communications in England and brought about fresh new ideas to a country going through massive change.

Beyond geopolitics, mass communications, and class changes, sexual mores among the provincial inhabitants of buttoned-down England were in for a change. In 1957 there was the release of the Wolfenden Report, which began a road toward an overdue acceptance and normalization of homosexuality in a country where even consensual homosexual activity could result in jail and public shame. In 1960, the trial that lifted the embargo on allowing *Lady Chatterley* by D. H. Lawrence to be published in England was a major victory for anticensorship.

And truly setting the stage for the major changes to come, the Profumo Affair in 1963 rocked the seat of government, became a scandal with international implications, and triggered a complete lack of confidence in the conservative party, which, along with a major economic downturn, would ultimately put Labour in power by 1964. After John Profumo, Secretary of State for War, resigned in June, Conservative Prime Minister Harold Macmillan resigned on October 18, 1963, and was replaced by Alec Douglas Home.

HOLLYWOOD ON THE THAMES

The commercial center of moviemaking in the 1950s was primarily based in Hollywood. American studio films dominated the movies, but in the aftermath of World War II, Europe, spreading its wings culturally, was becoming a hotbed of new types of film and artistic directorial visionaries. While most filmgoers are quite familiar with the Hollywood stars and American films that dominated the studio era, postwar Europe increasingly became an incubator of groundbreaking cinema.

Rome and Paris became the vortex of world culture. Fashion, art, style, and new modes of living and expression flourished in these two cities, and film, perhaps more than any art form from these two metropolitan destinations, was experiencing a zenith.

In Italy, Federico Fellini, Vittorio de Sica, Roberto Rossellini, Luchino Visconti, and Michelangelo Antonioni were creating a distinctly modern new Italian cinema,

France was going through a revolution captured under the Nouvelle Vague (New Wave) umbrella. While they all started their careers at different times, made films in differing styles and genres, and weren't all strictly from the Nouvelle Vague school, French film directors Robert Bresson, Jean Cocteau, Jean Renoir, Jean-Pierre Melville, Claude Chabrol, Louis Malle, Jacques Tati, Jean Luc-Godard, and François Truffaut collectively were some of the boldest and most exciting group of filmmakers in the world at this time. Godard would go on to spend some time hanging out with the Beatles but would ultimately end up making *Sympathy for the Devil* with the Rolling Stones in 1968.

Italy and France were not the only two European countries boasting daring new filmmakers. In Sweden, Ingmar Bergman was creating a haunting and austere style that at times could almost eclipse any of the filmmakers mentioned. Poland's Andrzej Wajda was also making bold new movies. There was also Austrian Max Ophuls, who worked in Hollywood and France. The films of Jules Dassin, an American who fled to Europe, were often produced in France, as were those of Russian-born Roger Vadim.

The British film world, on the other hand, didn't really have a any real unifying look, style, or trademark identity.

Prior to late in the 1950s some of the film genres that had taken hold in England included war films, comedies with a distinctive English quirkiness (mostly from Ealing Studios), crime dramas influenced by American film noir cinema, and horror films from Hammer Film Productions that appropriated and advanced some of the cinematic conventions of the American B movies, which would be picked up and imitated by American Roger Corman.

There were also films produced exclusively in England, or were American or European coproductions, that were either commercial international hits or were critically acclaimed. There are two films that must be considered two of the most successful British-American productions prior to the 1950s, and that often turn up at the top of the list of greatest motion pictures of all time, *The Red Shoes* and *The Third Man*.

The Red Shoes was released in the UK in 1948, and 1949 in the US. Adapted from *The Red Shoes* by Hans Christian Andersen, the film was the brainchild of the team of the English film director Michael Powell and the Hungarian-born Emeric Pressburger. The film starred the British ballerina and actress Moira Shearer, who was born in Scotland.

The second was *The Third Man*, released in the US in 1949 and England in 1950. The British connection runs deep. The film was directed by Carol Reed, with the screenplay by Graham Greene. Reed was also one of the film's coproducers, along with Hungarian-born and British-based Alexander Korda and American David O. Selznick for the production company London Films. The actor in *The Third Man* who received the most attention was American Orson Welles, playing Harry Lime.

The film included other American actors, including Joseph Cotten, who actually gets top billing in the film's credits. Some film scholars consider *The Third Man* the best film ever produced in England.

Of course, perhaps the most celebrated British filmmaker of all time was Alfred Hitchcock, whose film career began in the 1920s during the silent era and lasted well into the 1970s. Although none of his films from the 1960s were produced by British studios, or filmed in England, they often featured British actors as part of the cast.

Other esteemed British film directors, from the pre-1960s period, whose work was internationally recognized, included Basil Dearden, John Guillermin, Alexander MacKendrick, Ronald Neame, J. Lee Thompson, and especially David Lean. In 1962, Lean would become even more of a force when paired with his famed cinematographer Freddie Young. Some of these directors would also play an important part in the British film explosion of the 1960s.

The primary centers of film production for the major British film companies in the 1950s were Pinewood, Elstree, Ealing, Shepperton, and MGM's Borehamwood studio. Twickenham and Merton Park were primarily where B movies were produced. Bray was where Hammer's studio was located.

These studios would evolve to various degrees and either be part of the foundation of the new wave of British cinema or had already been active in solidifying the strengths of British moviemaking. The Ealing comedies, including the 1951 release *The Lavender Hill Mob* and the 1955 release *The Ladykillers*, which both starred British acting legend Alec Guinness, were a good example of a 1950s success story. *Halliwell's Film Guide*, one of the first comprehensive movie review reference books, called *The Lavender Hill Mob* "one of the most affectionately remembered Ealing comedies." But as the 1950s were coming to a close, Rank was also struggling and ceased their U.S. film distribution operation and like Shepperton, took on television series work to avoid financial problems.

Successfully collaborating or working on their own productions from the 1940s into the 1970s were the identical twins, John and Roy Boulting. One of their films would even intersect with Paul McCartney's career in the 1960s, when he worked on the soundtrack for *The Family Way* (1966).

Pinewood was perhaps the largest studio complex, and through the auspices of its proprietor, Rank, operated very much like a film factory. As the 1950s were giving way to the 1960s, Rank was the biggest film corporation in England.

Another key film distributor was Associated British Picture Corporation (ABPC). The company started in 1927 and closed in 1970. Significantly, it also operated a cinema chain starting in 1950 with 500 theaters. It became part of the Independent Television Authority (ITA) in 1955, a commercial television network of four stations. The principal film studio was located in various locations including at Elstree and Borehamwood, both north of London. Elstree has gone through many changes in ownership and is still active today. Elstree has a UA connection, as its Eldon Avenue Studios, Borehamwood location was bought in 1953 by Douglas Fairbanks Jr., one of the founders of UA, mostly for television production. Also, the BBC owned the studio, and when it purchased it in 1984, it began to be referred to as BBC Elstree Centre. Elstree Studios on Shenley Road in Borehamwood was where Hitchcock made *Blackmail* in 1929, the first British film of the postsilent film era. The studio eventually became part of EMI and continued to go through many ownership changes and further expansion.

There were many others producing films in this period, including British Lion Studios, which was located at Shepperton. Like much of the rest of the British film industry, British Lion was struggling, and to keep Shepperton open and operating, they took in television series work. British Lion existed as a film company in many ways since 1919, but in its modern heyday, between the mid-1950s and mid-1970s, it was primarily a film distribution company. It produced or distributed such classics as *The Third Man*, new British cinema entries such as *Expresso Bongo* and *The Entertainer*, British films with a music connection in the 1960s and 1970s, including *The Family Way* (with a soundtrack by Paul McCartney and George Martin) and *The Girl on a Motorcycle* (with Marianne Faithfull) in the 1960s and *The Man Who Fell To Earth* (starring David Bowie) in the 1970s. By 1964, the company was wildly expanding and developing relationships with independent film production companies and directors, as well as Brian Epstein.

The Woolf brothers, John and James, also produced many films in this period. They launched two production companies, the well-known Romulus Films, and the lesser-known Remus films. They also had a film distribution company, Independent Film Distributors (IFD). IFD distributed *The African Queen*, directed by John Huston and starring Humphrey Bogart and Katharine Hepburn in 1951, and their own Romulus-produced *Room at the Top* in 1959, which will figure prominently in the early unfolding of the new British cinema. Other film companies included Bryanston, a consortium of 16 independent producers run by former head of Ealing Michael Balcon. These new companies spearheaded a slow rebirth in British film in 1959, with Woodfall Films Production (cofounded by director Tony Richardson, playwright John Osborne, and producer Harry Saltzman) producing *The Entertainer* and Beaver Films producing *The Angry Silence*, both released in 1960. Allied Film Makers was set up by various filmmakers and producers, including Bryan Forbes, Richard Attenborough, Guy Green (who made *The Angry Silence*), Basil Dearden, Michael Relph, and Jack Hawkins.

THE BRITISH NEW WAVE

Finally, late in 1950s, three kinds of films emerged that laid the foundation for movies with a very definite new British film wave: realist films, social problem films, and what came to be known as "kitchen sink" films. The British Film Institute (BFI) defines kitchen sink films as, "predominantly focused on the lives of the working classes, with broad regional accents thankfully intact, the kitchen sink films had no time for traditional, rose-tinted celluloid visions of England's supposedly green and pleasant land. Instead, these raw human stories revolved around crumbling marriages, the drudgery of unskilled work, sexual orientation, stymied aspirations, backstreet abortions, disenfranchised youth, homelessness and gender, class and race discrimination."

These films were very much the result of British filmmakers realistically grappling with postwar, postimperial England's new place in the world.

This new cinema flowered simultaneously with the emergence of a slew of young British playwrights and novelists who were the first to artistically express the world of the new generation of Britons. Film organizations also sprang up that seemed to take their cue from the film societies and underground magazines in Europe, particularly in France.

Sequence was a film journal headed by future new British filmmaker Lindsay Anderson, who would join future new British filmmakers Czech-born Karel Reisz and Brit Tony Richardson in launching the *Free Cinema* group in 1956. *Sequence* would also include influential writings by British cinematographer Walter Lassally. Richardson was the cofounder of the English Stage Company. Between 1956 and 1959, the company presented the works of what were dubbed "The Angry Young Men"—John Osborne, Arnold Wesker, John Arden, Michael Hastings, and Shelagh Delaney (who actually was a woman)—at the Royal Court Theatre. Other new young English writers remaking British theater and included playwrights Harold Pinter, Arnold Wesker, John Arden, Keith Waterhouse, Willis Hall, Alun Owen, Robert Bolt, and David Mercer. These new young voices were seeking to breathe life into the stuffy, moribund, genteel state of English theater. Sometimes who these angry young playwrights exactly were depended on the day of the week. They were also not confined to playwrights and included novelists such as Kingsley Amis (father of novelist Martin Amis), Alan Sillitoe, Stan Barstow, and John Braine. Another one of these angry young men who happened to be a woman was novelist Doris Lessing.

Free Cinema screenings occurred between 1956 and 1959 and included six programs shown at the National Film Theatre in London, featuring three films from the US, France, and Poland, along with three British films—two documentaries and Lorenza Mazzetti's *Together*.

In 1959, the Woolf Brothers would produce one of the first big breakthrough British films of the late 1950s/early 1960s, Jack Clayton's *Room at the Top*. The film was released in the UK in January 1959 and the US in March. The film was adapted from John Braine's novel, who, along with Kingsley Amis, Joe Orton, and John Osborne were part of the fresh new crop of exciting young British writers who would go on to supply the source material for key British films of the early 1960s.

The novel *Absolute Beginners* by Colin MacInnes was published in 1959 and was in part loosely based on the 1958 riots in London's Notting Hill neighborhood, as well as taking a roman à clef approach in its depiction of the seedier Soho neighborhood. It was the middle novel in his London Trilogy and captured the youth explosion that was simmering underground. The author focused on big issues like race and family but also the fashion and jazz music that the new teenage generation was obsessed with at that time.

Room at the Top, starring Laurence Harvey (who was born in North Lithuania and grew up in South Africa but was always considered a major British actor) and French actress Simone Signoret, earned an X certificate in the UK. The X rating is different in the US and was introduced in 1968. The X certificate was introduced in the UK in 1951, and while the film would barely earn a PG rating today, it was a bold, new kind of British film. The film had two sequels, *Life at the Top* in 1965, about what happened to the characters 10 years later and the TV series *Man at the Top*, which became the film *Man at the Top* in 1973.

While *Room at the Top* kicked the door open for the British film new wave, *Look Back in Anger* became the film that was not a commercial success. This kitchen sink drama was about newly married Jimmy Porter, played by Richard Burton, and the torment he puts all around him as he grapples with his place in postwar England. The film opens with a brassy and exuberant jazz sequence, with Porter leading the frenzy on trumpet (this period was when England was in the grip of trad jazz). The excitement of the opening quickly gives way to the claustrophobic fate of Jimmy, his wife Alison, played by Mary Ure, and their flatmate Cliff, played by Gary Raymond. Burton's electrifying star turn reflects all the frustrations of young men of the era, with the stark black-and-white photography perfectly capturing the grim, gray, bombed-out England of the time. While Porter would go through many changes, including eventually taking up with his wife's friend Helena, played by Claire Bloom, the film's bleak ending would never make one think that in only a few short years England would be the center of the cultural universe. A few lines are telling in summing up the confusion of the time. When asked what he wants, Jimmy replies "everything and nothing."

Look Back in Anger, released in September 1959, was the result of the collaboration of many people whose careers in British cinema, together and apart, would contribute to important British films of the entire decade. The film was produced by Woodfall with backing from Associated British and Warner Brothers in America, who also handled its distribution. Harry Saltzman, who was a Canadian-born film producer living in England, supplied the money for John Osborne, whose play the film is based on, and director Tony Richardson to form Woodfall. Richardson, who would eventually marry Vanessa Redgrave in 1962 and divorce her in 1967, and whose children Natasha and Joely would follow their parents into a career in film, worked as a television director for the BBC. He made the film *Momma Don't Allow* with Karel Reisz. Richardson and George Devine also formed the theater group the English Stage Company at the Royal Court Theatre. Most famously, Saltzman, along with Albert Broccoli, would go on to produce the James Bond films. In 1956, British critic and cultural icon Kenneth Tynan championed the play the film is based on and rightly saw it as a major breakthrough in British drama.

It is important to note several characteristics of the people involved in *Look Back in Anger* and the unfolding story of new British cinema. It's no surprise that British theater would play a major role in the initial and continuing ferment of new British film, as British theater, going back to Shakespeare, plays a pivotal role in the superior dominant English dramatic tradition. Also, like *Room at the Top* with Laurence Harvey, this movie was a vehicle for Richard Burton to experience a breakout role that would further reinforce his career internationally. This large pool of acting talent in England, many of whom started out in theater, is one of many elements that made making films in England so attractive to American film companies, producers, and directors. Also, film studios such as Pinewood, Shepperton, and Elstree cost nearly a third less in booking fees to shoot interiors than American studios.

Finally, at the end of the year, *Our Man in Havana* would be released. Although not a new British cinema release, or noted as a British film classic, the film was highly entertaining, brought together many great talents, and in some ways foreshadowed the British spy craze to come. Several British acting legends were on hand, including Alec Guinness, Ralph Richardson, and Noel Coward, joined by Americans Maureen O'Hara, Burl Ives, and comedian Ernie Kovacs. The film was directed by Carol Reed, who, with previous films like *Night Train to Munich* and *The Third Man*, was a master at the suspense thriller. The screenplay was by Graham Greene from his book. Reed had previously worked with Greene on *Night Train to Munich* in 1940, which Greene adapted from his book; *The Fallen Idol* in 1948, which Green adapted from his book; and *The Third Man* in 1949, based on one of Greene's short stories and was cowritten by him and Reed. Another film that could run as a double feature with *Our Man in Havana* that was also released in 1959 was a remake of Alfred Hitchcock's *The 39 Steps* (originally released in 1935), one of the most popular films of the year.

The beginning of the 1960s began the slow trickle of American companies beefing up their production in England, with 20th Century Fox producing *The Innocents* in 1961 and the ill-fated *Cleopatra* in 1963. It was a mistake to film the Elizabeth Taylor spectacle in cold and dreary England and eventually production moved to Italy, but in many instances, that was almost the least of the problems of this ill-fated production.

The next major British film, *The Entertainer*, released in 1960, would include two names we're already familiar with; director Tony Richardson and writer John Osborne, whose play the film was based on. *The Entertainer* shared some of the same characteristics as *Look Back in Anger* but was in some ways a wistful throwback and had echoes of *Limelight* from 1952, which was directed by Charlie Chaplin. Like *Look Back in Anger*, the film was not only directed by Richardson, produced by Harry Saltzman, and based on a play by Osborne, the screenwriter of *Look Back in Anger*, but the prolific Nigel Kneale, writer of scripts for film and television, books and for newspapers and magazines, also shares screenwriting credits with Osborne. The film was primarily shot on location but primarily filmed outdoors at the northern England seaside holiday town Morecambe in Lancashire, with most of the interiors in the town's rundown music hall. While both Alan Bates and Albert Finney make their screen debuts (with Finney in one scene in the beginning of the movie), the real star of the film is Laurence Olivier, as the fading variety star and lecherous drunk Archie Rice, a role for which he received an Academy Award nomination for best actor. The film is also very much a family drama and backstage musical. While it retains some of the claustrophobic intrafamily squabbling of *Look Back in Anger*, Olivier is a lovable and mostly lighthearted old cad, whereas Richard Burton in *Look Back in Anger* was an out-of-control, venomous, and belligerent youth. The film also has a warm melancholy, thanks to John Addison's music. Near the beginning of the film, there are also youths dancing to rock 'n' roll, foreshadowing the importance that music would have in transforming British culture. Joan Plowright also has a substantial role in the film. Plowright, 20 years younger than Olivier, would marry him the following year, his marriage to actress Vivien Leigh having disintegrated over time.

For Richardson, these two British films were so critically acclaimed that Hollywood came calling, and he directed *Sanctuary* in the US in 1960, before returning to England to make three films that for many are the critical and commercial pinnacle of British films in the early 1960s.

While all of these British films reaped a mixed bag of commercial and critical success, the next major new British film, *Saturday Night and Sunday Morning*, released in 1960, would prove highly financially successful. The film was another Woodfall production, adapted from a novel by Alan Sillitoe, starring Albert Finney, and directed by Karel Reisz. Woodfall, however, would start to go through some changes, and after *Saturday Night and Sunday Morning*, Saltzman no longer worked with the company, apparently due to clashing with Richardson.

Other notable films from 1960 include *The Angry Silence*. *The Trials of Oscar Wilde*, directed by Ken Hughes, was one of two films Albert Broccoli produced in 1960, before joining Harry Saltzman to produce the James Bond films. Two of the film's British stars, Peter Finch and James Mason, began their acting career in the 1930s and would continue past the 1960s. Broccoli had set up Warwick Films in England in 1951 with Irving Allen, and for the next 10 years produced 22 films, and it is from these productions that several key people would be drawn to make the Bond films.

The next major new British film released in 1961 would also be a huge financial success and was also directed by Tony Richardson, *A Taste of Honey*, adapted from his Broadway-directed production. The film would be the breakthrough role for Liverpool actress Rita Tushingham as Jo and would continue to spotlight location shooting as a key to the new British film's aesthetic, with the almost-documentary feel of the movie spearheaded by cameraman Walter Lassally. Lassally worked on the film *Beat Girl*, which was a key film in the evolution of new British films with a pop music angle. *Beat Girl* was released in 1960 from Amicus Productions and was titled *Wild for Kicks* in the US. It featured Adam Faith in a typical British teen exploitation film formula. Notable cast members included Christopher Lee and Oliver Reed, in only his second credited film role. The crew also included assistant director Peter Yates, who would go on to his own long and distinguished career directing such films as *Bullitt*, *The Friends of Eddie Coyle*, *Breaking Away*, *The Dresser*, and many more. While just another teen B movie, *Beat Girl* is credited as having the first British movie soundtrack to be released on a vinyl album. It also included music from the John Barry Seven. Barry would go on to be one of the most critically acclaimed, successful, and prolific film music artists, not only in Britain but also throughout the world, particularly for his signature and influential work on the James Bond films. He won five Oscars and was nominated for original score in the 1960s, 1970s, 1980s, and 1990s.

Halliwell's Film Guide had much to commend about *A Taste of Honey*, calling it "a strange and influential film" and adding how the film was "lovingly photographed by Walter Lassally." The book goes on to say about the main character's two supporting role's screen personas, "it paints vivid sketches of her tarty mum and the harmless homosexual who looks after her when a sailor leaves her pregnant." It concludes by saying "it succeeds in its determination to wring poetry from squalor." The film actually received an X certificate because of its depiction of interracial love, homosexuality, premarital sex, and the overall unflinching portrait of an unwed woman getting pregnant at that time in England. Today, the film would probably be rated PG-13 in the US. While painting a grim portrait of postwar England and featuring the two main female characters living a hand-to-mouth existence, the film has tremendous heart, even with its sad ending where Jo's homosexual friend Geoffrey leaves her, thanks (or no thanks) to her overbearing mother.

In 1961, although exciting new movies and trends were emerging in the UK, surprisingly, British film attendance continued to decline, and some in the film industry continued to look for ways to break the duopoly of the Rank and ABC theater chains, who had a stranglehold on the exhibition circuit. There was lots of news out of the production umbrella company Bryanston, with John Osborne and Tony Richardson of Woodfall joining it, and the company later merging with Seven Arts-U.K, the UK arm of Seven Arts Productions, a company that invested in the British film industry and worked with Hammer Film Productions, best known for their horror films.

The year would also see the directorial debut of Bryan Forbes. Forbes was a true Renaissance man of the British arts. Prior to his directorial debut in 1961 with *Whistle Down the Wind*, starring Hayley Mills, Bernard Lee, and Alan Bates, Forbes worked as an actor. He began in 1949 with a small role in the Powell/Pressburger film *The Small Back Room*. He would act in 28 films prior to *Whistle Down the Wind*. Additionally, in 1955 he cowrote the screenplay for *The Cockleshell Heroes*, directed by Jose Ferrer. He would go on to cowrite three more screenplays, as well as write the screenplay for *Only Two Can Play*, starring Peter Sellers, which was adapted from the novel *That Uncertain Feeling* by Kingsley Amis. He would also continue to act, sometimes uncredited. He also wrote nearly 20 books, most of them novels, and for a brief time early in the 1970s, he was the head of EMI films. His screenplay for *The League of Gentlemen*, adapted from John Boland's novel, was directed by Basil Dearden and released in 1960. Forbes also acted in the film alongside the likes of Richard Attenborough.

Victim, by Basil Dearden was also released in 1961. It was a groundbreaking film about homosexuality with a bravura performance by Dirk Bogarde. The movie is the first time the word *homosexual* was included in an English-language film.

ELVIS PRESLEY AT THE MOVIES

The most famous star in the world who appeared in teen music rock 'n' roll music movies in the 1950s was Elvis Presley. Presley debuted in 1954 on the feisty, independent roots Sun Records and then moved to the large commercial major record label RCA in 1956 when his self-titled debut album was released and his first film, *Love Me Tender*, had its premiere. He would make two more films in 1957 and one in 1958, before entering the army that year. While his first few films offered mainstream moviegoers a chance to see the King of Rock 'n' Roll on the big screen, the movies, like some of the music he made after he left Sun Records and after entering the army, were sometimes poorly conceived and didn't often reflect the first flush of rebellious groundbreaking innovation that initially made Elvis the artist that broke rock 'n' roll wide open. He would make 30 feature films that only seemed to grow more insipid and formulaic as the 1960s went on. As much as the Beatles loved Elvis and considered him a touchstone, by the time they were garnering so much attention in Hamburg and Liverpool early in the 1960s, Elvis, and especially his movies, was not something they chose to emulate.

ON THE BEACH

The other teen movie phenomenon that burst on the scene not long after the birth of rock 'n' roll was the American beach movie, and music was a significant part of its youth appeal.

The genre's unofficial popular debut foray was *Beach Party* in 1963. Distributed by AIP, which had long made low-budget films, particularly with genre pictures that appealed to the burgeoning baby boomers and came to be most famously associated with Roger Corman, the film starred Frankie Avalon and Annette Funicello. Featuring music by Dick Dale and the Deltones and songs sung by the film's two stars, the film was a huge commercial success although beach movies had existed previously.

AIP quickly followed up with *Muscle Beach Party*, which added more current teen pop to its musical mix by enlisting Stevie Wonder and having Brian Wilson of the Beach Boys cowrite six songs. Again, the film did good business, but opening near the same time as *A Hard Day's Night*, the formula seemed a little dated, and by the next film, *Bikini Beach*, the producers were scrambling to interject as much of the British cultural touchstones as they could. According to Tom Lisanti, author of *Talking Sixties Drive-In Movies* and *Hollywood Surf and Beach Movies: The First Wave: 1959–1969*, "for *Bikini Beach*, William Asher, who directed the first two beach party films, stated in an interview, that AIP head James Nicholson had seen the Beatles perform in London and wanted them to co-star in this new film. It is not entirely clear how true that was, but the final shooting script had, instead of four British mop topped singers, just one called the Potato Bug who crashed the beach party. Frankie Avalon played the part complete with blonde Beatle hairdo, brush mustache, round spectacles and front tooth gap."

While the next beach film, *Beach Blanket Bingo* was surprisingly, especially at this point, the best of the beach movies, and Avalon posed as a Brit in *Bikini Beach*, Lisanti felt the next beach film *Beach Ball* was the most influenced by *A Hard Day's Night*, "The entertaining *Beach Ball* probably came closest in trying to ape *A Hard Day's Night*," with the focus on "four college boys who form a rock band." The film also includes some heavyweight musical guests such as the Supremes, the Four

Seasons, and the Righteous Brothers. While Lisanti doesn't exactly feel the first two films of the Beatles caused the complete demise of jukebox musicals, or even Elvis films, he did say that later on, "the innocence of the early to mid-sixties was being replaced by the cynicism of the late sixties and by 1967, the beach party movies washed away with the tide."

The British teen film with a rock music backdrop was still relatively new in 1962, outside of star vehicles for British Isles pop idols. One film that didn't rely on any British teen idols was *Some People*, part of the early oeuvre of director Clive Donner, which included David Hemmings, four years away from his star turn in the iconic 1966 Michelangelo Antonioni Swinging London staple *Blow Up*, in its cast.

The Loneliness of the Long Distance Runner would be yet another major new British film in 1962, directed by Tony Richardson, and the second time a work of Alan Sillitoe, this time a short story, would be the basis of a key new British film. The film would in some respects spell the end of the first wave of the new British Cinema, as its neorealist feel would soon give way to the frothy exuberance of the Swinging Sixties style. While most of these films would use non-British films as an influence here and there, *The Loneliness of the Long Distance Runner* seemed somewhat influenced by the French new wave, but again was a social problem film rooted in the grim state of provincial England. The film starred Tom Courtenay in his breakout role as Colin Smith, an angry young man grappling with the death of his father, manhood, and the reality of slim employment and financial prospects. The film slips back and forth in time but focuses on his incarceration at a boys' prison for the theft at a bakery and how the governor, played by Michael Redgrave, spots his running talents. Redgrave wants young Colin to win the upcoming race against a public school. Colin's place in the race is the film's denouement and is a metaphor for the rage, revolution, and change that would rewrite the lives of England's youth as the decade evolved. Courtenay won the prestigious BAFTA Award for Best Newcomer and was later nominated for Best Actor in a Leading Role for his next film *Billy Liar*. Still active today, with a list of movies, television, and stage credits to rival any of his contemporaries, Courtenay doesn't receive the same attention as some of the bigger international British star actors to emerge in this period, but that is not reflective of his talent, range, or ability not to be pigeonholed.

A Kind of Loving, released in 1962, would further introduce bright new talents to the British film scene who would be major players for years. Produced by Jo Janni for Anglo Amalgamated, the film starred Alan Bates and was directed by John Schlesinger. Schlesinger, like Richardson, started his professional career directing television programs, in his case documentaries, after making low-budget films at Oxford University. *A Kind of Loving* continued many of the themes of the kitchen sink, social problems, and new British films. Bates starred as Vic Brown, who falls for coworker Ingrid Rothwell, played by newcomer June Ritchie. Vic is unsure of whether Ingrid is the girl he wants to settle down with or if he should travel, see the world, and enjoy his youth, but when Ingrid becomes pregnant, the two marry. Their marriage quickly unravels while they are living with Ingrid's meddlesome mother. Ingrid falls, has a miscarriage, and eventually the couple must decide to reconcile or go their separate ways. The film's inconclusive ending, and equally unconventional title sequence, are emblematic of Schlesinger's deft directorial touch. Like many of the other films of this era, *A Kind of Loving* shows provincial English life in stark black and white. Again, it's hard to imagine that such a confused cultural milieu and grim country would soon come to embody the new 1960s freedoms. Schlesinger also adds some nice self-referential cinema touches, particularly when a movie marquee flashes the 1961 film *Victim*, starring Dirk Bogarde and Sylvia Sims. The Basil Dearden–directed *Victim* was the first British movie to utter the word *homosexual* and was one of the many new British films to deal with sex in a frank manner and not afraid to touch on controversial subjects. Prior to *Victim*, another film with a prestigious British director that dealt with controversial material was *Peeping Tom*, released in 1960 and directed by Michael Powell. The film, which dealt with a serial killer and voyeurism, was slotted in the horror genre, although it was more of a psychological thriller. The next year, Jack Clayton would also use the horror genre as the basis for a film that contributed greatly to the new British film explosion; *The Innocents*, based on *The Turn of the Screw* by Henry James, with a screenplay cowritten by Truman Capote.

The L-Shaped Room, another in the kitchen sink school of films, was also released in 1962, directed by Bryan Forbes. Leslie Caron's performance as Jane Fosset won her Best Actress honors at the BAFTA Awards and Golden Globes, along with an Academy Award nomination for Best Actress. The film was produced by Romulus with American backing from Columbia Pictures and was distributed by UA.

It's also interesting to note that many of these films were not set in England's capital city, London, but in the north of England.

Other notable 1962 films include *Live Now–Pay Later* and *The Wild and the Willing*.

Schlesinger returned in 1963 with *Billy Liar*, which A. O. Scott of the *Village Voice* called the best British film of the 1960s. The film centers on the life of troubled, disaffected Billy, was imaginatively shot, and featured fantasy sequences that offered new ways of filmmaking. It also featured new stars of British cinema, the previously mentioned Tom Courtenay and, in her breakthrough role, Julie Christie, which netted her a BAFTA Award for Best British Actress. Christie's star ascended quickly, and her next major film role in John Schlesinger's *Darling* in 1965 was produced by Anglo Amalgamated. For *Darling*, she received a Golden Globe nomination for Best Actress and won Best Actress honors at the BAFTA Awards and Academy Awards. She next starred alongside Omar Sharif in David Lean's epic adaptation of Boris Pasternak's *Doctor Zhivago*, which was released in 1965.

While *Darling* was directed by John Schlesinger, it was from an idea by Schlesinger, the film's producer Joseph Janni and Frederick Raphael, who wrote the screenplay. It was Raphael's second script. He cowrote the script to *Nothing But the Best* with Stanley Ellin, which was released in 1964, directed by Clive Donner, and starring Alan Bates. He worked again with Schlesinger in 1967, adapting the book by Thomas Hardy *Far From the Madding Crowd*. He would continue to work with such esteemed directors as Stanley Donen, Peter Bogdanovich, and Paul Mazursky and worked on what would be Stanley Kubrick's last film, *Eyes Wide Shut*.

The year 1963 would also see the release of *This Sporting Life*, adapted from David Storey's novel, directed by Lindsay Anderson, produced by Karel Reisz, and starring another major new talent, Richard Harris. Harris was in the throes of working on *Mutiny on the Bounty* in the South Pacific, which he loathed, when Anderson sent him the novel. Harris practically begged Anderson to let him star in the film. Tony Richardson had wanted Anderson to direct the film after reading the novel, but Woodfall did not have the commercial clout and were easily outbid for the film rights by Independent Artists through the Rank Organization.

Independent Artists initially envisioned Joseph Losey to produce, who had worked with them in 1959 on *Blind Date*, with Stanley Baker as the lead. Harris brought the same kind of gritty male anger and angst to the role that Richard Burton brought to *Look Back in Anger*. There were also echoes of Marlon Brando's star turn as Stanley in Elia Kazan's 1951 screen adaptation of the Tennessee Williams's play *A Streetcar Named Desire*. In a key scene late in the film, when he yells for Margaret (played by Rachel Roberts), Harris chillingly recalls Brando's agonizing yelling for "Stella" in *Streetcar*. It's wonderful seeing Harris sing in the film, and although it's no "MacArthur Park," hints of his Irish baritone seep through.

This Sporting Life, while not a box-office success, received multiple nominations from the Academy Awards, Golden Globes, BAFTA, and at the Cannes Film Festival. Richard Harris won for best actor at Cannes and Rachel Roberts won for best actress at the BAFTA awards. Anderson hadn't made any films between 1957 and 1962, but the work he did in these intervening years not only shaped his directorial talent and vision, but it also remained interconnected with the burgeoning success of the British film world. Before *This Sporting Life*, he directed eight plays for the Royal Academy of Dramatic Arts at the Royal Court Theatre. *The Lily White Boys* and *Billy Liar* both starred Albert Finney. *Progress in the Park* was written by Alun Owen who would go on to write the screenplay for *A Hard Day's Night*. *The Long and the Short and the Tall*, written by Willis Hall, was later a film, produced by Michael Balcon, released in 1961 and starring Richard Todd, Richard Harris, and David McCallum (who would go to play Illya Kuryakin in the American television 1960s spy classic *The Man from U.N.C.L.E.*).

Losey made three films with Harold Pinter: *The Servant, Accident,* and *The Go-Between.* The year 1961 would also see the release of *The Innocents,* directed by Jack Clayton, whose modest directorial output includes the aforementioned *Room at the Top;* Clayton was also a film producer. One of the film's stars was Michael Redgrave, who had a long and distinguished radio, television, and film career dating back to the 1930s, having appeared in such new British cinema releases as *The Loneliness of the Long-Distance Runner* and *The Go-Between.* Redgrave and his wife, actress Rachel Kempson, are the parents of three actors, Vanessa, Lynn, and Corin Redgrave. Vanessa's daughters Natasha and Joely, whose father was Tony Richardson, also entered the acting profession, as did Corin's daughter Jemma. Vanessa's son Carlo Gabriel Nero, who she had with actor Franco Nero, is a screenwriter.

Billy Budd, released in 1962, with Peter Ustinov directing, producing, costarring and cowriting the screenplay, was based on the Herman Melville novel and featured the screen debut of Terence Stamp. Stamp became one of the bright new young stars of British cinema in the 1960s, an actor who to this day remains vital and active and a fixture of the Swinging London in-set. His brother Chris was equally at the center of London 1960s' scene. After meeting Kit Lambert while working at Shepperton Studios (where they worked on such films as *The L-Shaped Room*), they went on to comanage the Who, from West London, in 1964. They also started Track Records, the label the Jimi Hendrix Experience recorded for in England.

It is important to note here that although primarily an American-made film, *Lolita* was released in 1962. Based on the novel by Vladimir Nabokov, two of the principal roles were by Brits (James Mason and Peter Sellers) and director Stanley Kubrick, though an American, was based and worked almost exclusively in England after completing *Lolita.* Like Richard Lester, who we will come to know quite well as the director of the first two films from the Beatles, *A Hard Day's Night* and *Help!* and many other films, he was also a musician (playing the drums) and was a classical music buff. Another major British film from 1962 to mention is David Lean's *Lawrence of Arabia,* starring Peter O'Toole and Alec Guinness.

NO, NOT THAT TOM JONES

Tom Jones was the moneymaking, postneorealist, post-kitchen-sink film that blew the doors open commercially and financially for the new British films of the time.

The film was based on Henry Fielding's novel *The History of Tom Jones, a Foundling,* published in 1749. It is regarded as one of the first true novels of English literature and fits into many literary subgenres. Its multicharacter, epic, 700-page tale of love, life, death, and hypocrisy is played more for comic and carnal fun in the film version and caught the tenor of the times to come in Swinging Sixties London.

After so many moody, dark, realist British films, *Tom Jones* was a rollicking affair and made an international star out of Albert Finney. *Halliwell's Film Guide* called the film "vivid and hilarious." One of the results of the film's success was a gushing spigot of American money that flowed into British movie production from American film studios such as Warner Brothers, 20th Century Fox, Columbia, Paramount, Universal, and MGM. It also spawned an eight-picture deal between Woodfall and UA. Oddly enough, it would be the last British art house film from Woodfall to make it in the US. It wouldn't be until *Women in Love* in 1969 that another British art film did good business in the States. *Halliwell's Film Guide* called *Tom Jones* "the spearhead of a new and successful drive to get British films a wider showing in the US."

The film completed a remarkable run for Tony Richardson that began in 1955 with *Momma Don't Allow*, a documentary short codirected by Karel Reisz with cinematography by Walter Lassally. Produced by the British Film Institute Experimental Film Fund, it was first shown as part of the first "Free Cinema" program at the National Film Theatre in February 1956. The short film captures a performance by Chris Barber's jazz band, featuring Ottilie Patterson, at a north London trad jazz club. While somewhat obscure, it gives an informed glimpse into the pre-pop-and-rock British era that would have a profound effect on the 1960s music scene. From there, Richardson went from strength to strength, with the aforementioned *Look Back in Anger*, *The Entertainer*, *Sanctuary*, *A Taste of Honey*, and *The Loneliness of The Long Distance Runner*, culminating with *Tom Jones*. Richardson would round out the first half of the 1960s with *The Loved One*, featuring a script cowritten by American Terry Southern, hot off his cowriting the screenplay for *Dr. Strangelove*, and with cowriting credits still to come on *The Collector*, *The Cincinnati Kid*, *Barbarella*, *Easy Rider*, and *The Magic Christian*, which features many Beatles and Richard Lester film connections.

The huge grosses that *Tom Jones* was accruing in the US in only a few dozen theaters weren't the only sign that America was waking up to the new British cinema. MGM had agreed to make nine movies at Borehamwood, and Paramount would make a whopping seventeen.

In 1963, the Basil Dearden film *A Place to Go* was a film that harked back to the era of stark kitchen sink films. This sometime grim, grainy black-and-white film shot mostly on location in Bethnal Green in East London was taken from a novel by co-screenwriter Michael Fisher called *Bethnal Green*. The story, like many kitchen sink films, centers on the unforgiving lower-class struggles of young men and their aging parents coming to grips with a changing, postwar England, just on the cusp of the invasion of pop culture. Petty crimes and young male characters seeking to break free of their humble station in life are at the core of the narrative.

There is also the emergence in British films of this period of a new, more assertive, yet somewhat confused female love interest, here played by the 1960s Brit film "It

Girl" of the period, Rita Tushingham, as Catherine Donovan. Ricky Flint, the lead, played by Mike Sarne, is a naïve young man deciding between getting married and getting a job or pursuing the carefree life of petty crime, escaping his claustrophobic circumstances. Sarne had a career that also included singing, directing, and TV roles, including directing the sexy 1960s cult favorite *Myra Breckinridge*, for which he cowrote the script based on Gore Vidal's book. In England, he was also known as a pop singer and hit the top of the charts in June 1962 with the novelty song "Come Outside." In *A Place to Go*, he opens the film singing the title song at his family's local pub. The film has one Beatles connection. Roy Kinnear, who plays the character Bunting, went on to play Algernon in *Help!* and also appeared in many other Richard Lester films. There's also a James Bond connection; Ricky's father is played by Bernard Lee, who played "M," the head of MI6, in 11 Bond films.

Stemming from the long British tradition of drama, it's no surprise that UK cinema produced some of the great film actors from the beginning of the birth of film. Whether from small regional theaters, or the country's esteemed Royal Academy of Dramatic Arts, actors grounded in Shakespearian plays or the vast theatrical Albion canon often made a smooth transition into film. In the postwar era and exploding in the 1960s, the number of these talented actors, many of whom would become major international movie stars, still resonates today.

2

They're Going To Put The Beatles in The Movies

Before the Beatles started filming *A Hard Day's Night* on March 2, 1964, they had been receiving feature film offers from as early as February 1963. In April 1963, the Beatles were in talks with promoter and manager Giorgio Gomelsky to work on a short film. Gomelsky is best known as an early manager of both the Rolling Stones and the Yardbirds, but in fact, he was an aspiring film producer, who only got into pop music as a backdoor route into film. The Beatles were hoping Gomelsky and Irishman Ronan O'Rahilly could produce a short, experimental film that would showcase the Beatles in a documentary style way, much like Richard Lester's *The Running, Jumping and Standing Still* film. The 1959 short film was directed by Lester and the legendary British actor and comedian Peter Sellers. Made on a shoestring budget over the course of a couple of Sundays, the surreal film featured equal contributions from one of Sellers's other *Goon Show* mates, Spike Milligan. Almost done as a lark, the film was nominated for an Oscar in the short-film category and would go on to have an enormous influence on *A Hard Day's Night*, Monty Python, and many British and eventually even American comedic films and television shows, throughout the 1960s and 1970s. O'Rahilly started out running the Scene Club in Ham Yard in Soho off of Windmill Street and would eventually go on to distinguish himself as the figurehead behind launching "pirate radio" on Easter Sunday 1964 with Radio Caroline, named after President Kennedy's daughter. Pirate radio broadcasting had existed almost since the advent of radio. These so-called pirates would broadcast from ships that were technically far enough out at sea to circumvent broadcasting laws. In the 1960s these kinds of stations sought to offer an alternative to the monopoly the BBC had over broadcasting in the UK but offering formats that appealed to the young fans of pop music. Whether it be what would have been termed Top-40 pop radio, earlier in the decade or more progressive and experimental formats later, the pirate stations broke the stranglehold the BBC had on radio programming and then became an influence on the BBC, forcing massive change at the BBC to add new channels and cater to the new youth music market. Another pirate radio station, Radio London, with American funding and an American-style Top-40 format, launched in December and would eventually be immortalized on *The Who Sell Out*, the group's third studio album, released in 1967.

The O'Rahilly film project never got beyond an outline, but the seeds of what would be were already taking root. Radio London ceased broadcasting on August 14, 1967, as a direct result of the passing of the Marine Broadcasting Offences Act. The success and ultimate shuttering of Radio London also led to the birth of the BBC's Radio 1, which launched on September 30, 1967, the first attempt by BBC radio to play the new emerging pop-rock music.

Another possible movie role for the Beatles was for them to appear in a feature film called *The Yellow Teddy Bears*. Although the Beatles never participated in the film, it was released in the UK in 1963 and was directed by Robert Hanford-Davis, coproduced by Tekli Films, and distributed by Compton Films, who also produced and distributed Roman Polanski's breakthrough film *Repulsion* in 1965. *The Yellow Teddy Bears* came out in the US in 1964. The film involves the promiscuity of teenage girls and attempts to moralize on abortion and premarital sex and, although preachy and dated, tries to seriously look at these issues, albeit strictly from the view of the older generation. The film was also called *Gutter Girls* and *The Thrill Seekers*, and there is allegedly a non-British "continental" version that contains nudity. The film has been repackaged over the years and marketed as a sexploitation film. To focus on that marketing angle, it is often paired on DVD as double feature with films easily categorized as sexploitation or with clips of 1960s British pop music artists, to make it appear to be a Swinging Sixties film. The Beatles never seriously considered being in the film. Paul McCartney has said that the group would have either had to perform the songs of other songwriters in the movie or give up the copyright on any of their own songs. The music in the film was eventually supplied by guitarist and bandleader Malcolm Mitchell. Mitchell led a jazz trio that backed American jazz musicians in England.

The Beatles did appear on film long before *The Yellow Teddy Bears* was released. On August 22, 1962, Granada Television filmed the group at a lunchtime session at the Cavern Club on Mathew Street in Liverpool. Interspersed with shots of the crowd, the group performed covers of Richie Barrett's "Some Other Guy" and "Kansas City," which the Beatles likely knew from Little Richard's version. Deemed too raw, the footage was not aired until November 6, 1963, after Beatlemania took hold in England. The concert occurred less than a week after drummer Pete Best was sacked and Ringo Starr had joined the group, and the day before John Lennon wed Cynthia Powell.

The group's first official television appearance occurred on October 17, 1962, at three different times during the day and at two different locations through Granada television: a lunchtime concert at the Cavern Club in Liverpool, in the evening at Granada's studios in Manchester, to appear on the regional television show *People and Places*, and then back to the Cavern.

The first time a newsreel movie was made of the group occurred on November 20, 1963. The film, titled "The Beatles Come to Town," was filmed by the Pathé News Service at the ABC Cinema in Manchester. The short features performances of the Lennon and McCartney-penned "She Loves You" and the Isley Brothers' "Twist and Shout," along with shots of hysterical fans, backstage footage, and more. There is also film of the Beatles performing on November 16, 1963, at the Winter Gardens in Bournemouth. Footage from the show was to be broadcast in the US on *The CBS Evening News* on November 21, but instead, it ran on the CBS Morning News on November 22 and was scheduled to also run in the evening, but the assassination of President Kennedy preempted it. Walter Cronkite did run it on the CBS Evening News on December 10. It also ran on NBC's *The Tonight Show*, then hosted by Jack Paar, on January 3, 1964.

The first official film of the Beatles in America, produced by CBS and distributed through National General, was a concert film of their performance at the Washington Coliseum in Washington DC, on February 11, 1964. The 12-song, half-hour set was shown in US cinemas on March 14 and 15, 1964, and also included performances by the Beach Boys and Lesley Gore.

Appearing in a feature film was an obvious next step in the Beatles' evolution as a pop music entertainment phenomenon. The group had been in the process of shedding their Liverpool roots, and their manager Brian Epstein had started to move the base of his NEMS operation to London as late winter/early spring faded into early summer 1963, eventually installing 10 phone lines to handle the unprecedented amount of work required to service his ever-growing stable of artists.

Epstein finally began negotiations with UA films in August 1963. The idea of the Beatles being signed by UA actually began with the company's music publishing division. Noel Rogers was the head of UA Music, British publishing division. Rogers knew that regardless of what kind of film was made and how it did at the box office, the song publishing and recording rights would be valuable. He had seen how well the soundtracks for *The Great Escape*, with music by Elmer Bernstein, and *Dr. No*, the first James Bond film, with the James Bond theme song written by Monty Norman and performed by the John Barry Orchestra, had done. Working in England's music industry, Rogers naturally knew Dick James, the Beatles' music publisher. While the Beatles recordings were released through EMI in England and Capitol in

America, the group had no specific recording arrangement for soundtrack albums in the US. It was this lapse on the part of Capitol Records in America, along with Roger's introduction to Epstein through James, that set the ball in motion for UA to land a three-picture deal with the Beatles and, initially more importantly to UA, have its record label release the official soundtrack in the US. It is interesting to reflect on how different the film career of the Beatles might have started if EMI and Capitol had secured the rights for any soundtrack albums in the US. In the final deal, UA would also split the lucrative song publishing rights of the Beatles songs used in the film through its subsidiary, Unart Music Corporation.

Rogers quickly brought his idea to UA's Mike Stewart, executive vice president of the music and record division, based in New York. Stewart brought the idea to David Picker, UA's vice president in New York, who bounced the idea back to London to George "Bud" Ornstein, the chief of UA's production operations for all of Europe (and who like *A Hard Day's Night* future director Richard Lester, was originally from Philadelphia). To give some insight into the swashbuckling producer, Ornstein produced *The Pride and the Passion*, a 1957 film shot on location in Spain starring Frank Sinatra, Gary Grant, and Sophia Loren and directed by Stanley Kramer. Being based in London, Ornstein was involved often in productions filmed in Spain and other parts of Europe, far from the costs, scrutiny, and sometimes backward, inbred nature of American Hollywood studio filmmaking of that time. He loved the sophisticated style of the English elite and did what he could to fit in, rather than stick out like the typically brash ugly American. Still, while in Spain helping along the troubled production of *The Pride and the Passion*, he ingratiated himself to some degree with the country's fascist dictator, General Francisco Franco, to work effectively in the country. He even had a relationship with mobster-in-exile Lucky Luciano. Luciano lived in Cuba and Italy and, in 1962, was considering allowing his life story to be made into a film. But upon arrival in Naples to meet with a film director to discuss the project, he had a fatal heart attack at the airport.

It is no surprise that Ornstein would be a key player in launching the film career of the Beatles. Another American in England, Ornstein was a central figure in the film *Tom Jones*, the movie that kicked the door open for the commercially successful new cinema in England. He also worked on another film that was key to the new British cinema, the first James Bond film, *Dr. No*. He started out as a postwar sales trainee with UA and was instrumental in getting Rank's British films picked up in the tough Irish neighborhoods in Brooklyn where he grew up. Given the dislike the Irish sometimes had for the Brits at the time, his successes in getting Rank's films accepted and exhibited in the Brooklyn theaters proved his value to the company. He was then transferred to UA's Latin American division, prior to a nearly nine-year stint in Spain, aided by his ability to speak Spanish. Early in the 1960s, he returned to England and moved into production. UA had long shed the roots of its original owners, making his relationship to his wife's aunt Mary Pickford, one of the UA's original cofounders, ultimately unhelpful.

Ornstein's London production office ran efficiently, and its streamlined approach made room for only four or five films a year. Once all the parties agreed that UA wanted to make a movie with the Beatles and an initial budget was drawn up, Ornstein and Picker got to work getting the film's production going. In *Things They Said Today*, a bonus documentary shot in 2002 that was on the Criterion Collection edition of *A Hard Day's Night*, Picker not only explained the way *A Hard Day's Night* was set up and executed and what factors made UA so successful in this period: "Our philosophy was, we chose the filmmakers we wanted to be in business with, we approved the scripts, we approved the budget, and they [the filmmakers] had final cut, as long as the film stayed within budget and followed the script, which we approved."

Though it's been said that Ornstein contacted producer Walter Shenson and Picker contacted director Richard Lester, this version has been disputed. Shenson already had a relationship with Lester, having worked with him on *The Mouse on the Moon* released in 1963. Also, Shenson was the real point person on the film, setting up his production company, Proscenium Films, to secure the songs from the group's publishing company, Northern Songs, and contract the Beatles to appear in the film, through NEMS, who represented the group.

RUNNING, JUMPING, AND STANDING STILL WITH RICHARD LESTER

Richard Lester's work with the Beatles influenced not only British cinema of the 1960s but also, to a lesser degree, the British rock scene of the decade, as well as having an enormous impact on the music video explosion of the 1980s. Neil Sinyard, Emeritus Professor of Film Studies at the University of Hull, and the editor of the *British Film Makers* series book on Lester (published in 2010 by Manchester University Press), summarized Lester's place in 1960s film: "In the 1960s Richard Lester was one of the most inventive and influential directors around. . . . John Schlesinger paid him the compliment of saying that with Jean-Luc Godard, Lester extended the freedom of cinema. Terry Gilliam said Lester was the reason he came to England."

Lester was one of those precocious children who came of age during a time of postwar affluence in America, growing up during the end of World War II and the immediate postwar period in Philadelphia. Lester was born with a high IQ and was a musical prodigy. He had not planned on a career in film, graduating from the prestigious Ivy League University of Pennsylvania with a degree in clinical psychology in 1951. Eventually working in television, Lester slowly worked his way up the ladder as a director with CBS TV. Feeling like America was a bit too staid for his adventurous spirit and curious intellect, he headed for England.

He would eventually be at the center of the seminal 1950s British TV comedy period, even briefly having his own program, *The Dick Lester Show* in 1955. The show, created by Lester with Philip Saville, costarring Lester, Alun Owen, and Reg Owen, and directed by Douglas Hurn, soon caught Peter Sellers's attention. Sellers was then a member, along with Spike Milligan, Harry Secombe, and Michael Bentine, of the landmark British comedy troupe the Goons, and it's more than coincidental that the Beatles would work with both George Martin, who worked on recordings of the Goons, and Richard Lester, who worked with the Goons on television.

Sellers's interest led to Lester's working with Sellers and Milligan on a television show. Unable to use the word *goon* in the title, the program was called *The Idiot Weekly, Price 2d.* After its initial airing, Sellers called to Lester and joked, "Either that's the worst television show I've ever, ever seen or I think you're on to something that we are aspiring to." *The Idiot Weekly, Price 2d* morphed into *A Show Called Fred* in 1956, which that same year became *Son of Fred.* Lester also worked with Michael Bentine on the television series *It's a Square World.*

Various members of the Goons had appeared in the films *Penny Points to Paradise* (1951), *Down Among the Z Men* (1952), and the short *The Case of the Mukkinese*

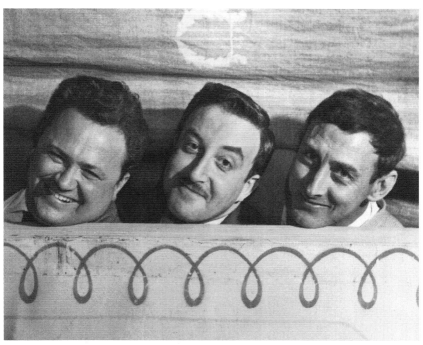

The groundbreaking comedy team the Goons were major influences on the surreal comedy of *A Hard Day's Night.* Pictured left to right: Harry Secombe, Peter Sellers, and Spike Milligan. Courtesy Photofest.

Battle-Horn (1956). All three films predate Lester's short with Sellers and Milligan, *The Running Jumping & Standing Still Film* (1959). Although many regard this as Lester's commercial breakthrough, Sellers actually filmed much of the movie with his Paillard Bolex 16-mm camera over the course of two Sundays in 1959 and was very much Lester's collaborator. Lester, Sellers, Milligan, and Mario Fabrizi cowrote the script. Lester also wrote the music for the film.

In 1959, Lester made the short *Have Jazz Will Travel.* The film was a 30-minute pilot that focused on the British jazz group the Tony Kinsey Quintet. Kinsey was a composer, drummer, and poet and played with a host of British and American jazz artists during his long career. It has also been released as *The Sound of Jazz* and is often confused with the 1957 American-made film of the same name, which focused on American jazz, and was broadcast on CBS, which was produced by Nat Hentoff, Whitney Balliett, and Charles H. Schultz.

Have Jazz Will Travel led to Lester's feature film directorial debut, *It's Trad, Dad!,* after producer Milton Subotsky caught a screening of the film. Subotsky, who'd co-produced the musical film *Rock, Rock, Rock!* (1956), was another American working in England, who formed Amicus Productions with fellow American Max Rosenberg, which produced *Dr. Who* films, horror films, and, much later on, adaptions of several Stephen King novels.

In many ways, *It's Trad, Dad!* was a perfect example of the kind of pop music film the Beatles didn't want to make. Released in the US as *Ring-A-Ding Rhythm,* the film included acts familiar to the Beatles, including fellow British musical artists such as Chris Barber, Acker Bilk, and Kenny Ball and those they would work with later, including Helen Shapiro and Sounds Incorporated. There was also a bevy of American rock 'n' roll stars in the film that the Beatles idolized, including Gene Vincent, Del Shannon, Chubby Checker, and Gary "U.S." Bonds. The thin plotline revolves around a group of teenagers who want to put on a jazz concert over the objection of the mayor. The teenagers enlist the help of some famous DJs, and in the end, the show comes off. Lester rescued the trite storyline with his innovative staging, lighting, camera work, and editing.

Another pre–*A Hard Day's Night* British film with a jazz angle was *Band of Thieves.* Released in 1962 as a vehicle for Acker Bilk, the film was directed by Peter Bezencenet. Bezencenet had been a film editor since the 1930s and directed a handful of thrillers in the early to mid-1960s.

The Beatles were well aware of *The Running Jumping & Standing Still* film, having seen it at the Tatler News Theatre in Liverpool on Church Street, unknowingly seeing the work of the man they would make films with in the future. The 600-seat theater opened in 1932 with the express purpose of providing a continuous bill of newsreels, cartoons, short films, and travelogues. The Beatles would often go to the cinema between lunchtime and evening shows at the Cavern, killing time in the plush old theater. The theater changed its name in 1968 and after, many subsequent name and program changes, closed in 1972 and became retail space.

Television, both in America and particularly in England, was very much still a developing medium run by young people. Although movies would take months, if not years to make, live television shows, especially in the age before videotape, reflected the world at that moment. In both countries, the dominant demographic was the baby boom generation (people born between 1946 and 1964). And key to the ever-changing English society was the end of national conscription, which started in 1957, as the first baby boomers were nearing their teen years. Men born on or after October 1, 1939, were no longer required to do national service, freeing them to pursue their careers at a younger point in their lives. National conscription formally ended on December 31, 1960. John Lennon has often said that this was an important factor in his being able to pursue his music career.

One of the many television shows that Lester worked on in England was the *Mark Saber* police television series, which had many incarnations in the 1950s and 1960s, both in the US and UK.

Lester worked as a codirector with another American living in England, who would be instrumental in the new British movie explosion, Joseph Losey. Losey was a theater and film director, producer, and screenwriter, who was blacklisted by Hollywood in the 1950s. The four key British films of the 1960s and early 1970s that he worked on, *The Servant, Accident, Modesty Blaise*, and *The Go-Between*, were all written or cowritten for the screen by British playwright Harold Pinter. Losey also had a connection with *A Hard Day's Night* screenwriter Alun Owen; the Losey-directed film *The Criminal* (1960) was written by Alun Owen. Lester wrote the original score for *The Criminal*, but it was replaced by a score written by Brit John Dankworth.

Lester's understanding of television and music, along with his ability to also produce commercials, made him ideally suited to be at the forefront of the new pop music film explosion, and his pairing with the Beatles on their debut feature film was a match made in heaven. He was also a key contributor to the new British cinema of the early 1960s, even though he was an American. *Halliwell's Film Guide* said of his film *The Knack . . . and How to Get It* (1965): "the running gags and visually inventive interludes shot in London's streets were almost undiluted joy." *Petulia* (1968) was in many ways the perfect extension and counterpoint to his other London films (*A Hard Day's Night, Help!*, and *The Knack*) because it was shot in San Francisco, which was, at that time, the new hip international world mecca. The film featured a score by John Barry, but it also featured performances by Big Brother and the Holding Company (featuring Janis Joplin) and the Grateful Dead, groups central to the San Francisco scene of the time. The film also featured a scene at an aquarium with performing penguins—one of the penguin's names was George, and the other's was Ringo.

BEATLES BUSINESS

Subafilms Limited was formed by Brian Epstein as December 1963 was fading into January 1964—perhaps as a result of how poorly the deal with UA turned out to be for Epstein and the Beatles. The company would produce the Gerry and the Pacemakers' film *Ferry Cross the Mersey* (1965) and the concert film of the Beatles' performance at Shea Stadium on August 15, 1965, which aired in England in 1966 and America in 1967. As for films unconnected to Epstein's NEMS stable, Subafilms (in conjunction with Selmur Productions), filmed the Fifth National Jazz and Blues Festival, held August 6 to 8, 1965, at the Richmond Athletic Association Grounds in Richmond, England. John Lennon and his wife Cynthia and George Harrison and his girlfriend Pattie Boyd attended the third night of the festival. Selmur productions was an American-based company that throughout the 1960s was involved in the production of many British films, including the Swinging London film *Smashing Time* (1967). The company also produced such television shows as *Combat* and the seminal pop music show *Shindig!*

Subafilms was just one of the companies formed by NEMS in the wake of Beatlemania. Two other companies connected with their business ventures were Stramsact and Seltaeb. Stramsact was set up to handle the Beatles' merchandising rights in England and Europe, working with companies who wanted to produce items like buttons, toys, dolls, and other items featuring the Beatles' image. Stramsact was also an attempt to curtail the slew of cheap, bootlegged items flooding the market, which only increased after the Beatles broke through in America. Epstein, who cared about the quality of merchandise associated with the Beatles, knew that NEMS was losing out on merchandising opportunities and needed someone to help stem the flow of unauthorized Beatles merchandising being produced.

David Jacobs, Brian Epstein's lawyer, recommended a young man named Nicky Byrne to run Stramsact, which launched in 1963. Seltaeb ("Beatles" spelled backward) was set up to handle US merchandising, which would prove to be even more lucrative but also more complicated in administering licenses and controlling the production and distribution of official Beatles merchandise.

Byrne was a curious choice to run companies. In the early days of pop in England, the industry was run by either the old school British upper class or the hustlers and show business veterans from Soho's Denmark Street. Byrne was part of the so-called Chelsea Set, who could be found at Alexander's restaurant, in the basement of Mary Quant's clothing shop Bazaar, the Fantasie espresso bar (the first of its kind in Chelsea), and the pub the Markham Arms.

He made his way in London thanks to his upper-crust pedigree and wife Kiki's fashion connections. But keen business acumen was not a part of his skill set, and he would ultimately lose millions for the Epstein and the Beatles. Beatles merchandise was selling like hotcakes, but because NEMS' share was initially only 10 percent, the loses were incalculable. This became another instance where the Beatles felt Brian had let them down and had been swindled due to this lack of tough business tactics. Jacobs was able to renegotiate the Seltaeb deals (with NEMS's share increasing to 45 percent), but wheelbarrows of money had been lost by that point. Then lawsuits started that went on for years, with Epstein deciding it made more sense to negotiate directly with companies who wanted rights. As for Nicky Byrne, he was sued by various parties, departed with money he paid himself from the company, bought a yacht, and went to live in the Bahamas.

Epstein negotiated with UA for the Beatles to appear in three films and brought the negotiations to a conclusion on October 29, 1963. On December 4, the Beatles Film Productions, Ltd. was formed. It's hard to imagine that at such an early stage in their recording career the group was on the verge of signing a three-picture deal with an important international film company like UA. Other than "My Bonnie" recorded with Tony Sheridan and issued on Polydor in January 1962, the Beatles had only released four singles, two EPs, and one album in England up to that point. "I Want to Hold Your Hand" was about to come out in November 1963, backed with "This Boy," along with the EP *The Beatles (No. 1)*, consisting of "I Saw Her Standing There," "Misery," "Anna," and "Chains" and their second album *With the Beatles*.

With the Beatles was released on November 22, 1963, in the UK, the day US president John Kennedy was assassinated. Although the album went to number 1 in the UK, the initial vinyl pressing came from a bad master that caused the phonograph needles to jump. It's not clear if this was a problem with the master or if the bass EQ was simply mixed too "hot" to play properly on the fairly primitive record players that most people in England owned at the time. In an odd coincidence, when Mobile Fidelity Sound Labs manufactured the album on vinyl for release in 1983, not as many records were pressed as planned of the audiophile reissue because the stamper broke at the factory in Japan, where the album was pressed.

BRITISH BEAT BOYS AND GIRLS

UA imagined the Beatles appearing in the kind of quickie teen B movie that had been a staple of American and British movies since the birth of rock 'n' roll, including such American films as *Rock Around the Clock* (1956), *Don't Knock the Rock* (1956), *High School Confidential* (1958), and films featuring Elvis Presley, such as *Jailhouse Rock* (1956), *King Creole* (1957), and *Love Me Tender* (1958). *The Girl Can't Help It* (1956) arguably may not fit on this list because it may not be considered a B-picture and had name stars and well-known musical acts, but it needs to be mentioned here.

In England, the rock music film may have had its birth with 1957's *The Tommy Steele Story* from Insignia Films. Steele would go on to star in similar pop music quickies, such as *The Duke Wore Jeans* and *It's All Happening*, along with higher-profile films. Although not regarded as any sort of great actor, he made many films throughout the 1960s (including appearing in *Finian's Rainbow* in 1968), along with television work in the 1970s. Quickly following in Steele's footsteps was Terry Dene in *The Golden Disc* in 1958.

The film that accelerated the sociocultural aspects of the genre, and was no mere quickie teen pop exploitation film, was *Expresso Bongo*, released in 1960, starring Laurence Harvey. Long before the Beatles, London had a thriving coffee bar scene. Italian movie siren Gina Lollobrigida started the craze, importing a Gaggia espresso machine to the Moka Bar, the coffeehouse she opened on 29 Frith Street in 1953. The coffee bar scene and the emergence of the British teen youthquake coincided and was one of the first distinctly British scenes that at times ran parallel with the trad jazz, skiffle, and emerging rock scenes. The 2 i's coffee bar, located at 59 Old Compton Street in Soho, opened in 1955 and billed itself "the home of the stars," with an even more pronounced interest in music, launching the career of the Vipers, who would be signed by George Martin at Parlophone.

Expresso Bongo, released in 1959 and directed by Val Guest, focused on the coffee bar scene and the rise of a budding pop star (perfectly played by a young Cliff Richard in his second film appearance). The film was adapted from a West End play that was written by Wolf Mankowitz and Julian More and that grew out of a newspaper article written by Mankowitz. Guest was a director and screenwriter who had been working in the British film industry since 1935. He had a fruitful association with the UK's horror movie company supreme Hammer, directing such films as *The Quatermass Xperiment* and *Quatermass 2*. He worked in many other genres, including such UK spy spoof's as *Where the Spies Are* and was just one of the five directors credited on the first *Casino Royale*. The film was adapted from the 1959 stage version. The story presents a somewhat jaded and cynical view of the pop music-making machinery behind the popular song (the backstage dramaturgy notwithstanding). Rather than be appalled by the seedier and more exploitative aspects of the film, a young Andrew Loog Oldham, future manager, producer, and kingmaker of the Rolling Stones, delighted in the shadier aspects of pop management and openly admittedly in his first memoir, *Stoned*, that he found his calling in the Harvey character. Oldham had worked for Mary Quant and one of his big music business breaks was working the hamburger stand at the Flamingo with Rik Gunnell's wife. The Gunnell brothers also owned the Bag o Nails and the Flamingo. Oldham briefly worked for Brian Epstein before becoming the manager and de facto producer of the first seven albums (and singles and EPs) from the Rolling Stones. Those recordings from the group in this period were credited as being produced by

Impact Sound, which was the production company that Oldham started with Eric Easton. Oldham had stopped producing the Rolling Stones after *Between the Buttons* and ceased working with them at all in 1967. Oldham started Immediate Records in 1965, signing such acts as the Small Faces from East London. The label would fold in 1970. A companion four-song EP was released on Columbia in the UK in January 1960 and quickly sold 1,500 copies. EPs at that time usually didn't reach 500 copies in sales.

Cliff Richard's next film, *The Young Ones*, released as *Wonderful to Be Young!* in the US and released in 1961, was the first of a trilogy of musical films that would launch Richard as a major star in England. The film would also be the first true British rock musical of the 1960s and became the second biggest box-office film in the UK. Much of the success of the film was the team assembled, including director Sidney J. Furie. Another non-Brit making his way in England at this time, Canadian Furie would have a long career in film, working in many genres. His major 1960s British film would have to be considered *The Ipcress File*, starring Michael Caine, released in 1965. The other key member of the team was choreographer Herbert Ross, another American having an impact of British films of the 1960s at this time. Ross would have a long career in theater and film, with his major American film career kicking off with *Funny Girl*, starring Barbra Streisand in 1968. With all the critical and commercial success of the film, the success of the music from the film is almost as important. The soundtrack album, released on December 15, 1961, through EMI's Columbia imprint and produced by Norrie Paramor, was number 1 for six weeks and became the first UK soundtrack album to have sales of one million copies. The third single from the album, the title track, also hit number 1.

Richard's next film, the 1962 film *Summer Holiday* directed by Peter Yates, was the second-biggest grossing film of the year in the UK, although many felt it didn't quite live up to the success of *The Young Ones*. Yates started as a graduate of RADA and worked in many roles in the theater before being one of the directors of *The Saint* television series, starring future James Bond, Roger Moore. Yates followed up *Summer Holiday* with *One Way Pendulum* (Woodfall's first movie filmed at a studio, in this case Twickenham), one of England's first new satirical films, which surprisingly ended up a commercial and critical flop. He went on to more distinguished work as the director of such films as *Bullitt* (1968), *The Hot Rock* (1972), *The Deep* (1977), *Breaking Away* (1979), and *The Dresser* (1983). The final film in what came to be known as the Cliff Richard's color musical trilogy was *Wonderful Life* (released as *Swingers Paradise* in the US) in 1964. Although Furie returned to direct, the film's troubled production and release after *A Hard Day's Night* led to its being deemed a failure.

Some of Richard Lester's early work would contribute to solidifying the early British pop music template, yet the genre would ultimately fizzle out as *A Hard*

Day's Night would completely change the game. It's hard to tell if the spate of British teen exploitation films that came out in 1963, a year before *A Hard Day's Night*, is merely a coincidence or partly set the stage for *A Hard Day's Night* to come along and refresh the genre. Several films fit neatly into the genre. *Just for Fun* was actually a follow-up to Richard Lester's *It's Trad Dad*, which was directed by Gordon Flemyng, who would subsequently direct two *Dr. Who* movies. *Just for Fun* featured a slew of rock and pop artists, including such American acts as the Crickets, Bobby Vee, and Freddy Cannon, and on the British side, Jet Harris and Tony Meehan from the Shadows, the Tornados, who scored a number 1 the previous summer with the Joe Meek–produced "Telstar," the Springfields, featuring a young Dusty Springfield, Joe Brown and the Bruvvers, the Vernons Girls, Louise Cordet, Brian Poole and the Tremeloes, and Sounds Incorporated—quite an impressive lineup of early British Invasion artists and other new young British popular artists.

Another film, *Live It Up* (1963), deserves more attention than it's received over the years. Featuring David Hemmings (future star of the quintessential Swinging London film *Blow-Up*) and a young Steve Marriott, who would go on to be a founding member and front man in the mod band the Small Faces and the harder-rocking Humble Pie. Other notable future British rock stars to appear in the film include Ritchie Blackmore (who plays lead guitar in one of the bands in the film, the Outlaws), who would go on to be a founding member of Deep Purple and work with numerous other musicians in a wide variety of genres. Also featured were the aforementioned Tornados, whose drummer, Clem Cattini, was one of the most important session drummers in early 1960s British pop scene. Producer Joe Meek is credited as the film's musical director. Adding yet another layer of authenticity, and presaging the English pop explosion that would be launched and galvanized by the Beatles in 1964, costumes were supplied by Mary Quant, whose short skirts, bold colors, and comfortable and casual young look would define 1960s British fashion for women.

Be My Guest (1965) was produced less as a follow-up to *Live It Up* and more as a supporting film on a double bill with the Morecambe and Wise comedy spy spoof *The Intelligence Men* (1965). Like *Live It Up*, it featured David Hemmings (as Dave Martin) and Steve Marriot (as Ricky). Musicians included Ken Bernard as part of the fictitious group Kenny and the Wranglers. John Carpenter, drummer of the mod band the Zephyrs, appears in a featured role as the leader of the fictious group Slash Wildly and the Cut-Throats, with the other members of the Zephyrs comprising the rest of the band. Three other groups—the Nashville Teens, the Plebs, and the Niteshades—all appear as themselves, as does Jerry Lee Lewis. The musical director was hit record producer Shel Talmy, yet another key American living in England, whose production on the breakthrough hits of the Kinks and the Who helped shape and define the sound of 1960s British mod pop. The Niteshades released the film's title song as a single, backed with "I Must Reveal," one of only two singles they ever released (both in 1964). The Zephrs also released a single from the film, "I Just Can't Take It," backed with "She Laughed."

Another film from the British teen exploitation genre that deserves more credit is *What a Crazy World* (1963). Notable British musical artists in the film include Marty Wilde, Freddie and the Dreamers (in their film debut), and Joe Brown and the Bruvers. Brown was a pre-Beatles, nonrock artist, whose instrumental sound had many fans, including Paul McCartney and George Harrison. In fact, Brown performed the last song of the *Concert for George* (2002) a cover of the 1920s chestnut "I'll See You in My Dreams."

It's All Over Town (1963) is another film that musically seems to have one foot in the past and the other in the future. The appearance of Acker Bilk represents the trad jazz and easy listening, mainstream music that Mum and Dad would listen to on the wireless. But like *Live It Up*, it also features appearances from pop artists who would define the British Invasion, including Dusty Springfield, as part the Springfields, and the Hollies and Freddie and the Dreamers. Freddie and the Dreamers would appear in their own pop music film vehicle *Every Day's a Holiday* (titled *Seaside Swingers* in the US), with *Cuckoo Patrol*, produced in 1965 but not released until 1967. Another film that features a British Invasion act is *Saturday Night Out* (1964), which features the Searchers and was released in April, when the Beatles were well into filming *A Hard Day's Night*. *Nothing But the Best* (1964), released in March 1964, the month the Beatles began filming *A Hard Day's Night*, is a film that would rate a mention as a movie with an appearance by British pop group the Eagles, from Bristol. Among production crew were several new British film mavens, including director Clive Donner, cinematographer Nicolas Roeg, and the film's star, Alan Bates. Donner, Bates, and Roeg would reunite in 1963 on *The Caretaker*, adapted from Harold Pinter's play.

Donner's *Some People* (1962) included elements of the British teen music exploitation genre. His next two films, although they would be considered light movie fare, fit right into the new British film scene. *What's New Pussycat* (1965) starred Peter Sellers, with music written by Burt Bacharach and Hal David; the title song was sung by Welsh heartthrob Tom Jones. His next film, *Here We Go Round the Mulberry Bush* (1967), was a slice of Swinging London and one of the Summer of Love's quintessential but ultimately forgettable films. The film included many of the players that made up the British pop scene at the time, including actress Judy Geeson and Adrienne Posta, who appeared in *To Sir, with Love* (1967). The latter film also featured Suzy Kendall and Michael Des Barres, in his first credited screen role. In addition to his work as an actor and musician, Des Barres would be married for a time to Pamela Ann Miller, former Frank Zappa protégé, member of the GTOs, and author of the popular rock groupie memoir *I'm With the Band*. The title song of the movie was sung by Scottish singer Lulu, although the version she sings in the movie (backed by the Mindbenders), is different than the one that became a number one hit in the US but reaching only number 11 in the UK. *To Sir, with Love* also features music from the Mindbenders on their own after Wayne Fontana had left the group to go solo.

Other than a small role in the 1957 film *No Time for Tears*, Posta started out as a British music pop singer in 1963, but other than a handful of singles, she mostly appeared in films, including not only *To Sir, with Love* but also *Up the Junction* (1968), which featured music supplied by Manfred Mann, and *Percy* (1971) with featured music by the Kinks. *Here We Go Round the Mulberry Bush* also featured a screenplay by official Beatles biographer Hunter Davies and a soundtrack that boasted music from and appearances by Steve Winwood, as part of Traffic; his previous band, the Spencer David Group also appeared.

Alan Bates was one of a crop of young new British acting talent who had already appeared in such key new British film releases as *The Entertainer* (1960) and *A Kind of Loving* (1962) and would subsequently appear in *Georgy Girl* (1965), *Far from the Madding Crowd* (1967), *Women in Love* (1969), and *The Go-Between* (1970).

Oddly enough, for all their popularity and visual appeal, the Rolling Stones never made a nondocumentary feature film. But it was not for a lack of trying.

Once the group broke through with "(I Can't Get No) Satisfaction" in June 1965, the first Mick Jagger/Keith Richards original to top the US and UK charts, their manager Andrew Loog Oldham began to make inroads into getting the group a movie deal, recruiting director Peter Whitehead to start filming the band while they were on tour in Ireland in September 1965. While Whitehead hoped to bring a fresh take to the still-new pop music documentary, Oldham envisioned the movie to be no more than an extended screen test. The film, titled *Charlie Is My Darling*, wrapped in spring 1966 and debuted in October the same year at the Mannheim Film Festival in Germany. But then, due to legal disputes between Oldham and the Stones' next manager, Allen Klein, it wouldn't see wider release until 2012.

In 1965, the Stones were set to star in a film called *Back, Behind and in Front*, to be directed by Oldham, Klein, and two American screenwriters who were currently following the group around while they toured to get ideas (as Alun Owen had done with the Beatles prior to writing the script for *A Hard Day's Night*). Mick and Keith were set to write the songs, and Mike Leander would do the incidental music. England and other European countries were planned as locations, and Jagger hoped über-photographer David Bailey would be the cinematographer.

Another photographer on the scene, Gered Mankowitz, was at the center. His photography studio was in Mason's Yard, where the hip clubs, the Bag o Nails and the Scotch of St. James, and the Indica Gallery were located. Mankowitz remembers the Stones "were under pressure" at this time, trying to finish the songs that would be on the *Aftermath* album, and after they finished writing, "they were going straight into RCA studios in Hollywood." *Aftermath* would be their first great album of the 1960s. Songs from the album were to be part of the film's soundtrack. But the film never happened. In 1966, the group planned on starring in a film adaptation of *Only Lovers Left Alive*, the third novel written by Brit Dave Wallis. The youth exploitation science fiction novel was published in 1964, and Nicholas Ray was set to direct and would cowrite the script with Gillian Freeman. Freeman had written the 1961 novel *The Leather Boys*, later made into a film directed by Sidney J. Furie and starring Rita Tushingham; Freeman herself wrote the screenplay. More on that film later.

Only Lovers Left Alive never made it off the drawing board because Ray's drug and alcohol problems were spiraling out of control. Next up, writers Keith Waterhouse, author of the novel *Billy Liar!*, and Willis Hall, who cowrote the script of the film version with Waterhouse, were approached to jump-start *Only Lovers Left Alive* or write a new script. But the film was not to be.

David Bailey was also planning to shoot a short film with Mick bizarrely titled *The Assassination of Mick Jagger*. But the film didn't happen, and Bailey ultimately made the short *G.G. Passion*, released in 1966 and starring Eric Swayne (Patti Boyd's boyfriend at the time she met George Harrison while making *A Hard Day's Night*), Chrissie Shrimpton (model Jean Shrimpton's sister), and Caroline Munro. Bailey cowrote the script with Gérard Brach, who had just come off writing *Repulsion* (1965) and *Cul-de-Sac* (1966), both directed by Roman Polanski, who was also one of the producers of *G.G. Passion*. Polanski's career is well-documented, and Brach would go on to a long career. Bailey had also wanted to direct Jagger in a film adaptation of *A Clockwork Orange*, published by Anthony Burgess in 1962, and which would eventually be made into a film in 1971, directed by Stanley Kubrick. In a footnote with a devilish twist, in 2013 Jim Jarmusch would come out with a rock 'n' roll vampire movie titled *Only Lovers Left Alive* that was not based on the novel but which Jarmusch said was inspired by the title.

UNITED ARTISTS

It many ways, it made sense that UA would end up producing and releasing the films of the Beatles. The company was the first film studio to be run by film artists rather than business people. It was formed in 1919 by actor/director Charlie Chaplin, the acting couple of Mary Pickford and Douglas Fairbanks, and director D. W. Griffith. While the company would go through many changes and ownership through the years, events that would unfold in the 1950s led to the company's working with the Beatles.

Early in 1951, lawyers-turned-producers Arthur B. Krim (of Eagle-Lion Films), Robert Benjamin, and Matty Fox came up with a new plan for UA. Griffith had dropped out in 1924, and Fairbanks died in 1939. Krim and company suggested to Chaplin and Pickford to set up UA as a company that bankrolled independent producers and not have an actual studio. Under Krim's and Benjamin's leadership, and with the continued financial backing of Fox Film Corporation president Spyros Skouras, this successful formula would result in such acclaimed films as *The African Queen* (1951), *Moulin Rouge* (1952), *High Noon* (1952), *Marty* (1955), and *12 Angry Men* (1957).

In 1957 the company went public, and almost simultaneously launched United Artists Records, after failing to buy an existing record company. Max Youngstein, who had worked for 20th Century Fox, the US Treasury, American film director Stanley Kramer's production company, and with Krim at Eagle-Lion Films, headed up the company. Initially, United Artists Records planned to just release soundtrack albums but eventually expanded into easy listening, instrumental, jazz, and recordings that showed off the new high fidelity and stereo recording possibilities of 12-inch, long-playing albums. Columbia Records had first manufactured long-playing albums in 1948, while stereo, which had been experimented with in various mediums for years, became commercially available in 1958.

One of the label's first soundtracks was *Paris Holiday* (1958), which starred Bob Hope and Anita Eckberg. *The Magnificent Seven*, with music by Elmer Bernstein, and *Exodus*, with music by Ernest Gold, proved to be hot sellers on their release in 1960. The soundtrack of *Never On Sunday*, an English/Greek/Russian coproduction featuring music by the Greek music genius Manos Hatzidakis, also became a surprise hit in 1960. Music from spy films and spoofs such as *The Pink Panther* and *Goldfinger*, both from 1964, were huge hits featuring two masters of film music, Henry Mancini and John Barry, respectively. By 1966, United Artists Records accounted for about one fourth of the company's revenue.

Much has been said about the Beatles' deal with UA. The initial budget of the film was £200,000 for a black-and-white film. UA hired Walter Shenson to produce; he would be paid £12,000, splitting the profits 50/50 with UA. His company, Proscenium Films, had two separate deals with Brian Epstein: one with Northern Songs for the songs Lennon and McCartney would supply for the film (and, most importantly for UA, for the soundtrack), and one with NEMS Enterprises on behalf of the entire group. In the original deal, Epstein had said he wouldn't accept less than an advance of £20,000, and 7.5 percent of the net profits (UA had been prepared to offer an advance of £70,000 and 25 percent of the net profits). Epstein then passed on the negotiations to his lawyer, David Jacobs. Jacobs quickly realized the number Epstein had floated was too low and eventually negotiated an advance of £25,000 and 20 percent of the net profits.

Many, including the Beatles, felt this was another example of Epstein not being a shrewd negotiator, ultimately costing the group potentially millions of dollars. Beyond the money, the structure of the deal itself was not beneficial to the group. Shenson would regain sole rights to the film after 15 years. Richard Lester has said that he was paid £6,000 by Shenson, who also generously gave Lester a percentage of 1 percent. Also, the original deal called for one film with an option for two more, which was not fulfilled until *Let It Be* was contracted by UA to be distributed in 1970.

UA launched its European division in 1961. Bud Ornstein, UA's man in London, was key to getting the Beatles to make movies for UA. Being in London, he witnessed firsthand the gradual soaring popularity of the pop group from Liverpool. His initial thought in signing the group was based more on the possibilities of their soundtrack sales for UA's record division than the potential box office receipts, given the fickle, short shelf life of pop groups. He was fortunate that Capitol Records, the American record label with first rights to release the group's music in the States, had waited until December 26, 1963, to release "I Want to Hold Your Hand," which was actually the group's fifth single.

Funnily enough, Capitol had already issued music from another group associated with the British Invasion. Capitol released "I'm Telling You Now" by Freddie and the Dreamers on September 2, 1963. It was the group's second single. The original Capitol single did nothing in the States, perhaps another contributing factor to Capitol's reluctance to release any of the Beatles' music up until that time because British music did not often achieve any commercial success in America. Despite its pop appeal, the Beatles' music had a bluesier edge, perhaps making the almost-novelty pop of Freddie and the Dreamers a safer bet. In the wake of the huge success by the Beatles and other British Invasion bands, Capitol would rerelease the song in 1965 on their budget Tower label, and this time it became a number one hit.

UA was able to acquire the soundtrack rights for *A Hard Day's Night* before Capitol even realized that they were sitting on top of what would become the biggest recording group in the world.

SWINGING LONDON

As the last cold days of late winter were unfolding into the early spring of 1963, London was already exhibiting the stirrings of what would come to be known as Swinging London. Homegrown British pop would become the central ingredient of the scene. Fashion, photography, and bold new ideas in design were already creating a new look. Cutting-edge hairstylist Vidal Sassoon, who'd opened his first London salon in 1954, was a huge influence on the fashion scene at large. His short bob-style mod cut, first made famous by fashion designer Mary Quant, later took flight when a more subtle variation of it was worn by Nancy Kwan in the 1965 British movie *The Wild Affair*, also starring Terry Thomas. It was Sassoon's surname that many years later prompted Paul McCartney to call "Rocky Racoon," which was on the White Album, Rocky Sassoon in the early stages of a song that Donovan helped him write. However, it was actually Leslie Cavendish that McCartney was thinking of when giving the song its title because Paul had spirited Cavendish away from Sassoon's employ to become the de facto in-house hairstylist for the Beatles.

Quant and her husband and business partner, Alexander Plunkett-Greene, had both attended the University of London at Goldsmiths College. Quant opened up her first Chelsea shop on the King's Road on the corner of Markham Square in the mid-1950s; she would eventually move to her second store in Knightsbridge.

John Stephen, from Glasgow, had started out at Vince's Man Shop on Newbury Street, the seminal new London's menswear shop (which also used a young male model named Sean Connery from Edinburgh for their adverts). He opened his first store, called John Stephen, on Beak Street in 1956. When his store was lost in a fire, it was his move to the then-undistinguished Carnaby Street in 1957 that began his ascension as a men's fashion trendsetter and earned him the nickname "The King of Carnaby Street." While the store initially attracted a more flamboyant gay clientele, it quickly caught on with the emerging Mods. With the brash, rough look of the teddy boys fading, Stephen's clothes were elegant yet casual and had a continental look perfect for the smart set of young men who were rejecting the stuffy old gray tweed look of their dads and wouldn't be caught dead looking like a teddy boy. The teddy boy style, that reflected a 1950s rocker look, with garish suits, hadn't completely disappeared.

By 1964, the mail-order business Biba's Postal Boutique turned into and would be another Swinging London clothing store that would put the UK on the fashion map and make a star out of its founder, Barbara Hulanicki, with the help of her husband Stephen Fitz-Simon.

Much later would come another King's Road boutique, Granny Takes a Trip. Instead of mod clothes, the shop would be one of the first successful psychedelic hippie clothes emporiums, known for an ever-changing building façade that at one time featured the front of an actual 1968 Dodge automobile. The shop was born out of designer Shelia Cohen's love of transforming Victorian clothing into hippie finery, partnering with her boyfriend, Nigel Waymouth, one-half of Hapshash and the Coloured Coat, who were a psychedelic-inspired design team who also recorded two albums, and London tailor John Pearse, who learned his trade working for Savile Row bespoke tailors. The shop was an immediate hit, attracting London's pop elite, including members of Pink Floyd, the Rolling Stones, the Who, the Small Faces, and the Beatles.

Granny Takes a Trip particularly appealed to Jimi Hendrix, whose career took off in London in 1967 with the release of the debut album by the Jimi Hendrix Experience. The Purple Gang, hailing from Stockport in northern England, even released a song named after the shop in 1967. It was one of only two singles the group released, and the song also appeared on their sole album *Strikes*, produced by Joe Boyd and released in 1968. Living upstairs at one time was an unknown writer who was born in India but educated in London, Salman Rushdie. The shop opened early in 1966 and, after a change in ownership, went out of business in the 1970s.

Hung On You, which took its name from a Righteous Brothers song, opened in 1966 and quickly joined Granny Takes a Trip as one of the hot new hippie clothing shops. Located at Cale Street in Chelsea, it was run by Michael Rainey and his wife, London scenester Jane Ormsby-Gore, the eldest daughter of Lord Harlech and sister of Alice Ormsby-Gore, who was romantically linked with Eric Clapton. The shop attracted the likes of the Beatles, the Rolling Stones, and the Who. The store moved to King's Road in 1967, and the old address eventually became Jane Asher's Party Cakes and Sugarcraft Shop.

While David Bailey's *Box of Pin-Ups* (with text by literary titan Francis Wyndham) wasn't released until 1964, establishing him as one of the preeminent forces of the Swinging London scene, he had long taken London by storm with his photography as far back as 1960. Photographers Terry O'Neil, Brian Duffy, and Terry Donovan were also representing a new, young, fresh photographic aesthetic.

Theater was also going through a massive change, beyond the dramatic writing of the new playwrights. Satirical comedy exploded in the form of *Beyond the Fringe*, which opened in London in 1961. While the Goons presented a zany, absurdist take on comedy, *Beyond the Fringe* offered something a bit more biting, topical, and satirical that went right for the throats of the stuffy old ruling establishment elite. After striking gold in London's West End, the revue quickly went to Broadway. Two of its members, Peter Cook and Dudley Moore, would go on to careers in mainstream entertainment, with Moore becoming a major Hollywood movie star. *Private Eye* magazine, which launched in 1961, would cast the same disapproving and jaundiced eye at the establishment elite and is still thriving today. In October 1961, Peter Cook launched the Establishment Club. The club was located at 18 Greek Street, and Cook co-owned the club with Nick Luard who also wrote for *Private Eye*. Cook and Luard purchased *Private Eye* in 1962. Unlike *Private Eye*, the club only lasted until 1964, and from the start, some of the older Soho hipsters felt the club commodified the bohemian scene and was very much one more example of the beginning of the end of the 1960s, before it was barely off the launching pad. Still, it was part of the orbit of changing London, and people like David Frost, of the television show *That Was the Week That Was*, were very much part of its fabric.

In August 1963, ITV launched *Ready, Steady, Go!* The program was not the first or last British music television show, but it came along at just the right time, with just the right look, to mirror the pop explosion in England spearheaded by the Beatles. The group made their first appearance on the show on October 4, 1963, the show's ninth episode. Although broadcast live, at 6:15 p.m. from Studio 9, Television House, in Kingsway, London, the musical acts mimed to their songs, so the Beatles lip-synced to "Twist and Shout," "She Loves You," and "I'll Get You." Other musical guests included Helen Shapiro, who performed "Look Who It Is," Peter Jay and the Jaywalkers, Tony Meehan, and Eden Kane. Dusty Springfield appeared as a copresenter, along with the show's regular host Keith Fordyce and interviewed the Beatles throughout the show. Paul McCartney also served as a judge during a "mime-time" contest.

A HARD DAY'S NIGHT: PREPRODUCTION

The first official meetings among Walter Shenson, Brian Epstein, and the Beatles took place in October 1963. It was a busy time for the Epstein and the Beatles. Having already moved to London, NEMS was scheduled to move from their cramped offices in Monmouth Street to larger, more posh surroundings at Argyle Square, right next to the London Palladium. But the move would be delayed, and the Monmouth Street office would be used as the rehearsal space for the group's *Sunday Night at the London Palladium* performance, which took place on October 13.

Although Alun Owen was not Richard Lester's first choice to write the screenplay for *A Hard Day's Night*, he was the first choice of the Beatles, who asked Brian Epstein to contact Owen on their behalf. Richard Lester originally wanted Johnny Speight, the creator of the British TV situation comedy series *Till Death Us Do Part*, to write the script, but although keen on working on the film, he backed out due to scheduling conflicts. The writing team of Alan Simpson and Ray Galton, cowriters of the British TV situation comedy *Steptoe and Son*, were also considered. Although they did not get the gig, one of the show's stars, Wilfrid Brambell, landed the role of Paul McCartney's cantankerous grandfather. Brambell was Lester's second choice for the role; he'd originally wanted to cast Dermot Kelly. Kelly, like Brambell, was Irish and was best known for his role in British television's *The Arthur Haynes Show*. He turned down the part as he was about to take on the role of Murphy in the British crime film *Panic*.

It's surprising that Lester hadn't considered Alun Owen previously. Owen had worked with Lester on four of his British TV shows, as an actor and not a writer, but Owen also had considerable theater writing credits at this point. Ultimately, a quirk of scheduling that cemented Owen's participation, when his work on Lionel Bart's play *Maggie May* (which, coincidently was set in Liverpool), was put on hold. Owen had also worked on other projects set in Liverpool, including *No Trams To Lime Street* (1959) and *The Strain* (1963).

In November 1963, Owen joined the Beatles on tour as part of his research for writing the script. In the 2014 documentary, *You Can't Do That*, Owen recalled his time in Dublin going from their hotel room to a press reception and to the theater where they would perform, noting, "At no time were they allowed to enjoy what was supposed to be success . . . the only freedom they ever actually get, is when they start to play the music and then their faces light up and they're happy."

Lester liked the basic framework of Owen's first draft but felt the script was too long and burdened with too much dialogue, and he sent Owen back to the drawing board. Owen came up with a draft closer to what Lester was looking for, but it was also one that Lester would occasionally use only as a blueprint to improvise from or to be revised on the spot.

Lester's television background would prove to be a major influence on the way he directed the movie. His use of multiple cameras, including extensive use of handheld cameras, although commonplace today, allowed for quick cuts, varied points of view, and freed the movie from the static shackles of commercial filmmaking.

POP GOES THE TELLY

Lester would certainly have been aware of the way pop music was being presented on British television, starting with the innovative and influential *Oh Boy!* The program, that debuted on ITV, was produced by Jack Good, who previously produced another UK television music show, the *Six-Five Special*, which spawned the 1958 film. Good would eventually leave England for America to produce the groundbreaking *Shindig!*, which would spawn other American teen music shows *Hullabaloo* and *Where the Action Is*, among others. Another show, *Cool for Cats*, may have been the first show on UK television to include music aimed specifically at teens. Produced by Associated Rediffusion, which, like *Oh Boy!* came from the ITV network, started in December 1956, coming along just before the first British pop films and lasted until February 1961.

THIS IS THE BEATLES

This multifaceted television influence would also contrast and reflect cinema verité documentary filmmaking, particularly in the Maysles' brothers *Yeah! Yeah! Yeah! New York Meets the Beatles*, commissioned by Granada Television in England. The film was first broadcast on February 12, 1964, only days after the Beatles appeared on *The Ed Sullivan Show* on February 9. A longer version, *What's Happening! The Beatles in the U.S.A.* aired in the US on November 13, 1964, on CBS. The footage was later incorporated into the DVD *The Beatles: The First U.S. Visit*, which featured the *Ed Sullivan Show* appearances as well as the footage shot by the Maysles. The US broadcast date (months after *A Hard Day's Night* was released) and limited exposure no doubt came as a relief to UA, given the similarities between *What's Happening* and *A Hard Day's Night*. Was life imitating art, or art imitating life?

In a press release from Mike Hunter, publicity manager for UA, announcing a Beatles press conference in New York on February 10, 1964, noted that the group would "soon be making their motion picture debut for United Artists." On February 19, another press release touted the success the group had during their two weeks in America, and stated that filming was set to begin on March 2, with Walter Shenson producing and Richard Lester directing from an original screenplay written by Alun Owen; Wilfred Brambell was also noted as one of the film's stars. It's hard to say if any members of the press who received the release had any idea who these key players were. A lengthy "Beatles Biographical Feature" was also put out by UA, continuing in the same overheated purple prose style. Although filled with lots of good information on the history of the group, one glaring error wasn't picked up; it was stated that Brian Epstein discovered the Beatles in Hamburg and not Liverpool.

Owen joined Shenson and Lester in Paris in January 1964 to further get to know them, spending a weekend with the foursome at the George V hotel. Shenson and Lester had also observed the four over the Christmas/New Year holiday while they were performing *The Beatles Christmas Show* at the Astoria Theatre in Finsbury Park, London. The London run (previews were held at the Gaumont in Bradford on December 21, and Liverpool on December 22), began on Christmas Eve, took a day off for Christmas, returned for Boxing Day (December 26), and ran through January 11, 1964. The show was presented in a variety show format, with a list of performers the included Cilla Black, Billy J, Kramer with the Dakotas, Tommy Quickly, the Fourmost, Rolf Harris, the Barron Knights, and Duke D'Mond. This format, which included skits and what Brits would refer to as pantomime, gave Shenson and Lester an opportunity to see the Beatles in light dramatic and comedy sequences and not just as musical performers.

A similar production, *Another Beatles Christmas Show*, would run during the 1964–1965 holiday season, featuring the Yardbirds, Freddie and The Dreamers, Elkie Brooks, Sounds Incorporated, the Mike Cotton Sound, Ray Fell, and Michael Haslam, a promising new artist and sister of future Renaissance lead singer Annie Haslam. Haslam was briefly managed by Brian Epstein and appeared to have a bright future with his outstanding vocal abilities. Sadly, he never became a major recording or touring artist and quickly faded into obscurity. The compère was Jimmy Savile.

Another Beatles Christmas Show opened on December 24 at London's Hammersmith Odeon and ran through January 16.

A HARD DAY'S NIGHT: CAST AND CREW

Although *A Hard Day's Night* was conceived as a quickie pop music movie, the crew put together to make the film were some of the best people in the film industry in England at that time; "top-flight people for a bottom-flight movie," as Denis O'Dell, the film's associate producer would put it.

Cinematographer Gilbert Taylor, who'd previously worked with Lester on *It's Trad, Dad!*, had begun his career in the silent era and, since 1949, had shot 29 movies. Prior to *A Hard Day's Night*, he'd worked on a film directed by another American living in England, Stanley Kubrick's *Dr. Strangelove, or: How I Stopped Worrying and Learned to Love the Bomb*, a film equally as culturally significant as *A Hard Day's Night*. Both films have a stark, flat black-and-white look, which Taylor would also employ on his subsequent film, *Ferry Cross the Mersey*, starring Gerry and the Pacemakers, another Liverpool group managed by Brian Epstein, and a film very much in the mold of *A Hard Day's Night*. Before Taylor's extraordinary career concluded in 1994, he worked with such talented directors as Roman Polanski on *Repulsion* and *Cul-de-Sac*, Alfred Hitchcock on *Frenzy* (1972), and George Lucas on the first *Star Wars* movie in 1977.

Long retired from the film business; in the Criterion Collection home release of *A Hard Day's Night* short documentary *Things They Said Today*, Taylor later spoke about his time working on *A Hard Day's Night*: "I don't remember the script being very detailed. Dick gave the impression that we've got to do something with it, but what, he wasn't always sure of." Taylor said his days began at six in the morning and didn't end until midnight and admitted the grueling schedule had him taking Benzedrine tablets. But going to work for Lester after working with Kubrick must have felt like a summer holiday. Kubrick meticulously storyboarded his films, creating a stylized, yet in some cases cold, sterile, artificial world, while *A Hard Day's Night*, although scripted, was filled with improvisation and chance (though *Dr. Strangelove* star Peter Sellers did improvise some of his dialogue). Taylor didn't work on *Help!*, having been thoroughly turned off by the Beatlemania surrounding the filming of *A Hard Day's Night*, making it surprising he did go on to do *Ferry Cross the Mersey*.

A Hard Day's Night was edited by John Jympson, the cinematographer on Michael Caine's breakthrough film *Zulu*, which came out in January 1964. He also had experience on British pop music films, editing Tommy Steele's film *It's All Happening*, released in 1963. Jympson had been working in movies since 1949, becoming a cinematographer in 1960, and continuing until 1999. He would go on to work on a wide variety of films including *Kaleidoscope* (1966) starring Warren Beatty, *Deadfall* (1968) starring Michael Caine, *A Fish Called Wanda* (1988), and the television series *The Martian Chronicles* (1980). He also worked with Taylor on *Frenzy*. Lester has said that although the two were good friends, he never felt in sync with him, and they never worked together again.

Assistant director John Merriman worked in the same capacity on *It's Trad, Dad!* and served as production manager on *Zulu* and the original screen version of *Casino Royale* (1967).

The camera operator was Derek Browne, who began his career in the 1940s. His first major British film credit was as camera assistant on *The Man Who Never Was* in 1956. He immediately started working on a slew of new British cinema films, serving as camera assistant on *Room at the Top* and focus puller on *Peeping Tom*. After *A Hard Day's Night*, he worked as camera operator on *The Bedford Incident* (1965) and *Stop the World I Want to Get Off* (1966). He continued on working into the 1990s on such films as *The Great Muppet Caper*, *The Trial of the Pink Panther*, *The Curse of the Pink Panther*, and Franco Zeffirelli's interpretation of *Jane Eyre* (1996).

Paul Wilson, the film's other camera operator, started in British film in the 1940s and worked on the classic film *Kind Hearts and Coronets* (1949). He also worked on *Help!* and such new British cinema films as *Petulia* and *The Bed Sitting Room*, all directed by Lester. He also worked with Lester on *Juggernaut* (1974), *The Royal Flash* (1975), *The Ritz* (1976), and *Superman II* (1980). His other work includes *Frenzy*, *Superman* (1978), *Labyrinth* (1986), and *Velvet Goldmine* (1998), as well as six James Bond films.

In the *Things They Said Today* documentary, Wilson discussed the then unheard-of use of six cameras at the time and how risky this was during the concert sequence: "Dick Lester said, 'You got to get the stuff when they're playing these numbers, so get a couple of these 10:1 zoom lenses and just do what you think.' So it gave us total freedom, because in those days there was no 'Video Assist.' You were the director's eyes. You were doing it and nobody else saw it until tomorrow. To be left to your own devices and get really good stuff was terrific. . . . We established a style that's still used today when they photograph pop groups. It's the best way of doing it." In another interview, he noted that noise from the screaming kids during the Scala Theatre shoot was so loud, his teeth vibrated and began to hurt, forcing him to see his dentist.

Ray Simm was the art director. He was probably the most seasoned senior crew member with experience working on new British cinema films, the four previous films he worked on were *The L-Shaped Room*, *A Kind of Loving*, *Billy Liar!*, and *Séance on a Wet Afternoon* (1964). He also worked on the British musical comedy *Jazz Boat* (1960), which starred Anthony Newley. Simm would stay on and work with Lester on *Help!* His next film was *Darling* (1965) and then the Michael Caine films,

The Wrong Box (1966) and *Deadfall*. It's important to note that John Jympson, Ray Simm, and Julie Harris (all of whom worked on *Deadfall*) also worked on *A Hard Day's Night*, and Simm and Harris worked on *Help!*

Costume design was done in an unconventional manner, befitting what would be such a breakthrough film. Julie Harris, who had only a handful of films to her credit, worked with the hip London tailor Dougie Millings and his son, who was already making clothes for the Beatles. Millings made five dozen suits for the Beatles for the film and also had a brief role as a tailor. Shoemakers Anello & Davide made the famous Beatles boots. *A Hard Day's Night* was a springboard into the new British cinema for Harris, who went on to work on *Help!*, *Darling*, *The Wrong Box*, *Casino Royale*, *The Whisperers* (1967), and *Prudence and the Pill* (1968). After two American films, Harris worked on *Live and Let Die* (1973), Roger Moore's debut as James Bond with music by Paul McCartney and George Martin.

Associate producer Denis O'Dell, who was credited as associate producer of *A Hard Day's Night*, would go on to head up Apple Films, as well as working on *Magical Mystery Tour* and *Let It Be*. He also worked with Lester and Lennon on *How I Won the War* (1967) and with Starr on *The Magic Christian* (1969). He also worked on Lester's films *Petulia*, *Juggernaut*, *Royal Flash*, *Robin and Marian* (1976), *The Ritz*, and *Cuba* (1979). O'Dell is name-checked by John Lennon in the lyrics of "You Know My Name, Look up the Number," a song they began working on as far back as May 1967; it eventually became the B side of the single "Let it Be," released in March 1970.

A Hard Day's Night was the first film that casting director Irene Lamb worked on. She would work on another British music movie of note, *Stardust*, released in 1974, directed by Michael Apted, produced by David Puttnam, written by Ray Connolly, starring David Essex and Adam Faith, and featuring other musicians such as Keith Moon, Marty Wilde, and Dave Edmunds in the cast. Her remarkable career includes working on *Get Carter* (1971), *The Music Lovers* (1971), *Jabberwocky* (1977), *The Lady Vanishes* (1979), *Time Bandits* (1981), *Brazil* (1985), *The Adventures of Baron Munchausen* (1988), and *The Roads Not Taken* (2020). She also worked with Woody Allen as well as with George Lucas on the fourth and fifth *Star Wars* movies.

Sound was naturally important for *A Hard Day's Night*. There were two sound recordists (Stephen Dalby and H. L. Bird) and one person responsible for the sound camera (Mike Silverlock). Dalby, like many members of the *A Hard Day's Night* crew, had been involved in British cinema for decades and worked on both classic British movies and the new wave of British films. Dalby worked on such key classics as *Kind Hearts and Coronets* (1949), *Passport to Pimlico* (1949), *The Lavender Hill Mob* (1951), and *The Ladykillers* (1955) as sound supervisor. His first major new British cinema assignment was working as director of sound on The *Loneliness of the Long-Distance Runner* in 1962. He was also an uncredited dubbing mixer on *Zulu* in

1965 and a dubbing mixer on *Alfie* in 1966. After working on *A Hard Day's Night*, Dalby would also work on *Help!* as sound recordist, as well and another Richard Lester film, *The Knack*, as director of sound. He also worked on the Gerry & the Pacemakers' *Ferry Cross the Mersey* as sound recordist in 1964, right after his work on *A Hard Day's Night*. In 1965 he also worked on Roman Polanski's *Repulsion*. In the 1970s he worked on such films as *The Apprenticeship of Duddy Kravitz* (1974), the musical film *Jacques Brel Is Alive and Well and Living in Paris* (1975), and *Lies My Father Told Me* (1975).

H. L. Bird would also work on both *A Hard Day's Night* and *Help!* after a career that stretched back to the 1940s. After working with Stanley Kubrick on *Lolita* in 1962, he worked with him again in 1968 as sound mixer for *2001: A Space Odyssey*. He died in 1968 at the age of 58. Mike Silverlock also died young, at the age of 46 in 1989. *A Hard Day's Night* was his first film. He also worked on *Alfie*, and his work as sound camera operator and boom operator went uncredited on his first eight films. Throughout the 1970s and 1980s, he primarily worked in television. In 1980, he worked on the Roger Daltrey vehicle *McVicar*. Sound editor Gordon Daniel also worked on the 1960s spoof *Modesty Blaise*, the Cold War classic *The Spy Who Came in from the Cold*, and the period drama *Far From the Madding Crowd*. Sound editor Jim Roddan also worked on *Modesty Blaise* and four Pink Panther films.

Along with Wilfrid Brambell, other members of the principal cast included Norm, the group's road manager and equipment handler, played by Liverpool native Norman Rossington. The combative, cliched relationship between Norm and the Beatles in no way reflects the warm relationship the Beatles enjoyed with their erstwhile road manager Neil Aspinall; in the original script, the character was actually going to be called Neil. Aspinall is also the man who would ultimately run Apple, nearly until his death. Aspinall would end up marrying UA's Bud Ornstein's daughter Suzy on August 30, 1968; the couple had four children. Aspinall eventually became the head of the Beatles' Apple Corps, where he worked until shortly before his death in 2008. They met and got to know each other through the period when the Beatles were making *A Hard Day's Night* and *Help!* for UA. Roag Best, who runs the Magical History Museum in Liverpool and is the brother of Pete Best, is Aspinall's son with Mona Best, who ran the Casbah Club in Liverpool.

Rossington was another cast member who had ties to the new British cinema movement of the 1960s and to Richard Lester. Rossington's career began in theater, where he rose from messenger to carpenter to draughtsman, eventually deciding on acting and training at the Bristol Old Vic. He also worked in television and had 10 films to his credit before working with Lester on *The Running Jumping & Standing Film*, going on to appear in *Saturday Night and Sunday Morning*, three British *Carry On* comedies, and such epics as *Lawrence of Arabia*. His second-to-last film appearance was fittingly in *The Krays* in 1990, a film about the famous British gangster twin brothers from London in the 1960s, when Rossington was at the center of 1960s British culture.

The bumbling equipment handler, named Shake, again was seemingly not modeled after Mal Evans, the Beatles' stalwart and lovable roadie and later Apple employee, who along with Aspinall, was a key insider and confidante of the group. Evans appeared to lose his way after the demise of the Beatles; he died in Los Angeles in 1976, after being shot by police during a confrontation.

John Junkin, who played Shake, had previously worked with Lester as a script-writer on *The Idiot Weekly, Price 2d*. He got the role of Shake when the actor originally cast fell ill. His previous on-screen film experience was mostly in small, often uncredited roles, and he went on to appear in such films as *The Wrong Box*, *Kaleidoscope*, as well as joining with Lester and Lennon in *How I Won the War*. He also worked in radio and television, appearing in *The Avengers, Mr. Bean, Inspector Morse, Coronation Street*, and *EastEnders*, among many other roles, wrapping up his film career in 2004. In the *Things They Said Today* documentary, Junkin fondly recalled working with the Beatles, calling his time working on the film as "six of the happiest working days of my life and I got paid as well. . . . they weren't Beatles and I wasn't an actor. We were all actors in a scene playing off each other and they were so brilliant and non-starry and so genuine it was no problem at all."

While seemingly in a small role as the TV director of the Scala Theatre concert sequence, Victor Spinetti must be given special attention. Spinetti's role in the film is quite memorable, and a close reading of a quote from Richard Lester in *The Beatles in Richard Lester's A Hard Day's Night: A Complete Pictorial Record of the Movie*, by J. Philip De, Franco, provides some clues on who he wanted Spinetti to emulate. Although Lester wouldn't name the individual, clues suggest it was Philip Saville, a British actor and director who had a long-distinguished career and is best known for his deft direction of early 1960s British television. In his memoir, *Victor Spinetti Up Front . . . His Strictly Confidential Autobiography*, published in 2006, the actor recalled how "between takes, the Beatles didn't go to their dressing room like film stars. They sat behind the set, chatting away. I've made lots of films but I've only worked with two other people like that, Richard Burton and Orson Welles. Richard recited poetry while Orson told stories."

But more importantly, Spinetti would be the actor most closely associated with the Beatles' films, having roles not only in *A Hard Day's Night* but also *Help!* and *Magical Mystery Tour*. He also can be heard in the Beatles 1967 Christmas fan club message flexi-disc and appears in Paul McCartney's promotional film for *London Town* in 1978. He appeared in such films as *Becket* (1964), *The Wild Affair* (1965), *The Taming of the Shrew* (1967), *Start the Revolution Without Me* (1970), and *The Return of the Pink Panther* (1975). He went through something of a film career renaissance long after the 1960s, appearing in Prince's *Under the Cherry Moon* in

1986 and *The Krays* in 1990. His extraordinary and beguiling career also includes work in the theater and television. His fellow actors, fans, and admirers felt much affection for him, and his adoration by the Beatles was without equal among all the actors they worked with on their films. Spinetti directed the play *Scene Three Act One*, based on John Lennon's two books. The National Theatre production at London's Old Vic Theatre opened on December 3, 1967, with music supplied by John Lennon and George Martin. The play was revived twice, for one-off productions in 2010 and 2012.

John Bluthal, who appears in the film, in the relatively small role as the car thief, would turn up in *Help!* in a larger, more memorable role as Bhuta. Bluthal had already appeared in Lester's *The Mouse on the Moon* and, after *A Hard Day's Night* but before *Help!*, appeared in *The Knack*. He also appeared in two more Lester films. His distinguished career lasted until 2017, shortly before his death. The Polish-born actor's career included work around the world in radio, television, and the theater. During his film career, he worked with such directors as Jerry Lewis, Richard Quine, Joe McGrath, Blake Edwards, Jim Henson, Luc Besson, and Joel and Ethan Coen.

Although in a small, uncredited role, don't miss Kenneth Haigh, who played Simon Marshall, the prickly television producer.

Some unique casting includes two actors who would both appear in *Goldfinger* (1964). Richard Vernon, who appeared as Johnson, the grumpy gentleman on the train, and in *Goldfinger* as Colonel Smithers. Vernon's train scene was apparently inspired by a real-life experience the Beatles had that Owen used for his script. Vernon also appeared in such classic British television shows as *Upstairs, Downstairs*, *Ripping Yarns*, and *The Hitchhiker's Guide to the Galaxy*. Margaret Nolan, the girl at the casino observing Paul's grandfather gamble ("I bet you're a great swimmer!"), played Dink in *Goldfinger*; dressed in a one-piece bathing suit, she gave James Bond a massage out by the pool. These two roles don't reflect the range of Nolan, who worked in theater, television, and film. Like Wilfred Brambell, she appeared in *Steptoe and Son*. Other TV roles included *Brideshead Revisited* and *The Saint*. As for other films, she appeared in such British 1960s fare as *Ferry Cross the Mersey*, *Witchfinder General*, and *Don't Raise the Bridge, Lower the River*. Her last film was *Last Night in Soho* directed by Edgar Wright from 2021, a film set in London in the 1960s, which also was the last film for Diana Rigg; the film was dedicated to both women.

In her screen debut, Anna Quayle had a small but amusing improvised scene with John Lennon and went on to appear in such key 1960s British films as *Smashing Time*, *Casino Royale*, and *Chitty Chitty Bang Bang* (adapted from Ian Fleming's children's novel) as well as television shows such as *The Avengers* and *Brideshead Revisited*. She won a Tony award for her role in the 1961 Broadway production of *Stop the World I Want to Get Off*, a role she originated in the London debut of the play. Talking about her scene with Lennon, in the *Things They Said Today* documentary, she observed, "John Lennon was very much a person to be reckoned with. He seemed to me to be an experienced actor. He knew exactly what he was doing."

Another woman with a small but eye-catching roles in *A Hard Day's Night* was Prue (Prudence) Bury. Bury played Rita, the schoolgirl on the train with Jean, another schoolgirl, played by Pattie Boyd. Bury's boyfriend at the time, Jeremy Lloyd, appears in the film as one of the nightclub dancers. He would also appear in *Help!*, reteam with Ringo Starr in *The Magic Christian*, and appear in a long list of 1960s British films including *Those Magnificent Men in Their Flying Machines*, *The Wrong Box*, *Smashing Time*, and the 1969 remake of *Goodbye, Mr. Chips*. "When the Beatles came to London they entangled themselves instantly into and became part of it and fashion trendsetters in it," he said in the *Things We Said Today* documentary. "The Beatles and the film melded in so well with the life of London that you got a good slice of what London was like in that small area of London. That was it; that was Swinging London. It was wonderfully reproduced in this movie."

A couple of extras who appeared uncredited include two titans of British entertainment. Charlotte Rampling is one of the dancers in the nightclub scene who would go on to a long film career that thrives as recently as this writing. Phil Collins of Genesis and his own blockbuster solo career appears briefly in the Scala concert scene as one of the young teen fans screaming at the show.

A HARD DAY'S WRITE

As the Beatles' fame spread around the UK, the members of the group made their way south to London to live. After temporary lodgings in hotels such as the Royal Court in Sloane Square and the President in Russell Square, in September 1963 the group took up lodgings in Mayfair at 57 Green Street, Flat L, on the fourth floor. Word quickly spread that the four were living there, and John Lennon was the first to leave in November, moving with his wife Cynthia and their son Julian to Kensington, at 13 Emperor's Gate, not far from the Gloucester Road tube station. Photographer Robert Freeman, who lived in Flat 2, had suggested the residence to the Lennons, who lived above Freeman in Flat 3, on the top fourth floor; the flat is where the songs for *A Hard Day's Night* first took shape. The building had no elevator. Freeman claimed in the Miramax special feature disc that Lennon would be playing Elvis Presley in his flat, while Freeman would be playing Charlie Parker. Freeman would shoot the cover for *A Hard Day's Night* in his photo studio located in the same building and create the photomontage for the closing credits of the film. In his Beatles biography *Shout!*, Philip Norman suggested that Lennon wrote "Norwegian Wood (This Bird Has Flown)" about Freeman's wife Sonny, a German model Freeman was married to at the time. Freeman would go on to direct the feature film

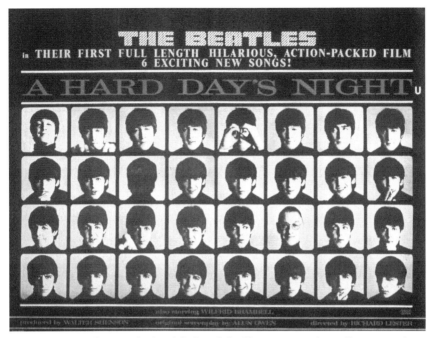

Robert Freeman photographed and designed the film posters and UK album cover for *A Hard Day's Night*. **Courtesy Photofest.**

The Touchables in 1968, from a script from Donald Cammell. Cammell would go on to write and codirect with Nicolas Roeg, the controversial 1970 film *Performance* starring Mick Jagger. The film's title song was provided by the English 1960s psychedelic group Nirvana. *The Touchables* was a decadent tale of a British rock star kidnapped by four women. Freeman's next film, released in 1969, was *Secret World*, which Freeman codirected with Paul Feyder, starring Jacqueline Bissett as the object of the infatuations of a teenage boy and was set in Provence. Feyder had been working in film since 1947 and it's his only feature film director's credit. However, his list of assistant director credits on many French and American films is voluminous.

John received a fan letter on audiotape recorded on New Year's Eve 1963 by a fan who had seen the Beatles perform in Coventry on November 17. Sometime in the first two weeks of January, Lennon used the tape to demo the song "If I Fell." The tape contains five takes, only one being an almost-full take. Part of the song required a high, nearly falsetto vocal that John couldn't quite reach, which eventually Paul would take on for the final recording.

It's also a unique demo in that within the song is a guitar riff that would eventually be the basis for "I Should Have Known Better." In his 1980 *Playboy* magazine interview with David Sheff, Lennon didn't make much of the song, saying: "That's me. Just a song—it doesn't mean a damn thing." It's interesting to note that these two songs would lead off the album, after the title track, which was composed at the last minute for the title sequence of the film. Also, like the first draft of the lyrics for the title track of the album, John wrote the first draft of the lyrics on a card, this time a Valentine's Day card.

The Lennons would not live long at Emperors Gate. Less than a year after they moved in, they relocated to suburban London in July 1964, where they would live until the house was sold in December 1968, shortly after John made his relationship with Yoko Ono public and the Lennons divorced. The large home, named Kenwood, was located in Weybridge, St. George's Hill, in the so-called "stockbrokers' belt," near the river Wey in the Elmbridge district of Surrey, some 16 miles outside of London. Walter Strach, the accountant for the Beatles suggested the Lennons purchase the 27-room mock Tudor manse, which was not far from where Strach himself lived.

Ringo Starr and his family followed the Lennons to Weybridge a year later, when he bought Sunny Heights, another mock-Tudor estate, in July 1965, where he lived until November 1968, counting Maurice Gibb of the Bee Gees and his wife, the singer Lulu, as close neighbors. Starr had previously lived in Knightbridge at Whaddon Street, William Mews, moving there in early 1964 at the suggestion of Brian Epstein, who had a flat there himself; George Harrison also lived at the same address. Starr also had a maisonette on Montagu Street, off Baker Street, in Marylebone, that he had moved into early in 1965. The flat would become a notorious lair of 1960s decadence with Starr leasing the basement and ground floor dwelling to Lennon, Jimi Hendrix and his manager, Chas Chandler, and oddly enough, even Lennon's wife Cynthia's mother. It was here that Lennon and Ono shot the nude photo for the cover of the *Two Virgins* album in 1968.

George Harrison also made the move out of London, when he left Whaddon Street in February 1965. His new home, Kinfauns, located on the Claremont Estate 15 miles outside of London, was a four-bedroom bungalow with a high gate and a garden that was nearly an acre, which had more recently been a girl's school. The psychedelic-inspired, The Fool, a Dutch collective, who lived with the couple to help paint the home's circular fireplace. Harrison loved being here, far from the glare of Beatlemania and the urban hurly-burly of London, although his wife Pattie liked to go out more and enjoyed the city social whirl. After returning from India in May 1968, the Beatles recorded their demos for what would become their double album *The Beatles* (the White Album) at Kinfauns. George and Pattie would live here until December 1969.

After living at the Green Street flat, Paul McCartney moved into the Marylebone area of London on Wimpole Street, home of his girlfriend Jane Asher, in November 1963. In 1965, he purchased a house at 7 Cavendish Avenue, St. John's Wood, around the corner from Abbey Road Studios, a home he still uses. McCartney became the only Beatle who stayed primarily in London throughout the Beatles years.

If all of the British Invasion recordings of the Beatles that were being released in the first flush of Beatlemania weren't enough, early 1964 saw a flood of releases from the music the Beatles recorded with Tony Sheridan in 1961 and 1962, along with their Decca audition material. Polydor in England had issued the *My Bonnie* EP to cash in on the group's growing popularity in the UK on July 12, 1963. The Beatles' debut EP for Parlophone, *Twist and Shout*, was released the same day; by July 26, it became the first EP to enter the *New Musical Express* Top 10. On January 31, 1964, Polydor issued the single "Sweet Georgia Brown," marking the UK debut of the recording; the B side was "Nobody's Child." Both tracks had been previously released. On February 28, Polydor issued the previously unreleased "Why," backed with "Cry for a Shadow." On May 29, Polydor issued the previously unreleased "Ain't She Sweet," backed with "Take Out Some Insurance on My Baby."

PARIS SESSIONS

Long before the Beatles started filming *A Hard Day's Night*, they began recording music for the film in the most unlikeliest of places, under odd circumstances. The Beatles flew to Paris on January 14, 1964, to play a series of concerts at the Olympia Theatre; after a warm-up show on January 15 at Cinema Cyrano in Versailles, the residency ran from January 16 through February 4, a run of three straight weeks.

The group shared the stage with a multitude of acts, performing two shows daily, with the occasional third performance tacked on. Outside of Germany and a short five-show run in Sweden in October 1963, it was the first time the group performed for any length of time on the continent. The audiences were not always enthusiastic, unlike the screaming fans in the UK and those they would later play for in the US and other parts of the world. Prior to one performance, the group also got into a scuffle with a French photographer, forcing the usually gentle Mal Evans to use his considerable size to set things straight.

Beatlemania was sweeping the UK and was scoring the group hits in places like Finland and Sweden, but the German market was surprisingly slow to catch on, given the many shows the group performed there. Although the group's debut recording came via their Bert Kaempfert–produced recordings on Polydor as the backing band for Tony Sheridan, they had no chart success in Germany.

To break into the German market, Odeon Records, the group's EMI subsidiary in Germany, wanted the group to rerecord "She Loves You" in German, along with a German translation of the single's B side "I'll Get You." Studio time was booked for a session on January 29 at EMI's Pathe Marconi Studios in Paris, located at

62 Rue de Sevres, Boulogne-sur-Seine, and was supervised by George Martin. Also in attendance were engineer Norman Smith, French tape operator Jacques Esmenjaud, and a German translator. It was the only time the four Beatles recorded together outside the UK.

As "I Want to Hold Your Hand" was the group's latest hit, it was decided to record German translation of that song instead of "I'll Get You." Norman Smith brought a four-track copy of the songs' backing tracks to Paris. But the group failed to turn up at the studio on the morning of the 29th. John and George had actually been in London the previous day and had only just returned to France; the rest of the group was sleeping in late at their luxury accommodations at the Hotel George V. After waiting impatiently, Martin went to their hotel, where, upon entering their suite, the group scattered in all directions like schoolboys caught raiding their parent's liquor cabinet; Martin scolded them like the stern headmaster he sometimes had to be.

The Beatles finally consented to going to the studio and, after settling in, ended up having fun recording the two tracks. While the group used the original backing track tape for "I Want to Hold Your Hand," they made an entirely new recording for "She Loves You" because the original multitrack had been destroyed. The original recording featured John playing his Gibson J-160; the new recording featured him playing the Rickenbacker 325 Capri that he had purchased in Hamburg at Steinway-Haus. When the Beatles first played in America, Rickenbacker would provide Lennon with a new 325, which had a distinctly brighter tone. The final single, "Komm, gib mir deine Hand"/"Sie liebt dich," was released on March 5 on Odeon in Germany.

Despite the late start, the group quickly completed their task and, with the extra studio time, worked on a song that Paul had composed at the George V: "Can't Buy Me Love." In *Many Years from Now*, written by Barry Miles with substantial input from McCartney, published in 1997, McCartney talked about writing the song: "'Can't Buy Me Love' is my attempt to write a bluesy mode. The idea behind it was that all the material possessions are all very well but they won't buy me what I really want. It was a very hooky song." In *Paul McCartney: The Lyrics*, again, McCartney referred to the song's musical structure: "It's twelve-bar blues, with a Beatles twist on the chorus, where we bring in a couple of minor chords. Usually, minor chords are used in the verse of a song, and major chords bring a lift and lighten the mood in the chorus. We did it the other way around here." It would be the true beginning of recordings earmarked for *A Hard Day's Night*, and "Can't Buy Me Love" became the final track on side A, following George Martin's dictum of having their strongest material as first track on each side of an album.

Originally slated as "Money Can't Buy My Love," which was the way it was called out by engineer Norman Smith before each take at the session, the song's arrangement was quickly changed by Martin to begin the song with the chorus. McCartney had been listening to a lot of Marvin Gaye, and no doubt the song's bass line was influenced by James Jamerson. There were also other songs written in Paris during the groups extended Olympia run.

The track would not be completed in Paris but would only require overdubs on February 25, at the band's first sessions for *A Hard Day's Night* back at Abbey Road.

ABBEY ROAD

It would be remiss at this point to not mention Abbey Road and give a sense of the legendary studio's history and its essential place in the Beatles' story. The studio, then named EMI Recording Studios, was located at 3 Abbey Road, not far from the Lord's Cricket Ground; it was renamed Abbey Road Studios after the release of the *Abbey Road* album. The name change occurred in 1970. While there are other well-known studios such as (Capitol, Electric Lady, Sound City, Sunset, the Record Plant, the Hit Factory, the Power Station, and Gold Star in the US, and Air, Olympic, and Trident in the UK), it's not hyperbole to say that Abbey Road is likely the most famous recording facility in the world. Located in the leafy residential neighborhood of St. John's Wood, the studio began operation in 1931 under the ownership of the Gramophone Corporation, a predecessor of EMI. The Georgian-style building became a designated landmark in 2010.

It was the *Abbey Road* album, along with the iconic cover shot of the group walking across the famous zebra crossing by Iain Macmillan, that prompted EMI to rename the studio and immortalize it forever, as well as inspiring countless homages and parodies. George Harrison's song "Apple Scruffs," though referencing the fans who hung out at the Beatles' Apple Corps headquarters in Savile Row, the song also refers to the recording studios where fans would wait to catch a glimpse of the members of the group. On completion of the song's recording, Harrison actually invited some lucky fans into Abbey Road to hear the finished track. The song appeared on Harrison's first proper solo studio album, *All Things Must Pass*, released on November 27, 1970. "Apple Scruffs" also appeared as the B side of non-UK versions of the "What Is Life" single, released on February 15, 1971.

The *A Hard Day's Night* sessions would yield the group's most formidable album to date. It was the first complete album they recorded on a Studer J37 four-track tape machine, which they first used on October 17, 1963, during the final sessions for their second album, *With the Beatles*. The group also began using the REDD.51 four-channel mixing desk, which replaced the REDD.37, a two-channel desk, installed at Abbey Road in January 1964 that had been in use at Abbey Road since 1958. REDD is an acronym for Record Engineering and Development Department. The REDD.51 desk, installed in 1964 would be used until the Beatles were in the midst of recording the White Album, when it was replaced by a Solid State MK desk. Both the REDD.37 and REDD.51 used vacuum tubes and were designed in house by EMI.

There were two important physical elements of Abbey Road that contributed to the Beatles' music sounding so special right from the start. Studio 2, where they recorded most of their music, was a big, cavernous room that allowed the group to have plenty of space to stretch out and allowed the music to resonate and breathe. Engineer Norman Smith made sure the overall ambience of the room would be felt on the recordings by employing a microphone to capture the sound of the room, placing the microphone about 20 feet from the amplifiers. They also used echo chambers. The echo chamber for Studio 2 is a small, tiled space that used moveable pillars to break up reflected sound.

The fact that so much of their music was primarily mixed for mono also adds to the electrifying punch and visceral directness of their music, particularly their works before *Sgt. Pepper*. The tape recorders used during this period included a mono ¼-inch EMI BTR2, then a twin-track ¼-inch EMI BT3, and finally a four-track 1-inch Telefunken M10, which the Beatles used well into the recording of the *Help!* album. Although there was also a four-track 1-inch Telefunken T9u available, it apparently was never used. The BTR2 and BTR3 were also used for mixdowns, as well as a mono tape copying ¼-inch Lyrec TR4. All of this equipment was designed, built, tested, and implemented by the staff at Abbey Road. The gear from Telefunken, which was a company based in Germany, and Lyrec, which was a company based in Denmark, were the only two pieces of equipment not designed and built by EMI.

The final recording of "Can't Buy Me Love" at Abbey Road on February 25 took place only days after the Beatles' triumphant conquering of America, highlighted by their appearances on *The Ed Sullivan Show*. The session would also feature work on the single's B side, "You Can't Do That," which would also appear as the penultimate track on the *A Hard Day's Night* album. This was the first track that Lennon played on the second Rickenbacker 325 Capri he owned, which had been given to him by Rickenbacker. The song was one John was proud of writing, saying that it was heavily influenced by Wilson Pickett.

While on tour in 1964, Lennon gave journalist Ray Coleman some insights into his guitar playing during this period: "I'd find it a drag to play rhythm guitar all the time so I always work myself out something interesting to play," citing "You Can't Do That" as the best example of that. He went on to say, "There wasn't really a lead guitarist and a rhythm guitarist on that, because I feel that the rhythm guitarist role sounds too thin or records. Anyway, it would drive me potty to play chunk-chunk rhythm all the time. I never play anything as lead guitarist that George couldn't do better. But I like playing lead sometimes, so I do it." After the single was released on May 22, George Martin added a piano to the track, perhaps with the intention of including it on the *A Hard Day's Night* album, but it was never used.

"Can't Buy Me Love"/"You Can't Do That" was released in the US on March 16, 1964, and in the UK on March 20. It's interesting to note that Capitol didn't want to release "Can't Buy Me Love" as a single, preferring "Roll Over Beethoven," which appeared on *With the Beatles* in the UK, and *The Beatles' Second Album* in the US. George Martin apparently convinced them otherwise.

The *A Hard Day's Night* album was the first to feature only Lennon/McCartney compositions, and no covers. Harrison's only composition on an album thus far had been "Don't Bother Me" from *With the Beatles*, and Starr had yet to contribute any songs himself.

With the single wrapped up by the afternoon of February 25, the group would now proceed in earnest recording their upcoming film's soundtrack, taking a break then commencing work on "And I Love Her." Most likely written for Jane Asher, it was one of Paul's first attempts at a ballad, written in the music room at the Ashers' house on Wimpole Street, just after Paul moved in with the family. Paul is quoted in *Many Years from Now* by saying, "It was the first ballad I impressed myself with. It's got nice chord changes in it. . . . I like the imagery of the stars and the sky. It was a love song really. The 'And' in the title was an important thing." Though Lennon has said he wrote the song's middle-eight, McCartney demurs; in his recollection, saying Lennon may have helped with the middle-eight but didn't write it. McCartney also singled out Harrison's guitar work on the track.

After perfecting the verses, John helped with the choruses, with the group providing only acoustic backing, and Ringo on bongos. In *Paul McCartney: The Lyrics*, McCartney said, "It starts with a F-sharp minor, not with the root chord of E major and you gradually work your way back." He added, George Martin was inspired to add a chord modulation in the solo of the song, a key change that he knew would be musically satisfying; "we shifted the chord progression to start with G minor, instead of F-sharp minor—so, up a semitone."

On February 26, the group convened at Studio 2 in the afternoon to begin recording on "I Should Have Known Better." In the evening session there was more work on "And I Love Her." The next day's morning and afternoon session was spent working on "And I Love Her" and a new song, "Tell Me Why"; they spent the late afternoon/evening session working on "If I Fell."

The evening session on March 1 was devoted to recording "I Call Your Name," "I'm Happy Just to Dance with You," and "Long Tall Sally." "I'm Happy Just to Dance with You" was the last song written by Lennon/McCartney that Harrison would sing on a Beatles album. "It was a bit of a formula song," McCartney admitted in *Many Years From Now*. "We knew that in E if you went to an A-flat minor, you could always make a song with those two chords; that change always pretty much always excited you." "I'm Happy Just to Dance with You,' that was written for

George to give him a piece of the action. I couldn'ta sung it," Lennon explained to David Sheff in *Playboy* in 1980.

"I Call Your Name" and "Long Tall Sally" were considered for the film's soundtrack but were instead issued on the *Long Tall Sally* EP, released only in the UK in June 1964. "I Call Your Name" had already been recorded by Billy J. Kramer with the Dakotas, appearing as the B side of the Lennon-penned number one hit for them, "Bad to Me." The song was written by John before he'd formed his first band, perhaps as early as late in winter 1957. One of the song's more unusual elements is its seemingly undetectable underlying ska beat, particularly in the instrumental break, very much in the style of records released by British label Blue Beat Records, which specialized in Jamaican sounds, a style that was popular in London at that time, particularly with Mods.

"Tell Me Why," while written to provide an upbeat rocker for the film's concert sequence, is yet another Lennon song of loss. "They needed another upbeat song and I just knocked it off," he explained to Sheff. "It was like a black, New York girl-group song."

"If I Fell" was one of John's best early ballads and a song that foreshadowed some of the subtle introspection of "In My Life," Paul told Barry Miles, "We wrote 'If I Fell' together, but with the emphasis on John because he sang it." John told Sheff, 'That was my first attempt at a ballad proper. That was the precursor to 'In My Life.' It has the same chord sequences as 'In My Life'—D and B minor and E minor, those kinds of things. And it's semi-autobiographical, but not consciously. It shows that I wrote sentimental love ballads—silly love songs—way back when."

Owing to the pressure of finishing up recording on the soundtrack album, doing live dates, and a myriad of media appearances, the Abbey Road session on March 1 was the first-ever Sunday the group spent at Studio 2. Filming for *A Hard Day's Night* was scheduled to begin the following day. The first songs that had been recorded were all intended for the film; the album's remaining songs would be completed after filming was finished.

LIGHTS, CAMERA, ACTION!

A Hard Day's Night would be filmed in black and white, with the negative and print at 35 mm. The aspect ratio would be 1.66:1, and the cinematographic process would be spherical. The sound mix was in mono (RCA Sound Recording).

There was much preplanning. Associate Producer Denis O'Dell was instrumental in saving the group considerable money when he was able to negotiate with the head of EMI to get free use of some equipment, when he indicated that Bush, a British-based electronics company, was supplying equipment free of charge for promotion.

He also was able to secure the use of a BEA helicopter, which was easily modified to say BEATLES in all capital letters on the outside. In his memoir, *At The Apple's Core*, he wrote that Twickenham Studios, conveniently located outside of the center of London, was chosen for many of the interior scenes because at the time it was closed, and the Beatles could film there in relative privacy.

It was Richard Lester's idea to start shooting the film on the train, so the Beatles would not have to worry about what came before the scene. Ultimately, Lester was not happy with the scene. In film director Steven Soderbergh's 2000 book, *Getting Away with It*, which is primarily made up of a long series of conversations between Soderbergh and Lester, Lester said of the train sequence, "we shot the train first, I think the train is the weakest." Yet in *Help!*, the closing scenes were filmed first. In response to Soderbergh's comment, "I can't imagine shooting the end of the movie first," Lester replied when speaking about *Help!*: "Well, there was some practical points of view. One, you couldn't easily get a long enough shooting day in the snow, for the snow scenes. Two, you couldn't get the hotel rooms easily. So that put it to the very end of ski season, and then the Bahamas worked because it was February/March, so it was between the big Christmastime and the Easter holidays. We had our own plane; we chartered a plane to take the crew and cast and all. I'm so used to it. It never bothered me. I've never shot anything in order."

On Monday, March 2, 1964, at 8:30 a.m., the Beatles began their journey into film history. After the formality of joining Equity, the actors' union, with the business conducted on the platform at Paddington Station, the group, cast, and film crew departed from Platform Five for filming throughout the West Country in the towns of Minehead, Taunton, and Newton Abbot. After the first day, it was realized that the daily departures could be more discreetly accomplished leaving from the Acton main line in West London and returning in the evening via London suburban stations as West Ealing, Westbourne Park, Harlington, and Hayes, the latter coincidentally where one of EMI's vinyl pressing plants was located.

On the first day of shooting their screen debut, Tollie Records released a new single of theirs in the US, "Twist and Shout"/"There's A Place." Tollie was a subsidiary label of Vee Jay that launched in 1964 and closed in 1965. The label also issued one more single from the Beatles, "Love Me Do"/"P.S. I Love You" in April 1964. Even though music by the Beatles was being released in the US through Capitol, many labels (Tollie, Vee Jay, Swan, MGM, Atco, Polydor), were all rushing out Beatles records, with some labels still putting out Beatles music well into July.

The film's opening was shot between April 5 and 12. The opening sequences of the film immediately convey the new youthful flowering of postwar England, as exemplified by the bustling capital city and the country's most striking example of the new exuberance and style of the Beatles. Fans of the French New Wave might detect a similarity to a key scene from François Truffaut's *Jules and Jim* (1962), when

Jules (Oskar Werner), Jim (Henri Serre), and Catherine (played by Jeanne Moreau and dressed as a man, complete with moustache and cigar) have a race running over a bridge. The youthful exuberance and sheer joy of both scenes reflect a freedom and carefree camaraderie of the burgeoning youth culture.

While it's been noted how many breakthrough films of the new British cinema were shot in the north and the Midlands, no film of the home turf of the Beatles, Liverpool, was used in *A Hard Day's Night*. Debbie Greenberg, whose family took over the lease of the Cavern Club in 1966 and is the author of *Cavern Club: The Inside Story*, remembers that the Beatles did film in Liverpool during the *A Hard Day's Night* shoot but said none of it was used. "The Beatles were being filmed around Liverpool for the film *A Hard Day's Night*. They filmed Ringo outside his home in Admiral Grove and then in a convertible car driven by George, with Paul and John in the back seat came out of Admiral Grove and turned left into North Hill Street. Our butcher's shop was situated diagonally opposite to Admiral Grove, and I was on the pavement in my butcher's coat and apron as the car (which was following a film crew in another car) went past very slowly but it seemed as if it was over in a flash. I believe that a lot of the film footage that was shot in Liverpool wasn't used in the film." She fondly remembers seeing *A Hard Day's Night* when it was released. "Seeing *A Hard Day's Night* for the first time was so exciting. To see The Beatles on the Silver Screen was incredible. We had often watched their playful antics on stage at the Cavern and the film brought it all back. I had witnessed their journey from their debut performance at the Cavern on February 9, 1961, to their final performance at the Cavern on August 3, 1963, and watched their meteoric rise to fame in America. Although we had lost them in Liverpool, we were still able to follow their journey to stardom."

Twickenham Studios came to be very much a second home for the Beatles. The rather nondescript group of seven buildings would also be where the Beatles filmed interiors for *Help!* and almost the entire first half of *Let It Be*. Many of their most memorable promotional films were also shot at Twickenham, including videos for the number one hit singles "I Feel Fine," the double A side "We Can Work It Out"/"Day Tripper," the *Help!* soundtrack's "Ticket to Ride" and the title track. The promos for "Hey Jude" and "Revolution," directed by Michael-Lindsay Hogg, were also shot at Twickenham, one of the key reasons Lindsay-Hogg was chosen as the director of *Let It Be*. Ringo Starr would also costar with Peter Sellers in the film *The Magic Christian* shot at Twickenham in March 1969. Denis O'Dell had hoped to produce *The Magic Christian*, through Apple Films, but ultimately, it was produced by Grand Films Limited and became the sole production of the company owned by Peter Sellers.

WJBK-AM, Detroit DJ Tom Clay, conducted the longest interview while the Beatles were filming at Twickenham, for nearly 12 minutes, on April 7, 1964.

The sequences shot on the train quickly established the cramped, hurried lifestyle of Beatlemania, which screenwriter Alun Owen stressed as one of the major running themes of the film. "That feeling of claustrophobia was how we tried to think of the whole first sequence, the whole first third of the film. In closed spaces: prisoners in space, prisoners of fans, prisoners by car, train, small hotel rooms—do this, do that, sign this," Lester observed in the book *The Beatles in Richard Lester's* A Hard Day's Night. The first time the group sings in the film (miming to "I Should Have Known Better"), it is basically in a cage. One of the early ideas for this scene was to actually let the live chickens in the compartment loose, but it was thought that the chickens might steal the scene.

The group's cheeky, antiauthoritarian stance, dry Liverpool wit, and ensemble interaction both reflected the group aura and each individual Beatle's own unique personality. In the book *The Beatles in Richard Lester's* A Hard Day's Night, Lester said: "The general aim of the film was to present what was apparently becoming a social phenomenon in this country [the UK]," said Lester. "Anarchy is too strong a word, but the quality of confidence that the boys exuded. Confidence that they could dress as they liked, speak as they liked, talk to the Queen as they liked, talk to people on the train who 'fought the war for them' as they liked."

These scenes also introduced some of the supporting actors who were integral to the plot, particularly Paul's gruff, yet very clean grandfather, played by Wilfrid Brambell. Brambell was well-known to British TV viewers as the father Albert Steptoe in *Steptoe and Son*; the "very clean" running joke was a reference to his Steptoe character, an old codger frequently referred to as a dirty old man due to his occasional lapses in hygiene, etiquette, and taste. Brambell was one of the few figures who stood out alongside the film's ostensible four stars. Prior to *A Hard Day's Night*, he'd appeared in such key new British cinema films as *Saturday Night and Sunday Morning*, as well as more commercial fare, like *Lawrence of Arabia*.

Another cast member on the first day of shooting may not have had as high a screen profile as Brambell but would become a major player in the story of the personal life of the Beatles. One of the two pretty schoolgirls that Paul McCartney chats up on the train was none other than Pattie Boyd, the future wife of not only Beatle George Harrison but also Eric Clapton. Boyd, who was to turn 20 on March 17, had previously worked with Richard Lester on a Smith's Potato Crisps (chips) commercial, her first commercial after enjoying a successful modeling career. She was so shy and nervous that after initially turning down the chance to audition for the commercial, the producers decided to dub her voice with someone else. Her audition for *A Hard Day's Night* took place at the Hilton Hotel on Park Lane, presided over by Walter Shenson and Richard Lester.

At the time of filming, she was dating photographer Eric Swayne. But Harrison was immediately smitten with Boyd, beginning a long courtship that resulted in their marriage on January 21, 1966. In her autobiography, *Wonderful Tonight*, published in 2008, Boyd says their first date was at the Garrick Club in Covent Garden, which also included Brian Epstein. However, in other sources, including the invaluable *The Beatles London*, by Piet Schreuders, Mark Lewisohn, and Adam Smith, recalling an interview she gave in 1964, she indicated it was more likely at Brad's Club, a basement club on the Duke of York Street in Central London.

The filming of the train sequences continued through April 12, with the cast and crew logging in thousands of miles in a mere six days. The comings and goings on the train were reported by an eager press as reporters flocked to the train whenever it made extended stops, especially when the cast and crew broke for lunch.

MEANWHILE, BACK IN THE STUDIO

Back at Abbey Road, producer George Martin was busy mixing the tracks the Beatles had recorded thus far. On March 3, he prepared mono mixes of "I Should Have Known Better," "If I Fell," "Tell Me Why," "And I Love Her," "I'm Happy Just to Dance with You" and "I Call Your Name." "And I Love Her" would be remixed again on June 22. These mixes would be used for the British *A Hard Day's Night* album and the film. On March 4, Martin prepared mono mixes of "I Call Your Name" for the American Capitol release *The Beatles Second Album*.

NEMS

On March 9, the gradual move of the Beatles entertainment empire from Liverpool to London was completed. Brian Epstein's NEMS office had finally shifted to its London base, its new headquarters on the fifth floor of Sutherland House at 5-6 Argyle Street; the NEMS press office moved to the same location. There was also an unofficial NEMS office, Hille House at 9 Stafford Street, set up in 1965. This small office was more of a private working escape for Brian Epstein, where he worked with his personal assistant Wendy Hanson and secretaries Judy Haines and Joanne Newfield. NEMS Presentations, an office that handled the Beatles television appearances, was located on Cork Street in Mayfair; the business there was handled by Vyvienne Moynihan and John Lydon.

On March 10, Ringo and the crew took over the Turk's Head, a small pub close to Twickenham Studios still serving up pints to this day. The scene shot here gave Ringo the first opportunity to flex his acting chops, in what would be the beginning of a long, fruitful but ultimately shortened film career, owing to the lack of success of the movie *Cavemen* in 1981. For now, Ringo was filmed in a series of slapstick sequences involving a beer bottle, a sandwich, a parrot, and a dartboard.

On the same day at Abbey Road, George Martin turned his attention to stereo mixing, including, "Can't Buy Me Love," "Long Tall Sally," "I Call Your Name," and "You Can't Do That." There was also some more mono mixing of "Long Tall Sally," "Komm, Gib Mir Deine Hand," and "Sie Liebt Dich."

There has been some debate over exactly who is playing on the final stereo mix of "Can't Buy Me Love" because the studio logs indicate a drum overdub and paperwork for a musician's studio fee. This appears to refer to engineer Norman Smith adding some hi-hat cymbal to the track on this date.

The Beatles would settle in at Twickenham Film Studios for the next two days, March 11 and 12, working on scenes that were supposed to be happening in a van and a hotel room. At Abbey Road, George Martin made stereo mixes of the two German-language tracks that were immediately sent to West Germany and America.

On Friday, March 13, the group headed roughly 30 miles outside of London to Gatwick Airport, the second-busiest airport in the UK next to Heathrow. The group arrived about 10 a.m. and shot scenes for the film's climax, a helicopter escape from the paparazzi. Cameramen positioned in a helicopter also shot the group from above, in footage that would be used in the first "Can't Buy Me Love" sequence.

On Monday, March 16, Ringo continued to shoot without the other Beatles at Twickenham. The day's scene included Wilfred Brambell, tweaking Ringo to stop moping about, get his rather large nose out of the book he was always reading, and break free for a change. The book he's reading, by the way, was *Anatomy of a Murder* by John D. Voelker, which was later made into a film by Otto Preminger in 1959, featuring a stirring film score by Duke Ellington.

Tuesday, March 17, saw the group filming at Les Ambassadeurs club at 5 Hamilton Place, near Hyde Park in London. The club served as the location for the film's fictional gambling establishment Le Circle Club, where Paul's grandfather is seen gambling. The club was also the setting for the first scene in the first James Bond film, *Dr. No*. The Beatles returned here for more filming on April 17.

Back at Twickenham on Wednesday, March 18, the scenes of the Beatles in their dressing room were filmed. On both March 18 and 19, they were interviewed for the BBC Light Radio Program show *The Public Ear*. The subjects covered included John's upcoming book, *In His Own Write* (published on March 23), and the film in progress:

GEORGE: Well, we just have been out for dinner at the Dorchester. And, Paul McCartney, would you like to say a few words to the listeners of Public Ear?

PAUL: Uhh, yes. What about them, George?

GEORGE: How are you enjoying filming? This is your first film, isn't it, Paul?

PAUL: (*laughs*) Yes. The first film we ever made, and uh, we're having a good time. We're not very good actors, but we're trying hard. That's the most important thing, really—having a try, isn't it?

GEORGE: (*mock seriousness*) Yes. I suppose it is, Paul. Well, are you having any trouble learning your lines, or anything like that?

PAUL: Well actually, George, I'm a bit lazy about that. I normally learn them about, uh, ten minutes before we do the scene, actually. (*jokingly*) I feel it gives an air of impromptuity. [SIC]

GEORGE: I see. How's the director of the film?

PAUL: Well, yes. Dick Lester's directing the film . . . uh, what's yer name? George?

GEORGE: George, yeah. BBC! I'm from the BBC, you see. Public Ear.

PAUL: Anyway, his name is Dick Lester. He's a good fella. He's bald, but don't hold that against him. He's one of the nicest fellas I've met, and he's a great director. I think he's gonna save the film in the cutting rooms. Great fella, he is.

GEORGE: (*continued mock seriousness*) What do you mean, "He's gonna save it in the cutting rooms?" What exactly do you mean by that, Paul?

PAUL: (*laughs*) Well you see, George, umm . . . The acting may not be very good, but if he can cut it up, and slice it around, and slop bits in here and slop bits in there, he may make it into a good film, you see.

GEORGE: I see. Well thank you Paul. And, uh, you'll receive your three-shilling fee at a later date.

PAUL: Don't mention it, George. Thank you.

The interviews aired on March 22.

John described *A Hard Day's Night* as "a comic-strip version of what was actually going on. The pressure was far heavier than that," a quote taken from an interview Lennon did and collected in the *Anthology* book. Ringo had an altogether different take in *The Beatles Anthology* book:

It was a lot of fun. It was incredible for me, the idea that we were making a movie. I loved the movies as a kid. I used to go to a hell of a lot, in the Beresford and Gaumont Cinemas in Liverpool. I have great memories from Saturday morning pictures. I'd be into whatever was showing; if it was a pirate movie, I would be a pirate, and if it was a Western I would be a cowboy; or I'd come out as D'Artagnan and fence all the way home. It was a great fantasy land for me, the movies, and suddenly we were in one. It was so romantic, with the lights and coming to work in the limo. I think because I loved films I was less embarrassed than the others to be in one; John really got into the movie, too. I felt a lot of the time that George didn't want to be there. It was something he was doing because we were doing it.

It is important to note that the *Anthology* project, which encompassed not only the book but also three 2-CD sets of material—also released on three triple-album vinyl packages, and three double-cassette packages, along with two 4-song CD maxi singles and a television special—kicked the whole project off. The television special was released in expanded form, first on VHS and Laser Disc and then on DVD. No Blu-ray release has been issued. "Free as a Bird," released in conjunction with *Anthology 1* and "Real Love," released in conjunction with *Anthology 2*, were released as the final single included on *The Singles Collection* box set released in 2019.

It was around this time that the film's name was settled on. Many titles had been suggested, most obviously *Beatlemania*; other innocuous titles included *Moving On*, *Traveling On*, and *Let's Go*. In one account, Ringo came up with the phrase after a particularly grueling day, remarking "It's been a hard day . . . ," then, on realizing the late hour, quickly correcting himself: "a hard day's night." However, the same phrase crops up in John Lennon's story "Sad Michael," which appears in *In His Own Write*: "He'd had a hard days night that day." Perhaps Lennon had heard Starr use the line at some point and borrowed it for his story.

Thursday, March 19, was a busy day. In the morning the group filmed scenes in the corridor of a fictional TV studio. For lunch, it was off to the nearby Dorchester Hotel in Park Lane, to attend the 12th annual Variety Club Silver Heart awards, where the current Labour opposition leader Harold Wilson (MP for Huyton, a suburb of Liverpool), presented the group with the award for Show Business Personalities of 1963. Wilson would become Prime Minister in 1964, serving through 1970, when he was defeated by Conservative Edward Heath, and then serve a second term as Prime Minister in 1974. Both Wilson and Heath would be castigated in George Harrison's "Taxman" from *Revolver* in 1966.

From central London, the group then went to the BBC's Television Theatre in Shepherd's Bush to tape their debut performance for *Top of the Pops*, miming to an empty house to their new single, "Can't Buy Me Love" and "You Can't Do That." Due to their tight schedule, the group did not have to travel to Manchester, where *Top of the Pops* was normally televised at that time.

On March 20, the group shot more TV studio corridor scenes at Twickenham before heading off to Television House, the central London studios and headquarters of Associated Rediffusion, to tape their appearance on the other important British TV music show *Ready, Steady, Go!* They mimed to three recordings: "Can't Buy Me Love," "You Can't Do That," and "It Won't Be Long." They also took part in a fashion show sendup with cohost Keith Fordyce, received an award from *Billboard* magazine, and were interviewed by the show's other cohost, Cathy McGowan, dubbed "Queen of the Mods." It was the group's second, and final, appearance on the show. Other guests included Dusty Springfield, Alma Cogan, and Marvin Gaye.

Beginning March 23, the group decamped for nearly a week at the Scala Theatre in London. The theater opened in 1772 and went through many name changes until finally settling on its final name. Located on Charlotte Street between Tottenham Street and Scala Street, it was yet another film location situated in or just north of a neighborhood that housed some of the group's London haunts in the 1960s such as the Speakeasy on Regent Street, where Paul McCartney took Linda Eastman after the two first connected at the nearby the Bag o Nails. It was also an area where many groups of the era performed, as well as ground zero for the later London underground music scene such as the Vesuvio club and the UFO club, both on Tottenham Court Road. It was also not far from seminal independent London recording studios such as Regent Sound and IBC. The BBC's Broadcasting House was also just around the corner and, like IBC, on Portland Place. The Scala Theatre was torn down in 1970, but stands in memory as the music venue where the Beatles played during the key concert scenes in *A Hard Day's Night*. Denis O'Dell had suggested using the theater as a stand-in for a real television studio because there weren't many television studios at that time in England.

Perhaps the most important day of filming was on Tuesday, March 31, which focused on the concert itself, the centerpiece of the film and probably at the time the favorite scene for the group's fans. The Beatles performed before an audience of 350 lucky fans who were recruited from the Central School of Speech and Drama, and because it was an actual movie shoot, they were all paid.

The concert featured the group miming to "Tell Me Why," "And I Love Her," "I Should Have Known Better," and "She Loves You," along with "You Can't Do That," which was ultimately cut from the film. All the songs except "She Loves You" (which had been released in 1963) would appear on the *A Hard Day's Night* soundtrack album. This sequence also features two cameos of Richard Lester, seen from behind the stage looking out on the audience and crossing the front of the stage during "Tell Me Why." Much harder to spot was a 13-year-old boy and unknown child actor, Phil Collins, future drummer of Genesis and eventually lead singer and mega-platinum solo artist.

The group would continue to film at the Scala through April 2, including a press party sequence that faithfully reflected the inane comments and clueless questions members of the establishment British press asked the group during the endless press conferences, interview opportunities, and other media appearances during the first flush of Beatlemania. This scene was very much improvised at the last minute and includes actual members of the British press.

On April 3, the group shot a movie trailer for the film at Twickenham, which featured the four sitting in two baby prams, acting out a surreal scene of typing and answering a phone that was obviously not connected.

Two Sunday shoots at Marylebone Station were held on April 5 and April 12 because Sunday was the one day when the station was closed to the public. The group was filmed running across the adjacent Melcombe Place into the station. Scenes of John, George, and Ringo using the telephone booths (since removed) and Paul, disguised in a moustache and goatee, sitting with Wilfrid Brambell, were also shot inside the station. Another shot of the group running on to the train was edited into the opening sequence along with footage shot early in March.

The scene of the group running down the street, where George and Ringo fall, was shot on Boston Place, another street adjacent to the station. The fans chasing them here and in previous scenes, like the fans at the Scala Theatre, were paid for the privilege of chasing their mop-top idols. Tony Bramwell, who knew John, Paul, and George, when they were all boys in Liverpool, eventually worked for NEMS, did record promotion, and was heavily involved in the group's promotional films, remembers how some of the fans were recruited. "Ada Fosters was the school to go, to book dolly birds for any teen thing for television, movies or theater. It just so happened that I had some of the students living in the same house as me. They regularly did *Ready Steady Go!* They appeared in *The Knack* and *The Dirty Dozen*."

On April 6 and 7 at Twickenham, the Beatles filmed the scenes in the mock TV studio's makeup room and the interior scenes at the police station. Some of the scenes of the Beatles and Bobbies running in and out of the police station may have been inspired by the silent Buster Keaton short from 1922 *Cops*, a favorite of Richard Lester. The filming on April 8 of the film's Strauss opera scenes didn't require the Beatles' participation.

Thursday, April 9, saw the filming of Ringo's big solo scene by the river. The sequence was shot on the Thames towpath by Kew Bridge in Surrey. Ringo sported a black wool fisherman's cap in the scene, which became a signature item for him, and more prominently for John, who probably borrowed the look from Bob Dylan. Ringo's mopey, hangdog appearance was genuine, the result of having stayed out late drinking the night before.

The TV production office scenes were shot at Twickenham on April 10. April 13 saw the filming of some of the film's most memorable scenes. In one sequence, George is mistaken for a model at a marketing company and, at one point, describing some new shirts as "grotty," a word Alun Owen actually made up. The scene's marketing executive, played by Kenneth Haigh, was based on the real-life magazine editor Charles Mark Edward Boxer, also known as Mark Boxer, who worked for *Queen* and *Tatler* magazines, and was best known for the much imitated, groundbreaking visual style he brought to *The Sunday Times Colour Supplement*.

In another scene, George demonstrates to Shake how to shave with a safety razor, while John plays war games in the bathtub. When the plug is pulled and the water drains, he disappears, one of the many surreal scenes in the movie and one that was

George Harrison introducing the world to the word "grotty" in *A Hard Day's Night*. Courtesy Photofest.

totally improvised. This scene encapsulates Lester's affection for surreal visual film-making and why his singular cinematic style at this time created his directorial vision on *A Hard Day's Night* and *Help!*, set him apart, and made the first two films of the Beatles so influential and successful.

On April 14 there was filming of a traffic jam scene outside Twickenham that was cut from the film. On April 15, there was more shooting at the Scala Theatre to film exterior shots on two different roads surrounding the theater, Tottenham Street and Scala Street, and the nearby Charlotte Mews. The Beatles spent the day of April 16 filming various chase sequences around St. John's Secondary School in Notting Hill Gate, with the school also serving as the exterior of the police station in the film. Scenes shot at the Portland Arms pub were cut from the film, leading Richard Lester to duplicate the exact scene and location for his next film *The Knack*.

The evening of April 16 saw the recording of "A Hard Day's Night," which had been confirmed as the film's title. Lennon had the lyrics scribbled on a discarded birthday card from his son's birthday party from April 8. Accompanying him to the studio that day was journalist Maureen Cleave, who was writing the column "Disc Date" for London's *Evening Standard*. Cleave was tipped off about the group by

Gillian Reynolds, a friend from Oxford. Cleave became one of the first members of the mainstream, establishment press to write intelligently about their music. As she wrote in the *Daily Mail* in 2009, she occasionally assisted Lennon with the lyrics: "The tune to the song 'A Hard Day's Night' was in his head, the words scrawled on a birthday card from a fan to his little son Julian: 'When I get home to you,' it said, 'I find my tiredness is through . . .' Rather a feeble line about tiredness, I said. 'OK,' he said cheerfully and, borrowing my pen, instantly changed it to the slightly suggestive: 'When I get home to you / I find the things that you do / Will make me feel all right.'" The birthday card is on display at the Manuscript Room at the British Museum.

During the three-hour session, the group recorded nine takes. The lyrics evolved slightly, and McCartney struggled to finally nail down his bass part on his Hofner, but Ringo quickly figured out his drumming. Harrison had been playing his new electric Rickenbacker 12-string guitar throughout the sessions, but it was concluded that the tricky part he was still working through would be best left to overdub once the basic rhythm track was in place. Ringo played cowbell for more rhythmic punch, Norman Smith added bongos, and George Martin played piano.

Given that the song would open the movie, George Martin felt that something really special and catchy was needed. The opening chord is the sound of John and George playing an F major with an added G, while Paul plucks a D on his bass. Additional overdubs of acoustic guitar and piano were added later. The track also had a unique George Harrison contribution at the song's end. Harrison had been struggling with the guitar solos, especially in trying to come up with something special for the end. After several failed attempts at nailing his part, the issue was resolved by Martin, as recording engineer Geoff Emerick explained in his memoir, *Here There and Everywhere*: "George Martin finally decided to instead employ the same 'wound-up piano' technique he had done the year previous on "Misery." I was told to roll the tape at half speed while the two Georges—Harrison and Martin—working side by side in the studio, foreheads furrowed in concentration—as they played the rhythmically complex solo in tight unison on their respective instruments."

George's distinctive electric Rickenbacker 12-string sound throughout the sessions would eventually become a major influence on a host of musical artists on both sides of the Atlantic. Across England, several British musicians started playing a Rickenbacker 12-string, including Gerry Marsden (Gerry and the Pacemakers) from Liverpool, Denny Laine (The Moody Blues) from Birmingham, Hilton Valentine (The Animals) from Manchester, and Pete Townshend (The Who) from London.

Harrison's use of the electric 12-string was revelatory, although others had been using the acoustic 12-string, primarily in folk circles in imaginative ways for some time. It is this recognition of the way the acoustic 12-string was used in folk music that may have caused Roger McGuinn of the Byrds to easily pick up on what Harrison was doing and adapt it to modifying folk music with the beat and jangle of the music of the Beatles. Across the pond, the acoustic 12-string had been a fixture of the folk scene as far back as Blind Willie McTell and Leadbelly, with Ramblin' Jack Elliot, Bob Gibson, and newer folk-inspired groups such as The Rooftop Singers also using the instrument. The Kestrels from Bristol, England, a group the Beatles crossed paths with in 1963, were using an acoustic 12-string as part of their sound. Also in 1963, noted British session god Big Jim Sullivan was playing 12-string acoustic on such albums as *Relax Your Mind* from Jon (Mark) and Alun (Davies). Mark and Davies would go on to form Sweet Thursday and The Mark-Almond Band, play with John Mayall and supply Marianne Faithfull with 12-string acoustic guitar backing in concert and on record early on, while Davies would play on all of the albums of Cat Stevens between 1970 and 1978 and be his primary instrumental collaborator for many years.

While Carl Wilson was an early American adopter of the Rickenbacker electric 12-string, it would have the biggest impact on another American musician, the aforementioned Jim (Roger) McGuinn of the Byrds, whose jangly, folk-rock hybrid sound was clearly influenced by the Beatles; one can easily trace a line from *A Hard Day's Night*–era Beatles, to the early Byrds album, to Tom Petty and the Heartbreakers, to R.E.M., finally culminating in The Traveling Wilburys, which included Harrison and Petty.

McGuinn had been toiling on the folk scene, working with the Limeliters, the Chad Mitchell Trio, Judy Collins, Bobby Darin, and Simon and Garfunkel, among others, both on stage and in the studio. After seeing the Beatles on the *Ed Sullivan Show*, McGuinn began playing "I Want to Hold Your Hand" on his acoustic 12-string at Los Angeles club the Troubadour on "hoot night." He quickly saw the possibilities of weaving folk music with the new brand of Beatles pop and how the 12-string guitar would be a key part of that sound.

While George was the first member of the Beatles to use a 12-string guitar, an acoustic 12-string would not be used on a Beatles album until Lennon played a Framus Hootenanny acoustic on *Beatles for Sale*. Lennon also played the instrument on *Help!*, *Rubber Soul*, and *Abbey Road*.

Harrison was not the first Beatle to enjoy the fruits of the Rickenbacker guitar sound. As early as 1960, Lennon played a 325 six-string that he bought in Hamburg in 1958; originally having natural (maple-glo) finish, John had it painted black. Lennon liked the guitar because it was small, and he could hold it up close to see his fingerings because he refused to wear his glasses on stage. His stance, holding his guitar up high on his chest, his legs spread apart, and his feet pointing outward, was borrowed from his Hamburg mentor Tony Sheridan. This typified the Lennon dichotomy. On the one hand, his provocative stance displayed an aggressive posture, and on the other hand, his refusal to wear glasses on stage covered up one of his many insecurities.

Harrison's first Rickenbacker was also a six-string that was given a black finish, which he purchased when visiting his sister in the United States in September 1963. It was a 425 solid-body from 1962, that as of this writing is on loan to the Rock & Roll Hall of Fame in Cleveland, Ohio. It was the acquisition of Harrison's second Rickenbacker early in 1964 that would radically change the group's sound. Harrison would refer to the instrument as the "Ricky 12."

While the Beatles were in New York in February 1964, representatives of Rickenbacker were anxious to present some of their new instruments to the Beatles. John Lennon was shown the company's new 360 twelve-string electric guitar, the first electric 12-string guitar Rickenbacker had ever built. George Harrison was sick in bed with the flu, but Lennon instinctively knew that Harrison would love the instrument. The guitar was duly taken to his room, and after playing the instrument, he did indeed want one of his own. Harrison was still playing his black-painted, Gretsch 12-string Country Gentlemen at the time, which he would eventually give to Jimmy Page. He was also playing another Gretsch, a smaller, red Tennessean, that, like the Rickenbacker, had a twangy sound, with a more country feel.

But this new Rickenbacker was the one that defined the new guitar sound of the group at the time. Harrison would play the instrument on seven tracks on the upcoming film soundtrack: "I Should Have Known Better," "Tell Me Why," "If I Fell," "I Call Your Name," "Any Time at All," and the title song. On the title track, Harrison would actually play the solo on one of his Gretsch guitars and the rhythm part on his 12-string Rickenbacker (also using the instrument to reinforce the final note). In an early take of "I'll Be Back," Harrison did use his 12-string Rickenbacker, but the song would take on a more acoustic feel, and the final version did not feature the instrument.

On Friday, April 17, the Beatles returned to Les Ambassadeurs to shoot the discotheque scene, dancing to their own recordings of "I Wanna Be Your Man" and "Don't Bother Me," both originally released on *With the Beatles* in 1963. The group also taped an interview with Ed Sullivan; Sullivan was also given a clip from the upcoming movie, which would be aired on May 24. This was from the concert sequence, showing the group miming to "You Can't Do That," a sequence eventually cut from the film.

As the filming wound down, the group worked on rerecording dialogue and doing postproduction sound syncing at Twickenham. Filming on Monday, April 20 featured Paul in a sequence meant to provide him with a solo spot in the film and was shot at the now-defunct Jack Billings TV School of Dancing. Even though Paul, along with Richard Lester did considerable work revising the script, it ended up being cut.

George Martin spent the afternoon at Abbey Road producing mono and stereo mixes of the title song to the film.

Tuesday, April 21, featured more filming at the dance school, with Paul continuing to chat up actress Isla Blair. The Beatles spent the morning of Wednesday, April 22, filming the opening of the first "Can't Buy Me Love" sequence, when they descend the fire escape at the rear of the Hammersmith Odeon (now the Hammersmith Apollo), when they momentarily escape from their confinement. In the afternoon, the group headed back to Notting Hill Gate, filming a scene where they are chased by the police on St. Luke's Road. From there, Ringo filmed his solo scene on Lancaster Road, being chased by fans, seeking refuge in a thrift shop, and emerging in disguise. Paul was also filmed this day on Goldhawk Road in Shepherd's Bush as part of his unused solo scene.

On Thursday, April 23, more footage was shot for the "Can't Buy Me Love" sequence. A helicopter landing pad was constructed at the Thornbury Playing Fields on Bridge Road in Isleworth not far from London Airport. The group was filmed jumping off a ladder and from a helicopter as they cavorted around the field

The morning shoot ended early for John, who headed to London's Dorchester Hotel to attend a literary luncheon held in his honor by Foyle's book shop, leaving the other three Beatles to complete filming for the sequence. John was somewhat the worse for wear, having spent the previous evening with his wife Cynthia at the Ad Lib, one of London's hip new clubs. The luncheon attracted a cross section of British musical artists, including Yehudi Menuhin, Helen Shapiro, and Marty Wilde, as well as Harry Secombe from the *Goon Show* and clothes designer Mary Quant. But the attendees were to be disappointed by John's lack of participation; he declined to give a speech.

At Abbey Road late in the afternoon, George Martin did a final mono mix of the title song, which became the released version; it's not known if any of the Beatles attended the session.

April 24 was the last day of filming, with Ringo shooting more of his solo scenes on Edgehill Road in West Ealing. In this sequence, Ringo chivalrously drapes his overcoat over a puddle for a woman crossing a muddy field, only to find the puddle is actually a hole when she falls in. This old gag appeared in another British film of the time, Ken Russell's *French Dressing*, released in April 1964, which had a similar scene.

With that final bit of whimsy completed, the filming of *A Hard Day's Night* concluded.

Richard Lester discussed the Beatles' close relationship with each other in an extensive interview with Peter von Bagh for the Cinema Rediscovered Cineteca of Bologna in November of 2014 in one of the most recent interviews that he has done, saying, "In essence they were very alike. They were very, very supportive of each other. If one of them had too much to drink and had a problem at home, the others would try to protect him and take over. They were the ones that would be doing the jokes that were aggressive and outrageous and the other one would recover. It was a very interesting thing to watch. I was privileged to be a part of it for three to four years."

Regarding the tricky transition from *A Hard Day's Night* to *Help!* he said:

To me it was the only way we could deal with what we had available to us. We didn't just want to make *A Hard Day's Night* in color. We didn't want to do a film about their private lives because it would have been X-rated. We therefore took the decision, rightly or wrongly, that we should find a story that attacked the four and use the story as a device to try and show them as they were in 1965. This as you probably know, led John Lennon to say very kindly, "We're extras in our own bloody film."

For Lester, the period working with the Beatles was the height of the 1960s, but he could see the fall coming.

Things were going terribly well until *Time* magazine had a cover saying "Swinging London" and from then on it was downhill. Everything was happening and it was all intertwined. The fashion was a big number. It was enthusiastic and optimistic and that sense that "If you really want to do it." All you have to do is to learn three chords on a guitar. It was a good time for that, and it really didn't last much beyond '66 or '67. Then you go to Vietnam and the May riots in '68. It was short honeymoon period, but God it was fun.

And he talked about the pleasures of film directing:

I think to be honest the most pleasure in being a film director is the editing process, at least for me. Preproduction is fine because everything is ahead and due. Shooting is agony because it's wasting money all the time. No matter what you do or think you are doing, you are burning money and if you have any sense of responsibility you hang your head in shame by the end of the film. I tried desperately not to overspend and to not waste time, but some things happen.

FILM WRAP

Once filming was completed, a wrap party was held on April 24 at Winchester Hall, which adjoined the Turk's Head, where they'd filmed on March 10. Among the cast and crew, American DJ Murray the K was a guest at the party. The pub and hall are both still open, and the hall, although not very big, hosts weddings and other events.

In other respects, April 29 could be considered the last day of filming. Since February 22, Adrian Console, a photographer for UA, had been shooting footage of the group without sound to be used for promotional purposes, and on April 29, they were filmed visiting Madame Tussaud's wax museum to pose with their wax effigies prior to departing for a show that evening in Glasgow, Scotland. This footage was used in the documentary short *Follow the Beatles*, which also featured two scenes from *A Hard Day's Night*, as well as interviews with Dick Lester, Walter Shenson, Alun Owen, Wilfrid Brambell, cinematographer Gilbert Taylor, hairdresser Betty Glasgow, choreographer Lionel Blair, and British film journalist Alexander Walker. There's wonderful footage of the group returning to the UK from America on February 22 and, a few days later, supposedly reading Alun Owen's script. The glimpses of the group inside Abbey Road recording "And I Love Her" and "Tell Me Why" are priceless. *Follow the Beatles* aired on BBC 1 on August 1.

THE DAYS AFTER *A HARD DAY'S NIGHT*

June 1964 was another busy month for the Beatles. Along with film work, concerts, recording, record releases, and radio and television appearances, Lennon and McCartney were always writing songs. "World without Love," mostly written by Paul, became a number one hit single in America on June 27 for the British duo Peter and Gordon, whom Lennon jokingly referred to as Peter and Garfunkel. It had previously topped the UK chart on April 23.

Following a vacation break, the Beatles entered Abbey Road on June 1 in the afternoon, the first of three productive days of recording. First came the Carl Perkins cover, "Matchbox." "I'll Cry Instead" was primarily written by John and partly influenced by Del Shannon's "Runaway." John didn't regard the track highly, telling *Hit Parader* in 1972, "A nice tune, though the middle is a bit tatty." The session's final song was "I'll Be Back."

June 2 saw the group recording "When I Get Home," which John described to *Playboy* in 1980 as "another Wilson Pickett, Motown sound . . . a four-in-the-bar cowbell song." June 3 began with a photo session, during which Ringo collapsed from exhaustion. With a tour set to begin the next day, Brian Epstein quickly drafted a replacement, Jimmy Nicol, who was brought in for a rehearsal that afternoon. Nicol had kicked around the London music scene since the late 1950s. He'd played drums on singles by Tommy Steele's brother's group, Colin Hicks and the Cabin Boys, as well as playing for Vince Eager, and serving as a session drummer for Ted Heath and Johnny Dankworth. He most recently was the drummer for Georgie Fame and the Blue Flames. His stint with the Beatles would encompass shows in Denmark, the Netherlands, Hong Kong, and Australia until Ringo rejoined the group.

Following the rehearsal with Nicol, John, Paul, and George worked on "Things We Said Today," "Any Time at All," and demos of "You Know What to Do" and "No Reply." In explaining the writing of "Any Time at All" to David Sheff in the 1980 *Playboy* interview, Lennon indicated it was another one of his songs that was sort of a follow-up to something he had previously written: "An effort at writing 'It Won't Be Long'—same ilk. C to A minor, C to A minor with me shouting."

"I'll Cry Instead," "I'll Be Back," "When I Get Home," "Things We Said Today," and "Any Time at All" would all end up on the *A Hard Day's Night* UK album. "When I Get Home," "Things We Said Today," "Any Time at All," and "I'll Cry Instead" would appear on *Something New* released by Capitol. The latter song also appeared on the UA version of the soundtrack released in the US, mistakenly titled "I Cry Instead" on the back cover of many copies. Varying mixes of "I'll Cry Instead" would surface over the years, the US mono version running longer than the UK version by repeating the first verse. The song was meant to be used in *A Hard Day's Night* but ended up being cut. "I wrote that for *A Hard Day's Night*, but Dick Lester didn't even want it," Lennon said in *Playboy*. "He resurrected 'Can't Buy Me Love' for that sequence instead. I like the middle-eight to that song, though that's about all I can say about it."

June 10 marked the last time any work was done on *A Hard Day's Night* related to music, with George Martin completing a mono mix of "I'll Be Back." Interestingly, the Beatles approved the album's mono mix but didn't hear the final stereo mixes until the stereo album was released. Another interesting feature of the album was the number of songs that ended in a fade out, in contrast to a cold ending, which had been the norm on their previous recordings.

Photographer David Hurn was lucky enough to be on the set while the Beatles were filming *A Hard Day's Night*. "I was in the army at Sandhurst, and had a friend, John Antrobus," he told the author. "We left at the same time, I to be a photographer, and he to be a writer. He went on to write with Spike Milligan, including the play *The Bed Sitting Room*. He joined an agency, Associate London Scripts. Peter Sellers was associated with Spike Milligan and wrote *The Running, Jumping & Standing Still Film* directed by Dick Lester—I worked with them all. When Dick was asked to direct the Beatles film, it was natural I worked on that."

Hurn spent about 10 days on the shoot, including the train sequences. "Most films had a unit photographer. I suspect it was a union requirement. Their pictures were handed out for free to the general press, etc. I was employed, but kept the copyright, to attempt to get space in major magazines—*The Sunday Times*, *Life*, *Newsweek*, etc. My agreement was that I would not pose any pictures. I basically had a free hand anywhere. My main worry was the enormous volume of fans. How the four lads coped is difficult to understand; the fans were quite frightening."

Also present throughout the shoot was photographer Bert Cann. Cann had been involved in the British film world since 1932, when he began his career as a pageboy at Gaumont Studios in Lime Grove. He eventually developed an interest in the still photo department and landed a job running the dark room at Pinewood Studios. After an apprenticeship under American photographer Lee Garmes and a stint in the army, he landed at Bush Studios and began his long career as a portrait photographer of British movie stars. He branched out working on nonmovie assignments, including photographing the queen, and his work for *Life* magazine beginning in 1951 is legendary. He was the still photographer on *The Mouse That Roared* and *Dr. No* before working on *A Hard Day's Night*.

POSTSHOOT

Editing the film required some important decisions. Perhaps in hindsight, the way Lester chose to edit the concert sequence might have been done differently, given that one song ("You Can't Do That") was dropped entirely and two ("I Should Have Known Better" and "If I Fell") were shortened. Surprisingly, Lester felt Wilfrid Brambell was stealing too many scenes, taking away from what was essentially a youth movie for Beatles fans. This led Lester to cut footage featuring the veteran actor and, in some cases, do reshoots.

As Paul's solo scene was cut, he ended up being the only Beatle without a solo spot. Lester felt that McCartney lacked the naturalness of the other three Beatles, feeling that perhaps due to his relationship with actress Jane Asher, he was a bit too exposed to the world of acting, making him somewhat self-conscious and less spontaneous. He felt quite differently about George's acting. As for George's acting ability, in the special features DVD that came with the Miramax Collector's Series edition released in 2002, Lester said, "The most accomplished actor is George. He never attempted too much or too little. He was always right in the center. He got out of the scene everything there was to get out of it. There wasn't a lot for him to do, but what there was he had to do, he did well."

There were numerous scenes where the Beatles went off script, ad-libbed, or set up a situation where they could be spontaneous, such as, according to George Harrison in the *Anthology* book, in the press party scenes and, according to John in the same book, the bathtub sequence. In the book, John indicated they were embarrassed by the train sequence because it was early in the shoot, and they were nervous and self-conscious. On a more enjoyable note, he said in the *Anthology* book: "The best bits are when you don't have to speak and you just run about. All of us like the bit in the field where we jump about like lunatics because that's pure film, as the director tells us; we could have been anybody."

One of the most innovative aspects of the film was the closing title sequence, which was conceived and photographed by photographer Robert Freeman, not Lester. Freeman had been a constant presence in the visual presentation of the group from nearly the beginning of their recording career, through *Revolver* in 1966. It was his black-and-white pictures of John Coltrane (including Coltrane playing the flute, which was not an instrument he was associated with) that prompted Brian Epstein to hire him to photograph the Beatles. His photography adorns the covers of the *Long Tall Sally* EP and the albums *With the Beatles*, *A Hard Day's Night*, *Beatles for Sale*, and *Rubber Soul*. He did the cover photos for John Lennon's two books, *In His Own Write* and *A Spaniard in the Works* and the cover photo for Brian Epstein's *A Cellarful of Noise*. Freeman photographed the Beatles on the set of *A Hard Day's Night* and *Help!* and accompanied the group to the US on their first visit.

Freeman photographed the Beatles at his home studio at 13 Emperor's Gate, and the pictures were then imaginatively edited into a montage that made it look like the group members were dissolving into each other; the photomontage played during the end credits of *A Hard Day's Night*, which featured a reprise of the title song. The photos also were used to create the 20 black-and-white frames that made up the unique look of the UK album cover, with each Beatle represented by five frames, looking like the celluloid frames of a movie minus the sprocket holes, bordered with a blue outline. Oddly, UA chose to use only one photograph of each Beatle from the shoot for the cover of their US soundtrack album, cropping each Beatle's face to show only their hair and eyes, emphasizing their "mop-top" persona. The bold use of red does add a more eye-catching look but pales in comparison to the more subtle and iconic UK album cover. Like his work for the cover shot of *With the Beatles*, Freeman created another iconic image of the Beatles that would be copied, imitated, parodied, and mulled over for years to come.

In an interview with the author, Freeman discussed his work on *A Hard Day's Night* and *Help!*: "There was no input on *A Hard Day's Night* or *Help!* All the ideas for the covers were mine. Being with the Beatles was being in the center of crazy activity, the eye of a hurricane—and surreal situations provoked by fanatics, fans! It was an altogether lively and amusing time."

UA actually proposed that the voices of the Beatles should be dubbed because they felt Americans wouldn't understand their Scouse accents. Thankfully, cooler heads prevailed, and unlike the *Yellow Submarine* movie and the Beatles television cartoon series, the group's actual Liverpool voices were on full display.

Part of the postproduction was coming up with all the ways music would be used in the film. Up to that time, music in movies was presented in various ways: accompanying the opening title sequence, performed (or usually lip-synched) by a group or singer, coming from a radio, record player, or unseen source, or combinations. What Lester did was revolutionary, using a recording of a song to accompany a scene, almost the way a live piano player would play a song during a scene in a silent film. This is commonplace today and not something anyone would even think about while watching a movie now, but at the time the way it was done it was distinctive and something that would go on to be a key component in later films of the 1960s like *Easy Rider*, *The Graduate*, and others.

In *A Hard Day's Night*, Lester had Beatles songs playing to underpin the action and not just songs that would be on the soundtrack. For the nightclub scene of the Beatles dancing, he used their own music taking, "I Wanna Be Your Man," "Don't Bother Me," and "All My Loving," from *With the Beatles* (in the UK) and *Meet the Beatles* (in the US). "Can't Buy Me Love" was used not only in the sequence when the Beatles romp around a field after escaping the confinement of the theater but also used effectively during the chase scene with the police near the end of the movie.

Lester and his crew and even the Beatles certainly enjoyed their time making *A Hard Day's Night*, but they may not have known exactly what they had. The basic plot is somewhat conventional. The Beatles play a television show in London and have various adventures and misadventures along the way. The opening train sequence, displaying the group's cheeky, antiauthoritarian attitude and using surrealistic narrative devices, sets the tone for the whole movie. The group's interaction with their various handlers, journalists, and those involved in the television show, not to mention Paul's grandfather, makes for great comedic moments but also underscores their fishbowl existence. It also provides insight into their distinct personalities and group interpersonal relationships; although not an actual reflection of the real Beatles, enough rings true to make the movie quite different from what had come before in pop music, youth-oriented movies.

The side plots, particularly Ringo's attempt to break free from the bonds of the group and its resolution offers some drama and allows for various songs to be played while the Beatles cavort about. Some of the plot does reflect the group's lifestyle, especially their being constantly chased by their fans and poked and prodded by adults, the media, and even each other. Ultimately, it is the group's Liverpool charm and the musical segments that makes *A Hard Day's Night* such a joyful delight. Repeated viewings yield nuances missed on first viewing, and certain memorable lines get repeated over and over again by the group's fans in the course of everyday life.

In an interview in 1989 with *Musician* magazine, George Harrison put the film into perspective" "*A Hard Day's Night* was just, I suppose in retrospect, it was just magic because of the timing—and because we were so rough, and at the time, Dick Lester being the person to do it. So it was just one of them little packages that wasn't really like these days when they say how are we going to package *Batman*, we'll get Jack [Nicholson]—it wasn't really like that kind of thing."

GEORGE MARTIN AT THE MOVIES

There was also what would be considered typical instrumental soundtrack music in the film. Three were instrumentals of songs from the film: "I Should Have Known Better," "And I Love Her," and the title song. "Ringo's Theme (This Boy)" was an adaptation of "This Boy." "This Boy" was the B side of "I Want To Hold Your Hand" and was released in November 1963; the song also appears on *Meet the Beatles* and the Capitol EP *Four by the Beatles*, released in May 1964. The original "I Should Have Known Better" along with "And I Love Her" also appeared on one of the two British EPs released in conjunction with *A Hard Day's Night*, titled *Extracts from the Film* A Hard Day's Night.

Music from the instrumental score, arranged by George Martin, was released on several albums, credited to the George Martin Orchestra. In addition to Abbey Road, some of the music was recorded at Cine-Tele Sound (CTS) in Kensington Gardens Square in Bayswater as early as June 8, 1964. The instrumentals featured session stalwarts like guitarist Vic Flick, drummer Clem Cattini, Big Jim Sullivan, and Yardbirds and Led Zeppelin guitarist Jimmy Page. The facility opened in 1956, primarily for film score work and television jingles. The studio boasted the most modern audio gear of any London studio doing soundtrack work at the time because these music-only studios tended to have equipment that predated the war. Because of that CTS also attracted bookings for nonsoundtrack work. Recorded at CTS are such landmark soundtrack albums as *Casino Royale* in 1967, featuring the music of Burt Bacharach, the soundtrack for 1967's *Two for the Road* with music by Henry Mancini, and John Barry's *The Quiller Memorandum* in 1966.

Off the Beatle Track, credited to the George Martin Orchestra, was released in the US on July 10 by UA and in the UK on August 3 by Parlophone. It was reissued on CD from One Way Records in 1994. The album features all instrumental versions of four songs featured in *A Hard Day's Night*, "Can't Buy Me Love," "Don't Bother Me," "All My Loving," and "This Boy." *A Hard Day's Night: Instrumental Versions of the Motion Picture Score* arrived in September 1964 on UA. *And I Love Her* includes six songs by the Beatles (comprising half the album), including five from the *A Hard Day's Night*—"If I Fell," "And I Love Her," "I'm Happy Just to Dance with You," "I'll Cry Instead," and the title track, making "No Reply" the only song not on the *A Hard Day's Night* album. The album was released in 1966 in the UK only on Columbia's Studio 2 Stereo label, an audiophile imprint that primarily released instrumental and easy listening records.

The UK EP *Music from the Film* A Hard Day's Night (UA), credited to the George Martin Orchestra, includes the film versions of the title track and "Ringo's Theme (This Boy)" and nonfilm versions of "If I Fell" and "And I Love Her." Because UA did not have the rights to release the Beatles songs on their soundtrack as singles, they released two singles of instrumentals: "And I Love Her"/"Ringo's Theme (This Boy)" in July 1964 and "A Hard Day's Night"/"I Should Have Known Better" in September 1964.

This was not the first time Martin worked on movie music. He'd produced the title song of the film *Smiley* (1956); wrote music for the title of *I Like Money* (1961) sung by Nadia Gray (originally titled *Mr. Topaze* and directed by and starring Peter Sellers); wrote and performed the song "Lover's Blues" for the 1961 low-budget American exploitation film *V.D.* (also titled *Damaged Goods*); composed the score for *Crooks Anonymous* (1962), which was Julie Christie's film debut; was the arranger and conductor of the film score for *Take Me Over* (1963); and served as music director for *Calculated Risk* (1963).

Recording the film's score was something that Martin had been looking forward to. But Richard Lester's presence at Abbey Road while Martin was conducting a 30-piece orchestra touched off an argument when Lester became critical of what Martin was doing. To avoid a battle, Martin made some adjustments to the arrangements at Lester's request. In the short term, this resulted in the two not being on speaking terms and, in the long run, prompted Lester to use Ken Thorne to work on the film score for *Help!* instead of Martin. Nonetheless, in a minidocumentary featured on the DVD in the 2009 box set of stereo albums, Martin had good things to say about Lester:

> *A Hard Day's Night* was the first big one I did. I had the benefit of having a director—Dick Lester—who was a musician, who was quite a good pianist. And of course we recorded the special songs for the film, as we just do ordinary recordings and Dick used a lot of the songs I already recorded on the past albums. 'Can't Buy Me Love' already had been recorded for example.

In *Things We Said Today*, Martin said, "I was glad [Lester] was on board because I really didn't want another *Summer Holiday*."

Martin was nominated for an Oscar for Best Scoring of Music, Adaptation of Treatment for his work on *A Hard Day's Night* (losing to André Previn for *My Fair Lady*). Alun Owen received a nomination for Best Story and Screenplay Written Directly for the Screen. UA, in their rush to release the album, didn't wait to get stereo mixes of the Beatles songs for the album, simply creating "fake stereo" mixes for the stereo version of the album; thus, only the instrumental tracks were in true stereo. It wasn't until a 2014 reissue of the UA soundtrack on CD, featuring both mono and stereo mixes, that a true stereo version of that album became available.

UA released the US soundtrack on June 26. Parlophone released the UK version, with seven songs from the film on side one and six nonfilm songs on side two, on July 10. The UK version is considered the definitive version of the album. Unusually, it contained only 13 tracks instead of the standard 14, which wouldn't happen again until *Sgt. Pepper's Lonely Hearts Club Band* in 1967. It would also mark the fourth and last time the group's press officer Tony Barrow would write liner notes for a full-length UK album. Barrow's usual prose didn't disappoint, but unlike past liner notes, he spent a great deal of time simply recounting the group's work on the film and writing and recording the album.

Parlophone also released the single "A Hard Day's Night"/"Things We Said Today" on July 10. Such is the quality of "Things We Said Today," that it's hard to believe the song ended up as a B side. In fact, Parlophone had announced in *Record Retailer* in July 2, 1964, that the group's next single would be a "new double-side hit single," suggesting that it would be a double A-sided disc. The advance demonstration discs even featured a red capital "A," on both sides; usually such singles had an "A" on side one and no letter on the other side.

But a week later, *Record Retailer* reported that despite being "originally planned as a double 'A' side release, EMI are concentrating on the film theme at the top side." Paul wrote "Things We Said Today" in May 1964 while on holiday with Jane Asher, Ringo, and his girlfriend Maureen Cox, composing the song on a new Epiphone acoustic guitar. In *Many Years from Now* he explained: "It was a slightly nostalgic thing already, a future nostalgia: we'll remember the things we said today, sometime in the future, so the song projects itself into the future and then is nostalgic about the moment we're living in now, which is quite a good trick. . . . It has interesting chords," he began. "It goes C, F, which is normal, then the normal thing might be to go to F minor, but to go to B flat was quite good. It was a sophisticated little tune." Between EMI and Capitol, 14 singles by the Beatles would be released as double A-sides.

More songs from *A Hard Day's Night* would appear on Capitol's *Something New* album, released on July 20 in the US. The same day saw the release of the Capitol single "I'll Cry Instead"/"I'm Happy Just to Dance with You." Closing out the year, *Beatles '65* featured the only song from the UK *A Hard Day's Night* album that had yet to appear on a US album, "I'll Be Back." Only Capitol Records, at that time, would have the temerity to release an album in 1964 comprised of mostly previously released music from other albums and singles and call it *Beatles '65*.

Parlophone released two EPs of the film's songs, *Extracts from the Film* A Hard Day's Night on November 4, and *Extracts from the Album* A Hard Day's Night on November 6. All the tracks on the *Extracts from the Album* EP appeared on the Parlophone album, but only "I'll Cry Instead" appeared on the UA album. "Can't Buy Me Love" would also turn up on the UK EP, *The Beatles Million Sellers*, released in December 1965. The four songs on the *Extracts from the Film* EP all appeared on the Parlophone and UA albums and were released on singles in the US Anyone who bought a UK first pressing of *A Hard Day's Night* would also get an insert, listing various Parlophone releases.

Through the years, the music from *A Hard Day's Night* would come out on numerous releases in various formats. Three significant releases worth mentioning are Capitol's *Reel Music* album, the "Beatles Movie Medley" single, and the CD release of the UA soundtrack album. The *Reel Music* album, released in 1982, featured four songs from *A Hard Day's Night*, three from *Help!*, two from *Magical Mystery Tour*, two from *Yellow Submarine*, and three from *Let It Be*. The album, with its garish artwork, was not favorably received on release but does come with a nice 12-page souvenir booklet, an inner sleeve featuring cover photos of the 25 Beatles albums Capitol had released up through the *Rarities* album, and a page with photos of film posters and lobby cards. The album also contained tracks that were rarities in the US: true stereo mixes of "A Hard Day's Night" and "Ticket to Ride," a unique stereo edit of "I Should Have Known Better," and the British stereo mix of "I Am the Walrus," which features a unique edit. Promotional copies also included "The Beatles Movies Medley," a medley of seven songs from the films in the spirit of hit medleys that were popular at the time. The single's B side featured an interview with the group from the set of *A Hard Day's Night*, titled "Fab Four on Film." But Capitol could not secure rights to the interviews, so the commercial version of the "Medley" single featured "I'm Happy Just to Dance with You" on the B side.

Anthology 1 (1995), features takes 1 and 2 of "Can't Buy Me Love," as well as alternate takes of "You Can't Do That," "And I Love Her," and Take 1 of "A Hard Day's Night."

Live versions of songs that were originally released on the *A Hard Day's Night* soundtrack album on UA, and the UK *A Hard Day's Night* album would also appear on official releases.

On the original *The Beatles at the Hollywood Bowl*, there were live versions of "Can't Buy Me Love," "A Hard Day's Night," and "Things We Said Today." The 2016 reissue of the album, in conjunction with the Ron Howard film *Eight Days A Week*, added "You Can't Do That."

There have been several official releases of BBC recordings made by the Beatles. Those releases include *Live at the BBC* released in 1994 and *On Air: Live at the BBC, Volume 2* released in 2013. The CDs were issued and reissued and these releases are also available on vinyl.

Six songs that appeared on the *A Hard Day's Night* albums turned up on these BBC recordings. "Can't Buy Me Love," the title track, and "Things We Said Today" are on *Live at the BBC* and "If I Fell," "And I love Her," and "You Can't Do That" are on *Air: Live at the BBC, Volume 2*.

The Beatles performed "Can't Buy Me Love" three times on BBC radio, twice on *Saturday Club* on March 30, 1964 and May 18, 1964, and once on *Saturday Club* on April 4, 1964. The version included on *Live at the BBC* was broadcast on March 30, 1964, from a recording made at Studio Number 1 at the BBC Piccadilly Theatre. "A Hard Day's Night" was performed twice on BBC radio on *Top Gear* on July 16, 1964 (the debut broadcast of the then important new radio show), which included a piano overdub taken directly from the single because George Martin wasn't able to make the taping and from the radio show *From Us to You* on August 3, 1964. *The Live at the BBC* release was from a *Top Gear* broadcast on July 16, 1964, that was recorded on July 14, 1964, at Studio S2 (BBC) Broadcasting House. "Things We Said Today" was also performed only twice on the same shows and dates as "A Hard Day's Night." The recording on *Live at the BBC* is from the *Top Gear* broadcast on July 16, 1964, that was recorded on July 14, 1964, at Studio S2, (BBC) Broadcasting House, like "A Hard Day's Night."

"If I Fell" was performed by the Beatles two times on *Top Gear* on July 16, 1964, and on *From Us to You* on August 3, 1964. The version of "If I Fell" included on the *On Air Live at the BBC Volume 2* release was from the *Top Gear* broadcast on July 16, 1964, that was recorded on July 14 1964, at Studio S2 (BBC) Broadcasting House, the same as "A Hard Day's Night" and "Things We Said Today" from the *Live at the BBC*. "And I Love Her" was only performed once on BBC radio, and the version on the *On Air Live at the BBC Volume 2* release was from a *Top Gear* broadcast on July 16, 1964, that was recorded on July 14, 1964, at Studio S2 (BBC) Broadcasting House, the same as "A Hard Day's Night" and "Things We Said" from the *Live at the BBC*. "You Can't Do That" was performed four times on BBC radio on *From Us to You* on March 30, 1964, on *Saturday Club* on April 4, 1964, on *From Us to You* on May 18, 1964, and *Top Gear* from July 16, 1964. The version on the *On Air Live at the BBC Volume 2* release was from the *Top Gear* broadcast on July 16, 1964, that was recorded on July 14, 1964, at Studio S2 (BBC) Broadcasting House, the same as "A Hard Day's Night" and "Things We Said Today" from the *Live at the BBC*.

According to an interview conducted with Kevin Howlett, the foremost expert on the group's BBC recordings, 81 of the 88 performances by the group for the BBC have been released. Two of those not released from the era of *A Hard Day's Night* because of inferior sound quality are "I'm Happy Just to Dance with You" and "I Should Have Known Better."

BEATLES BOFFO BOX OFFICE

With a budget of £200,000, *A Hard Day's Night* grossed £14 million worldwide in 1964. The film was at the center of an explosion in commercial and worldwide acclaim for British films. The third James Bond film, *Goldfinger*, was the number one box-office film of the year in England, followed by *A Hard Day's Night*, Michael Caine's breakthrough film *Zulu*, and Norman Wisdom's *A Stich in Time*, just ahead of the final film in Cliff Richard's starring musicals of the early 1960s, *Wonderful Life*.

This was a watershed moment for British films. Yet in many cases they were films financed with American studio money. There were also British films that, although not big moneymakers or much remembered today, were nonetheless important to this key moment in British film history.

A British film released in 1964 that actually had been in production since 1956 was *It Happened Here*, cowritten and codirected by Kevin Brownlow and Andrew Mollo. Mollo was an expert on military history, particularly uniforms, and he would go on to work on such key 1960s films as *Dr. Zhivago* and *The Spy Who Came in From the Cold*, continuing into the twenty-first century on *The Pianist* (2002). Brownlow is one of the world's foremost film historians, who, along with Mollo did one other feature film *Winstanley* in 1975. He edited *The Charge of the Light Brigade* in 1968 and has many documentaries and short films to his credit, as well authoring many books on film.

Work on the film began when the two were in their teens; Brownlow was 18, and Mollo just 16. Their passion, vision, and talent was quickly recognized, and they were aided by Tony Richardson, who provided money and equipment, and Stanley Kubrick, who gave them unused ends of film stock from *Dr. Strangelove*. The film was a dystopian alternative history, which has often been classified as a science fiction film, that explored one scenario resulting from the Germans taking over England, a perennially popular scenario that's been explored in the American miniseries *The Plot Against America* (based on the Philip Roth novel of the same name), the Amazon series *The Man in the High Castle* (based on a Philip K. Dick novel), and numerous other novels and films.

It Happened Here was filmed in black and white, giving it a gritty realism and documentary look (enhanced by the use of actual documentary footage). The film holds up well today and, given the rising of right-wing nationalism in the US and parts of Europe, makes it frighteningly relevant.

A Hard Day's Night would go on to have an extraordinary afterlife. But initially, UA didn't treat the film with the kind of care, respect, and moneymaking potential its producer Walter Shenson felt it deserved. Shenson's main gripe with UA was that they rented the film out cheaply. Of course, *A Hard Day's Night* would go on to have an extraordinary afterlife. Shenson would regain rights to the film in 1979. The rights to the film are now in the hands of the Karsh family, who also co-own the right to *Help!* with the Beatles. Martha Karsh explained how the rights to the film came to be shared by the Beatles,

> The deal with the estate of Walter Shenson included all of his interest in both films, as well as the memorabilia, photos and ephemera he had. It was common at the time *A Hard Day's Night* was made for the producer to own the film copyright, but when The Beatles made *Help!* they negotiated a better deal and split the copyright with producer Shenson. As we acquired all that Shenson owned, we ended up 50-50 partners with The Beatles and their respective heirs in the ownership of *Help!*

The film has had an extensive post-theatrical history beyond its initial release. Its US network television debut was on October 24, 1967, on NBC. It was first aired on television in the UK on December 28, 1970 on BBC 1, oddly airing on a Monday afternoon at 4:05 p.m. John Lennon was at his home in Ascot watching the movie and was inspired to write "I'm the Greatest" after viewing it, given to Ringo Starr to sing on his 1973 album *Ringo*.

Very little unused footage remains from the *Hard Day's Night* shoot at Twickenham because the studio's policy was to destroy all unused footage.

Walter Shenson regained the rights to *A Hard Day's Night* in 1979 because UA, thinking a teen pop music exploitation film would have a limited afterlife and, with no vision of possible new technologies that might emerge to show films, let their rights to the movie expire. Unfortunately, Shenson did not exercise the good judgment and taste he displayed during the conception, filming, postproduction, marketing, and exhibition of the film in 1964. Shenson granted rights to Universal to release the film theatrically in 1982, devising a new prologue, a photomontage of stills from the film set to "I'll Cry Instead." The prologue was then followed by the film's actual opening of John, George, and Ringo running down the street. This new cut was used on all subsequent releases through 1997.

In 1984, the film was released through MPI Home Video on VHS and other short-lived formats, Betamax, laser disc, and CED video disc. Janus Films issued a Criterion Collection package in 1984 that included a theatrical trailer, *The Running, Jumping & Standing Still Film*, and an interview with Richard Lester. The initial Criterion laser disc release has technical problems that were fixed on future releases of that format. The VHS version became the standard way most people watched the movie, along with the occasional television and midnight movie showings. In 1993, a CD-ROM version was released through Voyager, using the QuickTime video format and, along with the extras in the Criterion version, also included a text copy of the script. This proved to be yet another format, one for computers, that faded quickly. In 1997, the film would debut on DVD through MPI and include all the Criterion extras, along with newsreel footage.

Finally, in 2000, after 36 years, the film would have a theatrical release that restored Lester's original opening. Released through Miramax, the now-defunct company co-owned by disgraced film producer Harvey Weinstein. Miramax would also release the film on DVD in 2002. The two-DVD set, which also included CD-ROM extras, boasted seven hours of additional material. Some of special features included was a newly produced promotional special titled *Things They Said Today*, which featured interviews with Richard Lester, George Martin, Alun Owen, and Gilbert Taylor. It would be included on the Criterion Collection set released in 2014. But some material remained exclusive to the Miramax edition: the bonus features "Their Production Will Be Second to None," which includes interviews with Richard Lester, Sir George Martin, Denis O'Dell, and David Picker; "With the Beatles," which includes interviews with cast members John Junkin, Lionel Blair, Kenneth Haigh,

David Janson, Anna Quayle, Jeremy Lloyd, and Terry Hooper; "Working like A Dog," which features interviews with the production crew, including Gilbert Taylor, Paul Wilson, Betty Glasow and Barrie Melrose; "Busy Working Overtime," interviews with the postproduction crew members Pam Tomling, Roy Benson, Gordon Daniels, and Jim Roddan; "Listen to the Music Playing in Your Head," featuring George Martin on the *A Hard Day's Night* songs; "Such A Clean Old Man!" featuring memories of actor Wilfrid Brambell; "I've Lost My Little Girl" featuring an interview with actress Isla Blair; "Taking Testimonial Pictures" featuring an interview with photographer Robert Freeman; "Dressed to the Hill" featuring an interview with tailor Gordon Millings; "Dealing with 'the Men from the Press,'" featuring a Tony Barrow interview; "They and I Have Memories" featuring a Klaus Voorman interview, and "Hitting the Big Time in the USA," featuring a Sid Bernstein interview. The soundtrack was digitally restored, and there is a French-language track. The film is presented in widescreen (1.66:1) but is enhanced for 16.9 television.

On the DVD-ROM there is a "Screenplay Viewer," which includes a reproduction of the entire first draft of the screenplay; "Remember All the Little Things" *A Hard Day's Night* scrapbook; a roundtable discussion with the cast and crew; and two now obsolete features—access to the "DVD Destination Site" and the "Award Winning" *A Hard Day's Night* website archive. It's no coincidence that Miramax would have out the first quality, postdebut release of the film. Miramax began as a small company that primarily distributed and exhibited music films for college audiences. Their breakthrough success was when they released a UK and US version of the Amnesty International *Secret Policeman's Ball* fundraising concert in 1981.

On July 6, 2004, a theatrical 40th anniversary screening attended by Paul McCartney, Victor Spinetti, John Junkin, and David Janson, among others connected with the film, was held in London.

In 2014 Janus Films acquired the film rights from Miramax from the Shenson Estate, which is managed by Bruce A. Karsh. Janus Films, through Criterion, released the film again in 2014 to mark its 50th anniversary. The three-disc package included a DVD of the film and a DVD with extras and Blu-ray disc with the film and the extras. A 4k digital restoration was approved by Richard Lester, presented in 1.75:1 aspect ratio (previous releases had been in 1:66:1 aspect ratio). The 4K release was the first time the Criterion Collection worked in this format because all previous releases had been in 2K. In January 2021, a 4K UHD version of the film was released; the package has the same contents as the 2014 release.

The last time the film was restored was in 1995 by Paul Rutan Jr., who was part of the team that worked on the new transfer, and would work in some capacity on restorations of all the movies of the Beatles except *Let It Be*.

There were many challenges faced in creating the 2014 reissue. The camera negatives of reels 1 and 10 were missing. Also, for the sequence filmed at the Scala

Theatre, the use of television monitors in the scenes had forced the filmmakers to slow down the filming to 25 frames per second instead of 24 frames per second, so the rolling black bars on the monitors wouldn't be visible in the film. This meant the music played during the live concert sequence is actually slower than on the soundtrack albums.

There were other challenges as well related to audio. The three songs used from the *With the Beatles* album were recorded on a two-track machine, whereas the songs from the *Hard Day's Night* album were recorded on a four-track machine. And the original multitrack mono tapes for "She Loves You" were missing.

The audio track on the new release is presented in various configurations: an uncompressed mono audio track, a new uncompressed stereo track, and a 5.1 DTS-HD Master Audio surround mix. All were prepared under the supervision of Giles Martin, George Martin's son, at Abbey Road. There is also an audio commentary featuring the cast and crew

Several interview featurettes are included. "In Their Own Voices" features 1964 interviews with the Beatles, behind-the-scenes footage, and photos. This nearly hour-long documentary includes interviews with Richard Lester, George Martin, Victor Spinetti, and many others. The documentary *Things They Said Today* is included. "Picturewise" is a feature on Lester's early work. *The Running Jumping & Standing Still Film* is included. "Anatomy of Style" looks deeply at Lester's cinematic style. There's also an interview with acclaimed Beatles author Mark Lewisohn. The entire performance of "You Can't Do That," which was cut from the film, is included. The set's booklet has an essay by Howard Hampton and an excerpt from *The Beatles in Richard Lester's* A Hard Day's Night: *A Complete Pictorial Record of the Movie*, by J. Philip De, Franco.

According to Kim Hendrickson, executive producer with the Criterion Collection, Lester was involved in both the video and audio restoration: "Approved by director Richard Lester, this new digital transfer was created in 4K resolution on a Scanity film scanner from the 35 mm original camera negative and two 35 mm fine-grain master positives." As for the audio Hendrickson said,

> In consultation with Lester, the monaural soundtrack was restored from digitally archived optical elements. These sources include fragments of surviving production stems and the print master that yielded much of the dialogue and effects material for the new 5.1 surround mix. This restoration would not have been possible without the generous contributions of archivists and engineers who evaluated a vast range of surviving audio elements in Hollywood, at Abbey Road Studios, at the British Film Institute and in Lester's personal collection.

Some movie tie-in merchandise and promotional items were attached to the film, although nothing like that which would come later with *Yellow Submarine*. Aside from the Official United Artists' Pictorial Souvenir Book, magazine-styled, like a concert tour program, published by World Distributors, of Manchester, England, the one item that was the most visible that collectors can easily seek out is the paperback book novelization. The book, *The Beatles in* A Hard Day's Night, was published by Dell in the US and sold for 50 cents and came with an eight-page spread of black-and-white photos. John Burke, who wrote the novelization, was a prolific writer and wrote under pen names. He wrote many highly successful suspense and science fiction novels, along with short stories, screenplays, nonfiction books, and even edited various collections. He wrote many novelizations of movies, television shows, and plays. Many British films of the 1960s received the novelization treatment by him from kitchen-sink dramas, to Swinging London films and more popular films.

After his work on *A Hard Day's Night*, Alun Owen never worked on another feature film, working primarily in television. After his work on the libretto for Lionel Bart's *Maggie May* in 1964, he never again worked in the theater.

Upon its release, *A Hard Day's Night* received almost unanimous praise from film critics, perhaps surprisingly, at a time when there was no underground or rock music press. *The Village Voice* was ground zero for New York City's alternative arts and culture scene, and reviewer Andrew Sarris wrote one of the more glowing reviews of the film, calling it "the *Citizen Kane* of jukebox musicals," a phrase often quoted in connection to the film's significance. But even older critics, presumed to be either indifferent or openly hostile to rock 'n' roll, seemed to be able to come to the film with an open mind and found themselves not only impressed by Lester's deft direction but also by the uncanny appeal of these four young men from Northern England. On the other side of the Atlantic, with Lester being singled out, with *The Times* saying "a lot of his bright ideas come off very well: the way, for instance, that several of the numbers are treated as contrapuntal soundtrack accompaniments to screen action of quite another sort; the outbursts of Goonish visual humor; the freshly observed London locations."

When John Lennon spoke to *Rolling Stone*'s Jann Wenner in 1970, he was critical about the way the film was perceived. "I thought it wasn't bad. It could have been better." He complained about the perception that the group was seen as little more than the puppets of their manager and film director. And although he'd initially thought Alun Owen was a good choice as screenwriter, his glib approach to the Beatles' individual characters irked him.

The film gained cult status over the years, a favorite of art and revival houses, the weekend midnight movie crowd, and college campus film festivals, in the years before the demise of drive-in movie theaters, and the rise of cable TV and home VHS players. In Danny Peary's three-volume *Cult Movies* book series, he said of the film: "*A Hard Day's Night* is a real treasure. It is an impressionistic chronicle of a typical twenty-four hours in their hectic lives, a wonderful comedic-musical showcase for the talented foursome at their peak."

It's also interesting to see how the film has been re-reviewed over the years as successive generations of film scholars and new audiences discover the film and its endless delights. On the 50th anniversary of the film in 2014, the film community again, almost unanimously, offered its praise, demonstrating how well it has held up. Kenneth Turan wrote in the *Los Angeles Times*: "It is remarkable how much it continues to dazzle, especially the film's trademark mixture of music and imagery." In *The Atlantic*, Colin Fleming called it a "cinematic masterpiece. It's one of the rare works of art from the '60s that's in the same league as, well, the Beatles." In *You Can't Do That*, Roger Ebert said it was one of the best five musicals he had ever seen, up there with *Singin' in the Rain*. Among the newer tastemakers of film, Mike D'Angelo of the *AV Club* said, "The music endures on its own, and the movie endures because it offers so much more than the music."

The film would have an enormous influence on future generations of filmmakers. Cameron Crowe's *Almost Famous* is a film that fully captures the essence of the rock world, the people who inhabit that world, and the music of a golden era in rock, the 1970s. He always used music effectively in his movies, in addition to making documentaries on Pearl Jam, David Crosby, and the making of *The Union*, a collaboration between Elton John and Leon Russell. Paul McCartney wrote and performed the title songs of Crowe's *Vanilla Sky*.

In an interview with the author, Crowe talked about seeing *A Hard Day's Night* for the first time. "I saw *A Hard Day's Night* and fell in love with the train scene and the cool microphone that Lennon sang into. It remains the definitive rock movie in so many ways, along with *Dont Look Back*—it's a two-pack gut punch of rock cinema." He then said of Richard Lester's influence, "He was the first guy who really knew how to shoot rock and roll and cinema. He understood the gravitas beneath the giddy rebellion. Lester influenced pretty much everything that came after, especially the great Who movie *Quadrophenia*."

3

EiGhT ARMs To HoLd You

The first Beatles album to appear on the Capitol label was *Meet the Beatles*, a revamped iteration of the UK edition, *With the Beatles*, released on January 20, 1964. It was one of five Beatles albums the label would release that year.

Capitol didn't release the group's first album, *Please Please Me*. That honor went to Vee-Jay, a Chicago-based label, which issued a reworked version of the album, *Introducing the Beatles*, on January 10, 1964. Vee-Jay had gained the rights to the

The Beatles performing in *Help!* Courtesy Photofest.

Beatles' recordings as Capitol had passed on releasing the group's first two singles, "Love Me Do" and "Please Please Me," in the US. As a result, EMI hired Transglobal Music, a New York–based agency that had helped EMI find US labels for their recordings in the past. Vee-Jay released their first Beatles single, "Please Please Me" in February 1963.

EMI next offered Capitol "She Loves You," which was again turned down. Transglobal ended up licensing the single to the Swan Records label in Philadelphia, which had ties to Dick Clark.

Capitol's initial handling of the Beatles music set the tone for their rocky relationship with the group. The unique relationship between EMI, which owned Capitol, and the differences between the way British and American record labels are structured, were key factors that are often overlooked. But Capitol's Dave Dexter Jr. has been rightly criticized for the way he altered the mixes of the group's music and prepared their albums for release in the States, and we will explore that unfortunate series of events.

How royalty payments in the two different countries affected the Beatles is also significant. British record company royalties on albums are paid to the songwriter and music publisher, divided by the number of songs on an album. In the United States, royalties to publishers and songwriters are fixed. Therefore, the fewer tracks on a US album, the less the label paid in royalties. This was part of the reason why Capitol did not replicate the group's UK albums in the States. This difference in royalty structure contributed to Capitol altering the group's UK releases all the way up until the release of *Sgt. Pepper* in 1967. Though it is true that Capitol came to release the group's records late in the game, they also had to contend with the complicated legal mess that resulted from Vee-Jay having already released a full album of the group's music and UA having rights to the soundtrack for *A Hard Day's Night*.

Right from the beginning, Capitol took the group's UK albums and altered them or created entirely different albums. Capitol's *Meet the Beatles* was 12 tracks, whereas the UK's *With the Beatles* was 14 tracks. The US album included nine of the *With the Beatles* tracks, the hit single "I Want to Hold Your Hand," and the B-sides from the US and UK versions of the single. Part of this was due to different perceptions about how an album should be marketed. For the most part, UK albums did not include singles or tracks from EP releases because it was seen as cheating the record buyers by making them buy a song twice. In the US, labels felt albums were built around hit singles or, some would say, padded with filler around hit singles. And although Capitol did release two EPs of the Beatles' music, the EP format was by then more popular in Britain than in America.

EMI began releasing EPs in England in 1954. Once rock 'n' roll hit, EMI started seeing healthy sales of EPs, with the years 1958 through 1964 being the peak years for the format. The EP was seen as good value for the money because the four song 7-inch disc was not appreciably more than a two-track single, and the glossy artwork, photos, and occasional liner notes also were an attractive addition that spurred on sales. The Beatles early EPs were big sellers in England, but as EMI began to put out releases that started to duplicate tracks from other single and album releases and the album format grew in popularity, sales dipped. EMI released their last EP, Cilla Black's *Time for Cilla*, in 1968.

The Beatles' Second Album, released by Capitol on April 10, 1964, was something of a hodgepodge. The 11 tracks included five leftovers from *With the Beatles*, two of the four tracks from the UK *Long Tall Sally* EP, "She Loves You" and its B side, "I'll Get You," "You Can't Do That," the B side of "Can't Buy Me Love" (and an album track on the UK version of *A Hard Day's Night*), and "Thank You Girl," the B side of "Do You Want to Know a Secret." For all its faults, *The Beatles' Second Album* did include a track, "You Can't Do That," that was not released yet in the UK.

Capitol released the first of two EPs, *Four by the Beatles*, on May 11, 1964. It contained two songs from the Parlophone UK release *With the Beatles* ("Roll Over Beethoven," and "Please Mr. Postman") along with "All My Loving" and "This Boy," which both appeared on the Capitol album *Meet the Beatles*. The first US EP release of music from the Beatles was *Souvenir of Their Visit to America*, released on March 23, 1964, on Vee-Jay.

The next Capitol album, *Something New*, released on July 20, 1964, featured eight songs from the UK *A Hard Day's Night*, the other two tracks from the *Long Tall Sally* EP, and the German version of "I Want to Hold Your Hand," "Komm, gib mir deine Hand." To really milk the fans, Capitol released the double album *The Beatles' Story* on November 23, 1964, which featured interviews with the group, selections from press conferences, and brief clips of Beatles songs, including a snippet of "Twist and Shout" live, the opening song of their first Hollywood Bowl concert on August 23, 1964. The record was coproduced by Gary Usher (who also worked with the Beach Boys, the Byrds, and Dick Dale), and DJ Roger Christian (who wrote songs for the Beach Boys and Jan and Dean). Christian was also one of the album's narrators, along with John Babcock and Al Wiman. After being out of print for many years, *The Beatles' Story* was finally reissued on CD as part of *The U.S. Albums* box in 2014.

There could have easily been a live album from the group in 1964. The Beatles had performed at the Hollywood Bowl on August 23, and the concert was recorded for future release, produced by Voyle Gilmore (who was assisted by George Martin) with Hugh Davis engineering. A mono acetate mix was prepared by Gilmore and Davis, but Martin and the group felt the quality of the recording was poor, largely due to the band's performance being drowned out by screaming fans. The Beatles' subsequent shows at the Hollywood Bowl, on August 29 and 30, 1965, were also recorded. But Martin and the group still felt the sound quality was unacceptable.

So it wasn't until the 1977 release of *The Beatles at the Hollywood Bowl* that songs from the 1964 and 1965 performances were officially released and were produced by George Martin. These recordings represent one of the most unusual recording specifications in the group's entire career, as both three-track recording (for the initial recordings) and 24-track recording (for the 1977 production) were used, the only time these two methods were used together on recordings for the Beatles. In 2016, an expanded edition with four additional tracks, *Live at the Hollywood Bowl*, was released, which was produced by Giles Martin, as a tie in with the Ron Howard film *The Beatles: Eight Days a Week*.

Beatles '65, released on December 15, 1964, combined one track from the UK *A Hard Day's Night* album, nine from the group's next UK album, *Beatles for Sale*, and their latest single, "I Feel Fine"/"She's a Woman." The second and final Capitol EP, *4 by the Beatles*, released on February 4, 1965, featured four tracks from *Beatles '65*. It was the Capitol's next album, *The Early Beatles*, released on March 22, 1965, included 11 tracks from the UK *Please, Please Me* album. The next Capitol album, *Beatles VI*, released on June 14, 1965, will be covered later.

BRITISH INVASION

While Beatlemania had been raging in England since 1963, other groups from England were proving that the success of the Beatles was no fluke and that not only Liverpool but also London and other northern and midland towns in England had groups and artists that could also notch up number one hits on the British charts.

Billy J. Kramer (born William Howard Ashton), hailing from Bootle, a suburb of Liverpool, topped the UK charts with "Bad to Me" in 1963 and "Little Children" in 1964, under the name Billy J. Kramer with the Dakotas. The group had five Top-10 hits in England, with the tour-de-force "Trains and Boats and Planes" (in 1965) just missing the Top 10 at number 12. Four of those Top-5 hits were written by Lennon and McCartney: "Do You Want to Know a Secret" (1963), "Bad to Me" (1963), "I'll Keep You Satisfied" (1963), and "From A Window" (1964). All were produced by George Martin at Abbey Road. Brian Epstein served as the group's manager. John Lennon helped Kramer come up with his stage name. Ashton chose the surname Kramer, but it was Lennon who suggested adding the J.

Gerry and the Pacemakers, another Epstein-managed group from Liverpool, had six UK Top-10 hits, including three number 1s, with their first three singles—"How Do You Do It," "I Like It," and "You'll Never Walk Alone"—all topping the charts in 1963. Ironically, "How Do You Do It," a Mitch Murray composition, was suggested by George Martin for the Beatles to record; they demurred, preferring to record one of their own compositions, "Love Me Do." "I Like It" was another Mitch Murray composition, and "You'll Never Walk Alone" was from the Rodgers and Hammerstein musical *Carousel*. The song has since become the unofficial anthem for soccer fans of Liverpool FC, and Gerry Marsden would often make live appearances at the club's soccer stadium in Anfield.

The Pacemakers' next single, "I'm the One," hit number 2 in 1964. Their next two hits were probably their best-loved songs: "Don't Let the Sun Catch You Crying," written by Marsden and fellow band members Les Chadwick and Les Maguire, which went to number 6, and "Ferry Cross the Mersey," written by Marsden, coming in at number 8. The group's other Top-40 hits include "It's Gonna Be Alright," "I'll Be There," and "Walk Hand in Hand." "I'll Be There" was a Bobby Darin composition that he recorded in 1963 for Atlantic Records; it was traditionally the last record played every night at the Cavern Club. The group's records were produced by George Martin at Abbey Road Studios. Marsden was such a beloved Liverpool figure, the Mersey Ferry Terminal was renamed the Liverpool Gerry Marsden Terminal after his death in January 2021.

The Searchers were also from Liverpool and notched up six Top-10 and three number one singles. The debut single, "Sweets for My Sweets," a Drifters cover, went to number 1 in 1963; the same year, "Sugar and Spice," written by their producer Tony Hatch (best known for the string of hits he wrote for Petula Clark), reached number 2. In 1964, they had two number 1s with "Needles and Pins," written by Sonny Bono and Jack Nitzsche, and "Don't Throw Your Love Away." "When You Walk in the Room," written by Jackie DeShannon, hit number 3. "Goodbye My Love" went to number 4 in 1965.

The group initially recorded for Pye in England, and Brian Epstein always regretted not managing the group. Like the Beatles, the group were pioneers of the 12-string Rickenbacker sound that would influence the Byrds and later Tom Petty and the Heartbreakers and R.E.M., among many others. While the 1970s incarnation of the band did not score hits like Manfred Mann and the Hollies, two British Invasion–era bands that smoothly transitioned into a new hit 1970s sound, their two releases on Sire Records were critically acclaimed and further burnished their already growing reputation as one of the truly great bands of the British Invasion.

Another key Merseybeat band from Liverpool was the Swinging Blue Jeans. The group actually preceded the Beatles and helped them on their way up the ladder. The group scored a number-two hit in the UK in December 1963 with "Hippy Hippy Shake," their third single and the song they are best known for. The song was written by 17-year-old American Chan Romero in 1959. His original version, released in 1959 on the American Del-Fi Records, became a number-three hit for him in Australia. The Beatles had performed the song back in July 1963, and that version appears on their *Live at the BBC* album; another version, from December 1963, appears on *On Air—Live at the BBC Volume 2*. The group's fifth single, "You're No Good," another cover, released in March 1964, hit number 3. The significance of the group in the Beatles story is that the group, then called the Bluegenes, were the resident hosts at the Cavern Club in spring 1961, serving as the host band on Tuesday nights. The Beatles played their second and first evening show on March 21, 1961, at the Cavern, as the guests of the Bluegenes. The first performance by the Beatles at the Cavern was a lunchtime performance, on February 9, 1961. The Beatles would eventually take over the host spot from the Bluegenes on August 2, 1961.

Two other British bands from England who also hit the charts were Brian Poole and the Tremeloes and Freddie and the Dreamers. Brian Poole and the Tremeloes hailed from East London. They have the distinction of being the group Decca Records chose to sign instead of the Beatles, after the Beatles failed their audition for Decca's Dick Rowe. The group had four Top-10 UK hits, starting in 1963 with covers of "Twist and Shout" and "Do You Love Me," the latter of which hit number 1 and knocked the Beatles' "She Loves You" out of the top spot. In 1964 they recorded two Top-10 hits, "Candy Man" and "Someone Someone," which hit number 2. After lead singer Brian Poole left to pursue a solo career, the group reached the Top 10 seven more times between 1967 and 1971, hitting number 1 in 1967 with "Silence is Golden." Freddie and the Dreamers hailed from Manchester and scored four Top-10 hits in 1963 and 1964 but never had a number 1.

On January 16, 1964, the Dave Clark Five reached the top of the British charts with their debut single "Glad All Over." Hailing from Tottenham in North London, the song knocked the Beatles "I Want to Hold Your Hand" off the top of the UK charts. Although not a Liverpool band, the group became one of the biggest bands of the British Invasion and one with a punchy and powerful sound. Right through 1970, the group consistently appeared on the charts, notching seven Top-10 hits and two number 2s. The Dave Clark Five would also show up in a teen exploitation movie, *Get Yourself a College Girl*, released in December 1964. This American-produced film also included fellow British Invaders the Animals, as well as American jazz artists Stan Getz and Astrid Gilberto (then riding high with their Top-5 Bossa Nova crossover hit "The Girls From Ipanema"), American garage-rock group the Standells, and Nancy Sinatra. The Dave Clark Five would also have their own movie, following in the footsteps of *A Hard Day's Night*, with *Catch Us If You Can* (titled *Having a Wild Weekend* in the US), released in April 1965 in the UK and in August in America. The film was directed by John Boorman, who would go on to direct *Deliverance*, *Hope and Glory*, *Point Blank*, and *The Tailor of Panama*, among others, and is still active today. Boorman didn't just make another movie about a pop group but instead had the group play people who worked in the film industry, with Clark taking on his real-life role as a stuntman. Although Boorman made a movie a cut above the usual 1960s pop-group film fare, the movie didn't do well at the box office. A soundtrack album, like the US film title, *Having a Wild Weekend* in the US, included four songs from the film and eight other tracks. Of the many similar films that appeared in the wake of *A Hard Day's Night*, this was considered one of the better ones.

Ferry Cross the Mersey, starring Gerry and the Pacemakers, was also released in 1965. It was directed by Jeremy Summers, who, due to the Pacemakers sharing management with the Beatles, was able to visit the set of *A Hard Day's Night* for insight and inspiration. *Ferry Cross the Mersey* also featured Cilla Black and the Four-most (both managed by Epstein), along with two other Liverpool groups, the Black Knights and Early Royce and the Olympics.

Freddie and the Dreamers appeared in four films, including their own pop-music film vehicle *Every Day's a Holiday* (titled *Seaside Swingers* in the US), which also included other musical acts including the Mojos. The film is also noteworthy as Nicolas Roeg was the cinematographer. The iconoclastic filmmaker would work as a cinematographer on other British films of the decade as *Fahrenheit 451, Far from the Madding Crowd, A Funny Thing Happened on the Way to the Forum, Petulia, Perfor-mance* (which he also codirected with Donald Cammell), and *Walkabout* (which he also directed). His directorial resume also includes *Don't Look Now, The Man Who Fell to Earth* (starring David Bowie), and *Bad Timing: A Sensual Obsession* (starring Art Garfunkel).

Although not as well-known, the Bachelors, hailing from Ireland, hit the top of the British charts with their only number 1, "Diane" (produced by Shel Talmy) early in 1964. The group would have eight Top-10 hits for Decca between 1964 and 1966 and appear in two teen pop movies starring Billy Fury, *Just for You* (which also included Freddie and the Dreamers) in 1964 and *I've Gotta Horse* in 1965. Fury was also the star of the 1962 film *Play It Cool!* The film, directed by Michael Winner, also starred UK music favorites Helen Shapiro and Shane Fenton and the Fentones, along with American Bobby Vee. Winner would go on to direct *The Cool Mikado*, featuring UK comedy staple Frankie Howerd and appearances by the John Barry Seven, West 11 with Diana Dors, and jazz trumpeter Ken Coyler; *The System* with Oliver Reed and Julie Christie; *You Must be Joking* with UK comedy legend Bernard Cribbins; *The Jokers* with Oliver Reed and Michael Crawford; and *I'll Never Forget What's'isname* with Oliver Reed and Orson Welles.

The Four Pennies were from Blackburn, Lancashire, northwest of Manchester. The group's second single, "Juliet," went to number 1 in February 1964—the only British number 1 that year to not also hit the top of the charts in the US. The group also appeared in two British teen exploitation music films in 1965, the seminal *Pop Gear* (known as *Go Go Mania* in the US) and *British Big Beat*. *Pop Gear* does include live footage of the Beatles singing "She Loves You," which originally appeared as *The Beatles Come to Town*, which was released from newsreel footage from 1963.

The final UK act that topped the charts in this period were the Honeycombs from London, whose one and only Top-10 hit was the number 1 "Have I the Right?" The track was produced by mad genius British record producer Joe Meek. Meek scored four number 1s as a producer and "Have I the Right?" was the last. Meek's previous number 1 was the track he is most famous for producing, "Telstar" by the Tornados. Other British bands who had hits in this period include the Hollies, Manfred Mann, the Animals, the Rolling Stones, and the Kinks, all of whom would successfully transcend the sound of the British Invasion era.

The Hollies from Manchester would go on a spree of 16 Top-10 hits through 1970 (including a number 1 and three number 2s), even though losing Graham Nash, one of their key founding members in 1968. The group would reorganize themselves in the 1970s and return to the charts with another number 1 and number 2. Though leaving in 1968, Nash nonetheless appears on the Hollies track "Wings," featured on the *No One's Gonna Change Our World* charity album, released on EMI's budget Starline label in December 1969, to benefit the World Wildlife Fund (the album also features the Beatles' first version of "Across the Universe").

Manfred Mann from London would score 12 Top-10 hits, including three number 1s and two number 2s. The group also interjected jazz elements into their sound. Manfred Mann experienced innumerable lineup changes over the years, including successfully going from one lead vocalist (Paul Jones) to another (Mike d'Abo). Like the Hollies, they would remake themselves for the 1970s as Manfred Mann's Earth Band and score three Top-10 hits, including a number 1 in America.

The Animals, hailing from Newcastle, were swept up in the R&B scene and would score eight Top-10 hits, including a number 1. They would also experience various lineup changes, with members going on to other projects. Bassist Chas Chandler became Jimi Hendrix's manager. Keyboardist Alan Price pursued a solo career and worked extensively in film, including on soundtracks such as *Oh Lucky Man!* (1973), starring Malcolm McDowell, one of two films he worked on with director Lindsay Anderson. Eric Burdon, the group's lead singer, enjoyed a solo career, as well as working with War, recording the big hit "Spill the Wine" with the group.

The Rolling Stones, from London, were also initially part of the R&B scene and are still thriving today. In the 1960s they quickly shed their R&B roots and scored 15 Top-10 hits through 1970, including eight number 1s and two number 2s. Of all the groups and artists to emerge out of the early British pop music scene, no group has lasted as long with such success and, as of this writing, with no signs of stopping. The Rolling Stones came closest to the success and influence of the Beatles.

Finally, we must acknowledge the Kinks from North London. While never receiving the same acclaim or sales as the Beatles, the Rolling Stones, or the Who, the Kinks would score 14 Top-10 hits through 1970, including three number 1s and three number 2s. Sometimes associated with the mod scene in their early days, the group would quickly transcend pop and make richly drawn concept albums. They would reinvent themselves in the 1970s and, although one of the most quintessentially English groups, find even bigger American success at that time. Aside from the

Beatles and the Rolling Stones, their stature and influence has only grown bigger, with principal songwriter Ray Davies's skills considered peerless.

There were also solo British female artists from this period who hit the top of the charts, including Cilla Black, Dusty Springfield, Petulia Clark, Lulu, Marianne Faithfull, and Sandy Shaw.

Cilla Black from Liverpool was closely associated with the Beatles because she was also managed by Brian Epstein and produced by George Martin at Abbey Road Studios. It was actually at a Cilla Black session at Abbey Road that artificial double tracking (ADT)), a technique invented by EMI's Ken Townshend, was first used. ADT was regarded as a major technical innovation and was heavily used on recordings by the Beatles. The former cloakroom girl at the Cavern first hit number 1 in the UK on February 27, 1964, with "Anyone Who Had a Heart," a Burt Bacharach/ Hal David song originally released by Dionne Warwick. Her cover of the Righteous Brothers' "You've Lost That Loving Feeling," produced by Phil Spector, and cowritten by Spector, Barry Mann, and Cynthia Weil, reached number 2 in 1965 (kept from the top spot by the Righteous Brothers' version). Paul McCartney wrote the theme song, "Step Inside Love," for Black's television show, which she performed for the first time on March 5, 1968. The theme proved so popular, McCartney wrote additional music to flesh it out, and the song was released as a single, which reached the UK Top 10. Black had Top 10 hits through 1970; her last UK Top 10 was "Something Tells Me (Something's Gonna Happen Tonight") in 1971.

Dusty Springfield, from London, was considered by many to be the top female British singer of the 1960s. She would have 10 Top 10 hits through 1970, but surprisingly only one chart-topper. The number of hits doesn't fully reflect either her singular talent or the continuing influence Springfield has had in popular music. Her 1969 album *Dusty in Memphis* is a seminal work that paired the British pop vocal queen with the key team of Atlantic Record's production staff, producers Jerry Wexler and Arif Mardin and recording engineer Tom Dowd. While the album was indeed recorded in Memphis at the famed American Sound Studio, extensive overdubs were recorded at Atlantic Record's recording studio in New York.

Petulia Clark had been making music since the 1950s and was not a new emerging artist during the British Invasion. In fact, she scored number 1 in 1961 with an English interpretation of a German song, "Sailor." She would have two more Top-5 hits, before scoring a number 2 with her most well-known song "Downtown" in 1964. After two more Top-5 hits, she would hit the top of the charts in 1967 with "This Is My Song" in 1967. The song was originally written by, of all people, film legend Charlie Chaplin, early in the 1950s.

Scottish singer Lulu had six Top 10 UK hits in the 1960s. She is best known for the main title theme song for the film *To Sir, with Love* in 1967, which did not chart in the UK but went to number 1 in the US.

Much like Cilla Black, Sandie Shaw's success was very much a British phenomenon. Hailing from London, she would score eight Top-10 hits through 1970, including three number 1s.

Marianne Faithfull only had three Top-10 hits in the 1960s, with her best-known song being a cover of the Jagger/Richards song "As Tears Go By." However, she has a place as part of pop royalty in the 1960s for many reasons, including being Mick Jagger's girlfriend, having been married to gallerist and scenester John Dunbar, appearing in movies, and generally being considered one of the most beautiful and most desirable it-girls of the period. What's more remarkable though, is how she overcame her 1960s ingénue celebrity and a serious drug problem to go on to make groundbreaking albums that continue to this day.

As for duos, on February 28, 1964, the London duo Peter and Gordon hit number 1 with their debut single "A World without Love," written by Paul McCartney. Peter was Peter Asher, brother of Jane Asher, who was dating McCartney at the time.

On April 18, 1963, 17-year-old Jane Asher interviewed the Beatles at the Royal Albert Hall. Asher was an actress who began her career as a young child, appearing in films and on television, including a stint as a panelist on *Juke Box Jury*, the BBC pop music celebrity panel show. Asher was assigned to interview the Beatles for an article in the weekly *Radio Times*; the second half of the Royal Albert Hall concert was being aired live on the BBC in a broadcast called "Swinging Sound '63." The Beatles performed alongside American star Del Shannon, Australian Rolf Harris, and homegrown UK talent including Shane Fenton and the Fentones, the Vernons Girls, Kenny Lynch (one of the few black artists on the scene, who was the first person to record a Lennon/McCartney cover song, when he released "Misery" on Parlophone in March 1963; he would later appear on the cover of McCartney's *Band on the Run* album), Lance Percival (who would be one of the vocal talents on *The Beatles* animated series), and the Springfields, a group that included Dusty Springfield. The concert was hosted by Liverpool native George Melly.

Asher was also photographed at the show by the BBC's Don Smith, posing as a typical screaming teenage Beatles fan. After the concert, Asher joined the Beatles at the Royal Court Hotel in Sloane Square and then went to a party at the King's Road apartment of *New Musical Express* journalist Chris Hutchins. The evening saw the beginning of a long relationship between McCartney and the actress that lasted until 1968.

While McCartney was dating Asher, he lived at the Asher family home on Wimpole Street in Marylebone from 1963 to 1966, sharing the residence with Jane, her siblings Peter and Clare, and their parents, Richard and Margaret. Richard was an expert on various medical and mental diseases, wrote medical texts, was a broadcaster, and worked at Central Middlesex Hospital. Margaret was a professor at Guild Hall School of Music and Drama and had taught a young man named George Martin the oboe. Peter would eventually leave Peter and Gordon, join Apple Records as head of

A&R, and have a long, still thriving career as a record producer and manager. After discovering James Taylor, who recorded his self-titled debut album for Apple, which was released in the UK in December 1968, he would go on to work with Carole King, 10,000 Maniacs, and many other artists. Jane eventually married British artist Gerald Scarfe, best known by pop music fans for creating the art for Pink Floyd's *The Wall*.

THE BEATLES SELL OUT

The frenzied pace that is reflected and parodied in both real and surreal ways in *A Hard Day's Night* continued after the release of the film. Personal appearances, interviews in the media, and especially touring ground on relentlessly. What used to be exciting now started to take a real toll on the group, and this was reflected in their next UK album *Beatles for Sale*. Prior to the album, the group recorded an exciting new single, "I Feel Fine," which followed some of the jangly exuberance of the *A Hard Day's Night* album sound. Lennon has said he wrote the song and Bobby Parker's "Watch Your Step" was an influence. The single was followed by "Eight Days a Week," released in the US in February 1965 and "Ticket to Ride," released in April in both the US and UK. The US version of the latter single bore the notation "From their forthcoming movie 'Eight Arms to Hold You,'" on the record label, the original title of the film *Help!*

It was a run of singles that for many was a high-water mark for the group. This run would oddly come at a time when the group recorded and released what some have considered one of their weakest albums, *Beatles for Sale*. The cover of the album told the story. While the group had already struck a moody pose on the black-and-white cover of *With the Beatles*, this new color cover caught the group in the midst of the whirlwind of Beatlemania. In retrospect, perhaps some of the criticism of the album may have been somewhat harsh. *A Hard Day's Night* solidified the power of the Lennon and McCartney songwriting partnership, although *Beatles for Sale* included six covers, which was for some a letdown because it didn't reflect as full and abundant a composing maturation as their previous album, especially since some of the covers on *Beatles for Sale* were songs they were playing in Hamburg or even earlier. *Beatles for Sale* was released on in the UK on December 4, 1964.

The Robert Freeman cover photo, taken on October 24, 1964, a crisp fall day in London's Hyde Park, is strikingly at odds with the inner gatefold spread. On the left side of the gatefold were album credits and liner notes by Derek Taylor. Below the notes was a picture of the group on stage at their first American concert on February 11, 1964, two days after their *Ed Sullivan Show* appearance at the Washington Coliseum in Washington DC, happily swept up in their performance. On the right was a picture of the Beatles taken by Freeman in front of an eye-catching collage at Twickenham Studios, around the time *A Hard Day's Night* was being filmed. The collage features a bevy of movie stars, including such well-known film icons as Donald Pleasance, Simone Signoret, Jayne Mansfield, and Victor Mature. Also pictured are Rachel Roberts and Albert Finney in a publicity still from *Saturday Night and Sunday Morning* and Tommy Steele and Benny Hill in a publicity still from *Light Up the Sky*. There are also pictures of more obscure figures such as Ian Carmichael.

Only a few days after the Freeman shoot, the Beatles recorded their second Christmas fan club messages for release on flex-disc. Amid the scripted messages and cheeky ad-libs, the group thanked everyone for making the year so successful for the group, talked about *A Hard Day's Night*, and gave a clue about their next film. "Hi, there!" George Harrison began. "I'd like to thank all of you for going to see the film. 'Spect a lot of you saw it more than once." Spect may have been a playfully veiled reference to producer Phil Spector, someone who the Beatles were particularly enamored with as a record producer. "I did," Ringo interjects. "Did you? So did I," George replies. "Thanks anyway. 'Cause it makes us very pleased, ya know. We had a quiet (sic) time making it. Actually, we didn't. We had a great time making it. And we're glad it turned out okay. The next one should be completely different. We start shooting it in February. This time, it's gonna be in color," to which John adds, "Green."

In perhaps a foreshadowing of things to come, John and Cynthia Lennon joined George Martin and his future wife Judy Lockhart-Smith on a skiing vacation in St. Moritz, departing on January 25, 1965, and returning on February 7. On January 27, Martin either sprained his ankle or broke his toe and spent the rest of the vacation hobbled by a cast.

George Harrison and Pattie Boyd departed for a European holiday on January 28, while Paul McCartney and Jane Asher flew to Hammamet, Tunisia (where Paul would write "Another Girl") on February 4; befitting one of the most famous couples of her Majesty's empire, the couple stayed at a villa provided by the British embassy. Not to be outdone by all the holidaymakers, Ringo Starr married his girlfriend Maureen Cox on February 11, 1965, at the Caxton Hall Register Office in central London. Lennon, Harrison, and Brian Epstein all attended, but McCartney had yet to return from his African getaway. The bride was with child, and their son Zak, future drummer for Oasis and the Who, was the first of three children. Just like John, Ringo's honeymoon would quickly turn into fatherhood and a family in a little more than six months.

On February 10, it was announced that the third Beatles film would be an adaptation of Richard Condon's novel *A Talent for Loving*, produced by Epstein's own Pickfair Films. Though the project never materialized as a Beatles movie, *A Talent for Loving* was released as a film in 1969, starring Richard Widmark and Cesar Romero. A western that seemed to spend more time poking fun at westerns, the film was directed by Richard Quine, with a script by Condon. Walter Shenson was the film's producer. The film's other Beatles connection Ken Thorne, who wrote the musical score, also wrote the instrumental music for *Help!*

NIGHTS IN SOHO

Although a documentary short and somewhat obscure, *Wholly Communion*, released in 1965 and directed by Peter Whitehead, is an important film. The film captured a poetry event at the Royal Albert Hall featuring beat poets such as Allen Ginsberg. The event marked a major turning point in the burgeoning British countercultural underground scene. There had been cultural changes percolating for years in England that led up to this moment, many of them located in one particular locale.

London, and its Soho district in particular, had at different points in modern history been home to scattered pockets of bohemian living and those who pursued an artistic or avant-garde lifestyle. Even before the end of World War II ended, the area from Fitzroy Square to Soho Square became referred to as Fitzrovia, a partially imaginary geographical place of the mind, that unconsciously swept up all the artistic, literary, and alternative lifestyles and centered them in this area.

There were many denizens of the hip underground in Soho in this period; painters Francis Bacon and Lucian Freud, writers Roland Penrose and Colin MacInnes, actors Robert Morley and Diana Dors, multitalented artist bohemians like George Melly, and those, like Quentin Crisp, who made their life into a work of art.

Members of the Goons sprang from the most unlikely of circumstances and are part of this Soho history. A strip club called the Windmill Theatre on Windmill Lane located in Soho never stopped presenting its odd nude theatre revue, which really was a place for art students to have a place to further their art education by having nude models. The so-called nude classes alternated with comedy, skits, and other performances. It is here where Harry Secombe expanded on his wartime act and eventually met his fellow members in the Goons. He first met Michael Bentine, who introduced Secombe to Spike Milligan, although Secombe may have crossed paths with Milligan during the war. Secombe's act, when performed at other theaters sometimes didn't go well, but he finally debuted on British television in 1946, performing with Jimmy Grafton. Grafton was not only a scriptwriter, who helped Secombe write his act, but also an agent and more importantly, the owner of the former Grafton Arms, which had been renamed the Strutton Arms, located on Strutton Street in Westminster. It was here, just off Victoria Street, that Secombe, Bentine, and Milligan met Peter Sellers. Their meeting sparked the idea to do a radio show, which launched the foursome into history. Their BBC radio show actually started as *The Crazy People* in May 1951, but by June 1952 it was known as *The Goon Show*. The show would last until 1960, although Bentine left in November 1952.

The 1956 *This Is Tomorrow* exhibition at the Whitechapel Art Gallery in London was where the seeds of the pop art movement first began in England. More important was *Blake, Boty, Porter, Reeve*, which opened at the A1A Gallery in London on November 30, 1961. The show featured Peter Blake, Pauline Boty, Christine Porter, and Geoffrey Reeve. It is considered one of the first pop art exhibitions ever to be held in the world.

Various bars, cafes, clubs, restaurants, book shops, art galleries, and meeting places in London served as the hothouse social nexus that brought all of these people together to meet, talk, exchange ideas, have affairs, drink, and drink some more. American jazz was the sound that became the soundtrack for the writers, painters, scene-makers, and comedians; pop music would come along much later. Feldman's Swing Club was the first place where jazz denizens would congregate, before it relocated to Club Eleven, and finally settled in at Ronnie Scott's, then located at 39 Gerrard Street, prior to moving to its current home 47 Frith Street.

Although the beat poetry genre had been around since the 1950s, primarily in America, the event captured in *Wholly Communion* presaged the kind of events that the British psychedelic movement would later stage, including events that White-head would film including *Pink Floyd: London '66-'67 and Tonite Let's All Make Love in London*. Whitehead also directed the Rolling Stones, *Charlie Is My Darling*.

Late 1964 and 1965 would prove to be a period when the fortunes of the British movie scene would expand, with current releases reflecting the new British Cinema aesthetic and the international film scene, rivaling Hollywood and sometimes even enjoying box office success. *A Hard Day's Night* and the first three James Bond movies were the major reasons for this critical, cultural, and box-office UK movie success. The acceptance and success of British films around the world, especially in the US, was important; while England had roughly 2,000 cinemas in 1965, America had approximately 20,000.

Karel Reisz, who figured prominently in the birth, rise, and breakaway success of British films in the first half of the 1960s, directed *Night Must Fall*, released in 1964. This thriller, starring Albert Finney, was an official entrant in the 14th Berlin International Film Festival. Although not as commercially successful as the original 1937 version, it was another important 1960s film from Reisz.

The Pumpkin Eater, directed by Jack Clayton from a script by Harold Pinter (adapted from Penelope Mortimer's 1962 novel) starred Anne Bancroft, who won best actress at the Cannes Film Festival for her role as Jo Armitage, a seemingly endlessly fertile woman, unfortunately married to an adulterous husband played by Peter Finch. James Mason and Maggie Smith also appeared in the film, and the haunting score was supplied by French movie composer Georges Delerue.

Zorba the Greek, based on a novel by Nikos Kazantzakis and directed, produced, and written for the screen by Michael Cacoyannis, was one of the biggest films of the year. Although an American-Greek production, the film had many British connections.

Director Guy Hamilton had quite a year, directing not only *Goldfinger* but also the war picture *Man in the Middle*, based on the Howard Fast novel and featuring music by John Barry. Although not a commercial success, it bore his deft action directorial stamp. After working as Carol Reed's assistant on *The Fallen Idol* and *The Third Man*, he established his new British film credentials (and versatility) with *The Party's Over*. Starring Oliver Reed, it was yet another groundbreaking film on the new angry young men (and women) of late 1950s and early 1960s England.

Ken Russell made his directorial debut with *French Dressing*, a quirky comedy with a movie spoof backdrop that also featured a score by Georges Delerue.

King and Country, from Joseph Losey, came hot on the heels of his critically acclaimed *The Servant* from 1963. The stellar cast of *King and Country* included Dirk Bogarde, Tom Courtenay, and Leo McKern (who would appear the following year in *Help!*). The film was nominated for a BAFTA and a Golden Lion, and Courtenay won best actor at the Venice Film Festival. While initially faring poorly at the box office, since the 1970s the film has become somewhat of a cult classic.

Another film very much ahead of its time is *The Leather Boys*, one of two films from 1964 directed by the underrated Sidney J. Furie. Furie, a Canadian, was yet another non-Brit to help define the 1960s arts and cultural explosion in the UK, including directing two Cliff Richard vehicles, *The Young Ones* in 1961 and *Wonderful Life* in 1964. *The Leather Boys* featured Colin Campbell as Reggie, who was married to Dot, played by Rita Tushingham in the film, in yet another important era-defining role for the actress. The film that would be released prior to *The Knack* that Tushingham was working on was *Girl with Green Eyes*, costarring Peter Finch. Released in 1964, it often gets overlooked in this period of films from Tushingham and the company that produced the film, Woodfall. The film was directed by Desmond Davis, who would direct Tushingham and Lynn Redgrave (who is also in the film) in *Smashing Time*, in 1967. The May-December romance drama was written by Irish novelist Edna O'Brien and adapted from her novel *The Lonely Girl*.

Yet another American taking advantage of being part of the British cinema of the 1960s was Roger Corman, partnering with Britain's kings of horror, Hammer Films. Corman directed two films shot in England in 1964: *The Masque of the Red Death*, starring Vincent Price and Jane Asher, with Nicolas Roeg on board as cinematographer, and *The Tomb of Ligeia*, also starring Vincent Price and with a script by Robert Towne. Ten years later, Towne would win an Academy Award for his tour-de-force script for director Roman Polanski's *Chinatown*.

Gonks Go Beat, yet another seemingly silly teen exploitation film, presents itself as a cross between musical fantasy and science fiction, playing off the *Romeo and Juliet* theme. It was directed by Robert Hartford-Davis (who also directed the notorious *The Yellow Teddy Bears*) and, while it fared poorly on its initial release, has since become a cult film. The "gonks" in question were highly collectible, furry little toys that appeared in England at the time. Even famous adults, like Ringo Starr and Peter Sellers, were taken with the kiddie novelty items, and using them in a movie with a handful of pop music stars seemed like a quick way to make a buck. The film featured 16 songs, and the original Decca Records soundtrack album is a prized collectible. While pop artists of the day such as Lulu (with the Luvers) and the Nashville Teens are on the soundtrack, so is the Graham Bond Organization. This particular version of the seminal British blues group also included guitarist John McLaughlin and two future members of Cream, bassist Jack Bruce and drummer Ginger Baker; saxophonist Dick Heckstall-Smith also played in two other seminal British blues groups, Blues Incorporated and with John Mayall. He was a founding member of the seminal UK jazz-rock group Colosseum. Andy White, the drummer who briefly replaced Ringo Starr on one version of "Love Me Do," was also in the group.

On December 29, 1964, *The T.A.M.I. Show*, directed by Steve Binder, was released. This groundbreaking concert film took place at the Santa Monica Civic Auditorium, Santa Monica, California, over two nights late in October and still holds up remarkably well. While the Rolling Stones and James Brown stole the show, the concert included a perfect cross section of British and American pop and R&B acts, including Chuck Berry, the Beach Boys, Jan and Dean, Lesley Gore, Gerry and the Pacemakers, Billy J. Kramer and the Dakotas, Marvin Gaye, the Miracles, featuring Smokey Robinson and the Supremes, all backed by members of the Wrecking Crew, a group of studio musicians that included Hal Blaine, Jimmy Bond, Tommy Tedesco, Glen Campbell, Lyle Ritz, Leon Russell, and Plas Johnson, among others. The go-go dancers included future celebrated and versatile comedic actress Teri Garr and Toni Basil, who had a varied film career but is best known for her 1982 number 1 "Mickey," added to period feel of the concert. Binder would go on to direct the 1968 *Elvis* television special (also known as the "Comeback Special"), and Diana Ross's Central Park television concert in 1983, among many other television credits.

The Big T.N.T. Show, released in 1966, was a sequel to *The T.A.M.I. Show*, shared the same executive producer (Henry G. Saperstein), and appears as a bonus feature on DVD and Blu-ray reissues of *The T.A.M.I. Show*. With Phil Spector as the music producer, it was hosted by David McCallum, at the time playing Illya Kuryakin in the American television spy series *The Man from U.N.C.L.E.* The concert took place at the Moulin Rouge club in Los Angeles. The heavyweight lineup included Ray Charles, Petula Clark, the Lovin' Spoonful, Bo Diddley, Joan Baez, the Ronettes, Roger Miller, the Byrds, Donovan, and Ike and Tina Turner. The film was directed by Larry Peerce, who would go on to direct *Goodbye, Columbus*, *The Other Side of the Mountain*, and many other critically acclaimed films of the 1960s, 1970s, and 1980s.

There were also the films that reflected the new Swinging London milieu such as *The Pleasure Girls* in 1965, starring Francesca Annis as Sally, a provincial girl who comes to London and encounters Nikko, played by Klaus Kinski, and Keith, played by Ian McShane. This is yet another film about young British girls coming to the big city (London) of this time.

Bunny Lake Is Missing (1965) was a serious film from Austro-Hungarian director Otto Preminger. Categorized by some as horror or fantasy and one of the last British black-and-white films of the crime genre. It was given some 1960s pop veneer by including a brief clip of the Zombies, seen performing on *Ready Steady Go!* on a television set in a bar and heard later playing over the radio. Greeted with mixed reviews upon release, the psychological thriller is now considered one of Preminger's best and boasts an all-star cast including Laurence Olivier, Noel Coward, Carol Lynley, and Keir Dullea. Like Lynley, Dullea was American. It would be the second major role for Dullea, after *David and Lisa* in 1962, and coming three years before he played astronaut Dr. David Bowman in Stanley Kubrick's seminal sci-fi masterwork *2001: A Space Odyssey*, which was released in 1968.

The film was released after the Zombies scored two huge hits with "She's Not There" and "Tell Her No" from 1964, making them yet another major British Invasion group. The group would go on to make the psychedelic classic *Odessey and Oracle*, which was released in 1968. After member Colin Blunstone went solo, and Rod Argent formed Argent, the group reformed in the early 1990s and regained a huge following. They were inducted into the Rock & Roll Hall of Fame in 2019.

The year 1965 also featured some interesting British-American coproductions. *The Collector*, directed by William Wyler and based on the John Fowles novel, features Terence Stamp in a role that earned him the best actor award at the Cannes Film Festival. *Promise Her Anything* was directed by Arthur Hiller and starred Warren Beatty and Leslie Caron in a stylish, lighthearted comedy of the times. Like *A Shot in the Dark*, the film was cowritten by William Peter Blatty, who would go on to write the book *The Exorcist*. He would write the screenplay of his book and produce the 1973 film.

There was also *Lord Jim*, produced and directed by Richard Brooks, whose screenplay was an adaptation of the Joseph Conrad novel. It starred British movie legends Peter O'Toole and James Mason, along with American Eli Wallach, and the celebrated veteran Austrian actor Curt Jurgens, who would play one of the best Bond villains of the 1970s in *The Spy Who Loved Me*.

The year would also see the release of the final film from one of the titans of British cinema, director Anthony Asquith. He had been making films since the silent era, starting with the 1927 film *Shooting Stars*. His last film, *The Yellow Rolls-Royce*, was a frothy and imaginative jaunty ride starring Rex Harrison and Jeanne Moreau.

Other 1965 British films worth mentioning include *Four in the Morning*, directed Anthony Simmons from his screenplay, featuring Judi Dench in her breakout role after her film debut in *The Third Secret*.

THE BRITISH SPY MOVIES THAT CAME IN FROM THE COLD

Oddly enough, the film genre that had the most effect on the movie the Beatles were about to start shooting would be the British spy film, in vogue for some time but currently reaching an apex of popularity, primarily as a result of the James Bond films.

Three defining British Cold War spy films were released in 1965: the James Bond blockbuster *Thunderball*, *The Ipcress File*, and *The Spy Who Came in from the Cold*. *The Ipcress File*, starring Michael Caine, was based on Len Deighton's novel and directed by Sidney J. Furie, featuring music by John Barry, and was coproduced by one-half of the James Bond production duo, Harry Saltzman. Caine's role as Harry Palmer came after his breakthrough role in *Zulu*; his next film, *Alfie* (with the celebrated Sonny Rollins jazz score), concluded a trilogy that certified Caine's legendary movie star status for eternity. Caine would return to the role of Harry Palmer in 1966 with *Funeral in Berlin* and in 1967 with *Billion Dollar Brain*. He would revive the role again in 1995's *Bullet to Beijing* and 1996's *Midnight in Saint Petersburg*, but the films were not based on Deighton's novels. *Halliwell's Film Guide* called *The Ipcress File* "a realistic espionage picture which offered a useful corrective to the adventures of James Bond." *The Spy Who Came in from the Cold*, based on John le Carré's novel and directed by American Martin Ritt, drew similar praise from the guide, which called the film "a corrective to the James Bond cult."

While the Pink Panther films were not truly spy films, or exclusively British productions, they certainly reflect some of the same sensibilities as the spate of British spy spoofs, and the star of the films, Peter Sellers, figures prominently in this narrative. The debut film, *The Pink Panther*, masterfully directed by legendary American film director Blake Edwards, who also cowrote the script, focused more on the character Sir Charles Lytton, the thief, portrayed by David Niven, instead of Inspector Clouseau, brilliantly played by Peter Sellers. The film was released in the UK in December 1963 and March 1964 in America. The next Pink Panther film, *A Shot in the Dark*, put Sellers at the center of the film. Edwards directed and produced, as well cowrote the screenplay with William Peter Blatty. Henry Mancini was another key factor in the film's success. The film composer had already struck gold with "Moon River" from *Breakfast at Tiffany's* in 1961, but his theme song for the Pink Panther films will live on forever. He would write many unforgettable theme songs, particularly those he wrote for Franco Zeffirelli's *Romeo and Juliet* in 1969 and *Love Story* in 1971.

British spy films very much set the template for *Help!* Simply the fact that part of their second film would be shot outside of London showed an influence, one of the appeals of the Bond films being their exotic locations. When the Bond films first appeared early in the 1960s, international air travel was something that was not yet being enjoyed by the masses. *Dr. No*, released in 1962, was filmed partly in Jamaica, with some scenes shot not far from where Ian Fleming, the author of the Bond books, lived. At the time, Jamaica was not the common Caribbean tourist destination that it is today. Also, reggae music had yet to cross over to America, although Millie Small's 1964 cover of "My Boy Lollipop" would become a hit in 1964, reaching number 2 in both the UK and the US. Its success helped launch a small independent record label called Island Records, run by Chris Blackwell—who actually worked as gopher on *Dr. No.*

From Russia with Love, released in 1963, upped the international locations with shooting in Scotland and Istanbul, Turkey. There were few places in the world more appropriate to shooting a spy film than Istanbul. Located on the Bosporus and straddling the East and West, it was the perfect place for opposing sides of the Cold War to fight it out, and the location added an exotic atmosphere of intrigue.

Goldfinger, released in 1964, was filmed in Switzerland, Miami, Florida, and Kentucky as well as London. Switzerland was also another perfect international destination, with its history of neutrality, secretive Swiss bank accounts, and intermingling of French, Italian, German, and Swiss cultures.

Other British spy films of the period include *Master Spy*, released in 1964, with music by Ken Thorne, who supplied the incidental music for *Help!* and contributed to another Beatles-related project, *The Magic Christian*, starring Ringo Starr. He also supplied music for the film *Head*, starring the Monkees.

Another film, *Ring of Spies*, based on the real-life "Portland Spy Ring" a story that was a fixture for some time in the British press, starred Bernard Lee, who, along with playing M, the head of MI6 in 11 Bond movies, had a long and varied film career.

The Liquidator, from director Jack Cardiff, was a spy thriller released in 1965 starring Rod Taylor, Trevor Howard, Jill St. John, and Wilfrid Hyde-White, with music by Lalo Schifrin. The film is sometimes forgotten but well worth seeing. Cardiff also had a long and distinguished career as a cameraman on such films as *Black Narcissus*, *The Red Shoes*, and *The African Queen*, along with winning Academy Awards, a Golden Globe, and a British Film Institute award.

In 1965, the British spy genre exploded in England, particularly films spoofing the genre. Films like *Intelligence Man*, featuring the British comedy duo Morecambe and Wise, and *License to Kill* (not to be confused with the later James Bond film of the same name) took more from the spoof elements of the Bond films; most other movies, more liberally sprinkled in espionage, action, and thriller components. *The Liquidator* was based on a John Gardner novel and was clearly more than just a spoof. *Where the Spies Are*, produced and directed by Val Guest, was also primarily a spy spoof, starring David Niven, who had already appeared in *The Pink Panther* in 1963 and would appear in the ultimate James Bond spy spoof, *Casino Royale* (codirected by Guest) in 1967. *Halliwell's Film Guide* called the film "the ultimate in spy kaleidoscopes" but also added it was "the folly that killed off the fashion." While that may be true from an artistic and kitsch point of view, spy spoofs and the Bond films themselves, would continue for years to come. In many ways, the Bond films were deemed spy spoofs by some. When this author interviewed composer John Barry at his home on Long Island in 2000 for the *New York Times*, when asked about the Austin Powers movies he said: "How do you spoof a spoof?" One could argue that almost any James Bond film from the 1960s could appear on a triple bill, with *Casino Royale* and *Help!*

Of all the British spy films of 1965, other than the aforementioned *The Ipcress File* and *The Spy Who Came in From the Cold*, *Operation Crossbow* shied almost completely away from the spoof spy movie template and, although not in the same league as Bond or *The Spy Who Came in from the Cold* and *The Ipcress File*, was an excellent film. It was directed by Michael Anderson, who had a long career in film of nearly 50 years. He had directed such films as *Around the World in 80 Days* and *All the Fine Young Cannibals*, and his next film would be the 1966 spy film *The Quiller Memorandum*, followed by *The Shoes of the Fisherman*, and beyond the 1960s *Pope Joan*, *Logan's Run*, and *The Martian Chronicles*.

Based on the real-life "Operation Crossbow," a British intelligence effort to stop the development of long-range German weapons, the screenplay was cowritten by Emeric Pressburger (under the pseudonym Eric Imrie), Derry Quinn, and Ray Rigby; was produced by Carlo Ponti; and boasted an international cast that included Sophia Loren (Ponti's then-wife, in a cameo role), Trevor Howard, Tom Courtenay, and American George Peppard. Sets built for the film at MGM's British studios were the largest ever built there at that time.

During 1965, in England, Anglo Amalgamated and British Lion continued to boost production and, with the success of not only the Beatles and Bond, UA's profits soared. Universal now beefed up their production in England. Other American companies also expanded their British offices, including large studios like MGM and 20th Century Fox and smaller ones like Embassy and Filmways.

When Brian Epstein moved his NEMS operation to London from Liverpool in 1963, he hired an accounting firm to look after the Beatles' vast financial interests. The company was Bryce Hanmer, Isherwood and Company. Their office was located on Albermarle Street in Mayfair, not far from Epstein's Hille House office, the future home neighborhood of Apple Corps, as well as Asprey's, a film location in *Help!* Like NEMS, the accounting firm had ties to Liverpool. They did more than just provide financial services; one member of the company, Czech-born Dr. Walter Strach, helped John Lennon and Ringo Starr find homes in Weybridge.

Strach's more financial-oriented activities for the Beatles included helping them with their complicated and burdensome tax situation. While the motto of the 1960s might have been sex, drugs, and rock 'n' roll, if you were a British rock star, you would have to add figuring out ways of escaping England's high exorbitant tax rate for high earners. At the time, high earners like the Beatles could be taxed north of 90 percent of their income. Strach formed a limited company for the group with he being the treasurer and secretary, as the first step toward sheltering some of the group's British income.

It was Strach, who lived in Nassau in the Bahamas and helped the group form a partnership with Walter Shenson, to minimize their tax exposure. He formed a company for the two parties called Cavalcade Productions based in the Bahamas. But as a result of the devaluation of sterling in 1967, their investment took a huge hit, and the company lost £8,000. Geoffrey Ellis, in his memoir *I Should Have Known Better*, remembers that it was actually Jim Isherwood who came up with the tax dodge, with help from Strach, who had specifically located to the Bahamas to help with the firm's client's tax situations.

EIGHT ARMS TO HOLD YOU

Less than a year after they started filming *A Hard Day's Night* in March 1964, the group settled in at Abbey Road to begin recording tracks for their next film on February 15, 1965. Producer George Martin and engineer Norman Smith would return. Tape operator Ken Scott would work on all the sessions until Phil McDonald took over for the last track recorded, "I've Just Seen Her Face," which appears on the UK version of *Help!* Second tape operator Jerry Boys would only work on the single "Ticket to Ride"/"Yes It Is," with the A side appearing on the US *Help!* album, as well as working on two other *Help!* soundtrack songs, "Another Girl" and "I Need You."

There would be changes on the *Help!* film and soundtrack songs that weren't even hinted at on *Beatles for Sale*. In some respects, one of the biggest nonmusical influences that brought about this change happened when the Beatles were in New York for a two-night stand at the Forest Hills Tennis Stadium in Queens. It was on August 28, 1964, at the Delmonico Hotel that Bob Dylan turned the Beatles on to the pleasures of marijuana.

EVERYBODY MUST GET STONED

The meeting between Bob Dylan and the Beatles at the Delmonico Hotel has been told and retold in countless books. The cultural and countercultural implications have long outstripped any musical ones. The fact that it was Bob Dylan who turned the Beatles on to marijuana seems too good to be true, but it is. The Beatles were scotch and Coke drinkers (drinking, or going to the pub, was just part of British culture) and, ever since their days playing night after night around the clock in Hamburg, they were also, when needed, pill poppers. The group viewed pot as a serious drug associated with junkies. Their meeting with Dylan quickly changed this perception and altered their minds and music.

Arguably, the most likely and seemingly accurate account of what actually happened on that hot August night comes from Al Aronowitz in his written account that appeared in *Q* magazine's August 1996 issue. Aronowitz was a New Jersey–based journalist who wrote extensively about the Beat generation in the 1950s for the normally staid *Saturday Evening Post*. He is one of the few figures, along with Neal Cassady and Allen Ginsberg, who made the transition from the counterculture Beats of the 1950s to the hippie culture of the 1960s. Aronowitz interviewed and profiled both Dylan and the Beatles for the *Saturday Evening Post*, seeing early on that these artists possessed something new and, especially in the case of Dylan, were pointing to a new kind of music and artistic expression. This made him the obvious person to broker a meeting between the two.

John Lennon had expressed an interest in meeting Dylan to Aronowitz but wanted to do it when he felt he was ready. While the Beatles were certainly more popular than Dylan, Lennon knew that Dylan's songs were beyond where the Beatles were at the time. It wasn't until *A Hard Day's Night* that Lennon had been able to fully synthesize the influence Dylan's debut albums had on him, with the writing of "I'll Cry Instead." The song appeared on the UA and Parlophone *A Hard Day's Night* albums and, in the US, was released as a single and on the *Something New* album, both from Capitol.

In mid to late August, the Beatles were on an American tour with shows scheduled in the New York area on August 28 and 29 at Forest Hills Tennis stadium in Queens and on August 30 at the Convention Hall in Atlantic City, New Jersey. The Beatles were finally ready to meet Dylan, and Brian Epstein contacted Aronowitz to arrange it. Aronowitz informed Epstein that Dylan was at home in Woodstock but convinced the Beatles' manager he would be able to get Dylan to make the trip into the city. Aronowitz made good on his word, and Dylan and his road manager, Victor Maymudes, made the journey back to the city in Dylan's blue Ford Fairlane station wagon.

With Aronowitz in tow, the trio arrived at the Delmonico, which was mobbed by teenage fans and the police. They were met in the lobby by Mal Evans and escorted up to the floor where the Beatles were staying, which was also filled with police. The group and their manager were just finishing dinner, and in an adjacent room, the group's publicist Derek Taylor was entertaining various high-flying celebrities and hangers-on, including folk luminaries the Kingston Trio and Peter, Paul and Mary, the latter of whom were managed by Dylan's manager Albert Grossman.

Dylan and his posse were finally escorted into the Beatles' room. The historic meeting got off to a bumpy start. Brian Epstein, ever the gracious host, asked Dylan what he would like to drink, and Dylan answered "cheap wine," which wasn't available. Some reports of the summit said Dylan agreed to drink anything, and other reports have Brian Epstein asking Mal to go and find some cheap wine for the new bard. Dylan also had no interest in any of the pills the group had, and at first, the Beatles were reluctant to try pot. It's important to note that some have suggested that the Beatles, particularly Lennon, had already tried pot. Tony Bramwell, who worked for Brian Epstein and the Beatles for years, in his book *Magical Mystery Tours*, published in 2006 by the Griffin imprint of St. Martin's Press, said Lennon smoked pot with P. J. Proby in spring 1964 in England. Further muddying this theory, in the Beatles *Anthology* book, Harrison says they smoked it before in Liverpool, being given pot by an older drummer in another group, although the other Beatles have never supported this memory.

After some poor joint-rolling, first by Dylan and then Aronowitz, Dylan passed a joint to Lennon, who said to instead pass it to Ringo, Lennon's "royal taster." Starr, not knowing marijuana smoking etiquette, puffed away on the poorly rolled joint. At this point, Maymudes jumped into action, rolling perfect joints and passing them all around. Starr was the first to catch a buzz and began laughing hysterically, with the other Beatles and their guests following suit. Epstein began saying he was on the ceiling, and Paul McCartney became so enamored by his newfound stoned insights he had Mal Evans start writing down everything he said. Supposedly, these no-doubt insightful ramblings were kept in Evans's possession and will be part of his diary, scheduled to be published in 2023. Derek Taylor supposedly popped in, but it is not clear if he indulged in the group's new high. Taylor's future use of marijuana was notorious, and his insights while under the influence have been duly noted as insightful, funny, droll, and memorable. The group's marijuana intake would flower from here, and any time they wanted to indulge, they would say, "Let's have a larf."

Once the Beatles started filming *Help!* in the Bahamas in February 1965, they would be laughing quite a bit. Both John, in *Playboy* in 1980, and Ringo, in the *Anthology* book, referenced the group's pot intake during the filming. "The movie was out of our control," said John.

> With *Hard Day's Night*, we pretty much had a lot of input, and it was semi-realistic. But with *Help!* Dick (Lester) didn't tell us what it was about, though I realize, looking back, how advanced it was. It was a precursor for the *Batman* 'Pow! Pow!' on TV—that kind of stuff. But he never explained it to us. Partly, maybe, because we hadn't spent a lot of time together between *A Hard Day's Night* and *Help!* And partly because by then we were smoking marijuana for breakfast during that period. Nobody could communicate with us because it was all glazed eyes and giggling all the time. In our own world."

Ringo added: "A hell of a lot of pot was being smoked while we were making the film. It was great. That helped make it a lot of fun. Dick Lester knew that very little would get done after lunch. In the afternoon we very seldom got past the first line of the script. We had such hysterics that no one could do anything."

Like *A Hard Day's Night*, the Beatles needed to come up with songs for the film and the soundtrack album before filming would commence. There are basically two separate batches of songs from this period; the ones that would appear in the film and the ones that didn't. The songs that did appear in the film include the title song, "Ticket to Ride," "You're Gonna Lose That Girl," "Another Girl," "The Night Before," "You've Got to Hide You're Love Away," and the previously released "She's A Woman," briefly heard in the film, coming from a radio, which was the B side of "I Feel Fine." The song also appeared on the US Capitol album *Beatles '65*, but neither the US nor UK versions of the *Help!* soundtrack.

The *Help!* period songs were written by Lennon with McCartney, with the sole exception of George Harrison's "I Need You." Of "You've Got to Hide Your Love Away," Lennon said in his 1980 *Playboy* interview, "that's me in my Dylan period. . . . I am like a chameleon, influenced by whatever is going on." In first singing the song to Paul, John mistakenly sang the lyric "two foot tall" as "two foot small;" Paul told him he liked the impromptu mistake and suggested John keep it, which he did. Peter Shotton, John's childhood friend, is alleged to be on some of the "hey's" in the chorus of the final recording.

Lennon and McCartney songs that didn't appear in the film but which would be used as B-Sides include "Yes It Is," the B side of "Ticket to Ride" and "I'm Down," the B side of "Help!"

The Beatles filming *Help!* in the Bahamas. Courtesy Photofest.

George Harrison's "You Like Me Too Much" would also appear on the UK soundtrack album and *Beatles VI* in the US. It has been suggested that this might have been one of the songs that Lennon helped Harrison complete. The song features George Martin and Paul McCartney playing the same piano together. Other tracks include "Tell Me What You See," which would be on the soundtrack album and "Wait," which would appear on *Rubber Soul*, with George using his new Vox V-850 volume control pedal at the suggestion of Colin Maney of the Remo Four, another Liverpool group managed by Brian Epstein. "If You Got Trouble" wouldn't be released until the *Anthology 2* album in 1996. "Bad Boy," the only cover in this period, would originally be issued on the US-only *Beatles VI* album and then on *A Collection of Beatles Oldies* in December 1966 in the UK.

The initial round of sessions ran from February 15 to 20, with the group departing for the Bahamas on February 22. These sessions would be different from their earlier time in the studio. Previously, the group recorded a song until achieving a satisfactory performance and then add minor overdubs prior to mixing. Now, they rehearsed a song until it was tight, began recording by laying down a suitable backing track, and then taking their time overdubbing vocals and instruments.

The Beatles would also introduce new musical sounds they had never previously used on recording sessions. Both Lennon and Harrison used 1961 Fender Stratocasters. Leo Fender started with the Telecaster in 1950, followed by the Fender bass in 1951, and then Stratocaster in 1954, which may be the most ubiquitous stringed instrument in the history of rock. McCartney also got in on the new electric guitar action with his new Epiphone Casino ES-230TD. McCartney had been listening to B. B. King and was plugged into the burgeoning British blues and R&B boom, liking the guitar sound he was hearing. After going to a guitar shop to find an instrument that would provide some of the fuzzy feedback sound he wanted, he was told to try the Casino because it had a semi-acoustic sound due to its hollow-body construction. At the time, Dave Davies of the Kinks and Keith Richards of the Rolling Stones were using the instrument. Davies combined the guitar's buzzy sound with a distorted speaker to achieve the raunchy grit of the Kinks' early hits. As for acoustic guitars, Lennon and Harrison each played a 1965 Framus Hootenanny 12-string acoustic guitar. A 1965 Vox Continental organ V801J was another new instrument Lennon played.

On February 15, the Beatles recorded "Ticket to Ride" in the afternoon and worked on "Another Girl" and "I Need You" in the evening. Lennon called "Ticket to Ride" "one of the earliest heavy metal records made" and credited McCartney with suggesting how Starr should play his drum part. In *Many Years from Now*, Paul suggests that the song was more of a cowrite, although it was John's song, and says ride came from Ryde, in the Isle of Wight, where Paul's cousin Bett and her husband Mike Robbins ran a pub. During their skiffle days, John and Paul appeared at the pub as the "Nerk Twins" for one show on April 23, 1960. "We sat down and wrote it together," said Paul in *Many Years from Now*. "I remember talking about Ryde, but it was John's thing. We wrote the melody together; you can hear on the record, John's taking the melody and I'm singing harmony with it." Paul was particularly proud of the ending. "I think the interesting thing was a crazy ending; instead of ending like the previous verse, we changed the tempo. We picked up one of the lines, 'My baby don't care,' but completely altered the melody. We almost invented the idea of a new bit of a song on the fade-out with this song; it was something specially written for the fade-out which was very effective but it was quite cheeky and we did a fast ending. It was quite radical at the time." As much as George's chiming rhythm guitar dominated the song, it's actually Paul playing lead guitar on his newly acquired electric Epiphone Casino. "Ticket to Ride" would be the group's next single, released on April 9 in the UK and April 19 in the US.

"Yes It Is" was the single's B side in both countries; it was recorded on February 16 and is a song gloriously dominated by Harrison's chiming, ringing 12-string Rickenbacker. John was never a fan of the song. In the 1980 *Playboy* interview with David Sheff he said, "That's me trying a re-write of 'This Boy,' but it didn't work." The session also saw the group finishing work on "Another Girl" and "I Need You," the latter song featured Harrison on his 12-string Rickenbacker again stealing the show, particularly in the way he used the Vox V-850 volume control pedal again.

The session was also an occasion when the group had a visit from EMI's chairman, Sir Joseph Lockwood, who presented the group with several record sales awards, and on February 19, EMI would throw the group a lavish party at the Connaught Hotel.

On February 17, the group would work on and finish "The Night Before" and Harrison's other *Help!*-era track "You Like Me Too Much." "The Night Before" featured a new keyboard wrinkle, with John playing the Hohner pianet N electric piano, an instrument that would show up in imaginative ways on future recordings, including "Tell Me What You See," recorded the next day. This time, it would be Paul playing the instrument, with Ringo playing claves, and George playing a guiro, a gourd played with a stick that gave off a rhythmic sound.

On February 18, the tasty "You've Got to Hide Your Love Away" would be recorded, featuring John's new Framus Hootenanny 12-string acoustic guitar. "That's me in my Dylan period again," Lennon told *Playboy*. "I am like a chameleon, influenced by whatever is going on. If Elvis can do it, I can do it. If the Everly Brothers can do it, me and Paul can. Same with Dylan." It would also mark the first time an outside musician, flautist Johnny Scott, was used on a Beatles track (aside from when Andy White replaced Starr on one version of "Love Me Do"). George Martin's production notes disputes the date and indicate that Scott overdubbed his flute solo on February 20. Scott actually recorded two separate flutes, an alto and a tenor, perhaps resulting in the session date's confusion.

"You've Got to Hide Your Love Away" would later be recorded by the Silkie with George on tambourine and Paul playing his Epiphone Casino; the track was produced by John Lennon with assistance from Paul. The Silkie were signed to NEMS and were managed by Alistair Taylor, who had been one of Epstein's most-trusted assistants and had accompanied him when Epstein first saw the Beatles at the Cavern Club in November 1961. The Silkie track was produced at IBC Studios in London on August 9, 1965. The single was a modest hit in the UK, but hit number 10 in the US. It marked a rare occasion when members of the group produced another artist so early on in their career. It also was at this session that John Lennon spotted a mellotron and ordered one. The mellotron would show up much later on a memorable Beatles recording.

Also completed on February 18 was "Tell Me What You See." "If You Got Trouble," with Ringo on lead vocal, was also completed but wouldn't be officially released until 1996 on *Anthology 2*. During the evening, six songs were mixed for mono supervised by George Martin.

On February 19, "You're Gonna Lose That Girl" was recorded. The final recording sounds rushed with Paul flubbing some notes; apparently that is why it was used for the scene where the floor is sawed out from under Ringo at the recording studio, so the saw noise would make it so the track couldn't be heard clearly. The group attempted to do further work on the song on March 30 but eventually decided to stick with the previous version.

"That Means a Lot" was another song destined to remain unreleased until it was released on *Anthology 2*. The song was completed on the final day of recording before the group left for the Bahamas and was also the last song recorded on Abbey Road's trusty Telefunken M10. The song would be later recorded by Texas-born British Invasion artist P. J. Proby, who released it in September 1965.

On February 20, five more songs were mixed for mono, again supervised by George Martin. All 11 songs that had been mixed were then brought to Shenson and Lester for them to decide which tracks would be used in the film.

One immediate result of the new manner in which the Beatles worked in the recording studio was evident in how much better the stereo mixes for *Help!* sounded. The group's mono mixes were always given the most care and seen as the way the music was intended to be heard on record. Even as late as *Sgt. Pepper's Lonely Hearts Club Band* in 1967, John Lennon felt mono was the best way to listen to the group's music, going as far as saying that one hadn't really heard the album until they listened to it in mono. Still, *Help!* was a breakthrough in stereo mixes for the Beatles.

HELP! THE MOVIE

There was never a doubt that Richard Lester would return to direct *Help!*, and many of the people who'd worked on *A Hard Day's Night* also returned, including producer Walter Shenson, art director Ray Simm, and costume designer Julie Harris. Actor Victor Spinetti, the harried director in *A Hard Day's Night*, was given a larger role as Professor Foot in *Help!* The Beatles had quickly adopted Spinetti as one of their own and were eager to have him in their next film. Spinetti's character in *Help!* was even more over the top and received more screen time, accompanied by his bungling factotum Algernon, perfectly played by Roy Kinnear.

While George Martin was credited as musical director on *A Hard Day's Night*, on *Help!* he merely received a credit as producer of the songs on the film's soundtrack. As detailed previously, Lester and Martin had a falling out during the making of *A Hard Day's Night*, resulting in Ken Thorne brought in as musical director on *Help!* and as the composer of the film's incidental music. Thorne would work with Lester again on *A Funny Thing Happened on the Way to the Forum* (for which he would receive the Academy Award for Best Original Score Sound), *How I Won the War, The Bed-Sitting Room, Juggernaut, Superman II,* and *Superman III.* Recordists H. L. Bird and Stephen Dalby also returned from *A Hard Day's Night.* Robert Freeman, who created the closing title sequence on *A Hard Day's Night*, was credited as color consultant and titles on *Help!* Camera operator Paul Wilson, who hadn't been credited on *A Hard Day's Night*, was fully credited on *Help!* Dougie Millings, fully credited on *A Hard Day's Night*, was not so on *Help!* Jeremy Lloyd, who'd had a small part in *A Hard Day's Night*, returned in a slightly larger role; he was actually given a line of dialogue.

Some of the new faces involved in the film's production included production manager John Pellatt. Pellatt had worked on the 1964 Freddie and the Dreamers film *Every Day's a Holiday* (*Seaside Swingers* in the US) as production supervisor. His film and television career dated back to the 1940s. The director of photography was David Watkin. Watkin had many ties to Lester and the British spy genre. His second major film job was lensing the title sequence for *Goldfinger* in 1964, which was designed by graphic artist Robert Brownjohn. Ted Moore was the film's cinematographer and worked on seven Bond films. David Watkin had been the cinematographer on Lester's *The Knack and How to Get It.* After *Help!*, he worked again with Lester on *How I Won the War, The Bed-Sitting Room, The Three Musketeers, The Four Musketeers, Robin and Marian,* and *Cuba.* His remarkable career would continue through 2001, during which time he worked on such films as *Chariots of Fire, Out of Africa, Moonstruck,* Franco Zeffirelli's penultimate film *Tea with Mussolini,* and many other films. The film editor was John Victor Smith. Smith had a long career that started early in the 1950s. He worked on the *Guns of Navarone, The Saint* TV series in 1964, and *Ferry Cross the Mersey,* the film vehicle for Gerry and the Pacemakers. He would go on to work with Lester on *How I Won the War, The Three Musketeers, The Four Musketeers, Royal Flash, Robin and Marian, Cuba, Superman II, Superman III, The Return of the Musketeers,* and the Paul McCartney *Get Back* concert documentary. Special Effects were handled by Cliff Richardson. His career began in the 1940s, and he worked on such movies as *The African Queen* and *Lawrence of Arabia.* He would go on to work with Lester on *A Funny Thing Happened on the Way to the Forum* and what would be his last feature film credit, *Juggernaut*. He also worked on such other films as *Casino Royale* (1967) and *The Day of the Jackal*. The assistant director was Clive Reed. Reed began his career in 1956, and prior to *Help!*, he'd worked on *Dr. No*. He would go on to work with Lester on *The Three Musketeers*, *The Four Musketeers*, and *The Return of the Musketeers*. Other films he worked on include *The Bedford Incident*, *The Quiller Memorandum*, *Catch-22*, *Carnal Knowledge*, and many other films. Along with the aforementioned Paul Wilson, the other camera operator was Jack Atchelor. He started in 1941 as a clapper loader and eventually worked on such films as *Billy Liar* but was uncredited for his work on *A Hard Day's Night*. Rita Davison handled continuity. She had a long career that began late in the 1940s. She worked on such films as *Six-Five Special*, *Peeping Tom*, *A Taste of Honey*, *The Loneliness of the Long-Distance Runner*, *Tom Jones*, *A Hard Day's Night*, and *Seaside Swingers* and would work with Lester on *A Funny Thing Happened on the Way to the Forum*. She would go on to work on *The Saint* TV show and the films *Petulia* and *Goodbye, Mr. Chips*. One of the two sound editors, Bill Blunden worked on *Ferry Cross the Mersey*. His 40-year career consisted of working in various capacities, mostly for television. The other sound editor, Don Challis, began with some uncredited assistant editor work in the 1950s before moving on to working on such films as *Beat Girl*, *Sons and Lovers*, *A Taste of Honey*, *The Loneliness of the Long-Distance Runner*, and *Tom Jones*. He would go on to work with Lester on *The Knack and How to Get It*, *A Funny Thing Happened on the Way to the Forum*, *How I Won the War*, *Petulia*, *The Three Musketeers*, and *The Four Musketeers*. Makeup was done by Freddie Williamson who worked with Lester on *The Knack and How to Get It*. His long career included work on *Alfie*, *The Italian Job*, *A Clockwork Orange*, *Educating Rita*, and *The Killing Fields*. Hairdresser Betty Glasow worked on *Lolita*, *A Hard Day's Night*, *Alfie*, *Georgie Girl*, and *To Sir, with Love* in the 1960s, and such work after the 1960s as *Empire of the Sun*, *Titanic*, *Tomorrow Never Dies*, *Saving Private Ryan*, and three Harry Potter films. Arthur Newman handled wardrobe and had worked on *Our Man in Havana* and *Zulu*. The music editor was Barry Vince, who had a long career in film and TV. Prior to *Help!* he worked on the 1964 Cliff Richard pop music vehicle *Swinger's Paradise*, and after *Help!*, he worked with Lester on *A Funny Thing Happened on the Way to the Forum*. He would go on to work on *The Leather Boys* and *Smashing Time*.

The biggest changes as far as the production of *Help!* is concerned in relation to *A Hard Day's Night* is that the film would be in color, shooting would occur in two locations outside of the UK (the Bahamas and Austria), and rather than make an attempt at a day-in-the-life documentary-style cinema verité film, *Help!* would be a broad comedy, with spy overtones. While *A Hard Day's Night* was a film that would be considered a major influence on music and cinema and regarded as one of the best British films of all time, *Help!* was in color and was a more stylized film, with the group part of a larger ensemble cast in a movie loosely yoked to the current British spy film genre.

Director Richard Lester and director Joe McGrath, who had unofficially contributed some ideas to *A Hard Day's Night*, came up with the rough idea for the film. Like Lester, McGrath had come from the world of television, having produced and directed the British David Frost television special *A Degree of Frost* and *Not Only But Also*, a British TV comedy show that featured Peter Cook and Dudley Moore, among others, which ran from 1965 until 1970. Mark Behm wrote the original story for *Help!*, this time with Ringo playing more of the central character of the film's plot. Behm was yet another American living abroad, who had come up with the story idea for the 1963 film *Charade*, based on Peter Stone's 1961 short story "The Unsuspecting Wife" (Stone would ultimately write the screenplay). Lester then brought in Brit Charles Wood to assist, feeling that Behm had no feel for British dialogue.

The film's initial plot had Ringo, fed up with fame, deciding to have himself bumped off before changing his mind. But the storyline was deemed to be too similar to French director Philippe de Broca's upcoming film *Up to His Ears* (which would be released in December 1965) and was scrapped. Lester has said that the new plot had many similarities to the plot of British writer Wilkie Collins's novel *The Moonstone*, published in 1868 and considered one of the first modern detective stories. In that story, as in *Help!*, the owner of a mysterious ring is the target of an Eastern cult. In the novel, the ring is cursed. In the film, the ring is needed to carry out a human sacrifice.

But there was also another influential reference point: surrealism. The surrealism goes beyond the sight gags and eschewed viewpoints that had already been explored in *A Hard Day's Night*. In *Help!* the surrealism is in the bold use of colors that intensify the location shooting, particularly in the sun-soaked scenes in the Bahamas. Bolder uses of color in the age of modernism rendered brashly by the Fauves comes to mind. The brightly colored pop art of cartoons rendered by Roy Lichtenstein also appeared to be an influence, as well as the work of Andy Warhol, who also used bold colors in his artwork but also appropriated images from popular culture and was a pioneer in popularizing mixed-media approaches to art, which in some cases would be even more profoundly felt on *Yellow Submarine*. "My real interest from a visual point of view, would always have been the twenties to the forties European Surrealists," Lester said in Steven Soderbergh's *Getting Away With It*. "I'd rather put my finger on a Magritte look rather than a Jasper Johns look." Later, Magritte would be an influence on others involved in a Beatles film and on the Beatles themselves in many ways, as shall be seen.

In Soderbergh's book, Lester credited cinematographer David Watkin for revolutionizing color photography in *Help!*:

> I think it was the first serious attempt to make diffused lighting positive. In other words, I think people like Raoul Coutard were working with natural light and doing it fairly effectively, but David was making it into a dominant factor in the way that he

photographed people's faces. It was stunning and he was brilliant. Totally extraordinary. If you look at the way the images start, the out of focus images, this is what [Watkin] eventually did on *The Devils*.

The Devils was a 1971 film directed by Ken Russell, starring Oliver Reed and Venessa Redgrave, about Urbain Grandier, a French Catholic priest accused of witchcraft who was burned at the stake in the seventeenth century.

A Hard Day's Night certainly had a fine supporting cast, particularly Wilfred Brambell, Norman Rossington, John Junkin, and Victor Spinetti. But they really were not much more than a supporting cast, and Lester wanted to keep it that way, even going as far as reducing screen time for Brambell in editing. *Help!* was an entirely different matter. The day-in-the life of a pop group approach of *A Hard Day's Night* needed the emphasis to be on the Beatles. *A Hard Day's Night* was also a vehicle to introduce the group to the world, beyond their fans in Liverpool, London, and the US. Although the *Help!* cast would be smaller, the featured roles were more prominent and often more central to the plot than the film's ostensible stars.

Help! features two competing groups after the ring at the center of the film's action. The film opens with an exotic cult about to sacrifice a female victim to the Goddess of Kaili. She is spared at the last minute because she is not wearing the sacrificial ring, which, it turns out, is now in possession of our favorite Liverpool drummer, Ringo Starr. The scene introduces us to some of the members of the excellent cast. There is the evil leader, high priest Clang, played in over-the-top fashion by Leo McKern, and Ahme, his assistant with a soft spot for the Beatles, sympathetically played by the lovely, charming, and understated Eleanor Bron. Later we will meet Professor Foot, played manically by Victor Spinetti, and Algernon, his sidekick, played pitch-perfect by Roy Kinnear.

Leo McKern was a veteran Australian theater, television, and film actor, whose distinctive appearance was due to his suffering a factory accident as a teenager and losing his left eye. He eventually emigrated to England and began working at the Old Vic and later the Royal Shakespeare Theatre. Through the 1950s and 1960s McKern established his acting credentials and played roles in the theater that he then transferred to the screen. While Kern's comedic turn in *Help!* was spot-on, he would often play comedic roles, but he also appeared in serious roles in such films as *A Man for All Seasons*, *The Shoes of the Fisherman*, *Ryan's Daughter*, and *The French Lieutenant's Woman*. In England, his role as Horace Rumpole in *Rumpole of the Bailey*, which began airing in the mid-1970s solidified his place in British popular culture. His connection to the people behind the early films of the Beatles and Richard Lester include an uncredited role in *The Running Jumping & Standing Still Film*.

Like Victor Spinetti, Eleanor Bron was another actor the Beatles worked with that they felt great affection for. Her major breakthrough came in the Cambridge

Footlights revue production of *The Last Laugh* in 1959; she was the first woman to appear in a Footlights revue. She later appeared in the Footlights revue *A Clump of Plinths*, which transferred to London's West End, where it was renamed *Cambridge Circus* (the show's soundtrack album, released on Parlophone in 1963, was produced by George Martin). She worked with Peter Cook at London's Establishment Club and became part of the set of bright young lights of satirical British television, appearing on such shows as David Frost's *Not So Much a Programme, More a Way of Life* in 1964, *My Father Knew Lloyd George*, and *BBC-3*. *Help!* was her first screen role, and she subsequently appeared in such defining 1960s British films as *Alfie*, *Bedazzled* (with Peter Cook and Dudley Moore), *A Touch of Love*, *Women in Love*, and *Two for the Road*. Bron's extensive theater, television, and radio roles include appearances in *Doctor Who*, *Absolutely Fabulous*, and *Rumpole of the Bailey*. She later worked with Cook in *The Secret Policemen's Ball* charity shows for Amnesty International. Bron is a true Renaissance woman and has written several books on a wide variety of subjects, including her acclaimed, yet surprisingly out-of-print memoir.

Roy Kinnear also was on a satirical 1960s British TV show with a David Frost connection, appearing on the seminal *That Was the Week That Was* in 1962. Kinnear was one of a number of *Help!* cast and crew members that Richard Lester worked with, appearing in such Lester-directed films as *How I Won the War*, *A Funny Thing Happened on the Way to the Forum*, *The Three Musketeers*, *The Four Musketeers*, *The*

The Beatles loved working with actress Eleanor Bron, shown here with George Harrison. Courtesy Photofest.

Return of the Musketeers, and *Juggernaut*. Kinnear turned in many other memorable comedic roles, including his appearance in *Willie Wonka and the Chocolate Factory*. Kinnear reunited with his *Help!* costar Victor Spinetti for a part in a Mike + the Mechanics music video, a group that featured Mike Rutherford of Genesis. Kinnear's son Rory, plays Dr. Frankenstein in *Penny Dreadful*.

In 1988, Kinnear reprised his role as Planchet, d'Artagnan's servant, in *Return of the Musketeers*. Location shooting in Toledo, Spain, had seen a number of accidents, with both Michael York and Richard Chamberlain falling off their horses, though neither received any serious injuries. But such was not the case four weeks into the eight-week shoot, in a scene involving York, Kinnear, C. Thomas Howell, and Oliver Reed, riding horses over the Tagos River on the Alcantra Bridge. After stunt doubles tested the location in rehearsal, the actors themselves shot the scene. Kinnear's horse initially lagged behind the others, then sped up, stumbled, and ended up throwing the actor, who suffered a broken pelvis and internal bleeding. The actor was reportedly in good spirits after being transferred to a hospital in Madrid, but he died the day after the accident due to a heart attack. He was 54 years old.

Lester immediately wanted to shut down the film's production, but Pierre Spengler talked him out of it. York later criticized Lester over his silence about Kinnear's death. Lester, still not fully recovered from a bout of hepatitis A, withdrew each night

Paul with Eleanor Bron in *Help!* Courtesy Photofest.

after shooting and, according to Spengler, simply couldn't face what had happened to one of his favorite actors.

Universal was unhappy with the results of two early screenings of the film and abandoned a US theatrical release in favor of cable and video; its UK theatrical release did not receive good reviews. The matter ultimately ended up in a legal dispute over who was responsible for Kinnear's death, the film production company or the hospital. The actor's widow, Carmel Kinnear, was eventually awarded £650,000 in damages and court fees against the film's producer and director. In Andrew Yule's authorized biography of Lester, the director said:

> How do you go on after that? Roy was a wonderful man, the best, someone I'd spent twenty years making films with. For me the light has gone out of being a filmmaker. It's gone. There hasn't been a day in the years since that I haven't thought about it. The idea of doing anything again involving action, anything that carries an element of risk—and all comedy, has that element—is something I'm not yet able to face.

The film would be the last feature Lester worked on; McCartney's *Get Back* concert film became his last-ever work as a director. Kinnear's death proved to be the most agonizing chapters in Lester's career.

Actors playing the smaller roles in *Help!* were also major dramatic talents. Warren Mitchell, who played Abdul, one of Clang's henchmen, was a BAFTA TV and Laurence Olivier award winner. He began his television and film career in the 1950s and appeared in such British spy films of the 1960s as *The Spy Who Came in from the Cold* and *The Assassination Bureau*, with a role in the 1970s cult film *Jabberwocky*. His spy role credentials were further solidified with roles in the TV shows *The Avengers* and *The Saint*.

John Bluthal appeared in *Help!* as Bhuta, another of Clang's henchmen. Bluthal appeared in *A Hard Day's Night* and acted in Lester's films *The Mouse on the Moon*, *The Knack*, *A Funny Thing Happened on the Way to the Forum*, and *Superman III*. Known more for the many television shows he appeared in between 1958 and 2011 (*The Benny Hill Show*, *The Saint*, *The Avengers*, *The Kenny Everett Television Show*, and *Rumpole of the Bailey*), he also appeared in such films as the original *Casino Royale*, *A Talent for Loving*, *The Return of the Pink Panther*, *Revenge of the Pink Panther*, and *Labyrinth*.

Patrick Cargill was another British film veteran who seamlessly fit into the cast as Superintendent Gluck. Cargill appeared in *Around the World in 80 Days*, *Expresso Bongo*, *Inspector Clouseau*, and *The Magic Christian*.

Prior to *Help!*, Lester did not sit around and rest on his laurels in the wake of the unanimous critical and cultural juggernaut that was *A Hard Day's Night*. He plunged right back into the world of television, producing some 50 commercials with James Garrett. Also, during his work on *A Hard Day's Night*, he signed on to direct *A Funny*

Thing Happened on the Way to the Forum, which would be released in 1966, after *Help!* Lester was taking a much-needed rest with his family in St. Tropez when a telegram arrived from Oscar Lowenstein, the director of the Royal Court Theatre and a partner in Woodfall Films. Anne Jellicoe's play *The Knack* had been a major success, and Lowenstein had novice playwright Charles Wood prepare a film treatment that he used to entice director Lindsey Anderson to direct a film version. Anderson turned him down, and given Lester's success with *A Hard Day's Night*, Lowenstein arranged a meeting with him that also included Woodfall's partners Tony Richardson and John Osborne. Lowenstein asked the somewhat reluctant Lester to at least take a look at Wood's treatment and meet the fledgling playwright. Wood was still working his day job at a British newspaper as an artist and typographer. His only performed play was *Cockade*, which was staged at the Arts Theatre, which was actually a three-part series of short plays. Wood had no previous film-script experience, and Lowenstein had to show him some screenplay samples to see how it was done. Regardless of his inexperience, Lester got on well with Wood and agreed to work on the project.

The first thing Lowenstein did was sign up Rita Tushingham, who'd played the part of Nancy in the stage play, to reprise the role in the film. Like Wood, Lester immediately got on with Tushingham, beginning what became a lifelong mutual admiration society. For the three male leads, Lester initially interviewed Ian McKellan, John Hurt, and Peter McEnery but ended up casting different actors: Ray Brooks as Tolen, Michael Crawford as Colin, and Donal Donnelly as Tom. In an extraordinary trifecta of ingenue rolls, Jacqueline Bissett, Charlotte Rampling, and Jane Birkin all made their debut credited screen appearances, although if you blink three times you will miss them all.

Mindful of needing to be ready to shoot the next Beatles film in February 1965, Lester finished *The Knack* in six weeks, working with a budget of £100,000. The film was changed dramatically from the play with Lester's experimental visual ideas creating a more edgy satirical approach, and both UA and Charles Wood were unhappy with Lester's cut. Fortunately, Tony Richardson at Woodfall could see that Lester had made a funny, offbeat film that presaged the effervescent fizz that was to be Swinging London cinema, and the film reflected Lester's directorial and visual influence of *A Hard Day's Night* and a little of what was to come in *Help!* The film, with its surreal editing, Greek chorus of older Brits watching the four young people explore the changing sexual mores of the era, and the metamorphosis the four characters go through by the end of the movie, was a major cinematic breakthrough, and further illustrated Lester's deft comic touch.

Proving the UA executives and Wood wrong, not only was *The Knack* chosen as an official entry at the Cannes Film Festival, but it also won the coveted Palme d'Or that year, the first British film to win the award since *The Third Man* in 1949. Other British films that subsequently won the award and came just after *The Knack* include

Blow-Up (1967), directed by Michelangelo Antonioni (which was actually a British/American/Italian coproduction); *If* (1969), directed by Lindsay Anderson; and *The Go-Between* (1971), directed by Joseph Losey. There was no Cannes Film Festival in 1968, in a show of support for the May 1968 spring riots.

Award in hand, the producers realized they had a winner, and after renaming the film, *The Knack . . . and How to Get It*, the film went into general release, premiering on June 2, 1965, at the London Pavilion with John, George, and Ringo attending. While the film was met with mixed reviews, they were nonetheless unanimous in praising Lester's zany, comedic, improvisational style.

The Beatles left for the Bahamas on February 22, 1965, on a private chartered BOAC Cunard Boeing 707, dubbed the Beatles Bahama Special, from London's Heathrow Airport. On arrival at New York's Kennedy Airport, they had to wait on-board the aircraft (had they disembarked, they'd have had to go through customs) before it continued on to the Bahamas. Having their own private plane meant they could indulge in the pleasures of marijuana, provided to them by actor Brandon deWilde (who may or may not have joined them on the flight), once they left New York. Arriving at Nassau Airport early in the evening, the group did a interviews with Gene Loving of Tidewater, Virginia radio station WGH-AM, and Larry Kane of WFUN-AM in Miami. Paul, George, and Ringo at least attempted to answer their questions, but John, perhaps due to jet lag and his drug-induced state, kept interrupting the interview with non sequiturs. Lennon even confessed they all got stoned on their flight, but this seemed to go over the heads of their interviewers, thinking either that John was kidding or that he was referring to drink. "I Don't Want to Spoil the Party" came up in the conversation; the song was the B side of the US "Eight Days a Week" single, released on February 15 and topping the charts on March 13. The title "Eight Days A Week" was inspired by a comment McCartney heard his limo driver make.

Help! would be filmed in Eastman color, with the negative and print in 35 mm. The aspect ratio would be 1.66:1 and the cinematographic process would be spherical. The sound mix was in mono.

The Beatles, their entourage, the cast, and crew set up shop at the Balmoral Club, Nassau. Located on Cable Beach, the club began as a glitzy Caribbean destination for 1940s high society. The club was founded by Sir Oliver Simmonds, and the likes of the Duke and Duchess of Windsor were just two of the fashionable regulars, with the Duke having a private office at the club. Part of the 21-mile-long island of New Providence, today the hotel is a chain resort, Sandals Royal Bahamian, that celebrates the Beatles filming of *Help!* in a commemorative suite called Villa Oleander. It was in this villa that Paul McCartney composed "Wait," which would appear on *Rubber Soul*, thought to be one of the few 50/50 collaborations by John and Paul since "Baby's in Black" in 1964.

Little filming was done on the shoot's first day, February 23. Footage of Ringo listening to conch shells was shot but was never used. The scene where the Beatles emerge, fully clothed, from a swimming pool at the Nassau Beach Hotel after escaping from the Kaili cult was also shot on this day. The hotel was now named the Hotel Melia Nassau Beach.

February 24 was the first full day of filming, with an 8:30 a.m. to 5:30 p.m. schedule that the Beatles adhered to most days. The scene where the Beatles are shown cycling on Interfield Road, near the airport, was filmed; the road no longer exists due to airport expansion. Gene Loving also did more interviews with John, Paul, George, Walter Shenson, Richard Lester, and the film's hairdresser Betty Glasow.

The next day, February 25, saw further filming done at Interfield Road, as well as filming at the Bahamas Softball Association's stadium with Ringo and John and at the lime quarry caves in the area with Paul. The Beatles met Swami Vishnu-Devananda on this day. Vishnu-Devananda, a leader in hatha yoga, was a founder of Shivananda Yoga. He gave each of the Beatles a signed copy of his book, *The Illustrated Book of Yoga*, which helped spark George's lifelong interest in Indian religion, culture, and music. George celebrated his 22nd birthday at a party that evening and, receiving a book whose main theme was reincarnation on the day of his birth must have felt like a divine coincidence.

Friday, February 26 saw Ringo being filmed in front of the post office on Bay Street, Ringo and George shooting sequences at the Royal Victoria Hotel, and John filmed running out of the public library. The prison camp sequences, which didn't feature the Beatles, were also shot at Lake Cunningham. On February 27, the group shot the "Another Girl" sequence on Balmoral Island, renamed Discovery Island in 1992. More filming was done at additional locations in Paradise Island on February 28 and Café Martinique on March 1. The latter date also saw Ringo, Victor Spinetti, Roy Kinnear, and Eleanor Bron filming on a schooner.

The March issue of *The Beatles Book* featured an interview with Paul and Ringo, conducted by Fredrick James, in which they discussed the filming of *Help!*:

RINGO: I have a letter here.

PAUL: Yes, yes!

RINGO: No, seriously. It's a letter from a girl who asks if we prefer making films to doing concerts.

PAUL: What's her name?

RINGO: Barbara.

PAUL: Now then, Barbara . . . If you were lying about in London on a cold February day and some bloke said "Hey, let's fly off to the Bahamas to make a film," how do you think you'd feel about it?

RINGO: What about the snow bit in the alps?

The Beatles frolicking in the snow in the Austrian Alps in *Help!* Courtesy Photofest.

PAUL: As long as you wear enough gear you can get by in the snow. Ask John. He sat in enough of the stuff at St. Moritz!

RINGO: So naturally it's more interesting to film in places like Nassau and Austria than it would be in an ordinary film studio. But that isn't what this bird Barbara was asking.

PAUL: Well I like doing films for a change but the waiting around while they change cameras and all that gets boring. With a film you've got to wait months before you see how the whole thing has turned out. With a concert you get reaction from an audience right away.

RINGO: What about the rushes? Every day when there's a break in filming you get a chance to see "rushes" of the scenes they shot the previous day.

PAUL: And all that can be hilarious because you see all the bits of film where somebody mucked things up by laughing or forgetting some lines.

RINGO: To answer Barbara's question once and for all, filming can be fun . . . especially if it means escaping from the winter and seeing a bit of the sun. But we love doing "live" shows.

From March 2 through 4, filming continued on Cabbage Beach at Paradise Island and Victoria Beach on Rose Island. Still, the group did make time for interviews, speaking with Dave Hull from KRLA-AM in Los Angeles on March 2. Hull was joined by Derek Taylor, who'd briefly worked as the Beatles' publicist the previous year. The film was the primary topic of discussion:

DEREK TAYLOR: Why the red paint all over your suit, Ringo?

RINGO: Well, it's . . . the film is basically a chase film and it's about a ring, and it starts off where they're going to sacrifice a girl, and they paint everyone they sacrifice red, you see . . . this tribe . . . but they can't sacrifice the girl because she hasn't got this magic ring on which she sent to me because I wear rings. And so they're after me now and they can't get the ring off and so they're going to sacrifice me . . . and that's why I'm red.

DAVE HULL: Listen, this idol out there in the water that we're watching, is going to be a one-shot take, and it comes up and it's got ten arms. What has this got to do with the movie?

GEORGE: This is Kaili and . . . it's the sacrificial god or something. It's a bit involved. I'll wait until they finish making the film and then I'll go and see it and then I'll know what's happening.

DAVE HULL: How come it has to be a one-shot take?

GEORGE: This thing is twenty feet high and it's taken them two hours to submerge it under the water. They can do it again but they'll have to wait another two hours before they can get the thing down on the bottom again. It's a lot of work, so if they can do it in one take, it saves a lot of time and trouble. [It's interesting to note that the Kaili statue has 10 arms, not eight, and was made out of polystyrene blocks.]

Hull also spoke to John Lennon:

DAVE HULL: What about your part in *A Hard Day's Night*. You know a lot of it was spontaneous. The part in the bathtub, you recall you talked to me last time. . . . are you doing the same here or are you sticking to the script?

JOHN: We're sticking to the script until there's an opportunity of, you know, going away from it. We've done a bit that has nothing to do with the script. Filmed little bits that the director thought might come in handy for something or other. Whenever a situation arises we do it.

Sometime during the first week of March, legendary 1960s AM disc jockey Murray Kaufman, better known as "Murray the K," landed in the Bahamas to interview the group. Kaufman had pushed his way into the Beatles' entourage on their first US visit, crowning himself "the Fifth Beatle," due to his relentless promotion of the group, something not lost on Brian Epstein. Kaufman interviewed all four Beatles over the course of his stay, as well as Victor Spinetti. In addition to discussing *Help!*,

Kaufman also asked John about his upcoming book, *A Spaniard in the Works*, and discussed with George Ringo's marriage earlier in the month. Paul denied that he and his girlfriend Jane Asher had any wedding plans and stated that he'd like to write a musical with a rock score.

March 5 saw location shooting at Cabbage Beach, Victoria Beach, and the French Cloisters with John, Paul, and George shouting for Ringo. The French Cloisters location, part of a fourteenth-century French monastery, was also seen in two James Bond films, *Thunderball* and the 2006 James Bond movie version of *Casino Royale*. On March 6, shooting was held at Nassau International Airport, where the Beatles are seen photographing each other. On March 7 and 8, the group filmed the sequence at a deserted army camp. The facility was actually an old hospital that housed handicapped children and the elderly.

The group's final interview in the Bahamas was with Fred Robbins for Radio Luxembourg's "Assignment Hollywood." Robbins, an American, talked to George and Ringo, asking questions that were typical for pop stars of the era, such as what foods they liked to eat. Ringo's life as a newlywed and George's marital status were also a big topic of conversation. Ringo always had a weak constitution when it came to food and probably not only couldn't believe the Beatles were still being asked such inane questions but probably didn't even want to think about it, given that travel always affected his eating habits adversely. Ringo was at one of the most frenetic points in the early years of the Beatles, and somewhere along the way, during the filming of *Help!*, Ringo's left eyebrow went white. Even at this late date, Ringo revealed that the film still does not have a title. A number of titles had been proposed, some more for fun than actual consideration, such as *Beatles 2*, *Who's Been Sleeping in My Porridge*, *High Heeled Knickers*, and *Bahamas Ball* (Shades of *Blue Hawaii*, *Fun in Acapulco*, *Viva Las Vegas*, *Paradise Hawaiian Style* from the titles of Elvis Presley movies in exotic locations). The final day of shooting, March 9, was spent doing pickup shots on Paradise Island.

The Beatles departed the Bahamas on March 10, arriving back in London around 7 a.m. on March 11. They left for Austria the morning of March 13, accompanied by John and Ringo's wives Cynthia and Maureen, respectively, and George's girlfriend Pattie. Upon arrival at Flughafen airport, they were met by 4,000 fans, journalists, and a few protestors—students holding up signs that said, "Beatles Go Home." An impromptu press conference was held at a nearby hotel, as the group was unable to check into their own hotel, due a recent avalanche. An interview with a public West German radio station based in Cologne, WDR, was filled with the usual questions, except that Ringo admitted the group needed to wait until 6 p.m. to arrive at their hotel, as the aftereffects of an avalanche were still being felt. On March 2, falling rocks from the mountains above from an avalanche fell to the valley below, killing 14 students from Sweden who were traveling by bus on Radstadt Tauren Road.

Most location shooting took place at the ski resort where the group was staying, the Edelweiss Hotel, in Salzburg Land, Obertauren, at 75 Romerstrasse, the group occupying rooms 502, 504, 506, and 507. On March 14, 2015, 50 years to the day the group began filming at the resort, a statue of the four Beatles was unveiled on the site. The film crew was put up at the nearby Hotel Marietta, which is still in existence.

Filming officially kicked off the next day, though the first scene shot, featuring a toboggan, wasn't used in the film. The Beatles were filmed frolicking in the snow, while their doubles—Cliff Diggins (for George), Mick Dillon (for Ringo), Peter Cheevers (for Paul), and Joe Dunne (for John)—were filmed in a horse-drawn sleigh. The doubles had extraordinary careers of their own. Cliff Diggins did uncredited stunts for three Bond movies (*From Russia with Love*, *Goldfinger*, and *You Only Live Twice*) as well as the 1967 Bond spoof *Casino Royale*. His additional spy-related film work included appearances in the television shows such as *The Saint* and *The Avengers* (Patrick Macnee's double). Mick Dillion also worked uncredited on *Goldfinger* and *You Only Live Twice* and another film that sprang from the pen of Ian Fleming, *Chitty Chitty Bang Bang*. He worked on Richard Lester's *A Funny Thing Happened on the Way to the Forum* (as Buster Keaton's stand-in) and *How I Won the War*. Other work includes *The Charge of the Light Brigade* and *Dr. Who and the Daleks*. Joe Dunne had a lengthy film career. His Bond films résumé includes uncredited work in *From Russia with Love*, *Thunderball*, and *You Only Live Twice*. Also uncredited was his work on *The Dirty Dozen*. He worked again with Richard Lester on *Superman II*. His long list of credits includes work on *The Avengers* TV series, *Kelly's Heroes*,

Ringo Starr and John Lennon discussing where to take a tea break on the ski slopes of Austria in *Help!* Courtesy Photofest.

The Pink Panther Strikes Again, A Bridge Too Far, Revenge of the Pink Panther, S.O.B., Victor/Victoria, Flashdance, Chaplin, and *The Usual Suspects,* among others.

The ski resort attire the Beatles wore in the Austrian scenes would become iconic, especially due to their wearing the outfits on the soundtrack album cover. The clothing was all black, with poncho or cape-like coats, and for John and Ringo, the fisherman's style flat caps that would become their trademark. Conversely, George's chapeau, a top hat, struck a comic touch.

On March 15, the Beatles and their doubles were filmed on ski lifts and the slopes, a sequence completed on the following day. The next day, the shooting of one of the film's more memorable scenes, when the group is seen playing curling. The game involves sliding a stone, also known as a "rock" (rather like a lighter, cylindrical, squat bowling ball but made of metal and with a larger base), across polished ice toward a target, called the "house." At one point, the mad scientist Foot (Spinetti) substitutes a smoking bomb for one of the stones with George's unsuspecting deadpan countenance striking a perfect note. On the same day, it was announced that the new film's title would be *Eight Arms to Hold You,* suggested by Ringo. But a change was still to come.

On March 18, the group shot scenes at several locations, including at the Olympic ski jump site. The 1964 Winter Olympics was held in nearby Innsbruck, more than 100 miles west.

March 19 was spent doing pickup shots, with a wrap party held in the evening; it was also assistant director Clive Reed's birthday. The party, which featured a short performance by the group, was interrupted at 8 p.m. by an interview with Brian Matthew for the BBC's *Saturday Club* show, broadcast the following day.

The next day, March 20, was the final day of shooting for the Beatles, who shot one of the film's best sequences, miming to "Ticket to Ride" in a variety of outdoor settings, at one point clustered around the piano from their hotel, brought outside for the occasion. Ringo and his double shot a scene at a restaurant that was cut from the film. Ringo and John also did a telephone interview with Chris Denning, host of the Radio Luxembourg show *The Beatles.* On the final day of shooting, the Beatles' doubles shot sequences at Radstadt station and in a tunnel. The Beatles returned to London on March 22.

On the same day in the US, *The Early Beatles,* the first of four albums the label would release in 1965 came out. Though released in mono and stereo, the mono version was a "fold down" of the stereo mix. The album is an abridged version of Parlophone's *Please Please Me* album. The track listing of Vee-Jay's *Introducing the Beatles* album, released in January 1964, was also based on *Please Please Me,* featuring the tracks that Vee-Jay had the rights to, rights which eventually went to Capitol by the end of 1964. *The Early Beatles* left off "I Saw Her Standing There," which

Paul no doubt hiding his bloodshot eyes in Austria in *Help!* Courtesy Photofest.

Capitol had already released on *Meet the Beatles*. But "Misery" and "There's A Place" wouldn't be released by Capitol until the *Rarities* album in 1980.

Filming on *Help!* continued back in London at Twickenham Film Studios on March 24, with the Beatles generally working from 8:30 a.m. until 5:30 p.m. Some of the first scenes shot were the interior temple scenes. On March 26, Brian Epstein announced that the upcoming soundtrack album would include the incidental instrumental music as well as songs, just like the US soundtrack to *A Hard Day's Night*. But while this was the case in the US, the UK *Help!* album would only feature songs from the Beatles, including one side of songs not used in the film.

On March 27, the next chapter in the Beatles' mind expansion would unwittingly take place at a small two-bedroom flat at 2 Strathearn Place, Bayswater. John, Cynthia, George, and Pattie arrived for dinner at the home of George's dentist, John Riley, accompanied by his girlfriend Cyndy Bury. Riley, then 34 years old, was the son of a Metropolitan police officer and had studied cosmetic dentistry at Northwestern University in Chicago. He was considered the dentist to the stars, with his Harley Street office boasting the likes of Dudley Moore as one of his prized clients. He also had a supply of LSD, which was legal, that was manufactured at a farmhouse in Wales. After dinner, he secretly "dosed" his guests with LSD-laced sugar cubes put in their coffee.

On realizing what had happened, the four wanted to leave; their suspicions heightened by Riley's instance that they needed to stay. Undeterred, the four left to catch a performance by Paddy, Klaus, & Gibson (Klaus being Klaus Voorman, their friend from Hamburg) at a London club, but the effects of the drug made it a disorienting experience. They finally sought refuge at George's home in Esher. Though angry at being dosed unwittingly, both John and George enjoyed aspects of the drug. "God, it was just terrifying, but it was fantastic," John told *Rolling Stone*, while in a separate interview with the magazine, George said, "I had such an overwhelming feeling of well-being, that there was a God, and I could see him in every blade of grass. It was like gaining hundreds of years of experience in 12 hours." Though Bury claimed the Beatles had said they wouldn't mind taking the drug unknowingly, Riley was banished from the Beatles' entourage after the incident. He had a small, uncredited role in the 1966 western *The Texican* and much later died in a car crash in Ireland in 1986.

On Monday, March 29, the Beatles filmed the laboratory scene and interiors for the railway station scene. On March 30, they returned to Abbey Road after filming where they attempted to record "That Means a Lot"; they eventually gave up on the track, which wouldn't be officially released until *Anthology 2*. Filming continued on March 31, April 1, and April 2, though it's not known what scenes were shot.

On April 5 and 6, the Beatles filmed the scenes at an Indian restaurant, the Dolphin, renamed the Rajahama for the film. George was quite taken by the Indian instruments used by the musicians in the scene. As he later told *Billboard* in December 1992:

We were waiting to shoot the scene in the restaurant when the guy gets thrown in the soup and there were a few Indian musicians playing in the background. I remember picking up the sitar and trying to hold it and thinking, "This is a funny sound." It was an incidental thing, but somewhere down the line I began to hear Ravi Shankar's name. The third time I heard it, I thought, "This is an odd coincidence." And then I talked with David Crosby of the Byrds and he mentioned the name. I went and bought a Ravi record; I put it on and it hit a certain spot in me that I can't explain, but it seemed very familiar to me. The only way I could describe it was: my intellect didn't know what was going on and yet this other part of me identified with it. It just called on me . . . a few months elapsed and then I met this guy from the Asian Music Circle organization who said, "Oh, Ravi Shankar's gonna come to my house for dinner. Do you want to come too?"

April 7 featured shooting the pub cellar sequence where Ringo is confronted by Raja the Bengal tiger, who turns into a pussycat whenever he hears the fourth movement of Beethoven's Ninth Symphony, commonly known as "Ode to Joy." April 8 saw the shooting of the washroom scene, where the out-of-control hand dryers wreak havoc. Two other scenes were shot that were ultimately cut from the film; Ringo on his own in the washroom and an elaborate scene with all four Beatles, the Scotland Yard inspector, the high priest Clang, seven policemen, and 12 of Clang's henchmen.

On April 9, "Ticket to Ride"/"Yes It Is" was released in the UK, eventually topping the charts. The single was released in the US on April 19, hitting number 1 on

May 22. "Ticket to Ride" would appear on the US *Help!* soundtrack and close out side one on the UK *Help!* soundtrack.

The single's release was followed by numerous promotional appearances. The group mimed to both sides of the single for *Top of the Pops* on April 10 at Riverside Studios, airing on April 15, with "Yes it Is" repeated on April 22 and "Ticket to Ride" on April 29 and May 6. A brief clip of "Ticket to Ride" turned up in an episode of the UK television series *Dr. Who*, "The Executioners," on May 22. The small bit of the "Ticket to Ride" *Top of the Pops* segment that would be used in the episode, that was the first of a six-part Dalek story titled "The Chase" broadcast on May 22. The Beatles were actually to appear in the episode in the future made up to look older, but apparently Epstein turned the idea down. April 11 saw the group appearing at the *New Musical Express* Poll Winners All-Star Concert held at Empire Pool in Wembley, performing "Ticket to Ride," "I Feel Fine," "She's A Woman," "Baby's in Black," and "Long Tall Sally." Concert highlights later aired on ABC television in the UK on Easter Sunday, April 18. After their Poll Winners appearance, the Beatles went to ABC's Teddington Studio Centre where they mimed to "Ticket to Ride" and "Yes it Is" live on *The Eamonn Andrews Show*.

On April 1st, *George Martin Scores Instrumental Versions of the Hits* on UA is released in the US.

The Beatles spent April 12 and the morning of April 13 at Twickenham shooting the Buckingham Palace scenes, also fitting in interviews with Cleveland radio station KYW-AM on April 12 and with BBC's light program show, *Pop Inn*, on April 13.

The evening was spent recording the title song for the film, which had finally been renamed *Help!* Recording was completed quickly, with 12 takes and overdubs done between 7 p.m. and 11:15 p.m. The first eight takes were workmanlike attempts to nail down the instrumental backing track. By the ninth take, the group started overdubbing vocals and additional instruments, completing their work with take 12. Ringo and Paul provided the base, with John leading the way on his Framus acoustic 12-string and George on his Gretsch. A new vocal track for "Help!" was recorded specifically for the film at London's CTS Studios on May 24.

The US and UK stereo versions of the song used the original recording done at Abbey Road. But a new vocal track was recorded specifically for the film at London's CTS Studios on May 24. Stereo versions were from releases taken exclusively from the work done at Abbey Road, while mono mixes included additional vocal overdubs from the CTS session. From this one short evening session for one song, material would show up in official capacity on the multimedia presentation *The Beatles at Abbey Road* from 1983, George Martin's new CD mix of *Help!* in 1987, an EPK for the promotion of the Beatles *67–70* CD reissue in 1999, (even though the track is from 1965), the *Anthology* DVD in 2003, the *Love* CD from 2006, and the reissue of the film on DVD in 2007. The mono and stereo versions of the UK album each feature a different lead vocal.

On April 14, the group was filmed in Ailsa Avenue, Twickenham, for the scene where the Beatles are seen getting out of their Rolls-Royce. Two women passing by (played by Dandy Nichols, later of the BBC sitcom *Till Death Us Do Part*, and Gretchen Franklin) provide some dry commentary as they watch the lads enter what are apparently their separate homes; it's later revealed that the four doors actually lead to one communal home. In a further subtle touch, the color of their individual doors—Ringo's blue door (number 5), John's brown door (number 7), Paul's white door (number 9), and George's green door (number 11)—match the colors of their separate but open, living areas. Lester would imaginatively use colors in this metaphorical fashion in *How I Won the War* (1967), which featured John Lennon, as a means of distinguishing between four different World War II battles (Dunkirk, Dieppe, Alamein, and Arnhem), tinting newsreel footage of each battle in a different color.

The scenes in the group's shared flat were shot with the help of the person who actually lived at flat number 7, Beatrice Pennington, who served the group tea and was rewarded with an autographed photo. According to a newspaper article reproduced in Mark Lewisohn's *The Complete Beatles Chronicles*, the article chronicled how the usually quiet suburban neighborhood was filled with the noise of screaming girls, off from school for the Easter holidays, who staked out the neighborhood for days, hoping to get a glimpse of their idols. The scene undoubtedly fueled the fantasies of countless would-be rock stars—the idea of living in a swanky London flat, with getting up to fun and hijinks more than enough enticement to form a band. There's no doubt the producers of the television show *The Monkees* may have gotten some inspiration for their cool California pad where the Monkees all lived together from this scene, although the Monkees house was more shabby-California boho cool.

On April 16, John and George appeared on the *Ready Steady Goes Live!* television show to plug their new single "Ticket to Ride." April 18 saw the release of *Pop Gear*, with two performances by the Beatles. All four Beatles were back at Twickenham on Tuesday, April 20, filming, among other sequences, the scene where Ringo nearly loses his hand while trying to mail a letter. On April 21, the group filmed the Scotland Yard scenes at Twickenham, meeting Superintendent Gluck (Patrick Cargill). Gluck delivers one of the film's running jokes, which later became a catchphrase for Beatles fans, in his droll observation "So, this is the famous Beatles?" on meeting the group. Another of his lines was to become especially amusing in retrospect: "And how long do you think you'll last?" The next day, April 22, the group was filmed miming to the title song, as if for a television performance. The black-and-white footage is shown in an early scene in the film, when it's screened for Clang and the Eastern cult. Clang throws darts at the screen in frustration as he discovers the cult's ring is now on Ringo's finger. The clip (minus the dart throwing) would be used as a promotional clip when the "Help!" single was released—a proto music video. The rest of the day and all of April 23 was spent shooting a sequence with Frankie Howerd that was ultimately cut from the film. The scene with Frankie Howerd and Wendy Richards was filmed at the so-called "Sam Ahab School of Transcendental Elocution." This scene is actually included in the *Help!* novelization. The novelization was written by Al Hine. The Dell paperback was 50 cents and included an eight-page black-and-white photo spread. Hine was a journalist, who wrote for newspapers and magazine; an author, who wrote many film and television novelizations; and a film producer. His book, *Lord Love A Duck* was made into a film in 1966. He also wrote a novelization of Lester' *Juggernaut*.

Filming was held at Strand-on-the-Green, Chiswick, on April 24, where the Beatles were shot emerging from Post Office Alley and then encountering Clang's henchmen (disguised as bagpipe players) on the River Thames towpath. Seeking refuge, they duck into the City Barge public house, which still stands today (though the interior shots were filmed at Twickenham). When Ringo is trapped in the pub's cellar, the other three Beatles escape by jumping through the front windows. The afternoon was spent with Ringo and George filming scenes that were cut from the film.

On April 27, at Twickenham, the Beatles filmed the scene where they arrive at an airport on their way to the Bahamas, in heavy disguise, all sporting moustaches and, in the case of John, Ringo, and George, beards. They also shot a scene with Ahme on a tank turret. April 28, again at Twickenham featured more shooting of the Frankie Howerd sequence and interiors of the City Barge sequence. In non-*Help!* related business, the group were filmed receiving a Grammy for Best Vocal Group Performance for "A Hard Day's Night" from Peter Sellers. Sellers perfectly sets the silly scene up by calling the award a "grandma award." The Beatles respond in kind, John referring to Sellers as "Mr. Ustinov," and then all four speaking in French gibberish, which evolves into "It's a Long Way to Tipperary." The clip was broadcast on NBC on May 18 on the Grammy Awards program *The Best on Record*.

April 29 saw a reshoot of the washroom scene that had first been filmed on April 8. The scene where Ringo is threatened by Clang in the storeroom of a recording studio, before being rescued by Ahme, was also reshot. The four were also interviewed by Radio Luxembourg DJ Chris Denning for his Sunday-night series *The Beatles*. In the interview, Paul says that Richard Lester came up with the title *Help!* because the previous title, *Eight Arms to Hold You*, posed a problem for John and Paul, when trying to write a song using that phrase.

The Beatles were back at Twickenham on Friday, April 30, for a busy day. The scene at the recording studio where the floor is sawed out from under Ringo's drum kit while the group is performing "You're Gonna Lose That Girl" took up much of the day. There were also several scenes involving the unsuccessful attempts of Clang and his henchmen to get the ring from Ringo, including a scene inside what is supposed to be the famous Asprey's jewelers. In another sequence, John and Ringo are in an elevator whose walls become magnetized by Clang in another failed attempt to extract the ring from Ringo's finger.

Some of the most action-packed and vivid sequences of the movie were shot between May 3 and May 5 at Salisbury Plain, the site of Stonehenge, when the Beatles are seen miming to "I Need You" and "The Night Before." The filming was akin to making a war picture, with troops, tanks, explosions, shooting, and general mayhem, as the military (including the actual British army's Third Tank Division troops) provides protection for the Beatles while they record. The cold and windy weather added to the difficulties. The Beatles, cast, and key crew were billeted at the nearby Antobus Arms hotel in Amesbury.

On May 7, the sequence of Paul being accidentally shrunk was shot at Twickenham. Location shooting was scheduled for Sunday, May 9 in the hopes of avoiding crowds. First came exterior shooting at New Bond Street, where the group goes into Asprey's. Then came exterior shooting at the "Rajahama" Indian restaurant. Next, John and Ringo returned to Twickenham, where Ringo is seen mailing a letter in a postbox on South Western Road. Ringo was next filmed outside a grocery store on Winchester Road, stepping on a weighing scale and nearly losing his finger.

The Beatles wrapped filming on *Help!* with two days of location shooting on May 10 and 11 at Cliveden House in Cliveden, Maidenhead, the site where the seeds of the Profumo scandal were planted. The mansion's bucolic grounds were used as a stand-in for Buckingham Palace. In addition to its royal heritage, Cliveden House also has a long and still continuing film and TV history. In addition to the interior shots, the group shot a surrealistic "intermission" scene in a part of the grounds known as Bluebell Wood that wouldn't be out of place in their yet unimagined 1967 film *Magical Mystery Tour*.

On the evening of May 10, the Beatles headed to Abbey Road Studios to record two Larry Williams covers, "Dizzy Miss Lizzy" and "Bad Boy." Both tracks would appear on the US Capitol album *Beatles VI* released on June 14 and reached number 1 by July 10. The version of "Dizzy Miss Lizzy" on *Beatles VI* would differ from the version that appeared on the UK *Help!* album. "Bad Boy" would not be released in the UK until *A Collection of Beatles Oldies* in 1967—the last cover song to appear on a Beatles album. Larry Williams recorded for Specialty Records, and the Beatles had regularly performed his songs live, going back to their Hamburg days in 1960. They also recorded Williams's "Slow Down." Three tracks recorded during the *Help!* sessions, "You Like Me Too Much," "Tell Me What You See," and "Dizzy Miss Lizzy," would be released in the US before appearing on the *Help!* UK album.

May 11 was the last day of filming for the Beatles; footage shot on this day of the cast and crew playing a softball game later appeared as a bonus feature on the 2007 DVD release of *Help!* Photographer Bob Whitaker came to visit, bringing along DJ

Buddy McGregor from Houston, Texas, radio station KNUZ-AM. No press interviews had been scheduled, but John, Paul, and Ringo gamely spoke to McGregor. The interview later appeared on a 7-inch record titled "Buddy in Britain" that was sold at a local department store for 50 cents. The final day of filming, without the Beatles, was on May 12. Postproduction continued through May 18.

Ultimately, it took 11 weeks to shoot *Help!*, whereas it only took eight weeks to shoot *A Hard Day's Night*, given the bigger budget and more elaborate production.

On June 4, the EP *Beatles for Sale (No.2)* was released in the UK. With this EP and the previous EP *Beatles for Sale*, eight of the 14 tracks from the *Beatles for Sale* album were duplicated.

On June 11 came the momentous announcement that the Beatles were included in the Queen's Birthday Honours list and would be decorated as Members of the British Empire (MBE). Once the story broke, the news media tracked down the Beatles on June 12 at Twickenham Film Studios, where they were watching a rough cut of *Help!* To placate the press, they gave an impromptu press conference.

Two days later on June 14, the Beatles were at Abbey Road, where they recorded "I've Just Seen Her Face,"[32] "I'm Down," and "Yesterday." "I've Just Seen Her Face" was affectionately titled "Auntie Gin's Theme" in its early stages, as Paul's Auntie Gin—the same relative name-checked in the Wings song "Let 'Em In"—liked it so much.

"Yesterday" had been gestating for some time, Paul giving it the provisional working title of "Scrambled Eggs." As he told *Playboy* in 1984:

> I fell out of bed. I had a piano by my bedside and I . . . must have dreamed it, because I tumbled out of bed and put my hands on the piano keys and I had a tune in my head. It was just all there, a complete thing. I couldn't believe it. It came too easy. In fact, I didn't believe I'd written it. I thought maybe I'd heard it before, it was some other tune, and I went around for weeks playing the chords of the song for people, asking them, "Is this like something? I think I've written it." And people would say, "No, it's not like anything else, but it's good."

Paul eventually wrote the lyrics while vacationing in Portugal, staying at the home of Bruce Welch of the Shadows, borrowing Welch's guitar (a Martin 00-18) to complete the song. At the session, Paul played the song on his acoustic Epiphone Texan and sang solo, making this the first "Beatles" track that featured only one member of the group.

On June 15, the group recorded John's song "It's Only Love" at Abbey Road. It was a song he always disparaged, telling *Hit Parader* in 1972, "That's one song I really hate of mine. Terrible lyric." The original title of the song was "That's a Nice Hat." The US version of the George Martin Orchestra's instrumental album *Help!* used the alternate titles of "Auntie Gin's Theme" and "That's a Nice Hat."

The final touches were put on "Yesterday" at a session on June 17. Paul recorded an additional vocal track. Then came the song's most distinctive element, a string quartet. George Martin, with some assistance from Paul, worked out an arrangement for the musicians: Tony Gilbert, first violin; Sidney Sax, second violin; Francisco Gabarro, cello; and Kenneth Essex, viola. The strings were recorded very dry, with the musicians playing straightforwardly, almost muted in their subtle approach.

McCartney had made some inquiries for the BBC Radiophonic Workshop to do some kind of an electronic backing for the track, but it never came to be. He also considered having Marianne Faithfull to do the song. Faithfull had released the Jagger-Richards composition "As Tears Go By" in June 1964, with strings orchestrated by Mike Leander. While Faithfull was a pop and folk singer at that time, one could argue that both Paul or George Martin could have had Faithfull's recording of "As Tears Go By" in mind when producing "Yesterday." Faithfull did eventually record "Yesterday" for her third album, *Go Away from My World*, released in December 1965. It was also released as a single but barely dented the Top 40. It would be Matt Monro who first had the hit with the "Yesterday" in the UK, when his version, released in 1965, reached number 8, his fifth and last Top-10 hit in the UK.

With "If You've Got Trouble" deemed unsatisfactory, Ringo still needed a song for his contribution to the album. He settled on a cover of "Act Naturally," written by Johnny Russell and a hit for country music legend Buck Owens. With Ringo, for the most part the central character in *Help!*, and Ringo being a fan of country music, the song's theme was perfect. George's own affinity for country music is reflected in his guitar solo, while Paul helped out with vocal harmony. The evening was spent recording the song "Wait," which wouldn't be released until later in the year on *Rubber Soul*. At this point, the *Help!* album was complete.

The promotional push for *Help!* began in the UK when a clip from the film was shown on *Thank Your Lucky Stars* on ABC-TV on July 17. The "Help!"/"I'm Down" single was released on July 19 in the US and July 23 in the UK, quickly topping the charts in both countries. "I'm Down" became something of a "lost" Beatles track, not appearing on an album until the 1976 *Rock 'n' Roll Music* compilation, after it had been mixed for stereo.

The *Help!* soundtrack companion album was released in the UK on August 6, and the US on August 13, again topping the charts in both countries. The film opened on July 29 in the UK, and August 11 in the US. As with *A Hard Day's Night*, the UK and US albums were vastly different from each other. The UK album included the film's songs on side one: "Help!," "The Night Before," "You've Got to Hide Your Love Away," "I Need You," "Another Girl," "You're Going to Lose That Girl," and "Ticket to Ride." Side two featured five originals ("It's Only Love," "You Like Me Too Much," "Tell Me What You See," "I've Just Seen a Face," and "Yesterday") and two covers, "Act Naturally" and "Dizzy Miss Lizzy." The US album featured the film songs interspersed between five instrumentals that were in the film, three composed by Ken Thorne, and two arranged by him based on Beatles songs. There was also a short, uncredited instrumental, based on the James Bond theme, that provided an introduction to the title song. The instrumental also features sitar, the first time the instrument was heard on a Beatles album.

The American version had had its detractors, including the Beatles, especially as American record buyers only received half an album. Other tracks from the UK version appeared on various US albums: "It's Only Love" and "I've Just See Her Face" would appear on the US *Rubber Soul*, released in December 1965; "Yesterday" would appear on *Yesterday and Today*, released in June 1966: and "You Like Me Too Much" and "Tell Me What You See" had already appeared on *Beatles VI*. The Bond intro on "Help!" is fun, and it's nice hearing the instrumental music, all making the American release a nice curio.

While preparing the *Help!* album, a memo circulated at Capitol about the possibility of releasing a Paul McCartney solo album, inspired by the fact that "Yesterday" was essentially a solo McCartney song and performance and had been hugely successful. This idea was quickly rejected.

The *Help!* soundtrack albums came in a year when soundtrack albums were big business. Five of the top 9 albums of the year were soundtracks, the year kicking off with yet another Elvis Presley soundtrack, *Roustabout* (his last number 1 album until 1973). Like the *A Hard Day's Night* soundtrack album, one of the unique aspects of the *Help!* soundtrack was the inclusion of music not performed by the Beatles. Capitol Records' Dave Dexter made up song titles for some of these instrumental pieces. The film also included various classical pieces, music specifically to propel the plot. One example is the scene when Clang's men break into the Beatles' communal home, and "Prelude to Act III," from Wagner's opera *Lohengrin* is played. The "Prelude" was grafted to a Ken Thorne instrumental from the film and named "In The Tyrol." Other pieces of classical music were used in the film that didn't appear on the soundtrack: Tchaikovsky's "1812 Overture" in the scene where Clang's men blow up a tank in which the Beatles are; the fourth movement of Beethoven's Ninth Symphony (aka "Ode to Joy") in the scene when Ringo confronts a tiger in the pub cellar; and Rossini's "Overture," played over the closing credits. Music not performed by the Beatles that appears in the *Help!* film can found on sources other than the official Capitol soundtrack album. The composer of some of the incidental music, Ken Thorne, released a compilation album, *The Film Music of Ken Thorne Volume 2*, through the Belgium label of Prometheus Records in 1995. The CD contained music from soundtracks Thorne scored: *The Bed Sitting Room* released in 1969 and directed by Richard Lester and *Murphy's War*, a 1971 movie, directed by Peter Yates, and Thorne and John Barry both contributed music. The CD also includes a nearly 11-minute piece titled "Help!: An Orchestral Fantasy." The *Help!* music here does include music that can found on the soundtrack album, but pieces from the film not on the album are also mixed in with that music to comprise the piece. A 2010 US CD does include some of Thorne's score from *The Bed Sitting Room*, along with music from another Lester film, *Juggernaut*, which was released in 1974.

Capitol also capitalized on the fact that the album was a soundtrack, and as was the case with soundtrack albums, it was a higher price than previous albums from the Beatles. The mono album was $4.98 and the stereo album was $5.98, which at the time was a lot of money for a record album aimed primarily at young children or teenagers. The album again featured another iconic cover, which, although not as groundbreaking as the UK *With the Beatles* or as evocative as *Beatles for Sale*, is nonetheless a beautiful, simple design. But as with *A Hard Day's Night* album, the US release had a different cover. The UK album release featured the group standing in a row, dressed in the mod ski outfits they wore in the film, all, except Paul, wearing a hat. The group are supposed to be spelling out H-E-L-P in semaphore signals with their arms but are actually spelling out N (George)-U (John)-J (Paul)-V (Ringo). The back cover featured four individual black-and-white pictures of the band. On the US cover, the Beatles were shown in a different order—George, Ringo, John, and Paul—meaning they were now spelling out N-V-U-J. The group's name is spelled out in large red letters across the top, while the Beatles themselves are standing atop even larger red and orange letters spelling the film's title. The song titles were listed below. The back cover features film credits and additional recording information and a color photo of the Beatles on the beach in the Bahamas taken by Robert Freeman, who also took the cover photo. Probably the best feature of the US *Help!* album was that it was a gatefold (the Beatles' third album released in this fashion, following the US *The Beatles' Story* and the UK *Beatles for Sale*). On *Help!*, the inner gatefold featured stills from the film, a plot synopsis, and some fun liner notes.

The *Help!* album, like a handful of other Beatles albums, has had a fluid post-breakup history. In the case of *Help!* and *Rubber Soul*, the stereo versions on the 1987 CDs were dramatically remixed by George Martin. Martin attempted to create a more modern stereo mix that relied less on hard panning vocals on one side and instruments on the other and also using more reverb. Many welcomed correcting this approach to stereo mixing, but some did not like the use of digital reverb. The original stereo mixes were eventually released on CD in 2009, though oddly they were added to the *Help!* and *Rubber Soul* CDs in *The Beatles in Mono* box and not the 2009 stereo CDs. Even more frustrating for collectors, while the stereo CDs were available individually and in a box, the mono CDs were only available in a box set, meaning anyone who wanted the original *Help!* and *Rubber Soul* CDs would have to purchase the mono box. Another major change Martin made for the 1987 *Help!* CD was correcting a problem with vocal dropout during the first chorus of "It's Only Love."

The US *Rarities* album (1980) featured the UK version of the title track (the UK *Rarities*, released in 1978, did not feature any music from *Help!*). In 2014, the US

Yesterday and Today album (which featured songs from the UK *Help!* album) was issued in mono and stereo on CD for the first time. The CD had the infamous "butcher" cover and also included a sticker featuring the "trunk cover" artwork should anyone wish to cover up the "butcher" shot.

Seven months after the *Help!* album was released, the *Yesterday* EP was released in the UK in March 1966. All four songs on the EP were taken from the UK *Help!* album: "Yesterday," "Act Naturally," "You Like Me Too Much," and "It's Only Love."

Both *The Beatles at the Hollywood Bowl* (1977) and *Live at the Hollywood Bowl* (2016) featured the same live versions of songs from *Help!*, "Ticket to Ride," and the title song.

On *Live at the BBC*, there were two performances of *Help!* songs: "Ticket to Ride," which appeared on both the UK and US albums, and "Dizzy Miss Lizzy," which appeared only on the UK album, recorded on May 26 and broadcast on June 7 as part of the BBC radio special program, *The Beatles Invite You to Take A Ticket to Ride*, hosted by Denny Piercy. Piercy's exchange with Ringo during the interview was a stellar example of the Starr wit when he was asked a question about his character in the film. Piercy: "Are you a sort of 007?" Ringo: "No, no. I'm sort of double entendre!" It was their last BBC radio performance.

Anthology 2, released in March 1996, included alternative versions of five *Help!* tracks: studio versions of "You've Got to Hide Your Love Away" and "It's Only Love" and live versions of "Yesterday," "Ticket to Ride," and the title cut from the group's appearance on *Blackpool Night Out* on August 1, 1965. It was the group's second and last appearance on the Sunday night British television show, which also included performances of "I Feel Fine," "I'm Down," and "Act Naturally."

Help! was released in a year when soundtrack album sales were booming. The soundtrack for *The Sound of Music* was released in 1965 and remained on the charts in the UK and US almost through the end of 1969. Right from the beginning of his career, movies had been big business for Elvis Presley. Between 1956 and 1965, he appeared in 19 films and released 11 soundtrack albums. The soundtrack to *Mary Poppins* was the number 1 album of 1965, and five of the top 10 albums of the year were also soundtrack albums.

Both the UK and US versions of the *Help!* soundtrack, whether mono or stereo, are regarded as having mediocre sound quality. This appeared to be caused not by the stereo mix itself but because of mastering and pressing issues. The *Help!* stereo mix is viewed by some as actually being the first really good stereo mix of an album from the Beatles. American fans would continue to suffer with the inferior Capitol versions through *Revolver*. Although the American version of *Rubber Soul*, the last album worked on by Dave Dexter, is met favorably by some with its more folk-rock song selection, American record buyers couldn't buy British imported records until 1968. By then, it wouldn't matter as much, as starting with *Sgt. Pepper's Lonely Hearts Club Band*, Beatles albums would be identical in both countries.

The *Help!* film premiered in the UK on July 29, 1965. As with *A Hard Day's Night*, the film was given a royal premiere at the London Pavilion Theatre, attended by Princess Margaret and Lord Snowdon, who would normally have been on their annual summer holiday by that point in the year. The royal premiere was sponsored by the Variety Club Heart Fund of Great Britain and the dockland settlements. Doors opened at 7:30 p.m. for an 8:30 p.m. screening, and a crowd of 10,000 packed Piccadilly Circus. The Beatles arrived in a black Rolls-Royce, accompanied by John's wife Cynthia, Ringo's wife Maureen, and Paul's girlfriend Jane Asher. The film was followed by a party at the Dorchester Hotel's Orchid Room.

For *Help!* UA made the largest order to date for color prints of the film. On the same night of the London premiere, the film also opened in locations where summer holidaymakers would be, including such obvious choices as Brighton, but also Barnstaple, Canterbury, Clacton, Lowestoft, Plymouth, Ramsgate, Weymouth, and Worthing. The film's opening week's grosses were dramatically higher than for *A Hard Day's Night*.

Help! premiered in the US on August 11. None of the Beatles attended the premiere. The group arrived in the States soon after on August 13, giving a press conference the same day at their hotel. On August 14, they taped an appearance for *The Ed Sullivan Show* and then gave their historic Shea Stadium concert on August 15. On August 29 and 30, the group returned to the Hollywood Bowl. The shows were again recorded. On the first night, the recording was produced by Karl Engeman and engineer Hugh Davies. Due to technical issues, the second night was recorded by producer Voyle Gilmore and engineer Pete Abbott.

On September 4, the single "Help!" reached number 1 in the US, with the album topping the charts on September 12. On September 13, "Yesterday"/"Act Naturally" was released in the US, reaching number 1 by October 9. "Yesterday" was not issued as a single in the UK until March 1976, after the Beatles recording contract with Parlophone had elapsed.

In 2013, *Rolling Stone* magazine put *Help!* at number 1 in their list of the Top-25 soundtracks of all time; *A Hard Day's Night* was number 4, and *Magical Mystery Tour* number 9. Surprisingly, only three other soundtrack albums were on the list from the 1960s with *Easy Rider* at number 14, *The Graduate* at number 16, and the only other group from the 1960s on the list, the Monkees, with *Head*, at number 25.

The *Help!* film did not meet with the nearly unanimous critical praise that greeted *A Hard Day's Night*. *Time* magazine, in their September 3 issue, said: "The charm and experimental spontaneity of *A Hard Day's Night* has been replaced by highly professional, carefully calculated camera work and cutting, plus a story line made out of finely-wrought jack-in-the-boxes." By 2018, Jordan Hoffman in *The New York Times* echoed *Time*'s dismissive review but gives Richard Lester his deserved due: "Unfortunately, *Help!* is awash in cringeworthy Orientalism, more than can be laughed off as merely the Music Hall–style comedy of its day. But Lester is still in top form during the playful, snowbound 'Ticket to Ride' number and 'I Need You,' in which the Beatles play in a field surrounded by armed soldiers." David Pirie, in the *Time Out* film guide, said *Help!* "never really lives up to the engaging opening sequence." He also said, "Many of the gags fall flat."

Those connected with the film often agreed with the less than generous reaction to *Help!*, although over the years it has been viewed less harshly and is now considered as a fun, colorful, and highly entertaining film, especially by fans of the group. In *The Beatles in Richard Lester's* A Hard Day's Night*: A Complete Pictorial Record of the Movie*, Lester said of *Help!*, "I love *Help!* I, for very complex reasons, prefer *Help!* to *A Hard Day's Night*." Lester added that several noted European directors of the era preferred the film, including Federico Fellini and Jean Renoir, and that Franco Zeffirelli said *Help!* was one his favorite films. In an interview with Scott Muni for the syndicated radio show *Ticket to Ride*, producer Walter Shenson said that in relation to *A Hard Day's Night*, *Help!* "was more like a 'movie' movie. It was like a live cartoon. It was a bigger picture; we went to the Bahamas and the Austrian Alps for locations, it was in color, we had a long shooting schedule and a bigger cast of actors besides the Beatles. Things that add up to a more expensive movie."

"Love it," said filmmaker Cameron Crowe in speaking about *Help!* to the author. "Loved the villainy and of course . . . the Beatles' bachelor pad. That idea was brilliant." As for the soundtrack album, Crowe said: "*Help!* is one of the Top-3 Beatles albums for me. Lennon calls it his Fat Elvis period, I call it Everything."

The film ultimately grossed more than £12 million, with a budget of £1.5 million. It also won first prize at the Rio de Janeiro Film festival.

For all of the mixed reviews and even the dismissive remarks made by the Beatles themselves, *Help!* felt right at home with the tone, subject matter, and style of British films of 1965.

The film has been reissued many times over the years. Rights to the film are currently co-owned by the Beatles and the Karsh family. From 1965 through 1980, UA controlled the film's distribution rights. In 1980, those rights reverted to producer Walter Shenson. Shenson kept the film out of circulation until 1987. Along with *A Hard Day's Night*, *Help!* was issued on videotape by MPI Home Video in Betamax and VHS and again in a special edition in 1995, along with a laser disc edition. In 1997, the film was released on DVD at 16.9 aspect ratio and PCM Stereo and DTS 5.1 Surround Sound audio formats and again on DVD as part of *The Beatles DVD Collector's Set* in 2000, which also included *Magical Mystery Tour*, *The First U.S. Visit*, and *You Can't Do That: The Making of* A Hard Day's Night. In 2007, two double DVD editions were released. The Blu-ray was finally released in 2013 in 1080p and PCM Stereo, DTS-HD Master Audio 5.1, and Dolby Digital 5.1 audio formats. Guy Massey was part of the team that worked on new stereo and 5.1 mixes of the main songs that were in the film at Abbey Road. In an interview with the author, he said: "I guess my remit was to bring something new to them [the mixes] if at all possible, so I tried to create some extra depth and width and a slightly overall extended frequency palette." The stereo mixes were created first and then the 5.1 mixes, from the original analog tapes. In terms of input from others, Massey said: "Apple and 'the shareholders' were often present either during the process or at least when we were close to completing, to check and give us a thumbs up to the mixes. We of course took on their comments and would adjust accordingly. The main thing I remember having to change would be vocal levels within tracks."

One of those 2007 double DVD editions was available as a deluxe edition box made in Holland. Of all the post-theatrical releases of any films of the Beatles, no other film, including *A Hard Day's Night*, has been given such a bespoke release. The materials are housed in an oversized, hardcover book-like slipcase package. Inside are two discs. Disc 1 has the original film. Disc 2 includes a 30-minute documentary on the making of the film, a missing scene, an in-depth look at the film's restoration, reminiscences of the cast and crew, three theatrical trailers, and three radio spots hidden in the menus. There is also a 60-page hardcover book, a reproduction of Richard Lester's original script with his handwritten notes, reproductions of eight of the US theatrical lobby cards, and a reproduction of an original theatrical poster.

THAT WILD MERCURY SOUND

The year 1965 would begin a major shift in music that the Beatles would be at the forefront of. While the Rolling Stones were also part of this shift, with tracks like "(I Can't Get No) Satisfaction," "Get Off My Cloud," and "Lady Jane," another British group would even more profoundly point to change in the air—the Yardbirds. The Yardbirds had come up at the same time as the Rolling Stones in 1963 and were a part of what was loosely described as the British R&B scene. And like the Rolling Stones, they would quickly lose their R&B and blues purist roots, move past covering American blues and R&B songs, and establish a sound that initially lumped them in with the London pop scene. With singles like "For Your Love," "Heart Full of Soul," and "Evil Hearted You" in 1965, all written or cowritten by Graham Gouldman (later of the band 10cc), they were stretching pop boundaries, particularly with "Heart Full of Soul," which featured new guitarist Jeff Beck (original guitarist Eric Clapton having left due to the group's move in a more pop direction, as evidenced on "For Your Love").

But the musical shift at this time was felt more strongly in America with the continued evolution of Bob Dylan, particularly his "Like a Rolling Stone" single released on July 20. The previous singles, "Subterranean Homesick Blues" and "Maggie's Farm" (both released in 1965), featured Dylan's new "wild mercury sound," but "Like A Rolling Stone," clocking in at more than six minutes, actually reached number 2 on the charts and was a major leap for the one-time folk bard. And with his next single, "Positively 4th Street," Dylan bid a bitter farewell to the folk crowd. His influence launched what was America's first real challenge to the British Invasion with the Byrds, who almost singlehandedly invented folk-rock, along with, perhaps unwittingly, their Columbia Records labelmates Simon and Garfunkel. And while the Beatles were still using four-track recording, the Byrds were using eight-track recording.

There were others scoring hits with the popular new folk-rock sound in America such as Barry McGuire with "Eve of the Destruction," written P. F. Sloane and produced by Sloane, Lou Adler, and Steve Barri. Also, James Brown was simultaneously inventing funk and hitting the top of the charts with "I Got You" and "Papa's Got a Brand New Bag." And while not much known outside of underground music circles, and with music clearly not made for the charts, the Paul Butterfield Blues Band's self-titled debut album introduced a melding of blues and rock that had an immediate impact on the evolving music scene.

WHAT GOES ON

The promotion of songs from the *Help!* album continued.

On August 14, 1965, the band taped an appearance on *The Ed Sullivan Show* at Studio 50 in New York, performing "I Feel Fine," "I'm Down," "Act Naturally," "Ticket to Ride," "Yesterday," and "Help!" The show was broadcast on September 12, the day before "Yesterday" was released as a single in the US. This was the last episode of the *Ed Sullivan Show* taped in black and white.

On November 23, the Beatles produced black-and-white videos for five songs at Twickenham Studios, Stage 3, directed by Joe McGrath and produced by InterTel VTR, a NEMS company: "Ticket to Ride," "Help," and the non-*Help!* songs "I Feel Fine" (two versions), "Day Tripper" (two versions), and "We Can Work It Out" (three versions). The entire concept behind this long day of filming was so the videos could be made available for pop music television shows on both sides of the Atlantic because the Beatles no longer wanted to appear live or make special arrangements for television.

Nonetheless, the group would appear only days later on the BBC's *Saturday Club* with Brian Matthew at Aeolian Hall for a short interview on November 29. Matthew would go on to have the distinction of being the first person to interview John and Paul at Abbey Road Studios on March 20, 1967, for the BBC Transcription Service of *Top of the Pops* for use outside of the UK. He also prerecorded their acceptance speech for the 1966 Ivor Novello Awards because they would not be attending.

On December 3, the single "Michelle"/"Girl," both from *Rubber Soul*, was released in a handful of European countries to coincide with their upcoming tour. December 3 also marked the beginning of the group's final UK tour at the Odeon Cinema in Glasgow, Scotland; their December 5 concert at the Empire Theatre would be their last Liverpool show.

Rubber Soul was released in the UK on December 3 on Parlophone, and December 6 in the US on Capitol. Again, the track listings were different in each country. The UK version (and to a lesser degree the US version) reflected major changes for the group, with tracks like "Nowhere Man" and "Drive My Car," while the American version had a more acoustic feel, reflective of the folk-rock trend, although oddly it didn't include "If I Needed Someone," which would have fit right in.

On December 13, the Beatles rejected *A Talent for Loving* as their next film project. It would take until December 26, 1967, before *Magical Mystery Tour*, their next film project, would appear and not on the big screen in cinemas but on British television.

4

Roll up for The Mystery Trip

THEY'RE COMING TO TAKE YOU AWAY

"When a man buys a ticket for a Magical Mystery Tour, he knows what to expect. We guarantee him the trip of a lifetime. And that's just what he gets. The incredible Magical Mystery Tour!"

The time between the release of the *Help!* album and film and the *Magical Mystery Tour* film, EP in the UK, and full-length album in the US, can't be measured in days, weeks, months, or years due to the accelerated speed in which the group's sound changed along with the musical and cultural world around them. The release of *Rubber Soul*, *Revolver*, and *Sgt. Pepper's Lonely Hearts Club Band* is unmatched in popular music in the 1960s; perhaps only Bob Dylan (*Bringing It All Back Home*, *Highway 61 Revisited*, *Blonde on Blonde*) and the Jimi Hendrix Experience (*Are You Experienced?*, *Axis Bold as Love*, and *Electric Ladyland*) could boast equally seismic three-album runs. Neil Young, Stevie Wonder, the Rolling Stones, Bob Marley, Joni Mitchell, and others would later boast dazzling three-album runs as the 1960s gave way to the 1970s, but the three-headed monster that is *Rubber Soul*, *Revolver*, and *Sgt. Pepper's Lonely Hearts Club Band* may be the high-water mark of popular music album-making. While the group hinted at new directions in songwriting on *Help!*, nothing at that point indicated the level of composition that was to come. Concurrent with the group's composing prowess and growth, the studio innovations that were the results of the Beatles needing to push the envelope, and the Abbey Road team's ability to accommodate them within the limitations of four-track recording technology, is a testament to both George Martin and the team around him during this period.

The level of sophistication and change the Beatles brought to popular music during this time is in many ways still unmatched. There's no question that the continued influence of Dylan on their songwriting and willingness to mix musical styles was still evident. The Beach Boys' *Pet Sounds*, released on May 16, 1966, was an album clearly influenced by *Rubber Soul*. The band's landmark single "Good Vibrations," released in the US on October 10, 1966, was another major influence on the natural evolution from *Revolver* to *Sgt. Pepper's Lonely Hearts Club Band*.

RED DOGS AND WHITE BICYCLES

Psychedelia, flowing from folk-rock and the evolving counterculture, was both influenced by the Beatles and an influence on the Beatles, whose psychedelic period began with *Help!* and lasted until *Yellow Submarine*. Psychedelia and the hippies didn't just pop up overnight. The use of mind-expanding drugs, exploring alternative lifestyles, challenging authority, and creating new artistic modes of expression was not a new phenomenon. Vienna, Berlin, Paris, and even Chicago were hotbeds of new ideas going back as far as the nineteenth century, and in the recent past Greenwich Village and San Francisco were considered ground zero for the beat poetry scene, with San Francisco's City Lights bookstore opened by poet Lawrence Ferlinghetti and Peter D. Martin in 1953.

London would join San Francisco as one of the two epicenters of the psychedelic movement. But the real seeds of the new countercultural music scene were blooming far from those major cities. In the seemingly odd locale of Virginia City, Nevada, at what sounded like a place out of an old western, was the Red Dog Saloon, originally the Comstock House, which first opened its swinging doors in 1863. The Red Dog Saloon, which took on its name in 1963, was ground zero for the American psychedelic scene, with poetry readings and all night American Indian peyote ceremonies led by Chandler A. Laughlin III. Laughlin started out managing two of Berkeley's celebrated coffeehouses, the Cabale Creamery and the Jabberwock (a name borrowed from the poem *Jabberwocky* by Lewis Carroll) in 1960, prior to revving up the new scene at the Red Dog Saloon.

The groups that defined the new scene at the Red Dog were Big Brother and the Holding Company, the Charlatans, and the Wildflower. The Charlatans were a key group in the evolution of the scene and, like Big Brother, were from San Francisco. They wouldn't release a single until 1966, nor an album until 1969, but they were nonetheless central to the musical explosion to come. The original lineup consisted of George Hunter, Richard Olsen, Mike Wilhelm, Dan Hicks, and Mike Ferguson. Drummer Hicks would go on to form his own group, Dan Hicks and the Hot Licks, long before the Charlatans 1969 album came out. Their proto-hippie, folk-rock, psychedelic sound had more in common with old-timey jug band, country, and blues than hippie music, but the foundation of the American hippie and psychedelic music attitude was born with these cosmic singing cowboys.

At the end of summer 1965, Marty Balin opened the Matrix Club in San Francisco with a performance by his band the Jefferson Airplane. Almost simultaneously, novelist Ken Kesey was hosting acid parties at his northern California home. Kesey's novels, *One Flew Over the Cuckoo's Nest* (1962) and *Sometimes a Great Notion* (1963) were revolutionary tomes of antiauthority anger that raged against the institutional American machine. In 1964, he took cross-country trips in an old school bus, painted in wild colors, with the word "Furthur" in orange placed above the windshield, matched by a sign on the rear of the bus that declared: "Caution: Weird Load," with most of those onboard tripping on acid, high on pot or booze, or a combination.

After getting busted for pot, Kesey decided to stick it to the man by hosting "Acid Parties" at his home in La Honda, California, where he'd lived since 1962. He asked his friend, gonzo journalist Hunter S. Thompson, to introduce him to the Hells Angels motorcycle gang to further accelerate the level of anarchy of his revolutionary intentions. Thompson's *Hell's Angels: The Strange and Terrible Saga of the Outlaw Motorcycle Gangs*, a New Journalism tour de force and a true insider's account of the anarchist motorcycle gang, would be published in 1967.

Kesey became the catalyst to unite the antiauthority forces of the Hells Angels with the proto-hippie California acid heads, masterfully documented by the dandy of New Journalism, Tom Wolfe, in his epic *The Electric Kool-Aid Acid Test*, published in 1968, just as the acid scene was turning to violent revolution. Kesey also began hosting acid tests outside his home in November 1965; at the first show, the music was supplied by a local group called the Warlocks, who would morph into the Grateful Dead.

October 1965 saw the Family Dog collective hold a dance concert, billed as a "Tribute to Dr. Strange," at the Longshoremen's Hall in San Francisco, which included performances by the Jefferson Airplane, the Charlatans, and the Great Society. Chet Helms was the main organizer of the Family Dog. Like Bill Graham, he would put on shows, mostly at the Avalon Ballroom in San Francisco, that were a social gathering of the emerging hippie tribes. These shows featured the new underground bands in a concert or dance event in an atmosphere resplendent with the new psychedelic light shows and other groundbreaking ways to present music. In November 1965, Bill Graham would throw a benefit concert for the San Francisco Mime Troupe. Graham was the group's business manager and the event, held at the troupe's Minna Street loft and featuring the music of the Jefferson Airplane, Mystery Trend, and the Fugs, would ultimately be the catalyst for Graham to start staging concerts in the city, eventually leading to the opening of the Fillmore West. The Fillmore West (later joined by New York's Fillmore East) would become the unrivaled temple of rock music venues. Often offering triple bills that featured folk, blues, jazz, and other kinds of music along with rock, the venue offered superior sound, a psychedelic light show, and free concert programs and posters that are now collectible artifacts of the 1960s psychedelic scene. Graham was a stickler for creating a unique experience. Every night, while the strains of "Greensleeves" was played as the last notes of the last act faded away, free apples were placed in tubs for fans to take on the way out.

Graham held a second San Francisco Mime Troupe Appeal Party on December 10, with the Warlocks now appearing as the Grateful Dead, at the Fillmore, along with the Jefferson Airplane, the Great Society, the John Handy Quintet, the Mystery Trend, and Sam Thomas. On February 4, 1966, Graham held his first nonbenefit show at the Fillmore with the Jefferson Airplane. Starting in the spring, other key San Francisco venues, such as the Avalon Ballroom and Winterland, would present the new San Francisco groups and other hip new sounds.

Long before Kesey's parties and acid tests, Dr. Timothy Leary was turning on, tuning in, and dropping out in a nondescript enclave of rural New York innocuously called Millbrook. Leary had been turned on to acid and psilocybin in 1961 by an Englishman, Michael Hollingshead, who was a researcher at Harvard.

Hollingshead and New Zealand–born John Esam were key figures in helping London turn on to LSD at this time. Esam was a filmmaker (he's credited as an assistant director for his work on *Tonite Lets All Make Love in London*), poet, early exponent of what would now be called the new age, mind-body-spirit movement, acid evangelist, and the first person to be arrested in England for selling LSD, along with DMT, in 1966. LSD would be made illegal in England in 1966.

Dr. John Beresford, assistant professor of pediatrics at the New York Medical College, gave Hollingshead his first dose of LSD; Beresford later became a scientist researching the effects of psychedelics at the Agora Scientific Trust, which he also founded. And it was none other than fellow Brit, the writer Aldous Huxley, who suggested that Hollingshead pass on the drug to Leary. Hollingshead met with Leary in Cambridge, Massachusetts, where Leary was working as a clinical psychologist at Harvard University. The two, along with Ralph Metzner, a German psychologist, worked on the Concord Prison Experiment to see if psilocybin could be used to reform prisoners and those who displayed antisocial behavior.

In 1963, Leary came in contact with members of the Boston folk scene and Mel Lyman of the Jim Kewskin Jug Band. Lyman became an early advocate of LSD among the Boston folk community.

Leary, Hollingshead, Metzner, and Richard Alpert, an American psychologist, spiritualist, and author of the seminal *Be Here Now* who would later be known as Ram Dass, all gathered together at Millbrook to further their study, teaching, and experiments. Along with Jean Houston, an American author who along with her husband, Robert Masters, cofounded The Foundation for Mind Research and were part of the Human Potential Movement, supplied guided trips to volunteers and gathered data on their experiences. Hollingshead eventually moved to London in 1965 and opened up the World Psychedelic Center. It was there that Hollingshead helped turn England on, bringing with him copies of the books *The Psychedelic Reader*, edited by Leary, Metzner, and Gunther M. Weil, and *The Psychedelic Experience: A Manual Based on the Tibetan Book of the Dead* by Leary and Metzner.

London was ripe for Hollingshead's arrival. On June 11, 1965, at the Royal Albert Hall, a poetry reading boldly called Poets of the World/Poets of Our Time, International Poetry Incarnation was held—more a psychedelic awakening than a stuffy literary gathering. Allen Ginsberg, beat poet éminence grise, a key figure in the transition from 1950s beat to 1960s hippie and a budding Dylan crony, was one of the stars of the evening, which brought together the tweedy hip literati and the emerging woolly underground. While in London, Ginsberg gave an unadvertised reading at Better Books in Soho, run by Barry Miles. Better Books paperback section manager Bob Cobbing also launched the London Film Makers Co-op, along with several others, modeled after the New York Co-op, in October 1966. The Co-op would move to the Arts Lab, where alternative film fare was screened.

The Poets of the World/Poets of Our Time, International Poetry Incarnation event was standing room only and included Andy Warhol and his Factory superstars tragic trust-fund beauty Edie Sedgwick and wild man Gerard Malanga, along with music from Donovan and his running buddy Gypsy Dave. The Albert Hall event was a chaotic happening that saw dancing schizophrenic patients brought there by renowned psychiatrist R. D. Laing, together with a performance by English cult guitar hero Davy Graham; Indira Gandhi, the future prime minister of India; the cream of the San Francisco Renaissance poets, including Lawrence Ferlinghetti and Gregory Corso; and poets from Denmark and Russia. Of all those who performed, it was Austrian writer, translator, and experimental sound poem poet Ernst Jandl, who, by all accounts of those who were there, stole the show from Ginsberg.

Much later, Ginsberg would spend time at Paul McCartney's house in July 1967, beginning a lifelong relationship between the two that also resulted in musical collaborations.

Back at Hollingshead's World Psychedelic Center, his modest digs were becoming a haven for writers like beat novelist William S. Burroughs, the poet Alexander Trocchi, the surrealist artist Sir Roland Penrose, and budding British art scene-makers Christopher Gibbs and Robert Fraser. Fraser, who would come to be known by some as Groovy Bob, would introduce Paul McCartney to many artists, including Andy Warhol, who showed the Beatle his film *Chelsea Girls* at Paul's home on Cavendish Avenue. Gibbs would later be the set design advisor on the notorious film *Performance* starring Mick Jagger.

Donovan dropped in at the World Psychedelic Center, as did Eric Clapton, Paul McCartney, and Peter Asher, one half of Peter and Gordon (and Jane Asher's brother). In 1966, Burroughs did some experimental recordings at 34 Montagu Square. The flat was purchased by Ringo in 1965; though he soon left for London's suburbs, he retained ownership of the premises until 1969. While Ian Sommerville, William Burroughs's lover, cut-up collaborator, and computer software pioneer, was living at Montagu Square, he helped McCartney, set up an experimental sound studio in the flat for impromptu recordings, including his own. McCartney cut early demos of "Eleanor Rigby" at the flat. McCartney was also making short films, including *The Defeat of the Dog* and *The Next Spring Then*. It was a gathering place that attracted the Indica Books brain trust of Peter Ascher, Barry Miles, John Dunbar, and McCartney.

The two films that Burroughs did with Antony Balch, *Towers Open Fire* and *Cuts Up*, were screened regularly at UFO. The UFO Club was launched by John "Hoppy" Hopkins and the young American folk and jazz music business entrepreneur Joe Boyd. Although it was an Irish dance hall during the week, the UFO Club would offer the same kind of "happening" experience as the Fillmore in San Francisco, providing a space for the emerging British psychedelic counterculture kids to dance, drop acid, smoke pot, and listen to the newest bands, most notably the Soft Machine and the Pink Floyd Sound. Like the Fillmore, psychedelic art posters were made for various events, primarily by Michael English and Nigel Waymouth, who worked as a collective better known as Hapshash and the Coloured Coat, "Hapshash" partly taken from the Egyptian Queen Hatshepsut with the words "hash" mixed in. English attended Ealing School of Art with Pete Townshend of the Who. The duo also did album covers and even recorded several albums under their nom de plume. The UFO Club eventually moved to the Roundhouse in early August and folded in less than two months. Brit Balch distributed Tod Browning's cult classic *Freaks* in 1963. Other experimental films shown at UFO include the five-part *Dog Star Man* by Stan Brakhage, produced between 1961 and 1964, and the short *Bells of Atlantis* from 1952, featuring a naked Anaïs Nin and directed by her husband Hugh Parker Guiler, who was known as Ian Hugo.

World Psychedelic Center wouldn't last long, but a new bookshop/art gallery would become the destination for those seeking new modes of expression and lifestyle. Indica Books & Gallery grew out of the salon begun by John Dunbar who had been art critic for *The Scotsman* and his then-wife Marianne Faithfull. Dunbar, along with Barry Miles and Peter Asher, formed a company, Miles, Asher and Dunbar Limited (MAD), and opened Indica in March 1966. The gallery/bookshop was at 6 Mason's Yard, off Duke Street, just a few doors down from the club Scotch of St. James, though the bookstore would soon separate from the gallery and move to 102 Southampton Row. Anything was possible for the new space; Paul McCartney had invested £5,000 in the enterprise and helped out by building the shop's bookcases and designing its wrapping paper.

According to an advert, reproduced in *The Beatles London*, beginning on November 8, 1966, Yoko Ono held an exhibition at the Indica Gallery that ran through until the 18th. It was at this exhibit (*Unfinished Paintings*) where she officially met John Lennon. The specific date has been stated as November 9, with that date being a preview of the exhibit, prior to its official opening. If it had been at the so-called preview, it would have been on the 7th, but that's the day that John and Cynthia returned from Spain, where Lennon was filming *How I Won the War*. Barry Miles, a key figure connected to the Indica Gallery, in his book *The Beatles Dairy*, also states their meeting date as November 9th.

Going back to *Rubber Soul* and the seeds of the group's psychedelic flowering, the track "Norwegian Wood (This Bird Has Flown)," was an early indication of the group's future psychedelic direction. The track contains what has often been credited as the first use of a sitar on a Western pop recording (played by George Harrison), although sitar music not performed by the Beatles also appears on the US *Help!* soundtrack album. In fact, the producer on this session, George Martin, used sitar as back as 1959 on a track by Peter Sellers, titled "Wouldn't It Be Loverly."

"Norwegian Wood" and the single "Day Tripper," both largely written by John, were influenced by his increasing use of LSD. "Nowhere Man," from *Rubber Soul*, also fit in somewhat lyrically and more musically with the emerging psychedelic song genre.

A UK artist who was creating music even closer to the still-underground psychedelic sound was Donovan, who was from Scotland. While strains of psychedelia had been subtly emerging from the Yardbirds since Jeff Beck joined in 1965, with his guitar on "Heart Full of Soul," having been used to replace a poor sitar part. There also was the Kinks' track "See My Friends," which may have unintentionally had shades of psyche-delia. But Donovan's beatnik folk already reflected an underground sound, one that was initially heavily inspired by Bob Dylan, as his spring 1965 hit "Catch the Wind" readily illustrated. Donovan's album *Fairytales* (1965), with songs like "Sunny Goodge Street," reflected a more impressionistic sound that seemed to be moving away from his folk sound. It wouldn't be until his 1966 single, "Sunshine Superman"/"The Trip," that the full flowering of his popular psychedelic sound would emerge.

Another less well-known artist exploring psychedelia was New York–born folk artist Sandy Bull. Bull, who moved from New York to Boston, then returned to Manhattan's Greenwich Village, and then took off for San Francisco, released the album *Fantasias for Guitar and Banjo* on Vanguard Records in June 1963, and that, long before "Norwegian Wood," had a raga feel. He also came up with a dazzling follow-up *Inventions* in 1965.

The Fugs ("fug" being a euphemism Norman Mailer used for a certain four-letter word in his novel *The Naked and the Dead* [1948]) mixed folk with a myriad of other styles that foreshadowed underground music. Their debut, *The Fugs First Album*, was released in 1965.

Pink Floyd began in fall 1965 at Cambridge University as the Pink Floyd Sound, the name Pink Floyd borrowed from two American blues musicians, Pink Anderson, from South Carolina, and Floyd Council, from North Carolina and with Pink and Floyd, bestowed upon, respectively, Syd Barrett's two cats.

The Beatles remained very much out of the public eye early in 1966, as the locomotive that was the underground counterculture was picking up steam in myriad ways. In January 8, at the Fillmore auditorium, Kesey and his band of Merry Pranksters held the first official public acid test, with music by the Grateful Dead; among those in attendance was Neal Cassady, the real-life model for the character of Dean Moriarty in Jack Kerouac's beat manifesto *On the Road*. This was followed by the Trips Festival at the Longshoreman's Hall from January 21 to 23, featuring the Grateful Dead, Big Brother and the Holding Company, and the Loading Zone. The Family Dog collective, led by Chet Helms, put on a concert at the Fillmore called the First Tribal Stomp, featuring the Grateful Dead and Big Brother and the Holding Company. In April, Helms opened up the Avalon Ballroom, which, like the Fillmore, offered an eclectic mix of music in a rarified atmosphere; the venue operated until 1968. In June, Big Brother would go through a major change when they played their first gigs with their new lead singer, a raunchy blues singer from Texas named Janis Joplin.

Back in England, the London Free School opened in March 1966, an altruistic attempt to educate London's poor. Peter Jenner, who would go on to comanage Pink Floyd and the iconoclastic John "Hoppy" Hopkins, had returned to England from New York in 1965, having been inspired by New York's Free University. Hopkins's girlfriend was Suzie Creamcheese (Suzie Zeiger), immortalized by Frank Zappa in several songs and subsequently portrayed on Zappa albums and in performances by several women. The landlord of the building where the school was located was writer and underground culture iconoclast John Michell. Hoppy, who worked on the Free School's newspaper *The Gate*, launched England's first underground newspaper *The International Times*, which began in the basement of the Indica Books & Gallery, partially funded by Paul McCartney, in October 1966; Hoppy celebrated with a concert at the Roundhouse featuring Pink Floyd and the Soft Machine. He even played piano on *The 5000 Spirits or the Layers of the Onion*, the second album from the Incredible String Band, which was produced by Joe Boyd, who started up the UFO Club with Hoppy.

The Yardbirds continued to be at the forefront of the new sounds emerging on the scene with their single "Shape of Things to Come" released in February. From Los Angeles, the group Love released their self-titled debut album in March and immediately established themselves as a band with a new sound and a new look. With their second album, *Da Capo*, released in November 1966, they became a psychedelic force, particularly as the song "Revelation" took up the entirety of side 2, lasting nearly 19 minutes. The Byrds also continued to be the band that some thought were America's answer to the Beatles, releasing "Eight Miles High" in March.

While San Francisco was the epicenter of the emerging counterculture in America, *Time* magazine's issue of April 15 pointed out another locale, named in a diagonal banner headline on its cover: "London: The Swinging City." The accompanying article was by Piri Halasz, author of the book *A Swingers Guide to London* (no, not that those kinds of swingers). *Time*'s cover art collage was by Liverpool-born *Punch* magazine cartoonist Geoffrey Dickinson and featured references to the Who, the film *Alfie*, other images that reflected the new youth explosion in London, and iconic symbols of London like Big Ben, a red double-decker bus, and the Union Jack. The article, credited as the first *Time* magazine cover story to be written by a women, brought together all the strands of life, art, and culture that made London the center of the cultural universe, although oddly, some felt that *Time* was a bit late to the party, and the article, in typical *Time* fashion, did seem a little ground down to be understood by the masses.

Stateside, San Francisco had quickly supplanted New York and Los Angeles as the place to be. The Jefferson Airplane, whose live shows were gaining lots of attention, became the first of the local groups to land a recording contract, releasing the single "It's No Secret/Runnin' Round This World" in February 1966 and their debut album *Jefferson Airplane Takes Off* in August 1966. It was the only album to feature Signe Anderson as lead singer; soon after its release, she was replaced by Grace Slick of San Francisco group the Great Society, which included her husband Jerry Slick and Jerry's brother Darby Slick. Drummer Skip Spence would also depart Jefferson Airplane after the first album (replaced by Spencer Dryden), stepping out from behind the drum kit to form Moby Grape early in 1967; their seminal self-titled debut album was released in June of that year. The rest of the Jefferson Airplane lineup would consist of Slick's future husband Paul Kantner, the aforementioned Marty Balin, bassist Jack Cassady, and guitarist Jorma Kaukonen.

The Beatles began recording what was to become their *Revolver* album on April 6. They emerged from the studio on May 1 to play a perfunctory 15-minute, six-song set at the NME Poll Winners concert at London's Empire Pool. Their performance was not filmed, and they did not play any of the new material they were working on. The double A-sided single, "Paperback Writer"/"Rain," was released May 30. While "Paperback Writer" was not far from the catchy pop of such previous tracks as "I Feel Fine," "Ticket to Ride," and "Day Tripper," "Rain" was a continuation of the new sound they only hinted at on "Norwegian Wood"—a portent of the musical shape of things to come. Again, Lennon led the group in the new direction, but with George Harrison's evocative guitar and what is arguably the best interplay on any Beatles track between Paul's bass playing and Ringo's drumming make it one of the most sublime works in the entire Beatles canon. Unfortunately, the single's release would be a high-water mark for the group in that period, with their ill-fated Japanese, Philippine, and US tours lurking in the future.

While Beatles fans would have to wait until early August for the arrival of *Revolver*, the psychedelic album was becoming more ubiquitous. The West Coast Pop Art Experimental Band released their debut album, *Volume 1*, in June. Two other albums came out that, although not strictly psychedelic works, changed the game completely. The Beach Boys released *Pet Sounds* on May 16 and Dylan's monumental double album *Blonde on Blonde* followed on June 20. The Mothers of Invention, based in Los Angeles and led by the iconoclastic and satirical mad genius guitar god Frank Zappa, released their own double album, the aptly titled *Freak Out!* on June 27. The album both reflected and parodied the emerging hippie counterculture. Zappa relished pricking the hippies in the 1960s, as much as he did the right wing in later years.

While all the juice seemed to be coming from American bands, the Yardbirds came out with their self-titled album in 1966, often referred to as *Roger the Engineer*. Eastern musical influences, deft production by the group's bassist Paul Samwell-Smith, and Jeff Beck's experimental, innovative, dexterous, and revolutionary guitar playing made the album a work that would eventually transcend not only pop and psychedelia but also the 1960s. The Yardbirds too often are best known for creating a home for three of the greatest guitarists in rock—Clapton, Beck, and Page—while not being credited enough for creating inventive and forward-thinking music, long before almost all their psychedelic peers.

Albums that were not from musical artists per se include *LSD*, a cautionary spoken-word album about the new LSD cult, mixed in with music from the group Fire and Ice (released on Capitol Records in July) and Timothy Leary's first album *The Psychedelic Experience*. Leary would be immortalized on vinyl on the 1968 album *In Search of the Lost Chord*, the second album from the revamped symphonic British psychedelic group The Moody Blues. In the song "Legend of a Mind," written by Ray Thomas. The lyrics "Timothy Leary's dead / no, n-n-no he's outside looking in" reflected Leary's acid visions and philosophical mysticism. Until Thomas retired from touring with the group, the song was a favorite of the group's live shows. The Byrds released their most overtly psychedelic album, *Fifth Dimension*, in July, which included the previously released single "Eight Miles High" and the cosmic space pop of "Mr. Spaceman."

Another album not generally considered psychedelic was *East West*, the second album from the Paul Butterfield Blues Band. The 13-minute closing title track features guitar jamming by Mike Bloomfield and Elvin Bishop alongside Eastern influences that make it fit snugly with the psychedelic music movement. Simon and Garfunkel's third album, *Parsley, Sage, Rosemary and Thyme*, released in October 1966, was the one that solidified their sound and also a defining album of the folk-rock genre, showcasing new forms of songwriting that was reshaping the narrow definition of what constituted pop music, with shades of art-song and baroque pop.

The group that most defined the prevalent folk-rock sound were the Mamas and the Papas, who released two albums in 1966, *If You Can Believe Your Eyes and Ears* and *The Mamas & the Papas*. The songs by John Philips, the harmonies, particularly the singing of Cass Elliot and Denny Doherty, and Lou Adler's deft production transcended genres and defied the popular/underground schism.

Back on the East Coast, the Blues Project also released two albums in 1966, *Live at The Cafe Au Go Go* and *Projections*. While not strictly psychedelia, the group's long improvisations, New York underground influences, and Al Kooper and Mike Bloomfield's relationship with Bob Dylan marked the band as one of the hippest on the scene.

Then there was what on the surface appeared to be nothing, made-for-TV sellout and pale imitation of the Beatles and Beatlemania, the Monkees. The success of *The Monkees* TV show led to the program's characters becoming a real band, their music getting better with each album. They even had the Jimi Hendrix Experience open for them in July 1967. The Experience didn't last long on the tour because fans of the Monkees didn't like Hendrix, and he became embittered by the treatment. It has been suggested that Hendrix was kicked off the tour, but it may be that he quit. A line can be drawn directly from the explosion of the Beatles, particularly *A Hard Day's Night*, to the Monkees. *A Hard Day's Night* was the proof that producers Bob Rafelson and Bert Schneider used to get the television show *The Monkees* financed because they had already wanted to make a movie or television show about a pop group. While the conventions of situation comedy and the standards set by previous shows that used pop music as part of their format were part of the formula, Rafelson and Schneider tapped into the 1960s youthquake that the Beatles detonated. It helped that they enlisted Brill Building veteran Don Kirshner to recruit crack West Coast session musicians and mostly East Coast teen pop songwriters to create quality hits that have stood the test of time.

By the time the Monkees were ready to make their only film, *Head*, their TV show had been canceled (the final episode aired March 25, 1968). So rather than remaking *A Hard Day's Night* or *Help!*, they did a more revolutionary *Magical Mystery Tour*, that was just as surreal but more American in its antiauthority, antiwar stance. On its release in November 1968, it was met with little critical or box-office acclaim and must have been confusing for the teenybopper fans of the *Monkees* television show, but it had a great soundtrack album and over the years has become regarded as an important mainstream psychedelic film. It also launched the careers of its producers and Jack Nicholson, who cowrote the script with Rafelson and Schneider. Schneider would go on to produce such key American films of the 1960s and 1970s as *Easy Rider* (directed by Dennis Hopper), *Five Easy Pieces*, *The Last Picture Show* (directed by Peter Bogdanovich), *The King of Marvin Gardens*, and *Days of Heaven* (directed by Terrence Malick). Rafelson would also direct *Five Easy Pieces* and *King of Marvin Gardens*, and go on to do the 1981 remake of *The Postman Always Rings Twice* with Jack Nicholson. Nicholson's career would explode over the next several decades as one of the greatest screen actors of all time. It's also significant to note that while *A Hard Day's Night* was an early influence on MTV and music videos (*The Monkees* being another influence), former Monkee Michael Nesmith's specific contribution might be even more significant. In 1981 he wrote and produced *Elephant Parts*, a collection of music videos, sketches, and parody commercials that was the most direct and substantial antecedent of MTV.

As 1966 would draw to a close, Buffalo Springfield, like the Byrds before them, would lay out a blueprint for the merging of rock, pop, country, and folk that would resonate for years and spawn countless successful groups in the 1970s.

In England, *Blues Breakers with Eric Clapton*, the debut album from John Mayall's new band, put British blues on the map, solidified Eric Clapton's place as England's reigning guitar god, and alerted the music world to a group that through many lineup changes would be integral to the evolution of British rock. John McVie, Mick Fleetwood, Peter Green, Mick Taylor, and many others would eventually launch their own bands or go on to superstardom with others.

On the English folk scene, while Bert Jansch and John Renbourn were inventing and reinventing British folk, the self-titled debut album from the Incredible String Band set the group up to transcend English folk and be at the forefront of the new psychedelic sound within a year. The mod music scene, while part of the Swinging London pop scene with bands like the Creation, the Small Faces, and the Action, who formed in 1963, would never measure up to the success of the Who. The Who released *A Quick One* at the end of 1966, which pointed the way forward for the group. The album that really exploded at the end of 1966 was *Fresh Cream*, released on December 23, 1966. It was the debut album from the Cream, comprised of Eric Clapton, Ginger Baker, and Jack Bruce. While on the surface a continuation of the evolution of the British blues scene, the short-lived group would become integral to the British psychedelic explosion.

America has had a long history of alternative media sources. One of the key American media sources that was primarily born and flourished in California was Pacifica Radio, which started in the 1940s. By the 1950s, it was an important broadcast media force, giving voice to the burgeoning postwar generation and strongly championing the Beats in the 1950s. In New York, Pacifica station WBAI featured Bob Fass, one of the first people on radio to interview Bob Dylan.

In 1966, the FCC decreed that FM radio stations must stop simply duplicating their AM programming and create new programming to add diversity to the FM band. This couldn't have come at a more opportune time because the underground counterculture was flowering. Launching its new format in 1966, WOR-FM in New York is often credited as being the first commercial progressive FM radio station, although community radio stations were already adopting the elements that would drive underground and progressive radio for years, including playing a wide variety of music, often as long sets with no commercial breaks. The DJs were subdued, hip-talking, but sincere music avatars and the presentation of commercials (if there were any) and other information, such as news, was vastly changed to cater to the tastes of the burgeoning counterculture.

San Francisco was also the home of the burgeoning underground media with the launch of the *Berkley Barb*, which debuted in August 1965. In September 1966, the *San Francisco Oracle* published its first issue and, like the *Berkeley Barb*, offered a literary alternative that reflected the new countercultural underground.

The year that changed everything was 1967, and the counterculture reached a critical mass. In October, the psychedelic music movement continued to gain momentum through autumn 1966, with the Blues Magoos releasing their *Psychedelic Lollipop* album and the Beach Boys releasing the single "Good Vibrations." In November, the 13th Floor Elevators released *Psychedelic Sounds*, though the group still had an edgier garage rock sound. The Misunderstood released the single "I Can Take You to the Sun" in December 1966, England's second big psychedelic single after Donovan's "Sunshine Superman," although not as popular.

While all the psychedelic sunshine seemed to be burning brightly in London and San Francisco, another LA band joined major label band Love with an album that brought the underground one step closer to the mainstream. The group's members included two former UCLA film students, and their name was inspired by British author Aldous Huxley, who, like George Orwell was open to new ideas in chemical mind alterations. Like Love, they also recorded for what used to be an independent folk label, Elektra. That group was the Doors.

Huxley's book, *The Doors of Perception* was published in 1954. It was the idea of rearranging one's senses in a dramatic way that most appealed to Jim Morrison and his fellow film student Ray Manzarek when choosing the band's name. The self-titled debut album from The Doors appeared in January 1967 and joined *Revolver*, *Fifth Dimension*, and *Sunshine Superman* (not released yet in the UK) as major label psychedelic releases that spawned hit songs. "Light My Fire," although trimmed down from the album version for single release, was a major hit. Other songs on the album, such as "Crystal Ship" and the 11-minute "The End," reflected the darker elements of the burgeoning acid culture, but with songs like "Break on Through" and two covers, it was clear that this was a group that wouldn't be confined to psychedelia. Finally, the group's lead singer, Jim Morrison, was the first person to come along who could compete with or even rival Mick Jagger in pure rock sex appeal. The group would release their second album, *Strange Days*, in December.

February 1967 would see the next major label psychedelic album released, with the aforementioned *Surrealistic Pillow* from the Jefferson Airplane. Their second album now featured vocals from Grace Slick, formerly of the Great Society. The Great Society had previously recorded Slick's songs, "Somebody to Love" and "White

Rabbit"; now, rerecorded by Jefferson Airplane, both became huge hits. "White Rabbit" was yet another instance where Lewis Carroll, influenced an aspect of the psychedelic explosion, with *Through the Looking Glass and What Alice Found There* being the source for the Jefferson Airplane song.

Also in February, San Francisco followed in the footsteps of New York by launching its first commercial underground FM station, when KMPX switched formats with Larry Miller unofficially launching the format on his overnight show. The new sound then became the station's new format through the efforts of the man that truly put the format on the map, Tom Donahue.

Another entry in the underground magazine scene happened in February with the launch of the hip underground newspaper *Oz* in London, started by Australians Richard Neville and Marti Sharp. *Oz* was a bit more upscale and put a greater emphasis on its graphic presentation. The Australian *Oz* staff were a part of yet another group of people outside of England who became part of the British countercultural firmament, including such wide-ranging Aussies as Robert Whitaker, who would bring a zany edge to his photos of the Beatles (including their infamous "Butcher Cover" photo), the writer and feminist icon Germaine Greer, peerless art critic Robert Hughes, and writer Clive James.

WHAT'S IT ALL ABOUT?

In 1966, the movies would also go through a rapid change. The Beatles, the ever-expanding British Invasion, and Swinging London along with the British movie scene were all thriving. Two films of this time were era-defining movies that still resonate today: *Alfie* and *Blow-up*. While *Zulu* (1964) established Michael Caine's acting prowess, and *The Ipcress File* (1965) put him on the map with the role of Harry Palmer (and he'd return as Harry Palmer in two more pictures), *Alfie* made him an international star, and he has never looked back. The film was directed by Lewis Gilbert, who would go on to do *You Only Live Twice*, the first of three Bond films he'd direct, the 1970 film *Friends*, featuring a soundtrack by Elton John, and *Educating Rita*, among others. *Alfie*'s screenplay was by Bill Naughton, which was adapted from his own play. Otto Heller, who began his 50-year career in movies early in 1920s during the silent era, was the cinematographer. The title song, by Burt Bacharach and Hal David, was sung over the closing credits by Cher in the US release, and Millicent Martin (who also played Siddie in the film) in the British release. Dionne Warwick and Cilla Black also recorded hit versions of the song. The soundtrack also featured the music of Sonny Rollins. Interestingly, Shirley Bassey, of Bond themes fame, has a small uncredited role in the film. It is easily one of the best soundtracks for a British film produced in the 1960s. American Shelley Winters also starred in the film, and two other actresses have connections to the Beatles: Jane Asher, who was Paul Mc-Cartney's girlfriend, and *Help!* costar Eleanor Bron, making her second feature film appearance. The film captured the shifting landscapes of the sexual revolution, and Caine's portrayal of the swinging womanizer is one of the most important roles by an actor in a British film in the 1960s. Caine's first memoir, published in 1992, was named after the opening lyric of the title song, *What's It All about?*

The second movie that reflected a seismic change in film in the 1960s was *Blow-Up*, directed by Michelangelo Antonioni, released in the US on December 18, 1966, and in the UK in March 1967. An Italian/American/British production, and Antonioni's first all English-language film, the movie was set in London and starred British actors David Hemmings, Vanessa Redgrave, and Sarah Miles. The idea for *Blow-Up* actually began with producer Carlo Ponti. Inspired by a Francis Wyndham article on young Swinging London photographers such as David Bailey that he'd seen in the *Guardian*, he began developing a film idea. He also drew from the short story *The Devil's Spittle* by Julio Cortázar, a writer associated with a Latin American boom in literature from Argentina that also included Gabriel García Márquez, Mario Vargas Llosa, and Carlos Fuentes. At one point, Ponti even approached David Bailey to make the film, but it didn't pan out. Making a film with a photographer as the lead made the choice of cinematographer especially important, and Antonioni chose Carlo Di Palma. Like *Alfie*, the film's score was by a master of modern American jazz, Herbie Hancock. One track was by the Yardbirds, one of the few recordings when Jimmy Page and Jeff Beck were both in the group; the band's performance in the film features Beck destroying his guitar à la Pete Townshend. The Yardbirds were more or less a stand-in for the Who, as Hemmings was basically playing Bailey. Antonioni's trilogy *L'Avventura* (1960), *La Notte* (1961), and *L'Eclisse* (1962) established him as the European master of enigmatic cinema, and *Blow-Up* won the Palme d'Or for best movie at the 1967 Cannes Film Festival and made Antonioni a major influence on the films of the 1960s. The director would show the film to Paul McCartney at his Cavendish Avenue home.

Blow-Up was an amalgamation of many film forms and reflected both the nihilistic vapidity of the new permissiveness and the simmering political discontent to come. At its heart, it is a stylish, yet impressionistic murder mystery, with an emphasis on exploring and challenging visual meanings, and is filled with confounding and perplexing narrative detours. It's an existential voyeuristic parable of the new media age, and layers of meaning can still be drawn from the film today. Antonioni would explore some of the same themes in *Zabriske Point* (1970), with an impressive soundtrack that boasted music by the Rolling Stones, Pink Floyd, Jerry Garcia and the Grateful Dead, the Youngbloods, Kaleidoscope, and John Fahey. *Blow-Up* was partly an inspiration for parts of the Austin Powers movies—for example, when Austin Powers in the first film, *Austin Powers: International Man of Mystery*, parodies the photographer in *Blow-Up*.

One of the filmmakers who was a major part of the new British cinema was Karel Reisz, who directed *Morgan—A Suitable Case for Treatment* in 1966. Only the third of the four movies he directed in the 1960s, the surrealist film is a dark comedic fantasy that earned Vanessa Redgrave an Oscar nomination for best actress; the film was also nominated for best costume design. More importantly, it was also nominated for the Palme d'Or at the Cannes Film Festival, where Redgrave won the Best Actress award.

David Warner plays Morgan, whose wife is leaving him for his gallery-owning friend. The down-on-his-luck artist spends most of the film trying to win her back and going completely mad in the process. The film strikes the perfect chord of comedy and spiraling insanity. The ending is eerily similar in outcome and tone to *The Graduate*, no doubt coincidentally. Redgrave made her film debut in *Behind the Mask* in 1958, and spent the next eight years on the stage; in 1966, along with *Morgan* and *Blow-Up*, she also appeared in *A Man for All Seasons*.

Georgy Girl was another movie that fit in with the new British film wave. The film starred Vanessa's sister Lynn Redgrave, Charlotte Rampling in her first credited screen role, veteran actor James Mason, and Alan Bates in yet another star turn that began with his first credited screen role in 1960's *The Entertainer*. The film was very much in the same vein as *Smashing Time* (1967), which costarred Redgrave and Rita Tushingham, Redgrave playing the provincial ugly duckling heading off to the swinging big city of London. *Georgy Girl*'s theme song, by Australian group the Seekers, was a bubbly and frothy international hit that, like Lulu's recording of the theme song of *To Sir, with Love*, perfectly captured the spirit of the film and the times. Note that Lulu's hit single version differs from the version performed in the film.

Michael Caine's second turn as Harry Palmer came in *Funeral in Berlin*, a film that although not the equal of *The Ipcress File*, was much better than the third Palmer film, *Billion Dollar Brain*. Caine appeared in two other films in 1966: *The Wrong Box*, directed by Bryan Forbes, and *Gambit*, an American film directed by Brit Ronald Neame.

Modesty Blaise was emblematic of the Swinging London school of spy spoof films. The uneven, yet entertaining film was oddly directed by Joseph Losey, who normally made more dramatic films or witty comedies, and unfortunately was obviously out of his element. But the film's stars weren't. Italian actress Monica Vitti, British legend Dirk Bogarde, and hot newcomer Terence Stamp make the best of a script that was punched up by an uncredited Harold Pinter. The film was nominated for the Palme d'Or at the Cannes Film Festival, although it never had a chance.

Other 1966 British films worth noting include Roman Polanski's *Cul-de-Sac*, his follow-up to *Repulsion*; the stylish crime caper *Kaleidoscope*, starring American Warren Beatty; the uneven Peter Sellers comedy *After the Fox*; the family film *Born Free*; *Fahrenheit 451*, based on Ray Bradbury's novel, a British production directed by Francois Truffaut and starring Julie Christie; and *The Quiller Memorandum*, a spy movie that is rescued by great music (by John Barry), a smart script (by Harold Pinter), a host of fine actors whose backstories don't always mesh (George Segal, Alec Guinness, Max von Sydow, and Austrian bombshell Senta Berger), and deft direction by Michael Anderson. Although somewhat of a lightweight spy spoof, *Our Man in Marrakesh*, starring American Tony Randall, is a likeable film and also included Brits Herbert Lom, Wilfrid Hyde-White, Terry-Thomas, Senta Berger, and German bad guy Klaus Kinski hot off *For a Few Dollars More* and *Doctor Zhivago*. *The Jokers* was yet another caper satire, masquerading as a Swinging London film, with yet another deft directorial touch by Michael Winner and featuring an expansive cast led by Oliver Reed, Michael Crawford, and Ingrid Boulting of the British film Boulting family.

Richard Lester had now left the Beatles and John Lennon behind and come out with an adaption of the stage musical *A Funny Thing Happened on the Way to the Forum*, while Paul McCartney did the music for film *The Family Way*.

One would think by now that the American movie industry would start seeking to make changes in the kind of films they made, given the ever-increasing sophistication and awareness of the new generation of filmmakers and filmgoers in Europe and England. While youth exploitation films like *The Wild Angels*, films from emerging directors like Francis Ford Coppola (*You're a Big Boy Now*) and Woody Allen (*What's Up, Tiger Lily?*), documentaries like *The Endless Summer*, and even *Chelsea Girls*, Andy Warhol's first film to receive more than just underground attention all showed signs that American film companies were waking up and smelling the espresso (or marijuana) or at least the scent of money by 1966, things were still pretty much the same. Coppola's second movie, *You're a Big Boy Now*, was admittedly influenced by Richard Lester. He initially wanted the Mamas and the Papas to provide the film's music, but the New York–based Lovin' Spoonful actually worked better because the entire film was shot on location in Manhattan. Woody Allen also tapped the Lovin' Spoonful for one of his film soundtracks, and *The Endless Summer* featured the surf rock music of The Sandals.

While UA's profits continued to soar, Paramount continued to expand their British production, and Bud Ornstein was now firmly in place at the company. As Warner was expanding their British production, Seven Arts acquired a third of the company. There were several entries into the spy spoof genre with Dean Martin playing an American version of Bond, almost strictly for laughs and kisses, as Matt Helm in *The Silencers*. James Coburn as Derek Flint in *Our Man Flint*, while a clear Bond knockoff, was actually quite entertaining and more than just a spoof. *Arabesque*, with Gregory Peck and Sophia Loren and very much in the mold of *Charade* from 1963, sought to avoid the spy spoof genre and, although hardly very original or new, was also quite entertaining. Both films were directed by American Stanley Donen, who brought a glittering American polish to both films. The cinematographer on

Arabesque was Christopher Challis. He had been a cinematographer since 1947 and a director of photography since the mid-1950s. Along with spy films such as *A Shot in the Dark* and *Catch Me A Spy*, he worked on *Chitty Chitty Bang Bang*, adapted from an Ian Fleming story, and followed up *Arabesque* with the stylish, Swinging London, American-financed Warren Beatty film *Kaleidoscope*. Challis reteamed with Stanley Donen in 1967 on *Two for the Road*, yet another stylish British comedy starring Audrey Hepburn, Albert Finney, and Eleanor Bron.

Two films that really did the new Cold War spy genre justice were the thriller *Torn Curtain* and comedy *The Russians Are Coming, the Russians Are Coming*. *Torn Curtain* starred Paul Newman and Julie Andrews and was deftly directed by the master Alfred Hitchcock. *The Russians Are Coming, the Russians Are Coming*, directed by Canadian-born Norman Jewison, was a pitch-perfect Cold War comedy that featured a host of comedy legends including Carl Reiner, Alan Arkin, and Jonathan Winters.

There were two movies based on the Batman character in the 1940s, and since 1989, 14 more Batman-themed movies have been released as of this writing. But for some fans of a certain age, the 1966 *Batman* movie starring Adam West and Burt Ward from the American TV series is their favorite. Almost a perfect sequel to *Help!*, with villainous costars Cesar Romero, Burgess Meredith, Frank Gorshin, and Lee Meriweather, along with music by Nelson Riddle and Neil Hefti, the film takes all one loved about the TV series and blew it up for the big screen.

Not a British film, *A Man and a Woman*, directed by Claude Lelouch, was a romantic movie with a winning formula that included the haunting soundtrack by Francis Lai and was a new kind of French film that was fresh, yet old-fashioned and had wide appeal and influence around the world. Finally, a film that starred a new British film legend in the making and one of Hollywood's biggest stars, who happened to be married to each other, Richard Burton and Elizabeth Taylor, was *Who's Afraid of Virginia Woolf?* With a screenplay by Ernest Lehman based on Edward Albee's play, photographed by Haskell Wexler, and directed by Mike Nichols in his film directing debut, the wrenching, powerful, timeless movie, would set the stage for Nichols's next film, the groundbreaking *The Graduate* in 1967.

SUNSHINE SUBMARINE

While everyone was turning on, tuning in, and freaking out, what were those four pop princes of Liverpool doing? Since the group's final concert on August 29, 1966, John Lennon had rejoined director Richard Lester in the fall to appear in his anti-war satire *How I Won the War*, based on the 1963 novel by Patrick Ryan, which was filmed in Celle, West Germany, and Carboneras, Spain, and was released in October 1967. Paul McCartney also continued to work in film, joining George Martin for the soundtrack to the film *The Family Way*, released on January 6, 1967, in the UK and June 12, 1967, in the US. With no new album planned for the holiday season, EMI released *A Collection of Beatles Oldies* that unofficially and unknowingly marked the midway point in the group's career.

The psychedelic cover illustration of *Revolver* by Klaus Voormann, a spindly/spidery, Aubrey Beardsley–influenced, black-and-white pen-and-ink/photo collage, was the first clue that *Revolver* was going to be an even more adventurous and timely album than *Rubber Soul*, although that album's cover also hinted at sophisticated changes in the music contained within. *Revolver*'s psychedelic-flavored album tracks, particularly "Tomorrow Never Knows," the first song recorded, the most overtly psychedelic, and destined to be the album's last track, was the strongest clue as to what the Beatles would begin working on in November 1966, when they started recording "Strawberry Fields Forever."

Revolver included "Eleanor Rigby," musically a follow-up to "Yesterday," in its use of strings but with a much more inspired, complex, and evocative lyrical story. "I'm Only Sleeping" evoked a psychedelic dream and featured backward guitar, a sound that would be a staple of psychedelic music. "Yellow Submarine," for all its child-like playfulness was a trippy psychedelic singalong that could be an anthem for the 1960s generation. The track was recorded on May 26 and June 1; George Martin was absent from the May 26 session due to food poisoning, Geoff Emerick became the de facto producer. Engineer Phil McDonald was present at both sessions. The various sounds effects and made-up sounds that are part of the song were created with assistance from Martin, Emerick, Neil Aspinall, chauffeur Alf Bicknell, Pattie Harrison, Marianne Faithfull, Brian Jones, other hired musicians, and the Beatles.

In *Many Years from Now*, McCartney recalled writing the song, one of the many he wrote while living at the house of his girlfriend Jane Asher's family. He wrote the song in that netherworld between being awake and falling asleep. "I remember thinking that a children's song would be quite a good idea and I thought of images, and the color yellow came to me, and a submarine came to me, and I thought, well, that's kind of nice, like a toy, very childish submarine." When Paul showed Donovan the song at Donovan's Maida Vale flat in London, he helped McCartney with the lyrics and came up with the line: "Sky of blue and sea of green / in our yellow submarine." In *Paul McCartney: The Lyrics*, McCartney said, "A large part of the subtext of 'Yellow Submarine' was that, even then, the Beatles were living in our own little capsule. Our own microclimate. Our own controlled environment." The only Beatles single with a lead vocal by Ringo was released on August 5, 1966, with "Eleanor Rigby" on the B side. "Yellow Submarine" appeared in slightly different versions on the UK mono and stereo editions of *Revolver*. On the deluxe reissue of *Revolver* in 2022, one of the *Sessions* discs' songwriting work tapes indicate John Lennon had more to do with the writing of the song than had previously been thought.

"She Said, She Said," was a dark track, inspired by a conversation actor Peter Fonda had with Lennon at a party while they were both high on acid, saying that he knew what it is was like to be dead, recalling a traumatic incident from his childhood when he accidentally shot himself. "Doctor Robert" was a story of the underside of the new drug culture's medical establishment, enablers, and was based on a real doctor, Dr. Robert Freymann of New York, who gave potent "vitamin" injections laced with hallucinogens and other drugs. Lennon both glamorizes and holds the doctor up as a stand-in for the hypocrisy of the drug culture and those writing and enforcing the laws at the time.

The recording of "Strawberry Fields Forever" began on November 24, 1966, at Abbey Road with producer George Martin, engineer Geoff Emerick, and tape operator Richard Lush. Some of the instruments used over the course of recording the song to give it its distinctive dreamy quality include the mellotron, which was John's but which was played by not only by him but also Paul using the flute setting, George using the guitar setting, and George Martin. The track also included swarmandal (also spelled svaramandal), which was played by George Harrison.

On December 15, a marathon recording session ensued that included three cellists and four trumpeters. "Strawberry Fields Forever" was being recorded with the intention that it would be used for a proposed new album with a concept McCartney had hit on in November while flying back to London from Africa, wherein the group would essentially use a collective alter ego (an Edwardian brass band) of the four, as a way of hiding behind the fame of Beatlemania and allowing themselves to experiment and strike out in new directions. It was the Beatles' first opportunity to make an album with no touring commitments. "Strawberry Fields Forever" takes its name from Strawberry Field (Lennon added the s at the end), a Salvation Army orphanage a short walk from John's childhood home on Menlove Avenue. It was located at Beaconfield Road; the grounds feature a large Victorian house and an extensive wooded area filled with trees and lots of places to explore and get lost. The place evoked many childhood memories for Lennon, who spent hours there with his friends. He began writing the song when he was on holiday on Santa Isabel Island in Spain in fall 1966 and also worked on it while in in Almeria, Spain, doing location shooting for *How I Won the War*. In *The Playboy Interviews*, Lennon told David Sheff: "Yeah, I took it as an image. It's like *A Little Night Music* was from the Magritte painting of a black tree with a half silver moon on it. It's irrelevant to the musical, except to know that the guy saw the picture and got the idea for whatever."

The second song the Beatles would work on for the new album was "When I'm Sixty-Four," which McCartney had written years before; the Beatles had played it on occasion at the Cavern. As psychedelic and experimental as much of the music on the eventual album would be, there were also plenty of up-beat rock tracks, jazz, dancehall, and other styles used that don't freeze the album in the psychedelic 1960s. The Beatles had for some time been borrowing from the avant-garde music sounds of John Cage and Karlheinz Stockhausen, whose sounds featured dissonant music, advanced electronic effects, tape loops, treated instruments, and many other musical forms and ideas that would be the backbone of the music of the Beatles from *Rubber Soul* through the White Album.

The Beatles ended 1966 working on "Penny Lane" on December 29 at Abbey Road with producer George Martin, engineer Geoff Emerick, and tape operator Phil McDonald. The sessions for the song would go on for nearly a month. The session on January 9, 1967, included four flute players and two trumpeters, with some of the musicians doubling on piccolo and flugelhorn. Further orchestration was recorded in Studio 3 at Abbey Road on January 12 when Martin recorded two trumpeters, two oboists, a bowed double bass, and a cor anglais or English horn. But McCartney felt something was missing. On January 11, he was watching a concert by the English Chamber Orchestra on television. When the orchestra performed Bach's "Brandenburg Concerto No. 2," McCartney was struck by the sound of a piccolo trumpet played by David Mason. McCartney arranged for Mason to play a solo trumpet part on "Penny Lane," perhaps the most memorable musical part of the track. Promo copies of the single in the US featured a different mix of the song, mix 11, which featured a final trumpet line from Mason; the commercially released single featured mix 14. Mix 11 was later officially released on Capitol's 1980 *Rarities* album. A stereo mix of the track wasn't created until September 30, 1971.

"Penny Lane" was the perfect lyrical complement and musical counterpoint to Lennon's "Strawberry Fields Forever." While "Strawberry Fields Forever" was a dreamy, impressionistic track that fit right into the current psychedelic music sound, "Penny Lane" was another perfect pop-rock song that exhibited McCartney's un-canny penchant for writing catchy songs filled with pop hooks and unforgettable melodies. Like "Strawberry Fields Forever," McCartney wrote a song filled with af-fection for a slice of Liverpool nostalgia.

McCartney had written the song soon before recording it on his piano at home, which had recently been painted with a psychedelic rainbow by David Vaughn. Vaughn later asked McCartney to provide music for an upcoming rave, and on January 5, 1967, the Beatles recorded a nearly 14-minute track for the event called "Carnival of Light," one of the most mysterious unreleased songs ever recorded by any of the Beatles. Referred to as a sound effects tape of loops and electronic noises, it was played at the "Million Volt Light and Sound Rave" held at the Roundhouse Theatre in London on January 26 and February 8, 1967. Noted Beatles author Mark Lewisohn, one of the few people to have heard the track, described it in *The Beatles Recordings Sessions* as: "the combination of a basic track and numerous overdubs. Track one of the tape was full of distorted, hypnotic drum and organ sounds; track two had a distorted lead guitar; track three had the sounds of church organ, various effects with heaps of tape echo and manic tambourine. . . . But of all the frighten-ing sounds it was the voices on track three which really set the scene, John and Paul screaming dementedly and bawling aloud random phrases like, 'Are you alright?' and 'Barcelona!'" The track was under consideration to be released on the Beatles' *Anthology 2* album, but George Harrison vetoed its inclusion.

Like Lennon, inspired by the real Strawberry Field of his youth, McCartney added the reality of the actual Penny Lane by evoking the real-life roundabout, fire station, a fictious banker of the real-life bank, and how poppies were sold each year on British Legion Poppy Day to raise funds for veterans (held around Remembrance Day in November, a day that honors members of the armed forces who have died in wars) and the real-life barbershop Bioletti's. McCartney's sweeping panorama of the Penny Lane neighborhood is filled with vivid and evocative anecdotes about people who didn't really exist but that nonetheless enhanced the song. While there has almost continuously been a barber in the area, the roundabout shelter, once a *Sgt. Pepper's Lonely Hearts Club Band*–themed bistro, has long vanished. In *Paul McCartney: The Lyrics*, McCartney explained, "The characters in 'Penny Lane' are still very real to me. I drive past it to this day, showing people the barbershop, the bank, the fire station, the church I used to sing in, and where the girl stood with the tray of poppies as I waited for the bus."

The Beatles planned to spend the early months of 1967 working on songs for their new album, but it was quickly decided that "Strawberry Fields Forever" and "Penny Lane" would be released as a double A-sided single, as no new music from the group has been released since the previous summer. Pirate radio station Radio Caroline was the first station to air "Penny Lane"; the station would later go off the air in August. While "Penny Lane" did not diverge too far from some of McCartney's recently penned singles and album tracks, "Strawberry Fields Forever" had bold ideas that fit right into the new psychedelic music sound. The two sides would also be the first music released in 1967 that would later be on the US *Magical Mystery Tour* full-length soundtrack album.

Only a few days after the Beatles signed their new recording contract with EMI, they began making promotional film clips for their new single, filming "Strawberry Fields Forever" on January 30 and 31, 1967, and "Penny Lane" on February 5 and 7. The clips were produced by the Beatles' own film production company, Subafilms. Though part of the reason Subafilms may have been formed was due to the poor deal Brian Epstein had cut with UA for the three feature-length films, the clips produced by Subafilms were still distributed by UA. Tony Bramwell served as producer (as part of his apprenticeship, he directed a couple of episodes of *Ready Steady Go!*) of the promo films, which were directed by Peter Goldmann. Bramwell would also become involved in looking at scripts and considering books for Apple Films to produce. Goldmann, who was Swedish, had been recommended by Klaus Voormann, the Beatles' Hamburg friend who'd designed the cover of *Revolver*. As a member of Paddy, Klaus, & Gibson, Voorman was also part of Brian Epstein's stable of musical acts and also played bass with Manfred Mann.

Goldmann had been scouting locations, and it was decided, even though it was the dead of winter in England, that filming would be done outside. Goldmann chose Knole Park in Seven Oaks, Kent, some 20 miles outside of London. Owned by the National Trust, the park's vast expanse included a fifteenth-century house, a bird-house, and a golf course. During a break while filming "Strawberry Fields Forever," John Lennon wandered into an antique shop and found the poster that would be the inspiration for the song, "For the Benefit of Mr. Kite."

The "Strawberry Fields Forever" shoot resulted in a trippy clip filled with back-ward effects and showed the Beatles in their psychedelic finery. The promo film for "Penny Lane" was more grounded in reality. The scenes of the actual Penny Lane area were done without the Beatles, while the scenes of the Beatles were shot on February 5 at Angel Lane, Stratford, and Knole Park on February 7. The clips were telecast in their entirety or in part on such British TV shows as *Top of the Pops* and *Juke Box Jury*. American teen music shows like *American Bandstand* and *Where the Action Is* were pleased to show the clips and could look past their experimental ele-ments. While New York music show *Clay Cole's Discotheque* scored a coup by airing the clip (though the host would quit the show some months later due to his disdain for psychedelic music), one could only imagine what those watching the *Hollywood Palace* Saturday night variety show thought.

"Strawberry Fields Forever"/"Penny Lane" was released on February 13, 1967, in the US, and February 17 in the UK; the UK edition also boasted a picture sleeve, the first Beatles UK single to have one.

The cover of *Sgt. Pepper's Lonely Hearts Club Band* was shot on March 30. On April 2, the Beatles completed recording of the album.

YOU'RE EITHER ON THE BUS OR OFF THE BUS

While on a trip to the States early in April, Paul McCartney came up with the idea for what would become the *Magical Mystery Tour* film.

Once the Beatles finished *Help!*, they began to consider what their next film project would be. In the *Anthology* book, George Harrison gave a sense of the pos-sibilities: "I remember we had Patrick McGoohan around, and he'd written a couple of episodes of *The Prisoner*, which we liked very much. We thought 'Well, maybe he could write something for us.' Then there was David Helliwell, who wrote *Little Malcolm and His Struggle Against the Eunuchs*—we got him up and asked him to write up something." None of these ideas came to fruition.

Paul McCartney's girlfriend, Jane Asher, was traveling the US with the British Old Vic, and he'd decided to surprise her with a visit on April 5, her 21st birthday, when her mother Margaret planned to throw her a birthday party. He arrived in Los Angeles on April 3, where he phoned Derek Taylor. Taylor of course had worked for Brian

Epstein in 1964 and 1965 and even was the ghostwriter for Epstein's memoir, *A Cellar Full of Noise*. After a falling out with Epstein, Taylor and his family moved to California, where he became a publicist for the cream of West-Coast pop groups such as the Beach Boys, the Byrds, and the Mamas and the Papas. Taylor was one of the organizers of the upcoming Monterey Pop Festival and asked McCartney to join the advisory board; McCartney agreed and suggested they book the Jimi Hendrix Experience.

According to David Leaf's liner notes for the 1990 CD reissue of the Beach Boys' *Smiley Smile/Wild Honey*, Paul joined Brian Wilson behind the recording console at Sound Recorders in Los Angeles and offered encouragement to Al Jardine while he was working on the song "Vega-Tables," later changed to "Vegetables"; and it has also been suggested he added celery crunching sounds for the track. Paul then flew to San Francisco on April 4, where he jammed with the Jefferson Airplane. He then flew to Denver to meet Jane on April 5.

While flying back home on April 11, McCartney sketched out the idea for *Magical Mystery Tour*, getting stationery from a flight attendant, and, using a crude pie chart to represent an hour of film time, began the process of visualizing the film. Mal Evans, traveling with him, would later be credited as one of the film's writers. It is interesting to note that the Beatles had envisioned *Sgt. Pepper's Lonely Hearts Club Band* as a visual album and had filmed the "A Day in the Life Session" with this in mind, using seven handheld 16-mm cameras, with fashion photographer Vic Singh (introduced to the group by Pattie Boyd) and music film director Keith Green doing most of the shooting; Tony Bramwell served as producer. The clip fashioned from the footage mixed together shots of the orchestra in evening dress, accessorized with toy props like a gorilla hand, and stock footage.

As detailed in *The Complete Beatles Chronicle*, the proposed visual album of *Sgt. Pepper* was to begin shooting in mid-October 1967 and wrap a month later. The budget was £34,000 for a 52-minute film. The screenplay was to be written by Ian Dallas. Dallas was a Scottish actor (best known as Maurice, Maya's assistant in Federico Fellini's 1963 film *8½*), a playwright, and the author of several books. The film was to be directed by Keith Green and coproduced by Singh and Tommy Weber. Aubrey Dewar, one of the cameramen who would work on *Magical Mystery Tour*, was to be one of two cameramen on the visual album. When looking at the general loose shooting ideas and proposed cast, there are some echoes of how *Magical Mystery Tour* would play out.

A similar concept was used when the Beatles performed "All You Need Is Love" on the *Our World* broadcast, the first worldwide live satellite television broadcast produced by the BBC, with the group surrounded by their London elite pop fellow travelers on hand for the party. Mick Jagger and Marianne Faithfull were there, along with Brian Jones, Keith Richards, Donovan, Graham Nash, Pattie Boyd, Mike Nesmith of the Monkees, and two of the members of The Fool, Simon Posthuma and Marijke Koger.

ON THE BUS

The idea for *Magical Mystery Tour*—taking a motor coach ride around England—reflected both the old mystery trips that were popular in England in summer for decades and Ken Kesey's psychedelic school bus trip in 1964, later immortalized in Tom Wolfe's book *The Electric Kool-Aid Acid Test*, published in 1968. Kesey would cross paths with the Beatles when he was supposed to record an album for Apple Corps. Kesey had come over to London with the Hells Angels and sequestered himself in an office at Apple and, with a tape recorder, pad and pen, and wrote and recorded some spoken-word material for the Apple label. Although he gave a tape to Peter Asher, his work has never been released

In the *Anthology* book, Paul reflected on the improvisational aspect of *Magical Mystery Tour*: "There wasn't a script for *Magical Mystery Tour*, you don't need scripts for that kind of film. It was just a mad idea. We said to everyone: 'Be on the coach on Monday morning.' I told them all, 'We're going to make it up as we go along, but don't worry—it'll be alright.'"

Ringo happily remembered how spontaneous filming *Magical Mystery Tour* was: "We rented a bus and off we went. There was some planning: John would always want a midget or two around, and we had to get an aircraft hangar to put the set in. We'd do the music of course. They were the finest videos, and it was a lot of fun."

John Lennon gave a more nuanced look at how the film came to be: "We knew most of the scenes we wanted to include; but we bent our ideas to fit the people concerned, once we got to know the cast. If somebody wanted to do something, we hadn't planned, they went ahead."

The group started work on the "Magical Mystery Tour" song on April 25 at Abbey Road. George Martin was producer, with Geoff Emerick the engineer and Richard Lush the tape operator. The group had, for the most part, long abandoned coming to a session with a song completed and ready to record. On this first day of recording, they did no more than rehearse the song, while Emerick created a tape loop of motor coach sound effects that would be used on the final track. There was considerable work done on the track on April 26 in Studio 3, including contributions from Neil and Mal. More work continued on April 27 in Studio 3, with a mono mix ready by the end of the session.

On May 3, Martin put four trumpeters through their paces and the sound of a celeste was conjured from a Lowry organ. Seven mono mixes were completed on May 4; a stereo mix wouldn't be done until November 6.

More work would be done on the track that would be used in nonfilm versions of the song. Paul only had fragments of the lyrical idea and wanted to glean ideas from coach tour posters, but Mal Evans couldn't find any. Everyone pitched in ideas, and Lennon actually lit up a joint in the studio and passed it around, no doubt hoping it would provide some inspiration. In *Many Years from Now*, McCartney doesn't hide the drug references inherent in the lyrics: "Roll up!! Roll Up! . . . was also a reference to rolling up a joint. We were always sticking those little things in that we knew our friends would get; veiled references to drugs and to trips."

On May 11 at Olympic Studios, the Beatles began work on "Baby You're a Rich Man." The song, primarily by John, was originally titled "One of the Beautiful People," and the "Baby, you're a rich man" segment by Paul. John has said that Paul was referring to Brian Epstein in the song, whom they both felt complained too much, which given how wealthy they had all become was tiresome. George Martin was the producer, Keith Grant was the engineer, and Eddie Kramer was the tape operator. Kramer, who would go on to work extensively with Jimi Hendrix and Led Zeppelin, also played vibraphone on the track. Since Martin was no longer employed by EMI, he could produce the session, but others who worked at Abbey Road or were employed by EMI were forbidden to work in other studios. In contrast to Abbey's Studer J-37 four-track tape recorder, which used 1-inch tape, Olympic employed an Ampex AG-440 four-track machine that used half-inch tape. Many regard the sound of Paul's bass on this track as the best sounding of all the recordings of the Beatles.

Another unique aspect of this session was that members of the Rolling Stones may have been there and supplied handclaps, especially likely given that the Stones frequently worked at Olympic. Selmer Clavioline Concert keyboard, a French-made instrument, was also used on the session. It wasn't so much a cousin of the mellotron as it was a forerunner of the synthesizer. The keyboard is actually two pieces connected by a cord—basically a valve (tube) sound generator and a combination speaker with an amplifier. The instrument was prominently featured on the Joe Meek-produced Tornados hit "Telstar" from 1962 and was also used on the Graham Bond Organization album *The Sound of 1965*. John Lennon played the instrument on "Rich Man," giving the track a finishing touch. A mono mix was created, but only a mock stereo mix was released in the US, and no stereo version of any kind was released in the UK in the 1960s. The track, which would turn up on the full-length US *Magical Mystery Tour* soundtrack album, was initially slated for *Yellow Submarine*.

The next day, May 12, they were back at Abbey Road, where they swiftly completed "All Together Now" in around five hours, which would make it onto the *Yellow Submarine* soundtrack. The song was Paul's, inspired by the music hall songs of his youth, and meant to be a sing-along. As he said in *Many Years from Now*, "to encourage the audience to join in they'd say 'All together now!' so I just took it and read another meaning into it, of we are all together now." Engineer Geoff Emerick doubled as producer for this session because George Martin was unavailable. Richard Lush was the tape operator. A mono mix was created at the session with a stereo done on November 15.

While the Beatles were recording "All Together Now," pirate radio station Radio London became the first station in the world to air *Sgt. Pepper's Lonely Hearts Club*

Band (with the Beatles' blessing). The press launch for *Sgt. Pepper* was held at Brian Epstein's London home on May 19. Among those in attendance was a young American photographer named Linda Eastman, who had met Paul recently at the Bag O' Nails club.

Once again venturing outside of Abbey Road, the group spent May 25 and 31, and June 1 and 2 at De Lane Lea Studios working on George's "It's All Too Much," which would appear on the *Yellow Submarine* soundtrack. The engineer was Dave Siddel, and the tape operator was Mike Weighell; George Martin was only present for the June 2 session. The song evokes George's journey from experimenting with LSD to practicing Indian religion. In his memoir *I Me Mine* he said: "'It's All Too Much' was written in a childlike manner from realizations that appeared during and after some LSD experiences and which were later confirmed in meditation." In a foreshadowing of things to come, Harrison deliberately took a line from another song to describe his wife—"With your long blonde hair and your eyes of blue." The lyric came from the single "Sorrow" by the Merseys, a cover of a song by the American group the McCoys. Much of the June sessions were spent on instrumental jams.

On June 2, George Martin recorded the track's additional musicians: four trumpeters (including David Mason, who'd been featured on "Penny Lane") and Paul Harvey on bass clarinet. The trumpets on the track sound like they were inspired by "Prince of Denmark's March" by Jeramiah Clarke. Mono and stereo mixes were created at De Lane Lea on October 12. EMI prepared a copy of the mono mix for use in the *Yellow Submarine* movie edited down from 8:15 to 2:31 for use in the finished film. On October 16, mono and stereo mixes were created for nonfilm use.

On May 18, it had been announced that the group would be participating in one of two segments representing England in the first worldwide television broadcast, *Our World*, scheduled for June 25. The broadcast was the brainchild of Aubrey Singer, who had worked for the BBC since 1949, starting as a film editor in his teens, and eventually became the head of the Features Group.

Though Paul's "Your Mother Should Know" may have been in the running for the *Our World* broadcast, John's anthemic "All You Need Is Love" was the more obvious choice. Work on the song (with the plan being to have the Beatles sing live to a backing track) began on June 14 at Olympic Studios; subsequent sessions on June 19, 21, 23, and 24 were held at Abbey Road. As was the case when different studios were used in recording, the original Olympic Studios tape would be mixed for mono on ¼-inch tape and then played back on the EMI BTR2 machines at Abbey Road.

On June 21, mixes of the track in progress were prepared for the BBC to use for their preproduction of the broadcast and for George Martin to use for the score he was writing for the track. Martin called the score "a fairly arbitrary sort of arrangement since it was at such short notice," in his book *All You Need Is Ears*, and it was he who added in the snatches of "La Marseillaise," the French national anthem,

"Greensleeves," Glen Miller's "In the Mood," and a snippet from Bach's Brandenburg concertos. He completed the score with dispatch. On June 23 and 24, a 13-piece orchestra was brought in to record overdubs on the backing track; they also participated in the broadcast.

On the day of the program, which would show the Beatles seemingly recording the song at Abbey Road, partygoers were rounded up to join in on the festivities. The usual suspects were easy to find on such short notice. Naturally, Mick Jagger and his girlfriend Marianne Faithfull were there, along with Keith Richards, Donovan, Graham Nash and his first wife Rose, Gary Leeds (better known as Gary Walker of the American group the Walker Brothers, who were oddly considered part of the British Invasion), all four of the members of the Small Faces, and Eric Clapton, sporting his new teased and curly hairdo. Keith Moon of the Who supplied percussion and Mike Vickers, formerly of Manfred Mann, conducted the orchestra, as George Martin was busy in the control booth. Other friends and family included Pattie Harrison, Mike McCartney, Jane Asher, and Hunter Davies, author of *The Beatles*, the only authorized biography of the group.

Simon Posthuma and Marijke Koger, members of Dutch design collective the Fool, had designed the costumes for the performance, were also there. The two had launched themselves in England with Karma, a small boutique on Gosfield Street, where they sold some of their Moroccan finds along with the requisite psychedelic art posters before they became the Fool, bringing in clothes designer Josje Leeger, along with Barry Finch, who had done publicity for Brian Epstein's Saville Theatre, and eventually became Leeger's boyfriend. They had previously designed the graphics for the inner sleeve of *Sgt. Pepper*. When asked for this book what inspired their clothing designs for the *Our World* broadcast, Marijke said: "Where does any inspiration come from? It just comes or it doesn't. I guess from the astral spheres."

"We were big enough to command an audience of that size and it was for love," Ringo said of the broadcast for the *Anthology* book. "It was for love and bloody peace. It was a fabulous time. I even get excited now when I realize that's what it was for; peace and love, people putting flowers in guns." During the broadcast, Paul had a bit of fun, throwing in an ad-lib, singing a line from "She Loves You" during the fade-out.

Following the broadcast, John recorded a new vocal for the single version of the track. The following day, Ringo overdubbed a drumroll, and the song was mixed in mono. "All You Need Is Love"/"Baby You're a Rich Man" was released as a single on July 7. On November 1, a shortened version of the track was prepared for the *Yellow Submarine* film, with a stereo mix intended for the soundtrack completed on October 29. The version of "All You Need Is Love" on all three of the *Yellow Submarine* soundtracks (US stereo and UK stereo and mono) is shorter than the version on the US and UK singles and the US *Magical Mystery Tour* album.

While the Beatles' performance of "All You Need Is Love" has become iconic, the other segment has been overlooked. Reported by Magnus Magnusson, the segment focused on a Scottish town called Cumbernauld. The town was considered a "New Town" when it was conceived and developed in the mid-1950s, to meet the growing needs of safe and affordable housing in the area.

There were some who wondered if the Beatles would take part in the Monterey Pop Festival, held June 16 through18, and it was even rumored that they were there in disguise. But the group was in the middle of working on "All You Need Is Love" in London, though they did provide a piece of artwork that was used in the festival's program, an illustration of almost childlike simplicity, with psychedelic drawings spelling out "Peace to Monterey from Sgt. Pepper's Lonely Hearts Club Band."

On July 19, John and Paul dropped in at a Rolling Stones session at Olympic Studios, providing backing vocals for "We Love You," which would not appear on the Stones' *Their Satanic Majesties Request* album, released that December, but was released prior to that in mid-August 1967 in the UK and early September in the US. The song was the A side in the UK, with "Dandelion" on the B side and was on the B side of the single in the US, with "Dandelion" on the A side.

ELECTRICAL BANANAS

In January 1967, *More of the Monkees* was released, as well as the latest album by the Rolling Stones, *Between the Buttons*, a record album clearly influenced by the drug culture. February saw the release of *The Mamas and the Papas Deliver*, the Byrds' *Younger Than Yesterday*, and the Jefferson Airplane's *Surrealistic Pillow*. Donovan's *Mellow Yellow*, an even more overtly psychedelic offering than *Sunshine Superman*, was released in the US only; tracks from both the US *Sunshine Superman* and *Mellow Yellow* were later released in the UK on an album itself called *Sunshine Superman*, which was issued in June 1967. In March came the self-titled debut album by the Grateful Dead, as well as *The Velvet Underground & Nico*. This debut record by the Velvet Underground seemed to share some of the edgy freakshow trippiness of the Mothers of Invention and the Fugs but would ultimately stand outside of Day-Glo hippie music and become a major influence on music for years to come.

"The 14-Hour Technicolor Dream" took place on April 29 at Alexandra Palace in London. The event was a fundraiser for *the International Times* newspaper but was also an excuse for British freaks to drop acid, smoke pot, and dance to headliners Pink Floyd (who were working on their debut album *Piper at the Gates of Dawn* at the time) and the obligatory appearance of the Soft Machine, who were joined by Tomorrow. Tomorrow included a young Steve Howe on guitar, who would go on to join Yes. The group's Keith West also worked with Mark Wirtz, on the highly influential *A Teenage Opera* project in 1967. Drummer Twink would go on to join the Pretty Things for their concept album *S.F. Sorrow* before forming the Pink Fairies and John's Children (which included Marc Bolan).

Also in attendance were Denny Laine, newly departed from the Moody Blues, Pete Townshend in a rare solo show, the Crazy World of Arthur Brown, the Pretty Things, the Move, the Creation, American blues legend Champion Jack Dupree, British blues pioneers Alexis Korner, Graham Bond, the group Savoy Brown, comedian Dick Gregory, and poets, jugglers, and avant-garde artists. One such artist named Yoko Ono performed and was observed by John Lennon, who was there with John Dunbar. British director Peter Whitehead was on hand to film everything, and his work appeared in two different films: *Pink Floyd: London '66–'67* and *Tonite Let's All Make Love in London*.

In June came albums from Country Joe and the Fish (*Electric Music for the Mind and Body*), the Mothers of Invention (*Absolutely Free*), the Monkees (*Headquarters*), the debut album from the Jimi Hendrix Experience (*Are You Experienced?*), and Moby Grape's self-titled debut album.

June also saw the full flowering of what Otis Redding called the "love crowd," with three key events. But before mentioning those three events, a precursor to the Monterey Pop Festival should be acknowledged. The Fantasy Fair and Magic Mountain Music Festival was held at Cushing Memorial Amphitheatre in Marin County on June 10 and 11. Some of the big names who played at what amounted to the first pop-rock music festival of its kind, included a slew of San Francisco bands including the Jefferson Airplane, the Steve Miller Blues Band, Country Joe and the Fish, the Charlatans, the Sons of Champlin, and many more. Popular Los Angeles bands such as the Byrds (with Hugh Masekela) and the Doors performed, along with pop acts such as the Fifth Dimension, the Grass Roots, and Spanky & Our Gang also performed. Dionne Warwick was perhaps the most mainstream artist present, but her inclusion speaks to the fact that a wide variety of acts performed. Also, unlike Monterey, there were many still relatively unknown underground acts on the bill. Other acts on Day 1 included Canned Heat, the Jim Kweskin Jug Band, Kaleidoscope (the American group), and the Chocolate Watchband. Day 2 also included P. F. Sloan, Captain Beefheart and His Magic Band, the Seeds, and Tim Buckley. The first key event was the release of *Sgt. Pepper's Lonely Hearts Club Band* on June 1 in the UK (although the first pressing was rush-released in advance and had been available on May 26) and June 2 in the US. June 1 was also the day *Absolutely Free*, the second album by Frank Zappa and the Mothers of Invention, was released. The second key event was the Monterey Pop Festival, and the third would be the *Our World* global television broadcast. Many figures have circulated through the years, but it's believed that some 400 million people watched the broadcast.

While the flowering of the hippie underground had been percolating for several years, the Monterey Pop Festival, for however close it was geographically to San Francisco and how far away it was from Los Angeles, New York, and London, became the freaks' coming-out party to the world. Instead of debutantes being welcomed into polite society, rock gods, dressed in their most swinging finery, announced themselves to the world at Monterey. The event was organized primarily by record producer Lou Adler and John Phillips of the Mamas and the Papas, as well as Derek Taylor, now ensconced on the West Coast after his short stint with the Beatles. Not only was Monterey a chance for the flower children to graduate to adulthood, but it also brought together the musical artists from disparate geographical music scenes into one big happy (hippie) family. The festival made stars out of Janis Joplin and Otis Redding, as well as British imports the Who and, ironically, the Jimi Hendrix Experience (Hendrix was actually American). While there had been other festivals that brought together similar groups, Monterey became the festival that put the new music on the map, long before Woodstock.

1967 FILMS WITH LOVE

A film associated with the Swinging London film genre that often gets overlooked is *Privilege*, directed by Brit Peter Watkins and starring Paul Jones of Manfred Mann as the lead character, pop star Stephen Shorter. In 1968 Jones would star in *The Committee*, directed by Australian Peter Sykes, featuring music by Pink Floyd and Arthur Brown, with Brown playing himself. Jones also sang several of the soundtrack songs in *Privilege*. Given the role he plays in the movie and some of the themes explored, it's ironic Jones would convert to Christianity in 1984. The pseudo-documentary film's story centers on Shorter's place as the most popular entertainer in the world who has captivated the new youth culture. He's made his handlers rich, but his bizarre stage show and persona have made him depressed, while at the same time he becomes co-opted by the Church of England to brainwash the youth into conformity. With the casting of model and mod "it" girl Jean Shrimpton as the love interest (in her only nondocumentary film role), the film is surprisingly cogent and touches on many themes that still resonate today.

This is especially interesting because Watkins had no knowledge and was not a fan of pop music. He used the 1962 Canadian short about Paul Anka, *Lonely Boy*, directed by Wolf Koenig, as a blueprint to understand the new world of pop stardom. The film was written by Norman Bogner and based on a script by Johnny Speight. Speight was the writer of the British TV situation comedy series *Till Death Us Do Part* and was considered to write *A Hard Day's Night*, an offer he had to turn down due to scheduling conflicts. Bogner wrote novels, plays, and TV scripts, with *Privilege* his only film script. Brit Mike Leander wrote most of the music. Leander would go on to work with the Beatles on "She's Leaving Home" from *Sgt. Pepper* and also worked with them on *Magical Mystery Tour* and was an in-demand record producer and Decca Records staff producer, working with numerous British and American musical artists, including most fruitfully with Marianne Faithfull and Gary Glitter. His other film credit was the 1969 British TV movie *Run a Crooked Mile*. Two other key British films of 1967 that were the previously mentioned are *Smashing Time* and *To Sir, with Love*. *To Sir, With Love* would become the third-biggest UK film at the US box office in the 1960s, behind *Thunderball* and *Goldfinger*. A film that was essentially a sci-fi film but was awash in psychedelia was *Pop Down*, a satirical film filled with pop music performances by the likes of Julie Driscoll, Brian Auger and the Trinity, the Idle Race, Dantalion's Chariot, Blossom Toes, Luis Bonfa, and also in a starring role in the film, Zoot Money.

Though *Sgt. Pepper* captured the cultural zeitgeist, and other British pop music was storming the charts and paving the way for the new musical innovations, the comet that was the British film industry was starting to fade around the world, with cutting-edge American movies now beginning to move to center stage in cinema and culture around the world. The two American movies that really exploded were *The Graduate* and *Bonnie and Clyde*.

The Graduate, directed by Mike Nichols, featured Dustin Hoffman in his break-out role, as Benjamin Braddock, personifying the youthful confusion of the new age. *Bonnie & Clyde* was directed by Arthur Penn and starred Warren Beatty and Faye Dunaway. The imaginative take on the Barrow crime duo myth unleashed screen violence to a new level and became the launching pad for using violence in films as a metaphor to reflect the escalating war in Vietnam. The film came only months before the end of the long-running film US motion picture production code that began in 1934 and would be replaced by a new letter rating system.

Sex, violence, and politics were the primary grand themes of these movies; the other key preoccupation of the time, drugs, was met head-on in such films as *The Trip*. The film was produced and directed by Roger Corman, written by Jack Nicholson, and starred Peter Fonda and Dennis Hopper, along with Bruce Dern and Susan Strasberg. Nicholson, Dern, and Strasberg would reteam in 1968 for *Psych-Out*, another film about the drug culture. The year also saw Nicholson cowriting the script for the Monkees only movie, *Head*. More significantly, Nicholson, Fonda, and Hopper would reteam in 1969 for *Easy Rider*. *Valley of the Dolls*, based on the block-buster novel by Jacqueline Susann, was a movie that took an exploitative take on sex and tried to make a statement. *Guess Who's Coming to Dinner* took a fresh take on race relations. *The Love-Ins* tackled the drug scene and centered on a character based loosely on Timothy Leary. Two music documentaries, *Dont Look Back* and *Festival*, were imaginative music films that hold up well, with *Dont Look Back* perhaps the best music documentary ever—at least until *The Last Waltz* came along.

The Beatles met up in London on July 19, 1967, to discuss their next film project, *Magical Mystery Tour*. On August 1, George and Pattie were in Los Angeles, staying at the home of music business lawyer Robert Fitzpatrick, who was vacationing in Hawaii. Derek Taylor was to visit, but he got lost in the heavy fog and had difficulty finding the address—1567 Blue Jay Way. While waiting for their friend, Harrison noticed there was a Hammond organ in the house, which he used to write the song "Blue Jay Way." The original lyrics, on Robert Fitzpatrick Associates letterhead, are reproduced in *I Me Mine*, revealing four lines that were cut from the final version. Harrison said of the song: "The mood is also slightly Indian. Derek Taylor is slightly Welsh." On August 8, George, Pattie, and Derek wandered around San Francisco's Haight-Ashbury neighborhood, though George did not enjoy the experience.

On August 11, photographer Richard Avedon shot psychedelic portraits of the Beatles at his penthouse studio at Thomson House, which originally appeared in *Look* magazine in the US and then in *Stern* magazine in Germany. The iconic photos would have an influence on the animation in the *Yellow Submarine* movie.

On August 22 and 23, the Beatles began work on an early version of "Your Mother Should Know" at Chappell Recording Studios; George Martin was the producer, John Timperly was the engineer, and John Iles was the tape operator. Timperly also worked at IBC and Olympic and had worked on Cream's debut album. He would later work with McCartney, including on 1991's *Liverpool Oratorio*. "Your Mother Should Know" was another one of Paul's songs that harkened back to the jazz age, like "When I'm Sixty-Four" from *Sgt. Pepper* and "Honey Pie," which would be on the White Album. Paul may have written some of the song at his London home on the harmonium while relatives were eavesdropping from the next room. In *Many Years from Now*, McCartney said: "In 'Your Mother Should Know' I was basically trying to say your mother might know more than you think she does. Give her credit." In *Paul McCartney: The Lyrics*, he explained, "No one thought it at the time, but we really were big fans of the music that came out of our parent[s'] generation." After attempting a remake on September 16, the song was completed on September 29 at Abbey Road. Brian Epstein attended the August 23 session, and it would be the last time the Beatles would see him alive.

On the evening of the 24th, at the urging of Pattie Harrison and Alex Madras, the Beatles and their partners attended a lecture by the Maharishi Mahesh Yogi. Impressed by what they heard, the group immediately decided to attend the Maharishi's Transcendental Meditation retreat being held that weekend in Bangor, North Wales, and left by train from London's Euston Station on Friday, August 25.

Alex Madras, later dubbed "Magic Alex" by Lennon, was the son of a Greek army officer with a background as mysterious as his son's would become. He'd met the Beatles through John Dunbar; they provided funding for his company, Fiftyshapes Ltd., which became Apple Electronics. In an interview with the *NME* in 1969, Lennon credited Madras with helping to write the song "What's the New Mary Jane." Post-Beatles, Madras was a hair stylist on the 1973 cult classic film *Invasion of the Bee Girls*.

Beatles Limited was formed by Brian Epstein in 1963. In April 1967, as the first step in forming a new company to relieve their tax burden, an updated partnership entity was formed called Beatles and Co. On November 17, Beatles Limited then became Apple Music Limited and, finally, in January 1968, Apple Corps Limited was formed. Technically, the first Beatles project for Apple was the *Magical Mystery Tour* film, which was not part of the three-picture deal with UA.

The first reference to Apple appeared on the back of the *Sgt. Pepper* album. Apple would really take off in 1968 with the first releases on Apple Records, dubbed "Our First Four" and released on August 26 in the UK: "Hey Jude" by the Beatles, "Those Were the Days" by Mary Hopkin, "Sour Milk Sea" by Jackie Lomax, and "Thingumybob" (written by McCartney) by the Black Dyke Mills Band. Both "Hey Jude" and "Those Were the Days" were worldwide hits. The label's first album release was George Harrison's *Wonderwall Music*, with the White Album the first Beatles album on the Apple label. Any releases by the Beatles were still technically under the same deal the group had with Parlophone and Capitol; the Apple label on their records was just an aesthetic one. Apple Films would go on to produce nine films between 1967 and 1974.

Brian Epstein died on August 27. An inquest was held, and on September 8, it was announced he had died from an accidental overdose of the prescription sedative Carbrital. On the day of his death, the Jimi Hendrix Experience had been performing at the Saville Theatre, which Epstein had leased and used to put on rock performances; the Experience's second show was canceled. The Beatles didn't attend the private family funeral for Epstein on August 29, so as not to draw crowds, but did attend a memorial service held for him on October 17. Epstein was buried at Long Lane Jewish Cemetery in Liverpool.

On August 30, Epstein's brother Clive took over as head of NEMS, and the following day, the Beatles announced they would continue to be managed by the company. There has been much speculation over whether or not the Beatles would have continued to be managed by Brian when their business agreement expired in September 1967. In his book on the *Magical Mystery Tour*, NEMS press officer Tony Barrow said they had planned to let Brian's management of the group end and not renew the contract. George Martin echoed a similar sentiment in one of his memoirs, *All You Need Is Ears*, saying that it was inevitable that he would have lost the Beatles when his contract ran out. Others have said of Epstein how paranoid he was at this time about his future with the Beatles. Yet, if the Beatles were one thing, they were loyal and preferred to surround themselves with people from Liverpool and those who were with them before they become so big and famous because they knew that they could be trusted. Perhaps, the dangerous aspects of Epstein's lifestyle and the way the various drugs he took so negatively affected him may have been more the reason they might have let him go or reduced his role. Tomorrow never knows.

In the world of the Beatles, once their mammoth success set in projects came and went, and however prolific they were, some ideas never came to fruition and were never produced. This was especially true of their film projects; after *A Hard Day's Night*, coming up with suitable film vehicles was never easy. Although *Help!* may have been a letdown after *A Hard Day's Night*, the group had been fortunate to work with Richard Lester again, and in many ways it was a good follow-up for the time. Subsequently, up until the breakup, the Beatles always struggled with finding the right film vehicle to complete their three-picture deal with UA. While the Beatles were responsible for creating their own music, many seemed to want to have a hand in what their next movie would be. Film production also involved a great many more people in contrast to the handful of people they worked with at Abbey Road, meaning they were more reliant on others and not as in charge of their work as they were in the recording studio.

One film considered as a follow up to *Help!* was the western *A Talent for Loving*. A script was prepared by Richard Condon, a novelist whose book *The Manchurian Candidate* was adapted into the 1962 John Frankenheimer Cold War thriller starring Frank Sinatra. *A Talent for Loving* would have been produced by a production company called Pickfair Films, run by Brian Epstein, Bud Ornstein, and James Isherwood, though oddly it wouldn't have been part of the group's three-picture deal for UA, which became a moot point when it was decided the Beatles wouldn't make the film after all. *A Talent for Loving* did reach the screen in 1969, directed by Richard Quine and starring Richard Widmark. The British/American coproduction was released through Paramount and had two Beatle connections: Walter Shenson was the producer, and Ken Thorne, composer of *Help's* instrumental music, wrote the music for the film.

In summer 1966, another idea was put forward that seemed like a real possibility; *Shades of a Personality*. The screenplay was by Owen Holder, a television writer and actor, and there was a strong possibility that Michelangelo Antonioni would direct the film in Spain.

In January 1967, producer Walter Shenson handed off *Shades of a Personality* to another writer, British playwright Joe Orton, whose work was darkly comedic. Following the broadcast of his radio play *Ruffian on the Stair* in 1963, Orton's breakthrough came in 1964 with the stage play *Entertaining Mr. Sloane*. Subsequent works included the television play *The Good and Faithful Servant* and stage play *Loot*, which won the 1966 *Evening Standard* award for Best Play. McCartney had seen *Loot* and liked it and encouraged Orton's involvement in the next Beatles film.

Orton found *Shades of a Personality* "dull and of little interest" and completely transformed it. He drew on some of his previous works for inspiration: a novel, *The Silver*

Bucket, that he'd written with his longtime boyfriend Kenneth Halliwell in 1953, and his own novel, *The Vision of Gombol Provol*, written in 1959. "It had great faults as a novel, but as the basis of a film it was more than adequate," he observed in his diary.

Orton's new script was called *Up Against It*, and was an anarchic farce that saw the four leads joining a revolutionary movement, helping to assassinate a female prime minister, and fighting in endless wars. Brian Epstein was likely baffled by the script and rejected it without comment. Orton then rewrote it, changing the four characters who would've been played by the Beatles into three; "It's a much better script without the weight of stars hanging on it," he declared in his diary.

On August 9, Orton planned to meet with Richard Lester to discuss the film, but mere hours before, he was murdered while he slept by Halliwell, who then took his own life. "A Day in the Life" was played at Orton's funeral. *The Vision of Gombol Provol* would be posthumously published as *Head to Toe*. The revised *Up Against It* would also be published posthumously and later adapted into a stage musical by Todd Rundgren.

It's amazing how quickly things can change. For the Beatles and parts of the world, the seemingly endless summer of love of 1967 was a golden time. Throughout 1967, before and after *Sgt. Pepper*, new sounds, the continuing flowering of psychedelia, and most importantly, the concept album continued to develop. The summer soundtrack was not just confined to the underground's albums of choice. Even the Top 40 was filled with new sounds. While tracks from some of those underground albums became hits, like "Whiter Shade of Pale" from Procol Harum, "Light My Fire" from the Doors, and both "Somebody to Love" and "White Rabbit" from the Jefferson Airplane, there were also hits such as "San Francisco" from Scott McKenzie that encapsulated the 1967 summer of love and R&B and soul singers breaking through with such tracks as "Respect" from Aretha Franklin and "Alfie" from Dionne Warwick.

In July an album was released that quickly drew comparisons to the Beatles in favorable, flattering, and respectful ways: *Bee Gees' 1st* (which, confusingly, was actually their third album). Led by brothers Barry, Maurice, and Robin Gibb (who were born in the UK and raised in Australia), the album was a lushly orchestrated, nearly baroque pop outing, with tinges of psychedelia and Beatlesque sounds, and most beloved for its unforgettable three-part sibling harmonies. Not since the Everly Brothers and the Beach Boys had an album so thrilled the listener with its vocal gifts. The album would fuel one of the most successful careers in pop music and begin a run of albums in the 1960s that is surprisingly underrated.

Like Cream, the group was represented by the Robert Stigwood Organization, which in January 1967 become part of NEMS. Epstein actually floated an offer for Stigwood to buy NEMS. But after his death, the Beatles made it clear they wanted nothing to do with Stigwood and paid him off with £25,000, though Stigwood was allowed to take the Bee Gees and Cream with him. Stigwood also set up his own record label, R.S.O., which would release all but one of Eric Clapton's 1970s solo albums and enjoy phenomenal success with the soundtracks from the films *Saturday Night Fever* and *Grease*.

Spearheaded by the release of *Sgt. Pepper*, the Monterey Pop Festival, the *Our World* broadcast, and the "All You Need Is Love" single, a popular artistic and philosophical renaissance seemed at hand. But for the Beatles, the unexpected death of Brian Epstein was the true first salvo in the long, fraught war that would lead to the breakup of the group early in 1970.

John Lennon would later say that when Brian died, he felt it was only a matter of time before the Beatles would come to an end, but Paul McCartney was determined to rally the troops. The Beatles were at a creative peak; the culture around them was both influenced by what they were doing and provided the Beatles with new influences. They had to step up to the plate.

So Paul arranged a meeting at his home on September 1, so the four could discuss *Magical Mystery Tour* and other plans. Paul was convinced the idea to continue on with *Magical Mystery Tour* was the right one, and he had been coming up with ideas for songs and had met with Tony Barrow, the group's publicist, to discuss the storybook that would accompany the album's release.

George Harrison stated his wish to go to India and study with the Maharishi, with John and Ringo in agreement, a plan they postponed until the new year. In the meantime, the Beatles returned to Abbey Road to work on the *Magical Mystery Tour* songs over four sessions from September 5 to 8, with George Martin producing, Geoff Emerick serving as engineer, and Richard Lush and Ken Scott as tape operators. On September 5, 6, and 16 they worked on John's "I Am the Walrus," with an orchestra of eight violinists, four cellists, three horn players, and a contra-bass clarinetist recording their parts on September 27 in Studio 1, conducted by George Martin. The song was partially inspired by Lewis Carroll's poem "The Walrus and the Carpenter," which appeared in his book *Through the Looking-Glass and What Alice Found There*, published in 1871.

An underlying influence were Lennon's feelings about Dylan, whom he admired, but who he also felt sometimes wrote nonsense that was slavishly lauded by his followers and the press. The "element'ry penguin" phrase was in reference to poet Allen Ginsberg, whose excessive Hare Krishna mantra chanting Lennon disdained. The sound of a siren near his home in Weybridge inspired the rhythm for the phrase "Mis-ter c-ity police-man." He also drew on unfinished song fragments, such as the one about sitting on a cornflake. Silly wordplay was nothing new for John, but in this case, he also consciously came up with words he knew many would read deeper meanings into. He had recently received a letter from a fellow Quarry Bank student, Stephen Bailey, who wrote that they were trying to decode the deeper meanings of some of the songs on *Sgt. Pepper* in his literature class. In response, Lennon couldn't resist purposely writing something that had no meaning at all, just to prick those that Lennon felt were pretentious eggheads who overanalyzed his work. In this spirit, he also drew on a childhood nursery rhyme that directly inspired the yellow matter custard and dead dog's eye lines (and possibly gave name to the bootleg record label Yellow Dog).

But reading too much into some of the more surreal lyrics of the songs of the Beatles, especially during their psychedelic period, can be a tricky parlor game. A longstanding rumor claimed that Eric Burdon, the lead singer of the Animals was dubbed the "Eggman" by Lennon due to Burdon's predilection for cracking eggs on the bodies of naked women. In fact, it was the other way around, as Burdon revealed in his 2002 autobiography, *Don't Let Me Be Misunderstood*, in which he recalled how one of his girlfriends had surprised him one morning while he was cooking breakfast by breaking an amyl nitrate capsule under his nose. The fumes made him fall to the floor, where his girlfriend then cracked an egg onto his naked stomach. After relating the story to Lennon, he cracked "Go on, go get it, Eggman!"

In his *Playboy* interview, Lennon said of the song: "In those days I was writing more obscurely, a la Dylan, never saying what you mean, but giving the impression of something." In the *Anthology* book, he said: "*Magical Mystery Tour* is one of my favorite albums, because it was so weird. 'I Am the Walrus' is also one of my favorite tracks—because I did it, of course, but also because it's one of those that has enough little bitties going to keep you interested even a hundred years later."

Paul demoed "Fool on the Hill" on September 6, with further work on the track done on September 25. The group also worked on George's "Blue Jay Way" on September 6, the session produced by George Martin, with Geoff Emerick the engineer and Ken Scott as the tape operator. More work on the song was done on September 7. A copy of the mono mix was prepared on September 16 for preproduction of the *Magical Mystery Tour* film.

September 8 was perhaps one of the most unusual sessions the Beatles ever worked on, with George Martin producing, Geoff Emerick as engineer, and Richard Lush as tape operator. The group worked on the only composition credited to all for them, the instrumental "Flying" (initially titled "Aerial Tour Instrumental") that also featured them chanting as part of the number. In *Magical Mystery Tour*, the song accompanies footage that was actually comprised of outtakes from Stanley Kubrick's *Dr. Strangelove* that had been acquired by Denis O'Dell and tinted by hand.

The six completed tracks—"Magical Mystery Tour," "Your Mother Should Know," "I Am the Walrus," "The Fool on the Hill," "Flying," and "Blue Jay Way"—would comprise the *Magical Mystery Tour* double EP and appear in the film.

At this point, other tracks that would appear on the Capitol album—the double A-sided "Strawberry Fields For Forever"/"Penny Lane" single and the "All You Need is Love"/"Baby You're a Rich Man" single—had already been released. The only remaining song that would make its way onto the album was "Hello Goodbye," which the

Originally released in 1967 as a six-song double EP in the UK, the full-length, 12-inch US *Magical Mystery Tour* album became the official soundtrack album for the television movie in the UK in 1976. Courtesy Photofest.

Beatles wouldn't begin work on until October 2. George Martin was the producer, Ken Scott was the engineer, and Graham Kirby was the tape operator. Ken Townsend's tape-to-tape synchronization workaround would again be used on October 19, and on October 20 George Martin worked with viola players Ken Essex and Leo Birnbaum in overdubbing their parts to the track. A tape copy of the mono mix was prepared for Capitol Records and sent to them on November 7. "Hello Goodbye" would be released as a single with "I Am the Walrus" on the flip side. Like Lennon's equally trippy "Strawberry Fields Forever," there are many released versions of "I Am the Walrus."

Before the Beatles started filming *Magical Mystery Tour*, the only "script" they had was what Paul McCartney referred to as the "visual script" he sketched in flight while traveling back to London from Los Angeles in April 1967. The drawing is a pie chart divided into eight sections, and McCartney's sparse annotations don't seem like more than simple cues. The first section indicates the film would be set on a coach (bus), introduced by a courier and that there would be commercial introductions, perhaps an indication that the film was always intended to be shown on commercial TV. There is also a reference to Ringo's fat aunt.

The entire first section was referred to as first trip. Section 2 says "coach—people meet, recruiting and song—'Fool on the Hill'?" Although the Beatles wouldn't work on "Fool on the Hill" until Paul demoed it at Abbey Road early in September, Paul had obviously written at least part of the song the previous spring and had earmarked it for *Magical Mystery Tour*. The song was partially inspired by a mystical experience Paul had with Alistair Taylor of NEMS, when the two were out walking Martha, Paul's sheepdog, as the sun was coming up. In *Paul McCartney: The Lyrics*, he relates how he worked on the song at his father's house and that it was about the Maharishi. He did further work on the song during a writing session with Lennon at McCartney's home, when they were still in the process of writing "With a Little Help from My Friends" for *Sgt. Pepper*.

Section 3 only indicates "marathon and laboratory scene." Section 4 shows a drawing of a smiley face (with a nose), and Section 5 says "dreams." Section 6 was left blank. Section 7 says "stripper & band" (ultimately played by Jan Carson backed by the Bonzo Dog Doo-Dah Band), and Section 8 says "end song." Under the chart are various notes and directions; "order lunch"; the word *magician* in parentheses; "hire a coach," "busty hostess" (ultimately played by Mandy Weet), "fat woman," "small man," and "lads & lasses."

The Beatles were fully in charge of their film; they wouldn't have producer Walter Shenson, director Richard Lester and his crew, or UA to take care of the all the practical, logistical, financial, and creative considerations that go into making a motion picture. Nor would they have Brian Epstein's singular managerial expertise. But some folks who had previously worked on films with them returned to work on *Magical Mystery Tour*, including Denis O'Dell, who'd been asked to do the film by Paul. And Victor Spinetti, one of the Beatles' favorite actors, returned to play an officious army sergeant, based on his role he'd played in the stage show *Oh! What a Lovely War*, in both the London and Broadway productions.

Before getting to the people who worked on the film with the Beatles, the unofficial codirector of the film, Bernard Knowles, needs to be mentioned. The veteran British film director, who started out in the newspaper business in the 1920s, worked on his first film in 1922 and directed his first film in 1945. He made his name in the film business as a cinematographer, with his work on five Alfred Hitchcock films, including *The 39 Steps* and the first film version of *Gaslight* in 1940, his best work. His film career stalled in the 1950s and he went on to work more extensively in television. *Magical Mystery Tour* was the film he did before his last film, *Hell Is Empty*, also released in 1967.

Four cameramen were hired to shoot the film. Aubrey Dewar first worked in film as the uncredited still photographer on *The Loneliness of the Long-Distance Runner* (1962), *The Girl with Green Eyes* (1964), and *One-Way Pendulum* (1965) and was finally credited for his work on *Morgan* (1966). He also worked as an assistant cameraman on *The Committee* (1968). Tony Busbridge began his career as an uncredited clapper loader in 1953, moving up to focus puller, though still uncredited. Prior to *Magical Mystery Tour*, he worked on the film *Dr. Zhivago* and went on to work on the film *Downhill Racer*. Daniel Lacambre worked extensively with Roger Corman and was also assistant cameraman on *A Man and A Woman*. Michael Seresin worked on *If . . .* , right after *Magical Mystery Tour* and subsequently worked on the films *Bugsy Malone*, *Midnight Express*, *Shoot the Moon*, *Bugsy*, *Angel Heart*, *Angela's Ashes*, and *Harry Potter and the Prisoner of Azkaban*, and is still actively working today. Interestingly, Ringo Starr, credited as "Richard Starkey," is listed as director of photography.

Sound was handled by Michael Lax, who would go on to work on numerous documentaries on Monty Python and Sean Connery, among others, the Broadway play *Hair*, as well as working in television. He worked on several projects with a music component, including *Message to Love: The Isle of Wight Festival*.

Design was done by Roger Graham and Keith Liddiard.

The film's unofficial assistant director was Andrew Birkin. Birkin, brother of Jane Birkin and the uncle of Charlotte Gainsbourg and Lou Doillon, has had a fascinating life. He started out as a runner on films for director Guy Hamilton, writer/director Charles Crichton, and on Stanley Kubrick's *2001: A Space Odyssey*. After *Magical Mystery Tour*, he worked with film producer and one-time head of Columbia Pictures David Puttnam and French director Jacques Demy. In 1974 he worked on *All that Glitters*, a documentary about British glam legends the Sweet. He has continued to make feature films, documentaries, and shorts, as well as acting and authoring two books. He has won several major film awards and has been involved in various philanthropic causes.

The film's editor was Roy Benson, who began his career on *A Hard Day's Night* as an uncredited assistant editor. Prior to *Magical Mystery Tour* he was the assistant editor of *The Bedford Incident*, went on to work on *An American Werewolf in London* and *Shanghai Surprise* (produced by George Harrison's Handmade Films), and appears as an interviewee in *The Making of Magical Mystery Tour* and *The Beatles: A Long and Winding Road*. He had the arduous task of editing the 10 hours of film down to 52 minutes, working from film shot on three different film stocks.

The sound editor was Gordon Daniel, who worked on *A Hard Day's Night*, *Modesty Blaise*, *The Spy Who Came in from the Cold*, and the period drama *Far from the Madding Crowd*.

Sound Editor Jim Roddan also worked on *Modesty Blaise*, as well as four Pink Panther films. Denis O'Dell's assistant was Gavrik Losey, the son of Joseph Losey, whose connection with the new British cinema has already been chronicled in detail. Gavrik would go on to work on such music related films as *That'll Be the Day*, *Stardust*, *Slade in Flame*, and *Babylon*, as well as *If . . .* and *Ned Kelly*, which costarred Mick Jagger and was directed by Tony Richardson.

Seven technicians were also along for the filming.

Alistair Taylor secured a 60-seat coach for the journey from Fox's of Hayes, in Middlesex. The coach was a 1959 British Bedford VAL Panorama Elite with a Plaxton body, license plate number URO 913E. The bus was painted yellow, with "Magical Mystery Tour" spelled out in multicolored, bold capital letters on each side as well as the back of the bus, with a blue strip underneath on each side that featured stars, rainbows, eyes, and other colorful psychedelic adornments. The bus would also gain attention from film fans when it appeared in *The Italian Job* in 1969, starring Michael Caine. In 1988 the Hard Rock Hotel chain purchased the bus.

There were many eccentric and offbeat members of the cast. Along with Victor Spinetti, Scottish poet, actor, musician, and quirky and brilliant Renaissance man, Ivor Cutler was a perfect foil for the Beatles. Paul McCartney had seen him perform on the British television show *Late Night Line-Up* and asked him to be in *Magical Mystery Tour*, playing Aunt Jessie's love interest, Buster Bloodvessel (a name he came up with). His strange singing style was very much a part of his act, as was his poetry, and it was planned that he would sing in *Magical Mystery Tour*, but the sequence ended up getting cut. Cutler began his career on BBC radio late in the 1950s on the *Monday Night at Home* radio show. He later become a staple of John Peel's radio show, adding comic relief to Peel's erudite and eclectic program. He appeared on various television shows, recorded more than a dozen albums, and wrote more than 30 books of prose, poetry, and children's stories. In 1967, he released the album *Ludo* on Parlophone, produced by George Martin. He was also a member of the Noise Abatement Society, which still exists; on its website, the organization describes itself as "a dynamic UK charity whose aim is to share a better understanding of what sound is, how it affects us and how we can solve noise problems in a pragmatic and sustainable way."

Ringo's Aunt Jessie, the object of Cutler's affections, was played by Jessie Robins. Robins was another British comedy, television, and film institution. She often appeared on such British comedy shows of the time as *The Benny Hill Show* and other seminal British television shows, such as *The Saint*, *Coronation Street*, and *Cathy Come Home*, which was part of *The Wednesday Play* series directed by Ken Loach. Robins would also appear in key British films of the era, including *Billy Liar!*, *Up the Junction*, *Chitty Chitty Bang Bang*, and Roman Polanski's *Dance of the Vampires*, a British/US coproduction. She also appeared in *Woman Times Seven*, released in 1967 and directed by Vittorio De Sica. During a break in filming on *Magical Mystery Tour* the gregarious actress showed off her musical skills, playing drums during a dinner break.

Many of the people the Beatles worked with on their films had some association with the Goons or Monty Python, such as Derek Royle, who played Jolly Jimmy the courier and appeared in many British television shows, including *Fawlty Towers*. In 1968 he appeared in *Work Is a Four-Letter Word* starring Cilla Black.

George Claydon played the photographer. In 1967 he also appeared in *Berserk!*, starring Joan Crawford, and *Casino Royale*; he would later appear in *Willy Wonka & the Chocolate Factory* and in Ringo Starr's T. Rex doc, *Born to Boogie*. He was one of several *Magical Mystery Tour* actors who were picked (mostly by Paul) out of the weekly magazine *Spotlight*, a resource for actors and casting agents that's still published today.

Nat Jackley was another old-school British eccentric who appeared in the film, as "Happy Nat the Rubber Man." Jackley, whose career began in the 1920s, had appeared in the theater, on television, and was in two other films connected to major 1960s British pop groups: *Mrs. Brown, You've Got a Lovely Daughter*, starting Herman's Hermits, and *Waterloo Sunset*, written and directed by Ray Davies of the Kinks. He also appeared in such films as *The Ploughman's Lunch* and *Yanks*. Though seen throughout the film, his key scene in *Magical Mystery Tour* ended up getting cut.

Other entertainers who appeared in the film included the Bonzo Dog Doo-Dah Band, performing the song "Death Cab for Cutie," written by Vivian Stanshall and Neil Innes (and which a Pacific Northwest indie band of the late 1990s would take as their own name). The band is seen backing stripper Jan Carson in a nightclub sequence, Stanshall delivering his vocals with all the louche sleaze of a faded Las Vegas lounge singer. The sequence was filmed at the Raymond Revuebar in London's Soho neighborhood. The club, formerly the Doric Ballroom, was opened by Paul Raymond as Raymond Revuebar in 1958 and ran until 2004. Since then, it has operated under a variety of different names and is today known as the Box Soho, a cabaret nightclub. Some of the performers from the Revuebar appeared in the 1964 UK musical *It's All Over Town*, which included among others Ivor Cutler, the Hollies, the Springfields, the Bachelors, and a future voice actor who would appear in *Yellow Submarine*, Lance Percival.

The Bonzo Dog Doo-Dah Band formed in 1962. The group's surrealist musical comedy fit right in with the Goons, Monty Python, and the new television, theater, and comedy forces that emerged late in the 1950s and early in the 1960s. By 1967, the Bonzos had become the house band on the British television show *Do Not Adjust Your Set*, which featured future Monty Python members Eric Idle, Terry Jones, and Michael Palin. The band's debut album *Gorilla* was released the same year. Their sound had become more psychedelic and fit right in with the emerging counterculture. Their 1968 Top-5 hit, "I'm the Urban Spaceman" was coproduced by Gus Dudgeon and Paul McCartney, using the alias Apollo C. Vermouth.

Other cast members included Mandy Weet as the hostess, Wendy Winters. Her real name was Miranda Forbes, and *Magical Mystery Tour* launched her career, primarily in television, and she later appeared in *Coronation Street*, *Absolutely Fabulous*, and two episodes of *Agatha Christie's Poirot*.

Maggie Wright appeared as the starlet. Her first role, in *Goldfinger*, was uncredited; she would go to appear in the films *What's New Pussycat?* and *The Assassination Bureau* and the television series *The Saint* and *The Martian Chronicles*.

Neil Aspinall and Magic Alex also appear in the film uncredited.

The film shoot for *Magical Mystery Tour* began on Monday, September 11, 1967. Paul had arranged for those invited to be on the coach to meet up at Allsop Place, near London's Baker Street tube station, the same starting point where music package tours of the early 1960s, including Beatles tours, had started from. Unfortunately, the coach, which was still being decorated, was two hours late in arriving. Paul was kept busy picking up the costumes for the shoot until the coach was finally ready, heading out of London for the west country, stopping off at Virginia Water, Surrey, to pick up the other three Beatles. There were 33 passengers on board, along with the Beatles and the film crew.

En route to Devon, the coach stopped for lunch at the Pied Piper restaurant on Winchester Road, Basingstoke, in Hampshire. The bus finally reached Devon in the evening, and the tired travelers spent the evening at the comfortable Royal Hotel on the Den in Teignmouth. If the Beatles thought they could just show up, register, and retire to their rooms for the evening, that is not how it turned out. The press had been following the Beatles since they left London, and despite taking the precaution of leaving the bus and arriving in a private car at the hotel, the Beatles confronted a large group waiting for them. Paul, always the group's savviest PR man, held a hasty press conference to pacify them.

The first night at the hotel was like the beginning of summer camp, with everyone jostling for room assignments and not always pleased with whom they would be bunking. While Paul was busy with logistics and housekeeping, John and technical director Peter Theobalds worked on Tuesday's shooting schedule. Theobalds was a filmmaker friend of Barry Miles and had a 15-page outline to work with. Plans for the next day's shoot would be worked out every evening, often with little regard to what had been shot during the day.

Tuesday, September 12, illustrated the challenges that would plague the filming of the movie. Traffic delays often forced the Beatles to change plans, and the shoot generated its own traffic, given that the coach was followed everywhere by an increasing contingent of reporters. Traffic led to the cancelation of filming at the Dartmoor Village Fair, then taking place in the moors of Widecombe. The Beatles had been used to having their way paved for them by Brian Epstein and his management team; now, they were forced to confront these issues themselves. The group did accommodate the BBC, with John and Paul granting an interview to Hugh Scully of *Spotlight South West*; the interview ran the next day.

The coach then headed to Liskeard, where no filming took place, and then moved on to Bodmin. There was a stop at the West End Dairy, where the passengers were filmed enjoying ice cream and other treats, a sequence deleted from the film. The next stop was on Paull Road, where the scene featuring the courier welcoming everyone on board was filmed.

In the evening, the coach stopped at the Atlantic Hotel in Newquay, a Cornish resort by the sea. Though planning to stay for just one night, the difficulties they'd already encountered led to the decision to stay for three nights. The next day, September 13, John directed a sequence at the hotel, as noted in a press report: "A very lucky few holidaymakers and locals even got a chance to star in the movie, with scenes of beautiful girls in bikinis being chased around the clifftops and outdoor swimming pool by character 'Happy Nat the rubber man.'" The scene was cut from the film.

Also shot on the same day were scenes of the four Beatles each looking through a telescope; another sequence cut from the film. At nearby Tregurrian Beach, a romantic scene between Buster Bloodvessel and Aunt Jessie was shot, oddly excised by the BBC when the film was first screened, though subsequently reinstated. While John was directing the shoot at the hotel's pool, Paul and Ringo set out for Porth, with the argument between Ringo and Aunt Jessie shot on the coach, and Paul shooting a sequence on the beach with George Claydon ("Little George the Photographer").

Meanwhile, George Harrison had opted to stay at the hotel, doing an interview with Miranda Ward of BBC Radio 1. Sipping tea and signing autographs, Harrison talked about the movie: "We want everybody to be able to freak out as it were—but we don't want to frighten—you know, some people get a bit frightened when like, 'A Day in the Life,' that record, when the music suddenly goes strange, and they don't know what it is. The natural thing when people don't know about something—they tend to fear it . . . so we don't want them to be puzzled by what's going on. So this way we can do—we can freak out a little bit, but it's—the excuse is that it's a Magical Mystery Tour."

Two sequences were shot in a field on September 14: one of George meditating, which wasn't used, and another where an impossibly large group is seen entering a small tent, which later served as the introduction to the "Blue Jay Way" sequence. In the evening Paul, Ringo, and Neil met up with Spencer Davis at the Tywarnhale pub in Perranporth, where Davis was on holiday; Paul took advantage of the setting to lead a singalong. Davis would show up briefly in the film on the bus, and he indicated John Mayall's wife Pamela was one of the camerapeople.

On September 15, the coach left Newquay to head back to London. On the way, a lunch stop at a fish and chips restaurant in Taunton, Somerset, was filmed but not used, as was later filming at a country pub. But a sweet scene between John and a little girl named Nicola Hale, shot on the bus, did make it into the film, as did a scene of Shirley Evans playing for the somewhat inebriated passengers.

By September 16, the Beatles were back at Abbey Road doing further work on "Your Mother Should Know"; the day's seventh take would later appear on *Anthology 2*. A mono mix of "Blue Jay Way" was made, and a tape copy of "I Am the Walrus" was prepared for the Beatles to mime to when they shot the sequence using the song the following week.

The first week of filming was an improvisational affair that reflected the freewheeling nature of the mystery coach tour concept that was the linchpin of the movie's theme. The second week would be more organized and feature various set pieces that captured the action off the bus.

On Monday, September 18, the band found themselves at the Raymond Revuebar at the improbable hour of 6:30 a.m. to shoot the "Death Cab for Cutie" sequence with the Bonzos and Jan Carson, though the shoot ended up being delayed because the Bonzos had their instruments stolen the previous day. Carson stripped topless, with the word *CENSORED* flashing across her chest, which was added during editing, to avoid having the entire scene removed by network censors and maybe also as a joke.

From September 19 through 24, filming took place in Kent. Not having realized that studios like Twickenham or Shepperton needed to be booked well in advance, the Beatles were forced to improvise when their first choices proved to be booked by others, and so they ended up at West Malling Air Station in Maidstone. The facility was built in 1917, initially used as a landing area during World War I. In 1930, it became the home of the Maidstone School for Flying and was known as Kinghill; it was subsequently renamed West Malling Airfield, Maidstone Airport, and RAF West Malling. It eventually became a US Naval Air Station before reverting back to nonmilitary use in the 1960s. Today the area is known as Kings Hill, and most of the structures present at the time of *Magical Mystery Tour*'s filming are gone.

As an example of the surreal nature of the film, one of the exterior scenes shot at West Malling included a bizarre tug-of-war scene with 12 children and blindfolded members of the clergy. Many of the main interior scenes of the movie were filmed inside one of the large airplane hangars, including the "Aunt Jessie's Dream" sequence which had literally come to John in a dream. John plays a greasy-haired waiter in the scene (perhaps inspired by his stepfather John Dykins's occupation), with his hair slicked back and sporting a pencil-thin moustache and an inane smile, shoveling piles of spaghetti onto Aunt Jessie's plate. Other restaurant patrons in the scene include the coach's hostess Wendy, who's stripped down to her bra.

The Beatles filming the *Magical Mystery Tour* television movie at the West Malling Air Station in Maidstone, Kent. Courtesy Photofest.

The Wizard's laboratory scene was filmed on Wednesday, the 20th, along with the "I Am the Walrus" sequence. This is the Beatles at their psychedelic peak, attired in their summer-of-love finery, designed by the Fool. Adding to the surreal antics, four policemen are seen precariously perched on one of the airfield's walls, swaying back and forth to the music and holding hands. The Beatles themselves also appear in animal costumes. It's worth noting that this is one of two times George Harrison would be shown playing his 1961 Fender Stratocaster that he painted in Day-Glo colors, the other time being the "All You Need Is Love" broadcast. The guitar was named "Rocky," which was written on the headstock; the words *BEBOPALULA* and *Go Cat Go* are also written on the guitar along with the Hare Krishna symbol. It may be Harrison's most iconic guitar, and it's great that it is captured here on film for posterity.

The sequence was later brilliantly parodied in *All You Need Is Cash*, a 1977 British TV special that told the story of the pre-Fab Four, the Rutles—Ron Nasty (Neil Innes), Dirk McQuickly (Eric Idle), Stig O'Hara (Ricky Fataar), and Barry Wom (John Halsey). The film's "Piggy in the Middle" sequence was filmed at the same West Malling Airfield location as "I Am the Walrus."

Most of the "Blue Jay Way" sequence was filmed on September 21 at West Malling Airfield, but a short insert of each Beatles playing a white cello in the garden of Ringo's home was shot on November 3. Another sequence shot that day inside Ringo's house had film from the West Malling shoot projected on Mal Evans's bare chest and John riding on a child's rocking horse.

On September 22, a hut at the airfield was used as the setting for the army recruiting scene, featuring Paul as Major McCartney, seen reading what looks like an old, oversized pamphlet called *The Great War*, and Victor Spinetti the recruiting officer. The film's opening scene, where Ringo buys tickets for the mystery tour from a newsagent, played by John, was also shot this day. The scene was shot at the Town Newsagency, at 90 High Street, West Malling, after it had closed for the day.

Another scene that was shot was where Jolly Jimmy welcomes people to crawl into the "magic" tent where the "Blue Jay Way" sequence was shown, a follow-up to filming from September 14. George was not present for any of the filming on this day.

The marathon race sequence, featuring a mad scramble around the airfield, was shot on September 23. On September 24, the final day of filming at West Malling, the closing ballroom scene where the Beatles perform "Your Mother Should Know" alongside 160 dancers from the Peggy Spencer formation dance group. Additional filming for "I Am the Walrus" was also done on this day, along with a scene of Ivor Cutler performing "I'm Going in a Field," which was cut from the film.

It was clear that what the Beatles had shot on film had something of the same vibe of the music they had been making as far back as *Revolver*. But the surrealistic aspect of *Magical Mystery Tour* was lost on those who saw it when it was first broadcast on the BBC on December 26, 1967, an impression that was not helped by the fact that the film was broadcast in black and white.

SURREALISTIC PILLOW

The surrealist movement grew out of the Dada art movement of the early 1920s. Dada began a direct line from the cut-up literary works of Tristan Tzara, T. S. Eliot, and others to John Dos Passos and the beats, such as William Burroughs and Brion Gysin. There were also the Dada artists Marcel Duchamp, Man Ray, and many others, along with the two figureheads of the movement, Tzara and André Breton. Breton's *Surrealist Manifesto* is almost a handbook on the underpinning of the 1960s psychedelic explosion, though he died in 1966 and so missed experiencing the 1967 summer of love. While a rejection of cultural norms and a pursuit of rearranging the senses were linchpins of the psychedelic movement, Breton's political anarchism was only beginning to stir. It's interesting that René Magritte, one of the key surrealist painters, would be a favorite of Paul McCartney and his artistic style would partially influence the final design of the Apple label art. McCartney owned three Magritte paintings, and one, *Le Jeu de Mourre* (*The Game of Mora*, 1966), which Robert Fraser acquired for him, was a painting of a green apple with the words *Au revoir* written on it in white cursive script.

This surrealistic aspect of *Magical Mystery Tour* was welcomed by uncredited camera operator Michael Seresin, who was born in New Zealand and has a still thriving film career. He worked on many films with Alan Parker, including *Midnight Express*, *Fame*, and *Angela's Ashes*, along with working on *Harry Potter and the Prisoner of Azkaban*. Prior to working on *Magical Mystery Tour,* he had just come off working, again uncredited, on *If . . .* , directed by Lindsey Anderson.

He described the feeling of what it was like working on *Magical Mystery Tour*:

> Such a different energy from the typical well organized hierarchal film business. I loved it. Such great lateral and free energy. I don't recall any particular direction. Shots and sequences seemed to just evolve. And we filmed it. In many ways, the whole project was the antithesis of conventional film making, which I found stimulating. Not sure too many others in the crew did. It was an experimental home movie I guess . . . Paul was the most intense and interested in getting all the material we required. . . . My one abiding memory on the last evening, a huge generator broke down and we had to wait hours for two replacements. All the dancers in the final number wanted to leave. I recall John saying to the others, "We better get out there, sign a few autographs and entertain them, or we will lose them and won't complete the number." The others agreed and wandered out. The dozens of dancers remained and we completed the sequence.

Thinking they were done on September 25, the Beatles took the 10 hours of film that had been shot to Norman's Film Productions in London, where they were joined by the film editor Ray Benson. While Paul, and to a lesser degree John, was the most active in the editing process, George and Ringo were also occasionally on hand. Initial estimates were that it would take two weeks to edit the film; instead, the editing process ended up taking 11 weeks, and more footage would be shot.

There would also be soundtrack overdubs to be done. On September 25 and 26, they worked on "The Fool on the Hill" at Abbey Road, with George Martin producing, Geoff Emerick as the engineer, and Richard Lush as the tape operator. The Beatles played a variety of instruments on the final version of "The Fool on the Hill," including two acoustic guitars, bass and drums, along with harmonica and finger cymbals, among other instruments and studio effects; there were also three additional flute players.

Considerable work was done on September 27 on "I Am the Walrus," including orchestral work and, in Abbey Road's Studio 3, the recording of 17 vocalists from the Mike Sammes Singers. The Singers would subsequently work with the Beatles again, providing vocals on "Good Night" on the White Album. Despite claims that the singers are saying "Smoke pot, smoke pot, everybody smoke pot," the lines were actually "Oompah, oompah, stick up your jumper," and "Everybody's got one, everybody's got one," taken from a 1940s recording by the Two Leslies. More work on "The Fool on the Hill" was also done at this session.

On September 28, tape copies of "Magical Mystery Tour" and "Flying" were readied, along with further work done on "I Am the Walrus." The mono mix release version was also completed for "I Am the Walrus," with further work done on "I Am the Walrus" on the 29th. John came up with the idea of taking random elements from a radio broadcast of *The Tragedy of King Lear* on BBC Radio 3's *Third Programme*, featuring John Gielgud as the king. The actual dialogue used on the track are the performances of Mark Dignam as Gloucester, Phillip Guard as Edgar, and John Bryning as Oswald. Due to the use of this live feed, with some stereo mixing done on November 6 and 7, the song is essentially half in stereo and half in mono. Capitol would be supplied with mono, stereo, and mono/stereo versions of the track but would ultimately release it, as they had done often, in fake, duo-phonic stereo. More work on "Your Mother Should Know" was also done at the session on September 29, lasting until nearly sunrise the next day on Saturday morning.

There was more filming on October 1 at West Malling, shooting additional footage of the coach. On October 2, further work was done on "Your Mother Should Know" along with a new song, then titled "Hello Hello" (later changed to "Hello Goodbye"), for the group's next single. The song had been partially worked out by Paul and NEMS Alistair Taylor, as a sort of word game, which all four Beatles contributed to. Lennon was never a fan of the song, aside from the ad-libbed fade-out ending, especially chosen as the A side of the single, relegating "I Am the Walrus" to the B side. "It's just a song of duality, with me advocating the more positive," Paul later observed. "You say goodbye, I say hello, You say stop, I say go. I was advocating the more positive side of the duality, and I still do to this day."

On October 6, more work was done on "Blue Jay Way." On October 12, the Beatles began the day at De Lane Lea Studios to work on "It's All Too Much," which would end up on the *Yellow Submarine* soundtrack, with the song running slightly longer in the film, due to having an extra verse. Then the work moved to Abbey Road for the "Shirley's Wild Accordion" session.

Shirley Evans supplied accordion for the film and, even recorded a specific number for it, the Lennon/McCartney instrumental "Shirley's Wild Accordion" at a session at Olympic Studio on October 12. Paul and Ringo contributed to the track, and the session was produced by John, his first time as a producer. Though Shirley is seen performing in the film, "Shirley's Wild Accordion" wasn't ultimately used. It remains unreleased to this day.

The world premiere of Richard Lester's *How I Won the War*, featuring John in a minor role as Private Gripweed, was held on October 18 at the London Pavilion. All the Beatles, their wives, and Paul's girlfriend Jane Asher attended, along with the film's star, Michael Crawford, Beatles friends Pete Shotton and Alex Madras, as well as Jimi Hendrix and Noel Redding of the Jimi Hendrix Experience, the Mamas and the Papas' Cass Elliot, actor David Hemmings and his wife Gayle Hunnicut, and Cilla Black, who threw a party at her apartment after the opening.

The next day, overdubbing on "Hello Goodbye" was done at Abbey Road. Further overdubs to "The Fool on the Hill" and "Hello Goodbye" were added on October 20, with no involvement from the Beatles, though they were in attendance. For "The Fool on the Hill," George Martin worked with flautists Christopher Taylor and Richard Taylor. Because all four tracks of the reel that contained "The Fool on the Hill" were full, a second four-track machine was synchronized through an ingenious solution, which was to use a new tape with a reference mix of the newest mono mix and a 50-kilocycle tone that would be the basis of the synchronization. This method would be employed again on November 1 to create the stereo mix.

On October 24, *A Hard Day's Night* made its television debut in the US, airing on NBC. On October 25, Paul returned to Abbey Road to work on "Hello Goodbye." On October 29, more scenes for *Magical Mystery Tour* were shot on Acanthus Road in Lavender Hill, where Ringo and Aunt Jessie are seen arguing as they walk to where the coach is waiting.

On October 30, Paul flew to Nice, France, accompanied by cameraman Aubrey Dewar, to shoot footage for "The Fool on the Hill," capturing the sunrise and the mountains, returning to England the next day.

When looking back on photos or film footage that was not actually used in *Magical Mystery Tour* of the Beatles shooting at various locations along the way, one is struck by how easily fans were able to interact with the Beatles and the Beatles didn't seem put off by it at all. In many photos and film, they seem friendly, allowing autographs and photographs, and generally seem relaxed.

On November 1, work was done on the mono mixes of "All You Need Is Love" and "Lucy in the Sky with Diamonds" for the *Yellow Submarine* movie. Paul did some final work on "Hello Goodbye" on November 2. There was also work done on mixes of "The Fool on the Hill." The next day work was done on "Hello Goodbye" and "I Am the Walrus." On November 7, copies of mono and stereo mixes of "Magical Mystery Tour," "The Fool on the Hill," "I Am the Walrus," "Flying," "Blue Jay Way," "Your Mother Should Know," and "Strawberry Fields Forever" were made and given to Voyle Gilmore of Capitol Records.

On November 10, the Beatles taped two promotional video clips for "Hello Goodbye." A third was also prepared comprised of material from the two. *Magical Mystery Tour* film editor Roy Benson also prepared a still yet unseen fourth video that was more a montage then a promotional clip.

The "Hey Bulldog" animated sequence was cut from initial prints of *Yellow Submarine* in America. While working on a video for "Lady Madonna" in February 1968 at Abbey Road Studios, Paul suggested instead they should work on a new song. John had some of the seeds a song, eventually called "Hey Bulldog," and everyone chipped in to complete it. Though the lyrics mention a bullfrog, Paul's barking during the number led to "bulldog" being added to the lyric as well (in addition to providing the title). Erich Segal, one of *Yellow Submarine*'s screenwriters, made the farfetched claim that "Hey Bulldog" referred to the mascot of his own alma mater, Yale. It was the last song recorded before the Beatles left for India in mid-February. Lennon was more dismissive about it, telling *Playboy*, "It's a good sounding record that means nothing."

The "Hey Bulldog" sequence in *Yellow Submarine* was storyboarded by Jack Stokes and animated by Group 2 Animation. The segment was included in the UK prints of *Yellow Submarine* but eliminated from the US version. It was finally restored for the 1999 reissue of the film on DVD.

Sometime in November 1967 the Beatles took part in a seven-minute promotional film titled *A Mod Odyssey*. The film would be used to promote the *Yellow Submarine* movie. It was primarily filmed at TV Cartoons (TVC), the production company producing *Yellow Submarine*, located at 36-38 Dean Street in Soho in London on the second floor. The area buzzed with the work of many animation companies and film lab establishments frequented by the *Yellow Submarine* film crew, with film labs Kays, Humphries, Studio Film Lab and Technicolor also in the area. It was located in a part of London near familiar haunts of the Beatles, including clubs right on Dean Street such as the Groucho Club and the Gargoyle Club, on Cranbourn Street, the Talk of the Town club, and on Gerrard Street, Ronnie Scott's club, and also on Dean Street, two key studios other than Abbey Road Studios used by the Beatles, De Lane lea Studios and Trident Studios on Flaxman Court. The record company that turned them down, Decca Records, was located on Great Marlborough Street. TVC was run by George Dunning. Dunning was joined by his partner John Coates, an animation director, who had worked at Associated Rediffusion, an early component of ITV in London. Interestingly, *Yellow Submarine* would be produced by a company called Tarot Associates, who were contracted to do it by UA, even though *Yellow Submarine* did not count as the third film the Beatles owed UA as part of their contract. Film of the Beatles from January 25 at Twickenham supposedly looking admiringly at footage of *Yellow Submarine* would be shown on NBC, after the first American television airing of *Help!* on October 12, 1968.

The "Hello Goodbye"/"I Am the Walrus" single was released on November 24 in the UK. "I Am the Walrus" has always been regarded as one of Lennon's most intriguing compositions, and the resulting track is a major exponent of the group's psychedelic period. Both the "Hello Goodbye" single and the *Magical Mystery Tour* album were released in the US on November 27 (the *Magical Mystery Tour* double EP was released in the UK on December 8). While the UK double EP contained six tracks, the US LP contained 11; the six songs that appeared on the UK EP, as well as "Penny Lane," "Strawberry Fields Forever," "All You Need Is Love," "Baby You're a Rich Man," and "Hello Goodbye."

Given that incidental music from the Beatles' films had appeared on the US soundtracks, it's surprising none of the incidental music from *Magical Mystery Tour* was ever officially released. While the incidental music may seem inconsequential, fans might like to have this music as part of an expanded audio edition of the album: the mellotron music, "She Loves You" playing on a fairground organ (from *Irvin's 89 Key Marenghi Fair Organ Plays Lennon & McCartney* on Decca), "All My Loving" played by a string quartet (from *Beatle-Cracker Ballet* by Arthur Wilkinson and His Orchestra on EMI/HMV), John singing "Two Little Dicky Birds" and "There's No Business Like Show Business," and the Bonzo Dog Doo Dah Band's "Death Cab For Cutie." There's also the singalong on the coach, led by Shirley Evans and her accordion, which included "I've Got a Lovely Bunch of Coconuts," "Toot Toot Tootsie, (Goo' bye)," "The Happy Wanderer," "When Irish Eyes Are Smiling," "When the Red, Red Robin (Comes Bob, Bob, Bobbin' Along)," "Never on a Sunday," and the "Can Can" dance from Offenbach's *Orpheus in the Underworld*. Several instrumental passages, including "Circus Fanfare" by Keith Papworth from *The Big Top* and "Winning Hit" by Herbert Chappell from *Marching Highlights* are from de Wolfe, the stock music library company. Other instrumental music includes "Zampa Overture" by the G.U.S. (Footwear) Band with Stanley Boddington.

Capitol Records had continually botched many of their Beatles album releases, but with *Magical Mystery Tour* they came up with a better release than the Parlophone double EP. EMI finally released the *Magical Mystery Tour* full-length album in the UK in November 1976, though unfortunately, they used Capitol's duophonic fake stereo masters for "Penny Lane," "Strawberry Fields," "All You Need Is Love," "Baby You're a Rich Man," and "Hello Goodbye."

Another strong point of the US *Magical Mystery Tour* album was that the 24-page booklet was blown up to a 12-inch square size, as opposed to the UK EP, which was a seven-inch square size. The booklet included song lyrics, John Kelly's stills from the film, and colorful psychedelic illustrations by Bob Gibson formatted like comic strips. Some of the strips show illustrations of action that didn't appear in the film because the book was prepared well in advance of the final edit. Gibson was already known to fans of the Beatles from his work on *The Beatles Book Monthly*. The booklet was edited by NEMS press office manager Tony Barrow, with Neil Aspinall and Mal Evans as editorial consultants. The liner notes have some jokey asides, as in the credit "Produced by Big George Martin"—the only time Martin was credited in this fashion. It's in keeping with the jocular mood of the project but also a reference to how Martin was often referenced, wherein he was big George and Harrison was little George. And the title of "I Am the Walrus" is the notation "'No you're not!' said Little Nicola," referring to the little girl on the bus that John entertained. It's also interesting to note that all the songs from the movie were listed as being published by Maclen Music, Inc., BMI, on first pressings of the US release, and Comet Music Corp. and ASCAP on future releases. Finally, the cover itself is worthy of attention. On the cover, the Beatles are all dressed like they were in the film, in animal costumes with George as a rabbit, Ringo as a chicken (was that the best they could do?), Paul as a hippopotamus, and John as the walrus. Of course, in the song "Glass Onion," which would appear on the White Album, Lennon would say "the walrus was Paul." He also references two other songs from the *Magical Mystery Tour* album in "Glass Onion": "Strawberry Fields Forever" and "The Fool on the Hill." He would also mention "Lady Madonna."

On November 28, George Harrison started working on music for the film *Wonderwall* at Abbey Road, after The Fool connected Harrison with the director of the film, Joe Massot, yet another American living and working in England at that time. Harrison was simultaneously working on the music for the film at De Lane Lea studios and, in January, would go to EMI's studio in Bombay (now Mumbai) to do more work. As well as music by Indian musicians, Harrison played piano, mellotron, and acoustic and electric guitar on the album's western-style tracks, which also featured appearances by Eric Clapton, Ringo Starr, Big Jim Sullivan, Tommy Reilly, and the Liverpool group The Remo Four.

Harrison also worked on "The Inner Light" at the same studio on January 12, 1968, something of a follow-up to "It's All Too Much" and "Within You Without You," which were all influenced by Harrison's interest in Eastern religion and culture, with the *Tao Te Ching* text the primary lyrical influence on these songs. "The Inner Light," recorded in twin-track stereo, would first appear as the B side of the "Lady Madonna" single released on March 15, 1968 in the UK. A stereo mix first appeared on the US *Hey Jude* compilation, released in December 1969 and released in the UK a decade later. "The Inner Light" subsequently appeared on *Rarities*; *Past Masters, Volume 2*; and *Mono Masters*. An alternate instrumental take of the song is included on the *Wonderwall Music* CD in the George Harrison *The Apple Years 1968–75* box set released in 2014. In *I Me Mine*, George offers a detailed explanation on how and why he wrote the song. He references the *Tao Te Ching* but also the book *Lamps of Fire* given to him by Juan Mascaro, who at the time was the Sanskrit teacher at Cambridge University. In his notes on the song George says, "The song was written especially for Juan Mascaro because he sent me the book and is a sweet old man. It was nice, the words said everything. AMEN"

Amid all the activity in the world of the Beatles at this time, Ringo went to Rome, Italy, to be in the film *Candy*, and Paul fled to his Scottish retreat. Therefore, only two Beatles were at the private party held for the opening of the Apple boutique on Baker Street on December 5, which opened to the public on December 17 in the UK. It was very much modeled after the aforementioned Granny Takes a Trip, being a hip clothing store that dealt in the various antique clothing and new hippie styles, that the pop and rock stars of the day frequented. The boutique's exterior also stood out, covered by a three-story psychedelic mural by The Fool, that was ultimately whitewashed over after complaints from neighboring businesses. In an interview for this book, Marijke of The Fool recounted the direction from the Beatles on how to approach designing the mural. "The Beatles always gave us a free hand. The only suggestion was made by John for the promo poster for the boutique; 'the legend A is for Apple' but that was all."

On December 8, the *Magical Mystery Tour* double EP was released in the UK, their last such release in that format and the only UK EP issued in mono and stereo (all previous UK Eps were in mono). This EP contained six tracks: "Magical Mystery Tour," "Your Mother Should Know," "I Am the Walrus," "The Fool and the Hill," "Flying," and "Blue Jay Way." The stereo version of "Blue Jay Way" includes backward tape effects, the cello is treated with multiple echo, and there's a final organ note. The mono version of "Flying" has extra bass and piano, and the sound effects at the end come in earlier than on the stereo version. The stereo version has an ending vocal track not heard on the mono version. The stereo version of "Fool on the Hill" includes extra flute, and near the end, some vocals are missing that are on the mono version. On the title track there are subtle differences in the trumpet part of the mono and stereo versions.

THE WINTER OF LOVE

On December 8, 1967, the Rolling Stones released *Their Satanic Majesties Request*, featuring caricatures of all four of the Beatles, buried/hidden in the lenticular artwork on the cover, paying back the love the Beatles showed for the group, including a Shirley Temple doll with the words "Welcome Rolling Stones" written on the cover of *Sgt. Pepper's Lonely Hearts Club Band*. The album was the group's response to *Sgt. Pepper*, and although it was not greeted warmly on release, it has become more appreciated over the years, taking on a more cultlike status. The album at one time was going to be called *Cosmic Christmas*, and the last track on side one, "Sing This All Together (See What Happens)," includes a roughly 30-second piece of music taken from the abandoned title "Cosmic Christmas," which comes in near the eight-minute mark, and if the speed on a turntable is changed, it sounds like a drone-like version of "We Wish You a Merry Christmas," apparently the handiwork of Bill Wyman.

The year 1967 ended with some extraordinary albums being released. In November came such American albums as *After Bathing at Baxter's* from the Jefferson Airplane, *Again* from the Buffalo Springfield, and *Forever Changes* from Love. From

England came *Disraeli Gears* from Cream, *The Who Sell Out* from the Who, and *Days of Future Past* from the Moody Blues. In December, *John Wesley Harding* from Bob Dylan and *Songs of Leonard Cohen* came from the US, and in England came the release of *Mr. Fantasy* from Traffic.

Ringo was in Rome from December 7 through 16 and was based at Incom Film Studios to film *Candy*. The French/Italian coproduction was directed by Christian Marquand and was based on the Mason Hoffenberg/Terry Southern novel, with a screenplay by Buck Henry (who had a small role in the film as a mental patient). The cast of aging international heavyweights included Marlon Brando, Richard Burton, John Huston, Charles Aznavour, and even the boxer Sugar Ray Robinson; Ringo played the minor role of Emmanuel, the gardener. The lurid, yet lightweight sex romp focused on the sexual exploits of Candy, played by former Miss Sweden Ewa Aulin, primarily in a state of undress. Other women in this older, male-heavy cast, included Italian actresses Marlilu Tolo playing Candy's sister Conchita, Nicoletta Machiavelli playing Marquita, Lea Padovani playing Silvia Fontegliulo, and Brazilian actress Florinda Bolkan as Lolita. Elsa Martinelli playing Livia Christian probably had the biggest female role outside of Candy, and don't miss Anita Pallenberg as Nurse Bullock.

The film wouldn't be released in the States until December 17, 1968 and wouldn't be released in Italy until February 1970 and France until August 1970. Although receiving mixed reviews, the overlong, uneven, laughable, politically incorrect (by today's standards), mess of a film nonetheless eventually did good business at the box office over time and continues to rack up sales via disc and streaming and is considered a cult classic of late 1960s psychedelic international sex cinema. The soundtrack featured a score by jazz muso Dave Grusin, who had recently worked on the soundtracks for both *Kaleidoscope* and *The Graduate*, as well as tracks by the Byrds and Steppenwolf.

On December 17, a screening party for *Magical Mystery Tour* was held for the Beatles fan club secretaries at Hanover Grand Film and Art Theatre in London, attended by John and George, who just returned from Paris. And in a stark contrast to *Magical Mystery Tour* and the Beatles, the Shea Stadium TV special from 1965 was also screened late in 1967.

On December 21, a fancy dress party was held to mark the imminent televising of *Magical Mystery Tour* on British TV and doubled as a holiday party thrown by the Beatles. It was held at the posh and cavernous Westbourne Suite at the Royal Lancaster Hotel in London. It was one of the last big Beatles social events to happen before the group fractured and the business of the Beatles consumed them; more than 200 guests were invited, including nearly everyone connected with *Magical Mystery Tour*, as well as Apple and NEMS staffers. Five bands played, including the Bonzo Dog Doo Dah Band. Billy J. Kramer recalled for the author the evening:

I was at the *Magical Mystery Tour* fancy dress party. The party was at the Royal Lancaster hotel. We were told to wear something different. I went to a costumer's and got an old-fashioned costume. It was velvet and a typical old-fashioned, English costume. When John Lennon arrived, he had on a denim jacket, with John written in metal studs across the back and he had his hair greased up in a Tony Curtis, Teddy-boy style. I spent most of the time with John's wife Cynthia keeping her company while John was smushing. I can't remember her dress, but her hairstyle and her complexion made her look l like a cameo. The thing I liked in the *Magic Mystery Tour* movie was John shuffling spaghetti. I do remember I was sober which was unusual for me back then. Paul and Jane Asher were dressed up like what's known as the cockney Pearly King and Queen. I spoke with George and Pattie in passing and I can't remember Ringo.

Magical Mystery Tour debuted on BBC-1 on Tuesday, December 26 (Boxing Day in England) at 8:35 p.m., following *This Is Petula: A Petula Clark Christmas Special*. The BBC had paid £10,000 for the rights to the film, which drew more than 13 million viewers. The film was broadcast in black and white, and most were only able to watch the show on the small sets that were commonly available at the time. Unsurprisingly, then, the movie was initially panned by most critics. The freewheeling film didn't have a conventional plotline, which made it a hard sell to the average person expecting mainstream entertainment. Coming after the exalted triumph of *Rubber Soul*, *Revolver*, and most recently, "Penny Lane," "Strawberry Fields Forever," *Sgt. Pepper*, and "All You Need Is Love," the film was a real comedown.

It gave the Fleet Street press cranks their first chance to go after the mighty Beatles, and the movie was savaged by the critics. In the *Melody Maker* of January 6, 1968, Bob Dawbarn best summed up how the movie divided the freaks from the straights: "If the Beatles *Magical Mystery Tour* TV show achieved nothing else, it underlined the remarkable gap between the generations; between the today people and suburbia; between traditionalists and those who keep looking for something better." It was far easier for him to heap unqualified praise on the double EP, calling it "six tracks which no other pop group in the world could begin to approach for originality combined with the popular touch." In an interview for this book, director Cameron Crowe recalls seeing the movie the way most people first saw it in America. "I saw one of those midnight screenings and liked it a lot. It had a great odd vibe. It was a nice time piece, very specific to the era."

The movie was shown again on January 5 on BBC-2 and in color and received a more favorable reception. But the BBC had trouble selling rights to anyone, finally working out a deal with Dutch television station VARA, who broadcast the show on February 10, 1968, in a Saturday morning slot normally reserved for children's programming. NBC had planned to show the film in the US but canceled due to the poor reviews. ABC also passed on the opportunity to air the film in the US.

"They were all looking for the plum pudding special," Paul said in *Many Years From Now*. "That's what they were expecting, and they very much didn't get it!" He later went on the *David Frost Show* to defend the film on December 27. The critical backlash unnerved the Beatles, and a flurry of defensive activity was quickly put in motion through interviews, various statements put out by the Beatles through Tony Barrow, and with a separate statement from NEMS Enterprises going overboard about a television show that had yet to be seen by anyone outside of England: "*Magical Mystery Tour* is being accepted all over the world as an important and successful experimental film."

In May 1968, as John and Paul were appearing on *The Tonight Show* to promote their Apple Corps venture, *Magical Mystery Tour* was sporadically screened across America, meeting with a more favorable reaction. It was first shown in two midnight screenings on May 10 and 11 at the Los Feliz Theater in Los Angeles, with proceeds going to the Underground Radio Strike Fund (for the DJs at KPPC radio then on strike). The film print was supplied by former Beatles publicist Derek Taylor, then living in California. Admission was $3. The first night drew an appreciative audience of 550, with good word of mouth assuring a sellout crowd of 770 the following night. Other showings included a screening at the Royce Hall on the UCLA campus on Thursday, May 16 and the following weekend, May 24 through 26, at the Esquire-Pasadena theater. The film was also shown that summer at the Fillmore East on August 11, 1968. Apple Corps further advertised that the film could be rented and would be shown with the short film *Ingrid*, which featured music from the Beatles.

In 1974 New Line Cinema acquired theatrical rights and gave the film a limited release. Either because philistines run American television or because the Beatles purposely kept it off television in the US, the film did not receive a national network airing until December of 2012, when the *Magical Mystery Tour* box set was released, and the film was screened on PBS.

Work on "Only a Northern Song" began on February 13, 1967, in the middle of the *Sgt. Pepper* sessions, and was to be one of George's contributions to that album. It was a dig at George's unfair treatment in contributing songs to Beatles albums but also about Liverpool. "'(Only a) Northern Song' was a joke relating to Liverpool, the Holy City in the North of England," he said in *I Me Mine*. "In addition, the song was copyrighted Northern Songs Ltd, which I don't own." In 1967, there were various working titles of this song including "Not Unknown," "Not Known," "Anything," and "India."

After another session on February 14, the group wouldn't return to the song until April 19. Work on the track continued through April 21, but once it was dropped from *Sgt. Pepper*, no further work was done until November 15, when a tape copy of the final mono mix was copied for use on the *Yellow Submarine* soundtrack. Nearly a year later, on October 29, 1968, a stereo mix of the song was attempted. The mono mix had been achieved by synching two four-track machines, rendering a true stereo mix nearly impossible, thus forcing the Abbey Road team to create a fake stereo mix fashioned from the final mono mix. This mix appeared on the stereo *Yellow Submarine* soundtrack.

The track "Yellow Submarine" would appear in slightly different versions on the UK mono and stereo editions of *Revolver*. A remixed version of the original track was released on the CD version of the "Real Love" single in 1996. The stereo remix included a previously unreleased spoken introduction from Ringo, with marching sounds and other sound effects on the original release now mixed much louder in volume.

Other versions of tracks from *Magical Mystery Tour* appear on *Anthology 2*: "I Am the Walrus" take 16; "Your Mother Should Know" take 27; "Hello Goodbye" take 16; and "The Fool on the Hill" demo and take 4. There are three versions of "Strawberry Fields Forever," a nearly two-minute version of John Lennon's demo and takes 1 and 7. There are two versions of "Penny Lane," a mono edit and a remix version.

The 2017 *Sgt. Pepper's Lonely Hearts Club Band 6 Disc Super Deluxe (Anniversary Edition)* box set, celebrating the 50th anniversary of the album's release includes alternate versions of songs that didn't make the album. There are four takes of "Strawberry Fields Forever" and a 2015 stereo mix. There are four takes, the original mono mix, and Capitol Record's mono promotional mix of "Penny Lane." There is a Blu-ray/DVD audio of both promotional films. The two CD set includes two takes of "Strawberry Fields Forever," one take and the 2015 mix, and the 2017 stereo mix of "Penny Lane." None of the vinyl *Sgt. Pepper* anniversary releases had any bonus material. The two promotional films also appear on the CD/2DVD and 2CD/2Blu-ray *1+* box sets.

The afterlife of *Magical Mystery Tour* continues with a fond appreciation of the film's eccentricities. *Magical Mystery Tour* has been rereleased many times in the US and the UK. In the US it was rereleased on VHS and Betamax in 1978, on VHS and laser disc in 1988, and on laser disc again in 1992. The original VHS, released through MPI Home Video, was of poor quality and is even presented in an incorrect aspect ratio, though it does include some unique alternative vocals in part on the title track. The 1988 release has overall better sound, with a Dolby digital audio remix by George Martin. The unique vocal on the title track remains, now in true stereo, but included for the last time on this release. The proper aspect ratio was restored, and the overall film looks much cleaner and clear. The film was not given a rating. The run time is stated as 50 minutes, but the current box set gives a running time of 53 minutes.

The film debuted on DVD in 1997 with little change, except the use of the album version of the title song and the alteration of a special effect. It was reissued in a box set in 2012, which included the film on DVD and Blu-ray (its first release in that format), which was a replica of the original double EP released in the UK, and a ticket. The two 7-inch vinyl discs were remastered, appear here in mono, and, on the label, are dated 2009. When the original *Magical Mystery Tour* double EP was released, record buyers had the choice of mono and stereo. Special features included on the DVD and Blu-ray include a commentary track from Paul McCartney; a 20-minute *The Making of* Magical Mystery Tour documentary; a *Meet the Supporting Cast* documentary; a short *Ringo the Actor* documentary, two scenes deleted from the film, new edits of "Your Mother Should Know," "Blue Jay Way," and "The Fool on The Hill"; and the "Hello Goodbye" clip as prepared for *Top of the Pops*. There is also a clip of Traffic performing "Here We Go Round the Mulberry Bush," which was dropped from the finished film. The title of the song was taken from the 1965 novel by Hunter Davies that the 1968 film was based on. Davies is of course the author of the Beatles official biography released in 1968. Davies fondly recalled the film and music in an interview with the author: "I was not involved with the music. (Director) Clive Donner did all that. I only met Traffic and Spencer Davis once in a small viewing theater in Soho (in London) when Clive ran a rough cut of the film for me—and the musicians—to see it for the first time with music added. I thought it was fab—so impressive and professional and clever."

The aspect ratio is 1.33:1. The Blu-ray is presented in DTS-HD master Audio 5.1, Dolby Digital 5.1, and PCM Stereo. The DVD is presented in Dolby Digital Stereo, DTS 5.1, and Dolby Digital 5.1. Everything is housed in a 10-inch box and includes a 60-page book. This is perhaps the best reissue box set of a Beatles film, although the deluxe *Help!* set is also quite good.

Surprisingly, the film's nontheatrical release history in the UK has been rather checkered. The first VHS release was in 1981, followed by a VHS and laser disc release in 1988. As in the US, it debuted on DVD in 1997 and Blu-ray in 2012.

A final note on *Magical Mystery Tour*. Although this book is mostly concerned with US and UK editions of recordings from the Beatles, the 1973 German edition of the album, *Magical Mystery Tour Plus Other Songs* (from Horzu and on the Apple label), has been one of the most praised pressings of any recording by the group. Three songs not in the film, "Penny Lane," "Baby You're a Rich Man," and "All You Need is Love," appear on this edition in true stereo for the first time, and the overall sound quality of the mastering and pressing is exceptional.

5

It's All in The Mind, Ya Know?

"Once upon a time, or maybe twice, there was an unearthly paradise called Pepperland. Eighty thousand leagues beneath the sea it lay, or lie (I'm not too sure)."

Rapid cultural changes had been unfolding throughout the 1960s, with the apex of hope and the hippie ideal peaking in the summer of 1967. The year 1968 would prove to be one where the fragile and idealistic ethos of the young and the new began to break apart.

New British films reflected a wide array of genres and represented something new or caught the public or critics imagination. *Oliver!*, one of the biggest films of the year, was an example of a last gasp of the big-budget musical. *The Lion in Winter* was a historical epic with a heavyweight cast (including future James Bond, Timothy Dalton, in his screen debut). *Mrs. Brown, You've Got a Lovely Daughter*, featuring Herman's Hermits, seemed like a throwback to *A Hard Day's Night* and the gush of British pop group films that sprang up in the early to mid-1960s. *The Girl on A Motorcycle*, a somewhat underrated film, featured pop star Marianne Faithfull. *Up the Junction* had some of the stark kitchen-sink realism of the earlier part of the decade and featured a soundtrack that included the music of Manfred Mann. *Joanna*, nominated for a Golden Globe for best foreign language film, was very much a Swinging London film. *Isadora* met with mixed reviews. It featured another breakout role for Vanessa Redgrave, playing dancer Isadora Duncan, and reteamed her with Karl Reisz, who also directed her in *Morgan*.

Another fresh new film of the moment was *If...*, directed by Lindsay Anderson. Indian-born, Oxford-educated Brit Lindsay Anderson burst on to the scene with the seminal new British cinema film *This Sporting Life* in 1963. After *The White Bus*

213

The Beatles appeared briefly at the end of the *Yellow Submarine* movie. Courtesy Photofest.

in 1967, he scored with the timely *If . . .* in 1968, centered on the brutish English boarding school class warfare, used as a metaphor of the burgeoning revolution of the Prague spring.

The movie event of the year was the release of *2001: A Space Odyssey.* The film was produced and directed by Stanley Kubrick, an American living and working in England. The UK/US production, released through MGM, featured a screenplay cowritten by Arthur C. Clarke with Kubrick. Clarke worked on the novel at the same time he worked on the film with Kubrick, and the book was published after the film came out. The film premiered at the 1968 Cannes Film Festival on May 17, with George Harrison and his wife Pattie in attendance, along with Ringo Starr and his wife Maureen.

Roman Polanski's 1968 film *Rosemary's Baby,* an American film, was the middle picture of his "apartment" trilogy, which also included *Repulsion* (1965) and *The Tenant* (1976). Until the release of *Chinatown* in 1974, *Rosemary's Baby* was Polanski's most popular and successful film. There were two chilling postscripts to the film, both with a Beatles connection. *Rosemary's Baby* was the last film Polanski made before his pregnant wife, Sharon Tate, along with four others, was murdered on August 9, 1969, by followers of Charles Manson at the Los Angeles home Polanski was renting. The killers also daubed the words *Helter Skelter* in blood on the walls of the home, taken from the Beatles song of the same name from the White Album. Oddly enough, Manson misread the song. A helter skelter is a ride at a fairground shaped like a spiral staircase. Manson interpreted the lyrics as referring to a coming biblical apocalypse that would be sparked by some kind of race war. The song's sinister and careening heavy guitar rock sound may have had more of an influence on Manson's twisted theory than what the actual lyrics were about. The apartment building where *Rosemary's Baby* was filmed was the Dakota, where John Lennon was murdered on December 8, 1980.

While much of the groundbreaking *Revolver* album was written and recorded before the group stopped touring, the period from *Revolver* onward was quite fruitful in a relatively short period of time. The high points were the double A side single "Penny Lane"/"Strawberry Fields Forever" and *Sgt. Pepper's Lonely Hearts Club Band*. The group also produced the *Magical Mystery Tour* film and EP, with Capitol Records in America releasing a full-length *Magical Mystery Tour* album (which eventually became the official release of the album in the UK as well). All of these projects overlapped at times, illustrating the industry and creative energies the group had in abundance during this period.

Two visual projects related to the Beatles were also happening at this time, one reflecting more where the Beatles had been, and the other going on to be regarded as highly influential and still resonating with Beatles fans and the world until this day. These two projects were *The Beatles* television cartoon series, begun early in 1964, and the full-length animated feature film *Yellow Submarine* begun in mid-1967. What also made this latter period so productive, and consumed most of their time in 1968, is that while the Beatles were recording the White Album, they were also launching their own company, Apple Corps.

"WE ALL LIVE IN A YELLOW SUBMARINE"

With 1967 behind them, various individual film projects were being considered both for the Beatles to star in or to be produced through Apple Films, with no participation by the group. Meanwhile, production on *Yellow Submarine*, had been progressing since summer 1967, with the roots of the project dating back to February 1964.

The arrival of Al Brodax into the world of the Beatles is yet another instance of an American playing an important role in the way the group was visually portrayed. Like Walter Shenson and Richard Lester, Brodax would be involved in two visual-art projects connected with the Beatles, working on both *The Beatles* American cartoon television series and *Yellow Submarine*.

Two other Americans who would play a key role in the Beatles professional lives were director Michael Lindsay-Hogg and Apple honcho Allen Klein, head of ABKCO, Klein's company, with the acronym being the Allen and Betty Klein Company (Betty was Klein's wife). Both Allen Klein and Lindsay-Hogg were involved in the making and releasing of the *Let It Be* film. While Lester and Lindsay-Hogg were both accomplished television and film directors as well as being creative in other fields (Lester as a musician and Lindsay-Hogg as a painter), Shenson, Brodax, and Klein were businessman from the rough-and-tumble, old-school world of show business, who exhibited many of the stock movie traits of the cigar-chomping executive. While Klein was more the street-smart, casually dressed old-school music biz muso, Shenson and Brodax were much more refined and comfortable dealing with the creative forces they were involved with in their respective fields. Oddly, of the three businessmen, only one wrote of their time with the Beatles, Al Brodax. When Brodax penned his book, *Up Periscope Yellow: The Making of the Beatles* Yellow Submarine, published in 2004, it was his take on not only the making of *Yellow Submarine* but also of the conception and making of *The Beatles* cartoon series. Two previous books had offered the first full-length look at these two projects: *Beatletoons: The Real Story Behind the Cartoon Beatles* by Mitch Axelrod, published in 1999, and *Inside the Yellow Submarine: The Making of the Beatles Animated Classic* by Dr. Robert R. Hieronimus—at the time a definitive book on the film and, now with Volume 2, they are combined the definitive two books on the movie. Hieronimus sought out dozens of people who worked on *Yellow Submarine* and offered even more facts, history, and testimonies in his second volume *It's All in the Mind: Inside the Beatles Yellow Submarine Vol. 2*, which he cowrote with Laura E. Cortner, published in 2021. To add further to the story behind the making of *Yellow Submarine*, Denis O'Dell, in his book *At the Apple's Core: The Beatles from the Inside*, published in 2002, included a handful of pages about the making of the film.

The Hieronimus-Cortner and Axelrod books and, to a lesser degree, the Brodax book, are important in the story of the Beatles in that they provide a deep and wide look at two major visual presentations. Other books that solely focus on the films of the Beatles only offer a fine general look at and appraisal of these two projects, largely due to the fact that the Beatles themselves were not much involved in these ventures. While Hieronimus-Cortner offers a history from a panoply of voices on the making of the film, and Axelrod offers his history on the Beatles cartoon series, the Brodax book is an at times Runyonesque tale of luck, perseverance, nerve, and, mostly, innocent bravado told in colorful prose. While the book doesn't offer the kind of entertaining and informed insider look supplied by the likes of Derek Taylor or Richard DiLello, or the extraordinary autobiography of an insider that artfully transcends that person's time with the Beatles, like Michael Lindsay-Hogg's *Luck and Circumstance: A Coming of Age in Hollywood, New York, and Points Beyond* (2011), the Brodax book, in its own inimitable way, tells the story from an insider beginning at the initial stages of the possibility of a cartoon series on the Beatles to the conception, production, completion and long afterlife of *Yellow Submarine*.

Early in the 1960s, Brodax was working for King Features Syndicate, part of the vast Hearst media empire, based in New York. He and his team, primarily consisting of eight people, with his two closest associates being Mary Ellen Stewart and Abe Goldman, worked on popular and iconic television children's cartoons such as *Popeye*, *Blondie*, *Krazy Kat*, *Beetle Bailey*, *Barney Google* (no, not that Google), and other syndicated cartoons of the time. The way Brodax tells the story in his book, being in Manhattan and being plugged into the explosion of the Beatles in America, he and, to a lesser degree, others on his team got the wild idea of making a television cartoon series about the Beatles featuring their music in the cartoons.

At some point in his pursuit of this idea, the Beatles were in New York in February 1964 to make their historic appearances on *The Ed Sullivan Show* and appear live in concert at Carnegie Hall and the Washington Coliseum in Washington DC. As he tells it, Brodax tracked down Brian Epstein at the Plaza Hotel, where the Beatles were staying for their *Ed Sullivan Show* appearances and managed to get a meeting with Epstein's secretary Wendy Hanson, at the Plaza's Oak Room bar. Apparently, Hanson took a liking to the affable New Yorker, and after conferring with Epstein, the Beatles manager agreed to let Brodax make the cartoon.

After meeting with lawyer Walter Hofer, a representative for the Beatles in America, and then with Dr. Walter Strach, the group's tax advisor, a deal was hashed out. The deal was heavily weighed to the advantage of the Beatles, and initially Brodax and his team had some buyer's remorse. But eventually everyone realized that while the series probably wouldn't be a big moneymaker for them, King Features was now in business with the Beatles and that somehow the deal would bear fruit down the road.

With a deal in place, Brodax now had to find a network that would carry the show and a sponsor. After no luck in securing a sponsor, an ad in *Advertising Age* magazine alerted Brodax and his team to what appears to have been a desperate toy company named A. C. Gilbert. Based in Chicago, the company was endeavoring to relaunch their classic *American Flyer* toy train line for the Christmas season, and Brodax thought they might be desperate enough to hitch their fading star (sagging caboose) to the Beatles' gravy train. Brodax met with Anson Isaacson, Gilbert's president and CEO, who was so excited about the offer the two never made it into Isaacson's office, concluding the deal in the reception area. Isaacson then referred Brodax to a Mr. Duffy at ABC-Television. That would be James E. Duffy, vice president in charge of sales at ABC-Television. He evidently told Duffy about Brodax as well because by the time Brodax returned to his office, Duffy had left a message eagerly agreeing that ABC should carry the series, quickly confirming a time slot of Saturday mornings at 10:30 a.m., with September 25, 1965, as the proposed start date. Duffy also found additional sponsors in Quaker Oats and Mars Candy.

There would ultimately be 26 cartoons aired in the first season, seven new episodes in the second season, and six new episodes running in the third season. The deal was officially announced on November 11, 1964. Brodax now had to move fast to get the cartoons in production. He initially wanted to work with Canadian Norman McClaren, an independent filmmaker specializing in animation, but as McClaren was unavailable due to his duties as head of the Canadian Film Board, he recommended George Dunning take the job. Although Canadian, Dunning was based in London—yet another case of an American or Canadian based in England who ended up in the orbit of the Beatles. Dunning, who had worked for the UK office of United Productions of America (UPA), was running a small independent company, TVC, which had been in business since 1957 and, at one time, included Richard Williams, who would go on to be the animation director for *Who Framed Roger Rabbit?* Williams also did the animation credits for the original *Casino Royale*, was the title designer for *Here We Go Round the Mulberry Bush*, did the animation credits for Tony Richardson's *The Charge of the Light Brigade*, and did the opening credits for *The Return of the Pink Panther* and *The Pink Panther Strikes Again*. Dunning had been mentored by McClaren, worked for him at Paramount, and had done considerable commercial work and experimental short films, along with more conventional corporate, educational, and industrial films. He also worked uncredited on the main title animation for two Pink Panther films: *A Shot in the Dark* in 1964 and *Inspector Clouseau* in 1968.

Once the deal was secured, Brodax enlisted Peter Sander, a 21-year-old suburban London-based designer, to create the basic cartoon personas of the Beatles. From the very beginning, *A Hard Day's Night* became a major influence on the cartoon series. To write the scripts, Brodax hired Jack Mendelsohn, Dennis Mark, Bruce Howard, and Heywood Fischer "Woody" Kling, who was a veteran television writer for Milton Berle, Red Buttons, Jack Paar, and Jackie Gleason. Working basically from scratch, the storyboards were created by Joe Cal Cagno, who did work for King Features, and also worked for Marvel Comics and Paramount and several other writers.

Voice actors to play the Beatles included Paul Frees, who did the voice of Boris Badenov of the cartoon *Rocky and His Friends* and *The Bullwinkle Show* as well as voices for the beloved animated children's Christmas classic *Santa Claus Is Coming to Town*. The other primary voice actor was Lance Percival, who also voiced Old Fred, who had been part of the highly influential satirical 1960s British television show *That Was the Week That Was* and also voiced the Jolly Green Giant. In 1965 he recorded a cover of the song "Shame and Scandal in the Family," which was produced by George Martin, which became a hit and appeared in the film *Mrs. Brown, You've Got a Lovely Daughter*. The two voice actors also provided voices for other characters in the cartoons. All the female voices in the cartoons were done by Jackie Newman.

Incidental music was done by Bernie Greene, who also provided music for the American television shows *Mr. Peepers* in the 1950s and *The Sid Caesar Show* in the 1960s.

The original concept for the cartoons, conceived by Brodax, would be two stories within each 30-minute episode based on two songs from the group and two sing-alongs. Unfortunately, the animation was rather crude on some episodes, and when the group was performing a song, the wrong Beatle was often shown singing it. This wasn't the only example of often bizarre continuity. In a case of foreshadowing, the first episode included a submarine and an octopus, long before *Yellow Submarine* the song or movie was even an idea and years before Ringo wrote "Octopus's Garden."

The first show had a high rating, with more than half of all sets in America tuned in to the cartoon. All of the hard work, doubt, and less-than-stellar deals paid off. Thirty-nine episodes would ultimately be completed, with the final airing of an episode (as a rerun) on April 20, 1969. Half of the episodes were produced in London by TVC, while the other half were farmed out to freelance animators at Group Two Animation in London, Canawest Studios in Canada, Artransa Park TV Studios in Australia, and Cine Centrum, an offshoot of TVC, in Holland. The use of many animation companies sometimes resulted in an inconsistency in the look and quality of the episodes. The somewhat crude and childish nature of the cartoons caused Brian Epstein and the Beatles to only allow the show to be broadcast in the US. *The Beatles* did eventually air in England on Granada television (region of ITV Network) on Monday mornings, premiering on July 7, 1980, and the entire series aired on ITV's *Night Network* magazine show on Sunday, May 15, 1988.

By the time of the third season, it was becoming more and more difficult for Brodax and his team to get new songs from the Beatles. Also, by 1967, the Beatles had long since shed their mop-top image, which was still very much how they were portrayed on the cartoon series, and their new psychedelic sound was not ideal for little children watching cartoons on Saturday morning. Viewers would never even know that the Beatles had evolved into their style and look because the dress of the group in the cartoons all the way through retained their 1964 image.

Keen-eyed fans looking closely at some of the segments of the episodes would spot little inside jokes and surprises. In the "Hold Me Tight" segment of the episode from March 5, 1966, there is a poster on the wall for a group called the Rolling Rocks. In both the *Yellow Submarine* movie and on the cover of the *Sgt. Pepper's Lonely Hearts Club Band* album, the Rolling Stones would be specifically name-checked. Echoing the Shea Stadium performance by the Beatles, during the "I'm Down" song segment, that aired on September 26, 1966, John Lennon plays organ with his elbow. In a nod to James Bond and *Help!*, during the "Penny Lane" part of the episode that aired on September 16, 1967, there is a character named James Blonde, and Scotland Yard also makes an appearance. There is also an appearance of Private Gripweed (played by John Lennon) in animated form from Richard Lester's *How I Won the War*. Also in that episode, John Lennon utters, "It's all in the mind, ya know?," which was later a key catchphrase for *Yellow Submarine*.

The series also continued to spawn merchandising based on the Beatles. Much of it fell into gimmicky items that reflected more of the early Beatlemania frenzy, but this time, given that the series was aimed at children, anything that fit into the toy category made sense. One item that fit more into the strictly musical side of the group was a songbook, *Songs from A Music Adventure Cartoon Series.*

The initial success of the series prompted Brodax to consider doing a cartoon series for other British pop groups, with the possibility of animated shows on Herman's Hermits and Freddie and the Dreamers proposed but never produced. Jack Mendelsohn was lured away from the series to write an animated superhero series about a teenage rock and roll group for Hanna-Barbera called *The Impossibles.*

Long before all of these cartoons there were the Chipmunks. The brainchild of Ross Bagdasarian, an actor and songwriter who specialized in novelty songs, the Chipmunks were three animated singing sibling woodland creatures, featuring the mischievous Alvin, along with his brothers Simon and Theodore. Their father was David Seville (Bagdasarian), and through him manipulating tape speeds, the group's unique vocal sound was born, with Seville playing the maddened fatherly foil to the Chipmunks' childish pranks. With catchy songs that appealed to adults and children, the music spawned a short-lived television cartoon series, *The Alvin Show,* running from 1961 through 1962 and later rebroadcast in color through 1964 on NBC. The Chipmunks released 12 albums between 1959 and 1969 and would return to recording in 1975, with the most recent Chipmunks album released in 2019. The prefab, animated animal group released *The Chipmunks Sing the Beatles Hits* album in 1964.

The success of shows like *The Alvin Show* and *The Beatles* helped launch a slew of animated shows appealing to children with real or prefabricated pop music groups, including the Jackson 5, the Osmonds, the Brady Kids, the Archies, the Groovie Goolies, the Super 6, Josie and the Pussycats, and the Beagles. In the case of the Archies, the imaginary group scored two Top-10 hits, including a number 1 with "Sugar, Sugar" in 1969. The music was made by a team of seasoned studio heavyweights including Ron Dante, who would go on to produce big hits for Barry Manilow. Jeff Barry, a key member of the Brill Building scene who also worked with Phil Spector, Canadian Andy Kim who scored pop hits in 1969 and 1974, studio ace Chuck Rainey, and countless others were just some of the key names contributing to the Archies' pop success.

According to Brodax's book, at roughly the same time that the production of original cartoon episodes for the series had started to wind down, Wendy Hanson and Geoffrey Ellis of NEMS approached Brodax to see if he'd like to take a crack at coming up with an animated feature film idea for the Beatles. Brodax had already broached the idea of making an animated film of the Beatles back when he first started negotiating with Epstein to make the cartoon series. In his book *At the Apple's*

Core, Denis O'Dell wrote that part of the agreement that Brodax struck with Epstein was that if the cartoon series was successful, Brodax could produce a full-length animated film using the likeness of the Beatles and their songs.

Nonetheless, Brodax had mixed emotions about the viability of such a project. But at a meeting with Nat Lefkowitz, Brodax's agent, and UA president Arthur Krim, the three men quickly struck a deal to make the film with a million-dollar budget, King Features handling finances, UA guaranteeing distribution, and delivery of the film to be in one year. The film was to be a coproduction of King Features and Subafilms. Ultimately, thwarting the initial impetus for making the film in the first place, David Picker of UA would not accept *Yellow Submarine* as the third picture of the deal the Beatles had with the studio, though the company still distributed the movie for Apple Films.

The making of *Yellow Submarine* was quite different in comparison to the more conventional methods of producing *A Hard Day's Night* and *Help!*, and even the unconventional process of creating *Magical Mystery Tour*. The Beatles didn't like the animated television cartoon series and assumed *Yellow Submarine* would be more of the same and, thus, had little to do with the film, other than supplying four new songs and occasionally making suggestions. After the Beatles saw some of the initial animation for the film, they were surprised and delighted by the innovative work and agreed to be filmed for a short segment, which was tacked on at the end of the film.

The fact that the movie was animated meant that for the most part none of the staples of the British film world would be involved. Location shooting, either in England or abroad, would not be part of the production, nor for the most part would any filming be done at Twickenham or any of the other premiere British film studios of the time. All of this, combined with the fact that the film would represent an entirely new approach to feature-length film animation, made boarding the *Yellow Submarine* film experience truly like discovering a whole new world.

While there was talk Brodax would be the one to write the script, many heavyweight names were approached instead, including Joseph Heller, author of *Catch-22*, and Ernie Pintoff, who worked with Mel Brooks on the Oscar-nominated short *The Critic*. Jack Mendelsohn, who was one of four key script contributors to the cartoon series and had a background as a comic book artist, was also approached by Brodax, though more as a backup than someone who would end up being the script's main writer.

After Brian Epstein wasn't impressed with any of the suggested writers and ideas, time passed, and Heller begged off to work on his book *Something Happened*. Mel Brooks, who may or may not have been officially asked to get involved in the first place, was busy in Yugoslavia making his movie *The Twelve Chairs*. Brodax also met with up-and-coming British playwright Tom Stoppard, but his first theatrical production, *Rosencrantz and Guildenstern Are Dead*, was about to be produced. In the midst of all the musical chairs involving potential writers, word came from the Beatles camp that Ringo suggested calling the movie *Yellow Submarine*, which everyone thought was a great idea. The double A-sided single "Yellow Submarine"/"Eleanor Rigby" had been released on August 5, 1966, in the UK and August 8 in the US and also appeared on the UK *Revolver* album.

Mary Ellen Stewart of the King Features New York office suggested Phil Minoff to write the script. He wrote for New York's *Cue* magazine, a short-lived publication that would eventually be folded into *New York* magazine and then disappear entirely. Minoff begged off, but suggested his relative, Lee Minoff, a psychologist, who, in addition to being an aspiring playwright, also worked in the film world. He'd served as uncredited publicist on the 1963 film *The Leopard*, directed by Luchino Visconti, and worked as one of Stanley Kubrick's assistants.

Minoff signed on (receiving $15,000 for a script and $2,500 for a rewrite), and while he would not be the sole screenwriter, his contribution would be significant because he came up with *Yellow Submarine*'s original story. Screenplay credits would ultimately be split among Minoff, Al Brodax, Jack Mendelsohn, and Erich Segal, with additional (uncredited) dialogue written by Roger McGough. The official credits would read: "From an Original Story by Lee Minoff, based upon a song by John Lennon and Paul McCartney."

Minoff wrote a 20-page treatment in one night at his London hotel room. After meeting with Brodax and Paul McCartney, he then wrote an expanded 25-page version. He was also given an advance, reel-to-reel copy of the unreleased *Sgt. Pepper's Lonely Hearts Club Band* album as inspiration. Other key members of the team—director George Dunning, production supervisor John Coates, and coanimation director Jack Stokes—had been invited to Abbey Road Studios by George Martin to hear *Sgt. Pepper*.

By late in May or early in June 1967, Minoff had a 108-page script. In a meeting in August 1967, the Beatles told Brodax they didn't like the script. Nonetheless, several of his ideas would make their way into the final film: the characters of the Boob, the Nowhere Man, Old Fred the Sea Captain (who it was also speculated could have been partially modeled on Jack Stokes), Old Fred's sidekick the Shaggy Seal, the Count Down Clowns, and the Apple Bonkers.

Other ideas of Minoff's appeared in the finished movie, including the mix of animation, photography, and ingenious color and black-and-white contrasts and juxtapositions. The Seas of Phrenology and of Holes seemed to be inspired by British pop artist Bridget Riley and her famed geometric style. The Sea of Time's pulsating melting clocks were obviously heavily influenced by Salvador Dalí's 1931 painting *Persistence of Memory*. There would be many more seas to come, including the Sea of Green from the "Yellow Submarine" song, a line inspired by Donovan. Minoff also suggested various cameos: Peter Sellers and Spike Milligan as Punch and Judy;

Rat Pack pals Frank Sinatra and Sammy Davis Jr.; the Rolling Stones; and, in a case of turning the tables, Ed Sullivan appearing on a show hosted by the Beatles. It's not clear if these cameos would've been animated or live action and, if animated, whose voices would be used. Minoff also suggested songs that didn't make into the final cut, including "Lovely Rita," "Penny Lane," "Strawberry Fields Forever," "She's Leaving Home," "Wait," and most surprisingly "You Know My Name, Look up the Number." He also suggested possibly using clips from *A Hard Day's Night* and *Help!*

With Minoff now not involved any longer, Brodax really only still had Mendelsohn as a possible scriptwriter. Brodax actually hired Mendelsohn to write a backup script, and at the time, Mendelsohn thought he was the only screenwriter. It wasn't until the film was released that Mendelsohn found out his credit was shared by Erich Segal as if to indicate they wrote together as a team. Mendelsohn had never heard anything about Segal up to that point and, after seeing the film, was more than surprised to see the movie did not faithfully follow the script he wrote. Ultimately, material from what Mendelsohn wrote, for which he was paid $5,000, did make its way into the finished film.

This ongoing lack of a screenwriter, and the fact that Brodax and his team were still recruiting a team to make the movie, caused Brian Epstein shortly before his death to grow increasingly impatient. But Brodax was starting to make some headway in terms of the ideas he was considering for the look of the animation, including being inspired by Milton Glaser's famous poster of Bob Dylan and the style of Paul Signac. Brodax had even considered Glaser as the film's art director on the film, but Glaser was too busy.

It was director George Dunning who ultimately was able to get the production of the animated film off the ground by reaching out to a slew of independent animators. Roughly 40 animators and 140 technical people would be used to complete the film over the course of the 12-month production. The entire production ultimately enlisted more than 200 people, including the recruitment of art students in London in the final push.

Dunning's key team also consisted of British animation director Charles Jenkins (given the credit, special sequences) and Heinz Edelmann, who would be credited as the film's art director. Edelmann, a Czech/German designer who was based in Dusseldorf and was then working for the avant-garde German magazine *Twen*, was brought in by Jenkins to work on the movie even though he had no prior animation experience. The two would be the most responsible for the film's groundbreaking animation style. For design, Brodax had also considered Alan Aldridge, who edited and did illustrations for *The Beatles Illustrated Lyrics* book first published in 1969, did the cover art for the Modern Jazz Quartet's fist Apple album, *The Jasmine Tree*, in 1968, and whose trippy style would have fit in perfectly, may have even submitted some draft design samples.

When *Yellow Submarine* is discussed by film historians, animation experts, or even people who worked on *Yellow Submarine*, it is Edelmann who is singled out more than anyone for his visionary style that defined key aspects of the look of this groundbreaking animated film. While some of his ideas may initially seem subtle or random, they often defined the visual and subtextual feel of the film. For example, Edelmann originally wanted the Blue Meanies to be red as part of a metaphor for the Cold War. Because of his dislike of Mickey Mouse and Disney in general, he gave the Blue Meanies Mouseketeer beanies. The Dreadful Flying Glove, which had appeared in a slightly different form in an illustration Edelmann did for *Twen*, represented the accusatory pointed finger of authority.

Edelmann and Jenkins would room together in London's Soho Square near the rented Knightway House studio's location. Production had moved here from TVC's Dean Street location, when the team that worked on the film grew. Dunning was one of the few people who remained at the Dean Street location after the move.

David Picker of UA also made an addition to the film production team by assigning David Chasman to work with Brodax. Chasman was UA's representative in London brought in to oversee productions and make sure all the trains were running on time, on schedule, and on budget; in his book, Brodax affectionately refers to Chasman as "The Rabbi." Picker had stressed to Brodax and Chasman that *Yellow Submarine* must be done on time because the newest UA Bond movie would be coming out immediately afterward and all of the company's promotional and distribution resources need to be behind their biggest moneymaking franchise. Picker needn't have worried, as *On Her Majesty's Secret Service*, the first Bond film without Sean Connery, wouldn't have its London premiere until December 1969, more than a full year after *Yellow Submarine* had its world premiere in England in July 1968.

Picker also suggested that Brodax cowrite the script. Brodax, with no scriptwriter on board, realized he'd need help and contacted Charlie Baker at the William Morris Agency, who suggested Erich Segal. Segal (who later wrote the novel *Love Story*) was an assistant professor of Greek and Latin literature at Yale University. He had planned to work with composer Richard Rodgers, as a replacement for Rodgers' collaborator Oscar Hammerstein II, who'd died in 1960, but the project stalled, leaving him free to work on *Yellow Submarine*. Brodax and Segal hit it off and got to work on the script, first at chez Brodax and then at Segal's dorm room and at the Yale library. Segal would be paid $16,000 for his efforts.

George Martin became a key resource in helping the animators move forward with production. Without a clear-cut, full script and with a deadline to deliver the film in a short period of time, bogging down production, as mentioned previously, Martin kindly invited George Dunning, John Coates, and Jack Stokes to Abbey Road Studios to hear an advance copy of the *Sgt. Pepper* album. Ultimately, three complete songs and excerpts of two others were used in the film. The album's title also inspired the name for the film's mythical "Pepperland," after Brodax had been thinking of calling it "Strawberryland."

A short test pilot film was done early in production, introducing Harrison's character, with his sitar music used for inspiration. The art for the individual Beatles in this sequence seemed to be heavily influenced by the famed psychedelic photographs taken of them by Richard Avedon in London on August 11, 1967.

Although rotoscoping had been around since 1915, the innovative way it was used in the film during the "Lucy in the Sky with Diamonds" section made for one of the most memorable sequences in the movie. While with the Richard Williams studio, Charles Jenkins had worked with the Oxberry aerial image system and painted over live-action photography. Jenkins also did the "Eleanor Rigby," "Only a Northern Song," "It's All Too Much," and Sea of Science sequences as well as the film's end sequence. He even created the balsawood *Yellow Submarine* maquette that became the physical model used to better visualize the submarine when animating. Dunning also was heavily involved in the rotoscoping ideas used in the film and had been equally or even more influential in the use of rotoscoping on *Yellow Submarine*.

Other key additions to the production team included Barcelona-based and New York–born Bob Balser, who grew up in California and who, with his wife Cima, would be integral to the making of *Yellow Submarine*. Balser would go on to have a long career in animation, working on *The Jackson 5ive* television cartoon series, the *Peanuts* cartoons, and the 1981 film *Heavy Metal*. On *Yellow Submarine*, he became coanimation director with Jack Stokes, with both under director Dunning. He worked on the "Nowhere Man" sequence and, along with Edelmann, assembled a 143-page storyboard script that was completed late in May or early in June 1968. Essentially the codirector, Balser directed the film from the beginning through the Beatles in Pepperland, with an emphasis on storyboarding the travel sequences. Jack Stokes primarily directed the film from the point when the Beatles conquer the Blue Meanies. Stokes was also responsible for supervising the voice actors. He would go on to work on the *Jackson 5ive* cartoon. Stokes and Balser were greatly responsible for tying all of the disparate loose ends of the film together and were key to finishing what was a chaotic and rushed production.

Bob Godfrey, an old friend of Dunning, who coincidentally was also an uncredited extra in the pub scene in *A Hard Day's Night* and an uncredited member of Clang's henchmen in *Help!*, was a consultant on the *Yellow Submarine*, and much of the camera work for the film was done at his studio. Godfrey also directed three episodes of *The Beatles* cartoon series for the songs "I'm Happy Just to Dance With You"/"Mr. Moonlight" and "I Saw Her Standing There."

Paul McCartney, in a meeting with Broadax and Segal at his London home, suggested the film should be called *All You Need Is Love*. Always a Disney fan, he also encouraged the filmmakers to consider a more Disney-like approach, though he also contended that the film should be aimed more at adults than children. Regardless of his suggestions, the Disney approach was out of the question; for one thing, *Yellow Submarine* had to be made in a year, while a Disney animated film often took at least three years to be completed from start to finish.

The "Eleanor Rigby" section of the film forever immortalized some of the people that were part of the King Features/TVC teams. One of the first people we see animated in the sequence is a man smoking a pipe, who unsuspecting viewers would be surprised to learn was actually the film's producer, Al Brodax. Production coordinator Abe Goodman is next seen as the man bracing himself against the wind with his collar turned up. The man seen in the red telephone booth, who worked at the local pub the Dog and Duck, was known as Peter the publican. His surname may have been Jones, and his brother George, also worked at the Dog and Duck. Built in 1897 and still located at 18 Bateman Street (but now boasting an upstairs dining room, "The George Orwell Room"), the Dog and Duck was an almost adjunct to the film's production office.

Elsewhere in "Eleanor Rigby," the man standing on the rooftop in a rather precarious position is Bob Balser. The soccer players were voice actor Geoff Hughes, dressed in blue for Everton, and Tony Cuthbert in red for Liverpool. The two ladies eating chocolates from a box of Fuller chocolates are Ellen Hall, the taller woman with glasses and very large hat, who was a bookkeeper for TVC, and her friend Phyllis Davis. The man in the motorcycle helmet who sheds a tear is TVC messenger boy Brian Endel. Perceived by some to be the personification of "Eleanor Rigby" in the segment, the woman holding a bowl is Alison de Vere, the supervisor of backgrounds. The Jack Russell terrier dog in the scene is Scrumpy, owned by one of the bartenders at the Dog and Duck. The two men used for the scene where there are all the men holding umbrellas were George Dunning and Heinz Edelmann. The scene appeared to be influenced by a 1953 painting titled *Golconda* by surrealist Belgian artist René Magritte. In another case of art influencing a shot in the segment, the man who looks like Rodin's *The Thinker*, wearing butterfly wings, is technical assistant Dick Clements. Other people who were models for various characters in other segments in the film included the bearded man wearing a monocle near the end of the "When I'm 64" segment. This was footage of artist Iain Cowan, who worked on the film's cleanup committee.

Dunning and Australian animator Bill Sewell (whose son is the acclaimed British actor Rufus Sewell, born during the production of *Yellow Submarine*) scoured the London film vaults of American movie studios that had gone out of business. They came up with footage of Ruby Keeler, Ginger Rogers, Eddie Cantor, Rochelle Hudson, and Goldwyn girls that would all be rotoscoped as part of the "Lucy in the Sky with Diamonds" sequence. Partly how the final affect was achieved was by using 12 different film stocks. Sewell had been working on a movie of his own called *Half in Love with Fred Astaire*, and parts of that movie were incorporated into this sequence.

Heinz Edelmann created the basic look of the four Beatles. His primary assistants were Alison de Vere and Millicent McMillian. Because Edelmann wasn't an animator, his unique visual style prompted the TVC animation team to adapt to his vision by modifying their work methods. To animate Edelmann's imaginative, flat, cutout style, they struggled to adapt his two-dimensional characters into a three-dimensional look, so the characters could appear to be moving through space. In the Heirnonmus-Cortner book *It's All In The Mind*, Cam Ford explained an additional major change the animators adapted for *Yellow Submarine*:

> Traditional animation is hand-drawn on punched paper; usually within a standard 12 field (which refers to the 12 × 8.65 inch drawing area that will actually be photographed). The quality of the screen image thus produced is adequate for TV commercials, TV series and even the old seven-minute cinema shorts, but is not really good enough for feature cartoons, for which a higher standard of picture quality is required. This is why TVC decided at the outset that *Yellow Submarine* would be animated on a larger 15 field (15 × 10.8125 inches), which provided over 50% more drawing area. Because the animation camera films 15 field artwork from further back in order to cover the larger area, the detail of the drawing thus appears finer and small irregularities become less noticeable. For *Yellow Submarine*, all the artists had to be equipped with expensive new drawing boards, and the animators grumbled that the larger drawings and paper were unwieldy to work with. However, in the end, we all agreed that the final result was worth the extra trouble and expense.

Edelmann, who had never worked on a film before, proved to be revolutionary in his working methods. He secured a suitcase full of special paints from Germany called Doctor Martin dyes, highly concentrated liquid watercolors, common in graphic arts but normally not used for film, that the creative team were thrilled with, though King Features' Abe Goodman was concerned about what would happen when the paints were put under hot lights and filmed. Edelmann also came up with the invasion sequence, much of Pepperland, most of the monsters, and the counting animation in the "When I'm 64" sequence.

It is odd that so much animation occurred so quickly in the early stages of the production, as usually with animation, the script, voicing, and, in some cases, the music come before any animating is done. Even with animation production ramping up, Brodax and Segal continued to make slow progress on what was still a disjointed script, particularly the beginning and ending.

Secured for the movie were the voices of John Clive, who would do the voice of John Lennon, and Geoffrey Hughes, who would do the voice of Paul McCartney. Ringo Starr proved to be tricky to cast, but eventually Paul Angelis would get the job. He would also voice the chief of the Blue Meanies and the opening narration. George Harrison was the hardest voice to cast because none of the voice actors auditioned were able to nail his flat, dry Liverpool delivery. By chance, while members of the animation team were drinking at the Dog and Duck, they thought they overheard George Harrison talking. It turned out to be a rather tipsy patron, Peter Batten. Batten was asked to audition and nailed the gig. Unfortunately, it turned out he was wanted for being a deserter from the British army while stationed in Germany and was arrested. Paul Angelis ended up completing his voice work. In the most recent reissue of the *Yellow Submarine* film on disc in the bonus special features, Angelis talked about the approach the voice actors took when doing the voices of the Beatles, "We didn't imitate the voices. We tried to recreate what we thought were their voice." Not surprisingly, Harrison's voice in the film is the least like his real-life Beatle counterpart and almost sounded at times like he was voiced by Sean Connery, with his somewhat thick Scottish accent. Dick Emery was cast as the voices of the Boob and the Lord Mayor. Emery also accompanied Charles Jenkins and voice actor Paul Angelis to Liverpool to shoot the photos used in the "Eleanor Rigby" and Liverpool sequences in the film.

The animators modeled the look of the Beatles primarily from the "Strawberry Fields Forever" promo film. Early on in the process of drawing the Beatles, sketches of Paul with and without a moustache were drawn, but ultimately, he appears in the film sans moustache. According to animator David Livesey, the chief Blue Meanie was modeled after Adolf Hitler. Animators Anne Joliffe, Tony Cuthbert, Mike Stuart, and others animated the Sea of Monsters (created by Edelmann), Sea of Holes, and "Nowhere Man" scenes.

The pressure-cooker environment of the film's production became stressful, with Edelmann quitting many times, often coaxed back to work by Abe Goodman. He later declined to talk about the film, feeling that it overshadowed his other work and, also after working on the film, even occasionally used a pseudonym—Henri L'esclave—which, loosely translates to "Henry the slave" in French.

The lack of a completed script was an ongoing problem. The production crew grew frustrated with the situation, finding it difficult to understand how so many disparate and disjointed scenes would eventually be put together to make a cogent story. But what everyone did agree on, for the most part, was the quality and innovation of what was being produced.

Although John Lennon knew Roger McGough, when they both attended Liverpool Art College and McGough was a member of the British comedy group the Scaffold, which also included John Gorman and Mike McGear, the stage name of Paul McCartney's brother Michael, it was George Dunning who brought him on board to work on the dialogue for the film to give it more of an authentic Liverpool feel because the various iterations of the script were all sounding too American.

Regardless of all the difficulties, *Yellow Submarine* proved to be a roaring success. From the opening sequence, it was clear that this was an animated feature film like nothing that had been produced previously. While some could compare it to Disney fare such as *Fantasia* or the lesser-known *Make Mine Music* in its perfect melding of music and images, this was a wholly new kind of animation for a full-length feature film. Surrealistic, bold, and imaginative images were produced that combined various artistic styles and mixed art and animation, other forms of media including live-action film, photos, and found images such as postcards.

Yellow Submarine is a Homeric tale, and like *Magical Mystery Tour*, the storyline is borrowed from the time-honored literary device of the journey. It also portrayed a battle between the forces of evil, the Blue Meanies, who were negative, mean, and wanted to abolish music, and the citizens of Pepperland, who loved music and who, aided by the Beatles, would triumph—music living on to make the world a beautiful, loving place. "All You Need Is Love" became the film's central song, and the only one by the Beatles to appear in full on two of their soundtrack albums (*Magical Mystery Tour* and *Yellow Submarine*). The various songs of the Beatles gave the animators a chance to create the unique worlds, bringing the songs to vivid life, and helping to portray the individual personalities of the group. Ringo, as in the previous films, was the star of the show.

The film is a psychedelic trip though not overtly. There is a sweetness to the good characters, and some of the more cutting aspects of the Beatles personalities have a more subtle sense of humor. As previously mentioned, catchphrases from the past, like "It's all in the mind, ya know?" are repeated and fit perfectly with the story arc. That phrase, taken up by the Beatles and originally from the Goons, featured prominently on the film's poster. "Nothing is real," from "Strawberry Fields Forever," the newest song at the time, was included on the cover of the UK edition of the *Yellow Submarine* soundtrack album. Both phrases fit perfectly with the feeling of how the physical world was an illusion, and deeper meanings could be had by exploring other forms of consciousness.

The film is obviously more than a children's cartoon, offering existential forays into the unconscious and reflect some of the new thinking that was influencing the psychedelic age. The score by George Martin beautifully evokes the generosity of spirit that is at the core of the film. Martin's soundtrack music has a dreamy, timeless, and uplifting quality and holds up more than 50 years later.

The real Beatles' live-action segment at the end of the film was shot at Twickenham on January 25, 1968, by Dennis Abey. The reason the Beatles were dressed in black and brown is because the animators were going to add some animation to the segment, and they needed to wear dark clothing to make the special effects work. Some accounts claim the segment was mostly ad-libbed in one take, though others indicate that it was scripted, with much time taken to set it up. The segment was followed by the song "All Together Now" (the second time the song appears in the film) and the closing credits.

The details of the film's production and the people who worked on it can in no way evoke all that went into the making of the film. It is for this reason that the *Yellow Submarine* books from Hieronimus and Cortner are a joy to discover. Hieronimus has made celebrating, studying, researching, and chronicling the making of the film his life work. He doesn't just report on the making and the history of the film but also worked to revive interest in it, helping with the film's restorations and bringing it to new audiences. Most importantly, through countless interviews with every possible person he could find, he made sure most of the people that contributed to *Yellow Submarine* were given their due for their involvement in the making of a groundbreaking animated feature film.

One of the biggest controversies was the power struggle over completing the film. When the film was nearing what was thought the end of production in May 1968, King Features ran out of the budgeted funds from UA and temporarily stopped paying TVC's employees. George Dunning took matters into his own hands and, with the assistance of others, basically hijacked the completed reels and any cels and art in progress and removed them from TVC's two London animation headquarters. Dunning's camp felt that Brodax was attempting to wrestle control from TVC, with King Features then finishing the film any way they chose and taking all the artistic credit. They also feared that Brodax would botch the rest of the production, resulting in an inferior product.

Fortunately, the dispute was settled quickly; TVC employees got paid, and the movie was finished. George Elvin, the General Secretary of the Association of Cinematograph, Television and Allied Technician (ACTT), and the father of David Elvin, one of the film's animators, worked with John Coates to settle the dispute. Dunning and Coates put up £25,000 of their own money to complete *Yellow Submarine*, and TVC nearly went bankrupt after work on the film was finished. It took the company roughly 10 years of hard work, mostly making commercials, before they were solvent and could even consider working on making feature animated films again.

George Martin, credited as musical director of *Yellow Submarine*, worked on the score with a 41-piece version of what was called the George Martin Orchestra, which included members of the London Symphony Orchestra. The soundtrack album, which featured Martin's score and six Beatles songs (four composed specifically for the film), was nominated for a Grammy for Best Original Soundtrack Album. Martin would go on to other soundtrack work, including *Pulp* in 1972 and the James Bond film *Live and Let Die* in 1973.

Instead of being able to watch the completed movie, George Martin was only given various reels of film, incomplete and out of order, to use in composing the instrumental score. Although he had the freedom to do what he liked, he said the process was chaotic. In one of his autobiographies, *All You Need Is Ears*, George

Martin said of the soundtrack music he wrote and recorded for the *Yellow Submarine* movie, "I might get reel four followed by reel seven—and even then there might be a couple of scenes missing, with a little notice on the reel to tell me how long the scene would be. I spent a frantic month writing the music, fifty-five minutes of it, in this haphazard way, and there was no room for mistakes. Everything had to be tailor made to the picture."

He ultimately composed six instrumentals, with "Yellow Submarine in Pepperland" credited to Lennon and McCartney and arranged by Martin. Martin has said that the "Sea of Time" track was influenced by Harrison's Indian soundtrack music for *Wonderwall*, and "The March of the Meanies" was influenced by Bernard Herrmann's work on Alfred Hitchcock's movies, particularly *Psycho*, and also had influenced the string arrangement for "Eleanor Rigby." Composer Maurice Ravel was another inspiration, while a Hamlet cigar commercial that used a Bach piece was an influence in the Sea of Monsters that features the exploding cigar.

Martin rerecorded the soundtrack music on October 22 and 23 at Cine-Tele Sound (CTS) Studios in London, a studio he used in the past, on film music for previous Beatles films, assisted by Jack Clegg. Clegg, who had been at CTS since 1963, had previously worked on Burt Bacharach's soundtrack for *Casino Royale*, considered a legendary work in audiophile circles. He also worked on Bacharach's soundtrack for *After the Fox*, Elmer Bernstein's *Return of the Seven*, and the soundtrack for the 1969 musical version of *Goodbye, Mr. Chips*. In 1970, he went to work at Martin's AIR Studios in London. The recording was completed in two 3-hour sessions with a 41-piece orchestra.

"Once all the music had been recorded, we dubbed it onto the film, and even then there was messing about," Martin recalled. "In some places we cut out the music because sound-effects worked better; in others, we eliminated the sound-effects because what I had written sounded better."

According to Martin, there was talk of releasing a soundtrack album featuring his instrumentals along with dialogue from the film and narration to be written by Erich Segal. The four new songs the Beatles wrote for the film would then be released separately on a seven-inch EP. Without the Beatles knowing, a mono master was pressed on March 13, 1969, by engineer Edward Gadsby-Toni, featuring "Only a Northern Song," "All Together Now," "Hey Bulldog," "It's All Too Much," and "Across the Universe." Even at this late date, the EP was still something that could've received an official release in the UK. But the Beatles canceled the EP because they didn't do well in America, and the *Yellow Submarine* soundtrack album had already been released.

Some of the songs in the *Yellow Submarine* movie had already been used in *The Beatles* cartoon series. "Nowhere Man" was used in Season 2 (1966) as a sing-along in episode 32, and the main song in episode 33. "Eleanor Rigby" was used in Season 3 (1967) as the sing-along in episode 35, the main song in episode 37, and the sing-along in episode 39, the last episode of the series. This last episode had faint stylistic animation touches that gave a surprising preview of the kind of animation TVC would employ for the *Yellow Submarine* movie.

On April 26, 1968, an article in the London *Times* said Apple Films bought the rights to James Kennaway's novel *Some Gorgeous Accident* and were considering having Kennaway write the screenplay, though it wouldn't be a project for the Beatles. Other Apple film projects would later be announced, including *The Jam*, from a short story by Julio Cortazar, with film music composer John Barry producing, and was slated to go into production in July 1968 in England. Another projected project was *Walkabout*, based on the James Vance Marshall novel, which would go into production in Australia in November, directed by Nicolas Roeg, with a screenplay by Edward Bond, and starring Jenny Agutter. It was also announced that films would be made of John Lennon's two books. Other film projects being considered by Apple Films included a project starring the model Twiggy. Apple ultimately did not produce any of these films.

A press screening of *Yellow Submarine* was held on July 8, 1968, at the Bowater House Cinema in Knightsbridge, London and was attended by Paul, George, Ringo, and Peter Brown. The Beatles posed for photos at the screening with a cardboard cutout of John's animated alter ego and some real-life Blue Meanies. A press conference followed the screening. "The *Yellow Submarine* cartoon depiction of the Beatles isn't us," George Harrison told the press. "There's not a true image of us. You press people have given us an image which isn't us either." His attitude had mellowed by the time of his interview for the *Beatles Anthology* book, when he said "I liked the film. I think it's a classic. . . . That film works for every generation—every baby, three or four years old, goes through *Yellow Submarine*."

The British premiere of each Beatles film had always been an event. While for *A Hard Day's Night* and *Help!* it was more about the crushing crowds of fans who packed into Piccadilly Circus to see the mop-tops at the height of Beatlemania, accompanied by their wives, girlfriends, families, and closest business associates, in mid-1968, it was more of a "happening," populated by all of the beautiful people of Swinging London, although the crushing hordes of fans once again showed up to test the will and resources of the local bobbies.

Yellow Submarine's world premiere was held on July 17, 1968, once again at the London Pavilion. John attended with Yoko Ono, one of their first public appearances together, and Ringo and George were accompanied by their respective wives, Maureen and Pattie. Paul arrived alone. A few days later, it was announced that he'd broken up with his girlfriend, Jane Asher. It was the final time the four Beatles would attend a premiere of one of their films. Various members of the Rolling Stones attended, although Mick Jagger was out of the country with Marianne Faithfull. Others reportedly present included new Apple Record's signing James Taylor and members of the Bee Gees. Swinging London model Twiggy and her boyfriend Justin de Villeneuve attended and used the event as an opportunity to announce their engagement, but the two never married. Princess Margaret, who'd attended the London premieres of *A Hard Day's Night* and *Help!*, added a dash of royal presence.

Attendees connected to the film itself included David Picker and David Chasman from UA and a contingent from the production team and the cast, including voice actor Paul Angelis. *A Hard Day's Night* actor Norm Rossington attended. There were many others rumored to be in attendance from various press reports and histories of the Beatles.

A *Pink Panther* cartoon was shown before the film.

After the premiere, there was a lavish party for nearly 200 at the Dorchester Hotel in Park Lane and at the newly opened Royal Lancaster Hotel near Hyde Park, which launched a *Yellow Submarine* disco, a name it kept for many years. It was reported that guests were asked to wear yellow.

On July 18, *Yellow Submarine* opened at Studio One on Oxford Street in London and ran for 11 weeks until August 5. On August 4, it would go into general release around the UK. Rank only distributed *Yellow Submarine* in 12 theaters outside of London. Of the 200 Rank theaters, it was eventually only released in half, resulting in it not achieving its box-office potential, much to the irritation of the Beatles and Apple.

On July 31, the Apple boutique closed. For a glimpse inside what the hip boutique looked like at that time, check out the 1968 UK/US film *Hot Millions*, starring British film legends Peter Ustinov, Maggie Smith, and Robert Morley, which also stars American actors Karl Malden, Cesar Romero, and Bob Newhart; there's a scene in the film where Smith and Newhart go shopping at the Apple shop.

On August 26, "Hey Jude" was released as one of the first four official releases from Apple Records. The first unofficial Apple release, never intended for the public, "Maureen is a Champ," sung by Frank Sinatra, a takeoff on "The Lady Is a Tramp," with new lyrics by Sammy Cahn. Sinatra privately recorded the song for Maureen Starkey's 22nd birthday.

While *Magical Mystery Tour* debuted on British television in December of 1967, the first theatrical screening of *Magical Mystery Tour* in the US wasn't until May 1968. The first theatrical screening in the UK followed at the Roundhouse in London on August 23 and 24, part of an event billed as "Middle Earth presents Magical Mystery Tour" and promising a six-hour fireworks show and a whole 48 hours of freak-out, with the tagline: "The Magical Mystery Tour is Coming to Take You Away." Middle Earth, previously the Electric Garden Club, where many of the hip, new underground hippie groups and artists of the day performed, had moved from Covent Garden to the Roundhouse in July 1968. The Roundhouse event also featured performances by the Incredible String Band, Traffic, the Bonzo Dog Doo-Dah Band, Family, Fairport Convention, Blossom Toes, Free, Hurdy Gurdy, the Pretty Things, Deviants, and Blonde on Blonde.

The first official US theatrical screening of *Yellow Submarine* occurred at the San Francisco International Film Festival at a midnight screening on October 2, 1968. The film made its theatrical premiere on November 12 at the County Museum of Art in Los Angeles, now known as Los Angeles County Museum of Art (LACMA). The LACMA screening was the second time a film had premiered at the museum, the first premiere being John Frankenheimer's *The Train* in 1965. *Yellow Submarine* then opened on November 13 at the Forum and Tower East theaters (both now closed) in Manhattan and at Radio City Music Hall on November 26. The US version of the film was shorter, with the deletion of the "Hey Bulldog" segment. The film would win the 1968 New York Film Critics achievement in feature-length animation award.

While the initial merchandising of the Beatles may not have been as lucrative for the group as they hoped due to the clumsy handling by Brian Epstein, with *Yellow Submarine*, and although they were not the first, they were partially and seemingly unknowingly helping invent the explosion of movie merchandising tie-ins that is now commonplace, given the sheer number of different movie tie-in products that accompanied the release of the movie. There were also various book tie-ins, including a novelization, credited to Max Wilk, though Erich Segal claimed he cowrote the book's footnote section. Wilk may have gotten the job because he knew producer Walter Shenson, having written the book and screenplay for the 1968 film *Don't Raise the Bridge, Lower the River*, which Shenson produced. Wilk also wrote a screenplay for the Beatles called *Here Comes the British* that was never produced.

While the movie tie-in book is a fun curio of the film and its time, like other tie-in items including magazines and comics, it doesn't completely parallel the storyline of the finished film because the movie wasn't completed while the various books were being readied for publication.

The film also spawned exquisite film poster art, certainly the most colorful of all the posters of the films of the Beatles. And while the posters indicated United Artists Entertainment from Transamerica, with UA as the film's distributor, they more prominently announced "Apple Films Presents a King Features Production," a phrase that was also clearly displayed in the film's end credits, a result of Denis O'Dell's negotiations.

The Beatles (the White Album) was released on November 22, 1968. The White Album was proof the Beatles were heading toward some kind of major group dynamic change because the album often felt like a collection of songs from four solo artists. It signaled a break from their previous psychedelic period (*Revolver, Sgt. Pepper's Lonely Hearts Club Band*, and *Magical Mystery Tour*), a four-sided Rorschach test that reflected the splintering, increasingly violent culture emerging across the world in 1968. The album reflected not only the violence of the era, including protests against the war in Vietnam and nuclear proliferation and the assassination of political and social leaders, but also meditations on a variety of subjects, originally written on acoustic guitars in the tranquil days the group spent in India. It's interesting to note that the album was initially to be called *A Doll's House*, the name of the acclaimed 1879 play by esteemed Norwegian playwright Henrik Ibsen. That was changed when the English group Family released their debut album, *Music in a Doll's House*, on July 19. The change in title also prompted what would become the stark, iconic all-white album cover; previously, the album was going to use the art that eventually adorned the UK compilation *The Beatles Ballads*, released on October 13, 1980. The art for *The Beatles Ballads* was by John Patrick Byrne, a Scot who would go on to be a respected playwright and theater designer. The painting of the Beatles depicted them as Lewis Carroll–like mythical psychedelic avatars surrounded by animals, with a small illustration of Yoko Ono in a circular object on John.

The *Yellow Submarine* soundtrack album was released on January 13, 1969, in the US and January 17 in the UK. The US soundtrack album was only released in stereo; the UK release was issued in mono for a limited time but was a fold-down of the stereo mix. In addition to the eight-track edition, there was also a four-track cartridge release. It was a format that never really caught on; the sound quality was better than on eight-track, but given there were only four tracks, the tapes held half the amount of music. The US album notes were by Dan Davis, who wrote liner notes for many other Capitol albums, most notably Glen Campbell's *Wichita Lineman* as well as albums from Bobbie Gentry, Lou Rawls, Frankie Laine, and Sandler & Young, for the album *Music from Big Pink* from the Band, and the self-titled debut album from the Quicksilver Messenger Service. He was with Capitol for 24 years, eventually becoming vice president of creative services in 1977. The UK edition features a different cover design and had liner notes by Derek Taylor.

Yellow Submarine marked the first time the Beatles had so little involvement in one of their films, so any evaluation of it could only really be about the acting, writing, direction, or general production. *The New York Times* had a review of the film by Renata Adler. A radical intellectual author and cultural firebrand with no film criticism experience, Adler was a surprise choice to succeed Bosley Crowther as the *Times*' chief film critic after he left in 1967; she was quickly succeeded by Vincent Canby in 1969. In her review on November 14, 1968, Adler was dazzled by the imagery of *Yellow Submarine* and, with her deep intellectual background, easily picked out all the artistic—high and low—touchstones in the film. "Not a great film. after all, but truly nice." she wrote. "*Yellow Submarine* is a family movie in the truest sense . . . it's a film to be enjoyed by children and adults." Two other key New York film critics, Pauline Kael at the *New Yorker* and Judith Crist at *New York* magazine, were both more unabashedly effusive in their praise of the film. In a review titled "Metamorphosis of the Beatles," Kael wrote, "The Movie is a nostalgic fantasy—already nostalgic for the happy anarchism of 'love.'" She went on to praise the film, along with giving a potted history of the evolution of Disney animation but also seemed saddened, though not surprised, by the multitude of movie tie-in products.

The *London Observer* turned to their art and dance critic Nigel Gosling to review the film. Along with praising the film and simultaneously disregarding current pop art trends, he coined a new phrase when describing the look of the film, calling it "mop art," and went on to add that the film "succeeds in soaking up acres of the fringe material thrown off by serious painting developments and putting them to such effective use that they are at the same time both valid and exhausted."

In a review marking the 50th anniversary reissue of the film, which included a new 4K restoration being shown in more than 80 theaters across the US, Owen Glieberman in the *Chicago Tribune* called it a "dazzling revival everyone should see, especially the new leaders of Pixar." *Time Out* magazine, in choosing the 100 best animated films of all time, slotted *Yellow Submarine* in at No. 12. Tom Huddleston wrote, "The script is silly, the story is cringeworthy, and the Beatle characterizations are a bit soft. But visually it's breathtaking, one of the few genuinely hallucinatory cinema experiences, and fully deserving of its high placement here."

Cameron Crowe reflected on *Yellow Submarine* in an interview with the author: "Loved it. It's especially creative, and creates a world all its own. What felt like a smaller project in between bigger efforts is in fact something that increases in value over time. Sometimes one project adds luster to an entire body of work, and that's the case for *Yellow Submarine*. A look back at the film and music gives many gifts. Especially the beyond gorgeous track 'Pepperland.'"

There have been various *Yellow Submarine* soundtrack album reissues through the years on LP, CD, in box sets (*The Beatles in Stereo* CD box set), on a multivinyl set (*Mono Masters*), and the *Yellow Submarine Songtrack* release, which eliminated the George Martin score and included all the songs in the film, with the exception of "A Day in the Life."

The *Yellow Submarine Songtrack* was the first remix project of music by the Beatles, done by Peter Cobbin and Paul Hicks. Cobbin, along with Geoff Emerick, Guy Massey, Allan Rouse, and Peter Mew, along with six others, was also involved in the sound of the film's 1999 restoration.

The *Mono Masters* CD and three-LP edition released in 2009 are significant because they contain the five tracks that were initially intended for the previously mentioned EP of Beatles songs from the film. The songs, mixed by engineer Edward Gadsby-Toni, were true mono mixes of "Only a Northern Song" (mixed in April 1967), "All Together Now" (mixed May in 1967), "Hey Bulldog" (mixed May in 1968), "It's All Too Much" (mixed May in 1968), and "Across the Universe" (a previously unreleased March 13, 1969). It was a long time before a true stereo mix of "Only a Northern Song" appeared on the *Yellow Submarine Songtrack* album in 1999.

Some of the *Yellow Submarine* characters adorned the *Wings Over Europe 72* tour bus, proving Paul McCartney's continued affection for the film.

Yellow Submarine was first shown on television in the US in October 1972 and in the UK in 1974. The first home video release on VHS arrived in the UK on August 28, 1987, released by MGM/UA; US release followed on October 20. This release presented the movie in full-screen format and not letterboxed. There are noticeable differences in the "Baby You're a Rich Man" scene. During what is known as the "Beatles to Battle" scene there is marching band music and music with a dissonant jazz feel. The US theatrical version cut the "Hey Bulldog" segment. This release prompted Subafilms and Hearst, who owned King Features, to contend that MGM/UA did not have nontheatrical rights, to sue the company and were awarded $2.28 million in damages. But the case remained unresolved. In 1994 MGM/UA claimed Subafilms did not have nontheatrical rights outside of the US. MGM/UA won their case and half of the damages from the first suit were paid back to them. King Features sold the rights to *Yellow Submarine* to Subafilms in the 1990s. As for the fate of TVC, the company closed in 1997.

A large team was responsible for the 1999 restoration of the film, which cost $600,000 and required extensive work, particularly on the film's first 40 minutes. Released to the home market on VHS and DVD, it featured a new digitally restored picture and a remixed soundtrack. The DVD included the *Mod Odyssey* behind-the-scenes featurette, audio commentary, three storyboard sequences, including two not used in the film, original pencil drawings, behind-the-scenes photos, interviews with the crew and vocal talent, a music-only track, the original theatrical trailer ,and a collectible booklet. There was a limited theatrical rerelease in 1999.

All of the new 1999 releases—album, VHS, and DVD—featured updated artwork by Apple employee Fiona Andreanelli. Andreanelli had worked on books related to the Beatles before joining Apple while working for Genesis Publications, which publishes limited-edition music books with a fine-art flair. Andreanelli pestered Apple chief Neil Aspinall to do a new *Yellow Submarine* book. "Neil Aspinall was a stubborn man," she told this author: "who knew what he wanted, and didn't want? As I came from a publishing background, prior to joining Apple, I loved working on *Yellow Submarine*, but missed doing what I'm best at, so I pestered him continuously to let me design a book, and eventually he struck a deal with Walker Books to do a children's storybook, probably just to shut me up."

Andreanelli talked about how the new visual concept for the various media came to look, with her directive from Aspinall being: "Only to bring it to a new audience. I had months of piecing together salvaged screens [screenshots] from the original film and watching it frame by frame to screenshot missing content." As with the original film, the Beatles' own involvement with the reissue was minimal. "They didn't have much involvement in the day-to-day business," Andreanelli says. "Ringo and Paul might come in [to Apple] but only ever to see Neil Aspinall. George Harrison however, was the only one who made the effort to come down to the basement where I worked to meet me and see what I was working on, as he took an interest in design. A moment treasured forever."

Bob Balser, director of animation who worked on the original *Yellow Submarine* movie, helped Paul Rutan Jr. with the 2012 restoration. As stated on the back of the DVD/Blu-ray releases, the new restoration was "restored digitally in 4K by hand, frame, by frame." In a press release, Heinz Edelmann explained part of his aesthetic approach to the animation of the film: "I thought from the very beginning that the film should be a series of interconnected shorts. The style should vary every five minutes or so to keep the interest going until the end."

The restored soundtrack offered true stereo versions of some of the songs for the first time. As was the case from the start, the instrumental soundtrack music score by George Martin in the film is different from the original soundtrack album instrumental music.

In 2018, there was a 50th anniversary theatrical release of the film for one day only in the UK (July 8) and an extended run in the US beginning on the same day. Amazon offered an exclusive stream of the film beginning July 13. Once again, the 5.1 surround sound mix was by Peter Cobbin.

Due to the COVID-19 pandemic, a worldwide sing-along of the film was held virtually, on April 25, 2020, on the Beatles' YouTube channel. This sing-along version was first shown during the 50th anniversary celebration of the film in 2018.

Interest in the film has been ongoing. The influence *Yellow Submarine* has had on animated feature-length films is incalculable. One of the first film directors to not so much emulate *Yellow Submarine* as to see the potential to create an adult animated feature-length film for a new audience was Ralph Bakshi, best known for directing *Fritz the Cat*. In an interview with the author, Bakshi said of *Yellow Submarine,* "I saw it when it first came out. I liked it very much for lots of reasons, especially because it wasn't another Disney fairytale that everyone else was making." While *Yellow Submarine* was generally well-received on release, full-length animated films for adults were still not fully accepted. On this subject Bakshi said, "The biggest problem I had was that somehow certain people resented the fact that I was doing my films in animation, destroying their childhood memories of animation. Live action directors could do what they wanted." Though Bakshi denied *Yellow Submarine* had any effect on his work ("I was more interested in personal biographical expression"), the Beatles, particularly the *Sgt. Pepper's Lonely Hearts Club Band* album, did have a subtle influence on *Fritz the Cat*. "The music was spectacular," he says. "The entire *Fritz* film used those Beatle tracks as temp music as I was cutting the film. I'll never forget how perfectly Fritz and the Beatles worked together."

And while the Beatles had wanted to make the first film adaptation of *The Lord of the Rings*, it was Bakshi who got to do it, coming on board as director after John Boorman, who was originally going to write the screenplay and direct. Bakshi's animated version, released in 1978, was also released through UA. Bakshi had wanted the Beatles to be a part of the film: "On *Lord of the Rings* I wanted the Beatles to do the voices of the Hobbits. But in animation when you need a voice, you need it that day. I couldn't get a clear answer from the Beatles about their availability, even though they wanted to do it." Bakshi did get to work with the Rolling Stones, directing their 1989 video of "Harlem Shuffle," originally released by the duo Bob & Earl in 1963. "Jagger called me to ask if I had any interest in writing and directing the 'Harlem Shuffle' music video. The bad boy of animation meeting the bad boy of music. On the set, which was packed with hundreds of people making noise, I asked Keith Richards what he thought about the Beatles; amazingly the entire set got quiet waiting for his answer. We both laughed. He never said a word."

While the making of *Yellow Submarine* was hectic, chaotic, and stressful, those who worked on the film nonetheless had fond memories of the experience. However, there were some sad epitaphs to the production. One of the key members of the Brodax team, associate producer Mary Ellen Stewart, died at age 34, long before film production had even begun. Director George Dunning also suffered major health problems near the end of the film, perhaps related to alcohol. He passed away in 1979, and from that period on, John Coates kept TVC afloat and over time reinvented the company.

For many who worked on the film, *Yellow Submarine* became a launching pad for long careers in animation and film.

Norm Drew, one of the young animators who worked on the film, would later work on the *Jackson 5ive* cartoon. In an interview with the author, he recalled: "Given the impossible deadline and equally impossible budget, mixed with the revolutionary design of this feature film, it was—for me—a Dickensian experience; 'The best of times; the worst of times,' and therefore unforgettable."

Cam Ford, another young animator, began working on *Yellow Submarine* early in June 1967. In an interview with the author, he talked about his initial work on the film:

> There was no script or even a story at the time, no characters, no overall design; not even a studio space large enough to house the almost two hundred artists that would be needed to produce the film—nothing except an agreement that we could use any songs from the then-new *Sergeant Pepper* album, plus four "new" and unreleased Beatles songs. I was given a couple of TV commercials for a Canadian bank to animate while things were hectically being assembled in order to meet the September 1968 deadline.

Eventually, the story began coming together.

Yellow Submarine was a groundbreaking animated film for children but, more importantly, for the adults of the psychedelic era. Courtesy Photofest.

It had quickly been agreed that the song "Yellow Submarine" would provide the basic
idea for the story, which would take the Beatles on an epic voyage through weird and
musical worlds, each suggested by another Beatles song, to a happy and harmonious
ending. All this on a budget of about one million dollars and a production time of about
one year—both about a quarter of a Disney feature schedule at the time. As a rough
story began to emerge, and a series of scripts and list of songs were chosen and discarded,
a marvelous German designer, Heinz Edelman, was asked to provide a different visual
"look" for the film. I was in the studio when his first drawings of the Beatles arrived,
and, as soon as they emerged from the envelope, we all immediately knew that this was
going to be the visual style that would give the film the totally new, psychedelic "look"
that we were after.

Balancing work on animating the movie with an incomplete script was the basic
working method of the film. Ford recalled, "Even before the story was finalized, we
began working on sequences inspired by the selected songs; hoping that subsequent
scripts—and there were many of those along the way—would somehow coherently
link up to the overall story. It was a chaotic—but challenging—way to work." Ford
also remembers the Beatles dropping in at the animation studio. "They did come in
once, with an escort of Apple photographers, to see how the film was going, and to
talk to the animators. I believe they were mightily impressed by how the totally dif-

ferent style of the film compared to the previous low budget TV series, which they hated. I got to meet Paul and John very briefly." Ford has fond memories of working on the film. "In my almost 50-year animation career, I would rank the year I spent working on *Yellow Submarine* as the most challenging, funny, frenetic, bewildering, and yet satisfying experience of my life."

Lucy Roberts Elvin worked as a trace and paint artist on the film; her future husband, David Elvin, had tipped her off about the job. She has been a trace artist, draftsperson, and worked for the British government in telecommunications. After working on *Yellow Submarine*, she became an animator and art school lecturer. She worked on many projects over the years, including *Who Framed Roger Rabbit?*

I joined the *Yellow Submarine* team in February '68 and worked in Maggie Geddes trace and paint unit alongside about six or seven other painters," she says. "Every morning a pile of cels arrived. We worked on scenes that included the Beatles in their complicated costumes—trouser legs and sleeves painted in different colours. Now and again the door would open and a head appeared asking "Anybody got Paul's left leg?" or "Any more of John's right sleeve?" It did make me smile. We must have painted hundreds of Blue Meanies, Apple Bonkers and Bulldogs etc. The volume of work was relentless.

Many of the people who worked on the television cartoon of *The Beatles* became the driving forces behind the *Yellow Submarine* animated movie. Courtesy Photofest.

David Elvin also worked on the film. "David was hired to work on *Yellow Submarine* in autumn 1967. He was really happy. Prior to this he'd spent three years working in the London studio of Halas and Batchelor (H&B). A lot of fellow artists from his time at H&B were also recruited to work on *Yellow Submarine*, which pleased him. One of David's qualities was his great sense of humor. It made him good company.

> As a background artist, David worked with Alison de Vere, head of background. The background artists produced the scenery—Pepperland and the interiors of the *Yellow Submarine*. David also worked on the inside of Ringo's house, which appears at the beginning of the film where we see all the statues of superheroes, other stars, and comic book characters. Alison gave him free reign to include the characters of his choice—Buffalo Bill, Flash Gordon, and the Phantom, etc. It was all his work. Later on, David did the background sequence for "Lucy in the Sky with Diamonds" working with another old friend, Bill Sewell.
>
> When the film was finished and everyone had dispersed David and Ted Lewis were paid to stay on as "troubleshooters," "tidy-uppers" and pick up anything that had to be re-done or was overlooked. They were the last two artists to leave the building. David said it felt very odd to be rattling round an area that had been so busy and vibrant just a short while ago.

Though production on *Yellow Submarine* was seemingly over, as the hundreds of people who had worked on it going on to other projects, it soon became clear that the film did not have a proper ending. The ultimate animated ending came together long after the main production was completed over the course of a weekend.

One of the extras on the 1999 DVD reissue of *Yellow Submarine* revealed what could have been yet another possible animated ending to the film. This storyboard shows the Beatles flying away on a sort of flying bird. The reason this storyboard was produced was that King Features didn't like what ultimately became the final end of the film but evidently didn't care for this alternative concept either.

Yellow Submarine was in many respects purposely produced with an "anti-Disney" aesthetic, so the announcement in 2009 of a three-dimensional computer animated remake produced by Disney could have been considered blasphemous. The remake would have been produced by ImageMovers Digital and distributed by Walt Disney Pictures. Director Robert Zemeckis had acquired rights to the 16 songs and recordings of the Beatles used in the original film from Sony/ATV Music Publishing.

A joint official announcement by Disney and Apple about the remake was made at the inaugural D23 Expo held at the Anaheim Convention Center in Anaheim, California, on September 11, 2009. The three-dimensional remake would be produced using performance-capture animation, which is sometimes called "motion capture."

Four actors were cast to provide the voices of the Beatles: Peter Serafinowicz as Paul McCartney, Dean Lennox Kelly as John Lennon, Cary Elwes as George Harrison, and Adam Campbell as Ringo Starr. While it was never confirmed if they would have been involved in the film, David Tennant and Paul O'Grady also auditioned for voice roles in the film. An American Beatles tribute band, Fab Four, would be the models for the motion-capture animation portrayal of the Beatles.

The film was to premiere at the 2012 Summer Olympics in London. But late in 2010, Disney had the production closed down. Part of the reason the film was ultimately canceled is that other animated productions headed by Zemeckis, such as *A Christmas Carol* and *Mars Needs Women*, weren't successful. Although Disney backed out, Zemeckis hoped the production would eventually be picked by another studio. There was also a planned theatrical presentation of *Yellow Submarine* that also never got off the ground. It's probably just as well that the film never happened in that as much as those close to the original didn't want to see a new remake; Zemeckis had at least tried to make a unique cinematic approach to a story connected to the Beatles. His debut directorial effort was the affectionate *I Want to Hold Your Hand,* cowritten by him and Bob Gale and released in 1978, which followed the exploits of several teenagers attempting to meet the Beatles while they are in New York in 1964 primarily to appear on *The Ed Sullivan Show.*

There's no way to fully assess the enormous influence *Yellow Submarine* continues to have on animation and popular culture. Over the years, many people from various creative fields have drawn influences from the film. Terry Gilliam of Monty Python fame was strongly influenced by *Yellow Submarine. Sesame Street, The Electric Company*, and *Schoolhouse Rock* have all at times reflected the influence of *Yellow Submarine*. Like Richard Lester's directorial and visual innovations for *A Hard Day's Night* and *Help!*, and even the work of the Beatles for *Magical Mystery Tour*, music videos were and still are heavily influenced by *Yellow Submarine*. And *Star Wars* actor Mark Hamill has said that the Chief Blue Meanie was the inspiration for him when he played the Joker in *Batman: The Animated Series.*

6

Posters, Incense, and Strobe Candles

What is it about *Let It Be*, the movie and album, that has made it the source of so much confusion and revisionism? No other film or album connected to the Beatles has gone through so many stages and changes and remained living history.

A wise man once said that all things must pass, and such is the case with the Beatles. Like a movie shot out of sequence, the end of the Beatles—their historic rooftop concert in London on January 30, 1969, as seen in the *Let It Be* movie—was not really how it all ended but was how many would remember the Beatles for decades. Unfortunately, the joyousness of the concert and the wonderful, ragged music the Beatles made on that chilly, gray day, was overshadowed by the relative gloominess of the film. Other than the rooftop concert, much of the film was shot with minimal mood lighting at Twickenham soundstage number 1, giving it a grainy documentary look. Even the staged sections of the group in their basement studio at Apple at 3 Savile Row were static, dark images of the group mostly performing two of their most weighty late songs, "The Long and Winding Road" and "Let It Be."

Aside from the *Let It Be* album cover (with its funeral black borders) and the book that came with the UK and Canadian pressings of the album (UA declined to publish the book in the US), the last time most people had a chance to see the *Let It Be* movie, officially, was when the VHS, Betamax, and laser disc editions of the film were released in 1981 and the RCA CED video disc edition in 1982. All of these releases were taken from the 16-mm film version.

When the *Let It Be Naked* album was released in 2003, the cover was an eerie photonegative of the four portraits that had adorned the original cover, as if to further reflect the fractured nature of the sessions. The words *Let It Be . . . Naked* ran across the top, in black except for the word *naked* in red. Apple had intended to reissue the *Let*

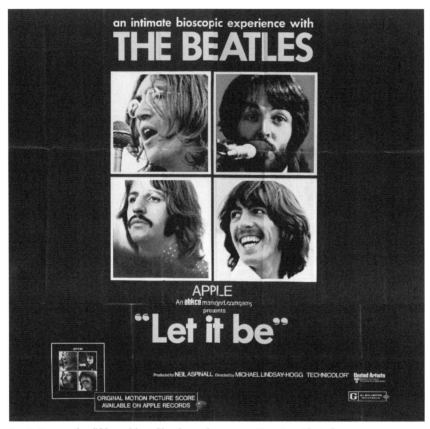

Let It Be was the fifth and last film from the group. Courtesy Photofest.

It Be film at the time of *Let It Be Naked*'s release, with new interview material shot for DVD bonus material. But no reissue happened, and *Let It Be* remained out of print.

As the years passed, no news of an imminent release of the film in any format was forthcoming. As much as the film was not the favorite from the Beatles, many fans clamored to have the film released, even starting an online petition to lobby Apple to release the movie. On the 50th anniversary of the rooftop concert, January 30, 2019, it was announced that a new film about the sessions, ultimately titled *The Beatles: Get Back* and directed by Peter Jackson, would be released, followed by the release of a restored *Let It Be* film.

As for the involvement of Jackson, it is also well-documented that the Beatles were enamored with J. R. R. Tolkien's book *The Lord of the Rings* and wanted to star in a film adaptation of it. More than 30 years later, Peter Jackson's two film trilogies of *The Lord of the Rings* and Tolkien's other masterwork, *The Hobbit*, were wildly successful.

Director Peter Jackson's *Get Back*, a three-part television series from Disney, resurrected countless hours of film and audio from *Let It Be*. Courtesy Photofest.

Jackson's Beatles film would be an entirely new movie, using the film shot during the sessions but crafting a different story that would in some ways paint a rosier picture of the events.

As established in the opening sequence of *The Beatles: Get Back*, the success of the mostly live "Hey Jude" videotaping was perhaps the single-most important motivating factor in the idea of a return to live performing and the concert/television show. Filming began in January 1969 initially at Twickenham Film Studios. Preliminary production for *The Magic Christian*, in which Ringo would costar, was already in progress at Twickenham's Stage 2. *The Magic Christian*'s producer, Denis O'Dell, secured the use of Stage 1 for the Beatles. When the Beatles were finished filming, *The Magic Christian* would begin using that stage as well.

The emphasis of this new project on the group performing live and becoming a documentary was concurrent with how live rock music sound and performance was evolving and how the pop music movie was about capturing the live concert. One of the first pop music movies to capture the new rock sound was *Monterey Pop* in 1968, following the concert in 1967. Some concert music movies in the pop-rock era were categorized as documentaries, such as *Festival* directed by Murray Lerner, released in 1967, and featured performances from the Newport Folk Festivals from 1963 to 1965. The film captured Bob Dylan's then heretical electric set at the 1965 festival and was nominated for an Oscar for best documentary in 1968.

It also worth mentioning the 1959 film *Jazz on a Summer's Day* a groundbreaking live concert film document directed by Bert Stern. The year 1969 would see the filming of *Let It Be*, *Woodstock*, and *Gimmie Shelter*.

There were plenty of youth movies, and the counterculture had firmly established a place in the movie world, particularly with the July 1969 release of *Easy Rider*, directed by Dennis Hopper, starring Hopper, Peter Fonda, and Jack Nicholson. The script was written by Hopper, Fonda, and Terry Southern and produced by Bob Rafelson and Bert Schneider. They featured the luminous cinematography of Hungarian László Kovács, which would launch his brilliant career. The film was infused with the countercultural divide that pitted the heads against the straights, a metaphor for the escalating war in Vietnam and student protests. Imbued with the spirit of rock music culture, the Hopper and Fonda characters were loosely based on David Crosby and Roger McGuinn of the Byrds, and the soundtrack made more effective use of rock or pop music than the Beatles did with *A Hard Day's Night*. The Byrds, good friends with Fonda, were featured prominently on the soundtrack album, along with Steppenwolf, the Holy Modal Rounders, and others. Made for less than $400,000, it would go on to gross $60 million and, like the Woodstock music festival, signal the arrival of the youth movement as a force to be reckoned with.

Thursday, January 2, was the first day of what would at first come to be known as the *Get Back* project. It was certainly different than anything the Beatles had done before. Throughout their career, the group would perform live and record. Since August 1966, they had stopped touring, and their recording process had not changed substantially. While they occasionally recorded outside of Abbey Road and began exploring recording at other London studios, change had been gradual. As for making movies, *A Hard Day's Night* and *Help!* had followed a conventional filmmaking process. With *Magical Mystery Tour*, the group took the moviemaking process into their own hands and in a leisurely, almost naïve way, made what basically boiled down to their own home movie. With *Yellow Submarine*, they had little at all to do with the movie and only came up with four new songs.

With *Get Back*, the group found themselves on a somewhat dark soundstage at Twickenham with little idea of exactly what they were doing. Given it was January, it was also quite cold. The only real idea was that the group would get back to playing live, recording songs without any overdubbing or studio trickery, in preparation for a live show. Whether the show would feature any of their older songs or cover songs was not clear. Nor was it certain where the show (or shows) would even be held.

The *Let It Be* album would include one of the oldest songs John and Paul had written. The young Lennon and McCartney were quite prolific as songwriters, almost from the beginning of their playing together in the Quarrymen in 1957. The two would often write songs at McCartney's home on Forthlin Road, and "The One after 909" was one of what is believed to be more than 100 songs Lennon and McCartney wrote long before the group's first single, "Love Me Do" was recorded. The group actually attempted to record the song in March 1963, but George Martin didn't like it. McCartney has claimed the Beatles recorded the song in 1958 at Percy Phillips's studio in Liverpool, at the same time they recorded "In Spite of all the Danger" (an original by McCartney and Harrison) and "That'll Be the Day" (by Buddy Holly and Jerry Allison and released in 1957), but it has yet to surface, and McCartney's recollection could be incorrect. According to the liner notes in the 2021 reissue of the *Let It Be* album, Lennon also said in 1968 that the Rolling Stones were offered the song before "I Want to Be Your Man" but turned it down. The song had the kind of lyrical theme that had been prevalent in folk, country, blues, and skiffle, with an emphasis on the romance of train travel. The group probably didn't have the song slated for their next album, but when the concept for a stripped-down musical approach was hit on for the *Get Back* sessions, and with Lennon not having much ready for the filming, the song was dusted off. The song no doubt provided the name for the 910 Newsletter, by Doug Sulpy, whose book *Drugs, Divorce and a Slipping Image: The Complete, Unauthorized Story of the Beatles' 'Get Back' Sessions* grew out of Sulpy's chronicling the *Get Back/Let It Be* period. The title is also in line with a series of songs throughout Lennon's career that includes, what must be his favorite number, number 9, most obviously on Revolution 9, # 9 Dream, along with a host of other occurrences where the number is significant to him, including his birthday October 9, 1940.

The Beatles had first worked on "Across the Universe" on Sunday, February 4, 1968, a session that also saw them working on "Lady Madonna." It was felt that "Across the Universe" called for female backing vocals—and where to find female singers late on a Sunday night? Right outside of Abbey Road Studios, where the group enlisted two fans, Lizzie Bravo, a 16-year-old from Brazil currently living in the area, and hometown London girl Gayleen Pease, to provide the backing vocals. Further work was done on February 8, but John wasn't happy with the track; when "Lady Madonna" was chosen as the band's next single, he nixed the idea of having "Across the Universe" as the B side.

Spike Milligan was in the studio on this day and asked if the track could be used on a benefit album for the World Wildlife Fund he was helping to put together. Lennon agreed and sound effects were added to the track on October 2. The album, *No One's Gonna Change Our World*, took its title from a line in "Across the Universe" and was released in 1969.

The version of the track from February 8 would be used as the basis for the version of the song that appeared on *Let It Be* album. Lennon recalled in the 1980 *Playboy* interview:

> I was a bit more artsy-fartsy there. I was lying next to me first wife in bed, you know, and
> I was irritated. She must have been going on and on about something and she'd gone to

sleep and I'd kept hearing these words over and over, "flowing like an endless stream." I went downstairs and it turned into sort of a cosmic song rather than an irritated song.

Lennon felt the Beatles didn't make a good track out of the song:

It was a lousy track out of a great song and I was so disappointed by it. . . . The guitars are out of tune and I'm singing out of tune. . . But the words stand, luckily, by themselves. They were purely inspirational and given me as boom! I don't own it, you know; it came through like that. I don't know where it came from, what meter it's in, and I've sat down and looked at it and said, "Could I write another one with this meter?" Such an extraordinary meter, and I can never repeat it! It's not a matter of craftsmanship; it wrote itself.

In the *Playboy* interview, David Sheff asked Lennon if writing the song was like a catharsis, to which Lennon answered: "It's like being possessed; like a psychic or medium. The thing has to go down. It won't let you sleep, so you have to get up, make it into something, and then you're allowed to sleep. That's always in the middle of the bloody night. When you're half-awake or tired, and your critical facilities are switched off."

McCartney started work on "Let It Be" during the White Album sessions in 1968 (an outtake would later appear on the White Album box in 2018). It was another song that came to McCartney in a dream, much like "Yesterday." As he explained in *Paul McCartney: The Lyrics*:

The context in which the song was written was one of stress. It was a difficult time because we were heading towards the breakup of The Beatles. . . . I fell asleep exhausted one day and had a dream in which my mum (who had died just over ten years previously) did, in fact come to me. She seemed to realize I was worried about what was going on in my life and what would happen, and she said to me, "Everything will be all right. Let it Be."

"The Long and Winding Road" is another song of McCartney's that dates back to the White Album era. McCartney wrote the song at his High Park Farm in Scotland that he'd purchase in 1966. In *Paul McCartney: The Lyrics*, McCartney explained the road that is evoked in the song. "From the bedroom window of my farmhouse on the Mull of Kintyre in Argyllshire, I could see a road that twisted away into the distance towards the main road. That's how you get into town. Campbeltown, to be precise." When writing the song, he envisioned Ray Charles singing it. In *Many Years From Now* he said: "It's a rather sad song. I was a bit flipped out and tripped out at the time. It's a sad song because it's all about the unattainable; the door you never quite reach. This is the road that you never get to the end of." "The Long and Winding Road" eventually was covered by Ray Charles on his album *Volcanic Ac-*

tion of My Soul. The album was released in April 1971 and also included a cover of "Something," written by George Harrison.

"For You Blue" was written by George Harrison sometime late in 1968. The song was musically inspired by Harrison's time spent in Woodstock, New York, with Bob Dylan and the Band over the last two months of 1968, but the lyrics were inspired by his wife Pattie. In his autobiography, *I Me Mine*, Harrison gave a succinct description of the song: "'For You Blue' is a simple twelve-bar song, following all the normal twelve-bar principles except it's happy go lucky!"

"I've Got Feeling" dates back to at least December 15, 1968, as footage from that day, filmed by Hans Preiner of ORF, Austria's national television station, shows Lennon playing the "Everybody had a hard year" part of the song on an acoustic guitar at Kenwood, his home, on the grounds of St. George's Hill estate in Weybridge. The rest of the song was written by McCartney. Though Lennon and McCartney now wrote together less frequently, this was a song where they did work together and finished the song at McCartney's home.

"Maggie Mae" was a traditional folk song that dates back to the 1750s, with the most popular version occurring in the 1850s, written by American Benjamin Russell Hanby. The British Isles version is believed to have originated in Liverpool and is about a prostitute who robs a sailor, when he returned from being at sea. It was given a skiffle feel by London group the Vipers as the B side of their single "The Cumberland Gap" (produced by George Martin). In 1964, Lionel Bart wrote a musical based on the song, *Maggie May*, setting it at the Liverpool docks. The Quarrymen also used to perform the song.

The Beatles were certainly all a bit groggy on the first day of filming at Twickenham. Projected dates for the live concert were discussed, and it was decided that they would perform on January 19 and 20, with a dress rehearsal on the January 18, though it wasn't clear at all what the setlist was to be.

John didn't need to travel into London each day from Weybridge because the home he had lived in there with his wife Cynthia and Julian was put up for sale, just prior to the beginning of the *Get Back* sessions and because John was with Yoko. John and Yoko had been living in Ringo's flat at 34 Montagu Square since July 1968. Paul also was still in London at his Cavendish Avenue home. George was out in Esher at his bungalow. Ringo moved to Sunny Heights in Weybridge in November 1968.

George, who would face the most challenges, go through major changes in his life, and at one point, quit the band, talked about his frame of mind going into the *Get Back/Let It Be* period in the *Anthology* book, which was surprisingly upbeat:

> I had spent the last few months of 1968 producing an album by Jackie Lomax and hanging out with Bob Dylan and The Band in Woodstock, having a great time. For me, to come back into the winter of discontent with The Beatles in Twickenham was

very unhealthy and unhappy. But I can remember feeling quite optimistic about it. I thought, "OK, it's the New Year and we have a new approach to recording." I think the first couple of days were OK, but it was soon quite apparent that it was just the same as it had been when we were last in the studio, and it was going to be painful again.

Early on the first day, the Beatles comment about the poor acoustics of the sound-stage. Talk of where the concert should be performed leads to a general suggestion of filming outside, specifically filming at the Theatre of Sabratha, a Roman amphi-theater in Sabratha, Libya. It's an idea that neither Paul nor Ringo like and becomes something of a running joke throughout the session. It's always a bit amusing when this idea is brought up, long after the fact, as something to scoff at. But in October 1971, Pink Floyd filmed a concert at the Roman amphitheater at Pompeii in Italy. David Gilmour of Pink Floyd must have enjoyed the experience so much that he returned in July 2016, this time as a solo artist, and was filmed. Another idea for the concert was filming at the Giza pyramids in Egypt, where in 1978 the Grateful Dead would be filmed.

Many of the key players of the *Get Back*/*Let It Be* saga are present on this first day. Most prominent is the film's director, American Michael Lindsay-Hogg, who got the job due to his directing the promotional films for "Hey Jude" and "Revolution" on September 4, 1968, at Twickenham. The group enjoyed the quasi-live format, and the intimacy and participation of the live audience for "Hey Jude" reminded the Beatles of how much fun performing was at one point in their career. After these successful videos, Paul asked Lindsay-Hogg to direct the TV show. It wasn't too long after the taping of "Hey Jude" that rumors began circulating that the Beatles would soon be playing live again. *Melody Maker* ran a story on September 14 about the possibility of a live performance for a television audience, quoting McCartney as say-ing, "The idea of singing live is much more appealing to us now—we are beginning to miss it. We will be doing a live TV show later in the year. I don't know about a concert, but it might lead to that. I love the idea of playing again—and I know the others feel the same way." In *Melody Maker* on November 16, Beatles press officer Derek Taylor said, "The group will be playing tracks from their album, old rock and roll tunes, anything they feel like or can play. It'll be informal and flexible." In refer-ring to "their album," Taylor presumably meant the White Album, which was to be released on November 22.

The notion that the show, or shows, would promote the White Album was quickly dropped in favor of learning new songs, with the rehearsals shot on film instead of videotaped and used for a documentary about the preparation for the live performance. The *Melody Maker* article said there would be three shows at the Roundhouse in London, which "will consist of a run-through, a dress rehearsal and a final show, each before a special invited audience." Further word out of Apple and in the press indicated that James Taylor, Mary Hopkin, and Jackie Lomax might also perform. These reports and articles throughout the end of the year offered a shifting set of dates. The Beatles were so sure these shows for television were going to happen, they even reported the news in *The Beatles Book Monthly* issues that came out in December 1968 and January 1969. The December issue also included a full-page advert, complete with entry form, where fans could win one of 50 pairs of free tickets to the show.

The "Hey Jude" taping and the idea to perform live again renewed the group's collective spirit. While they knew that their concert in San Francisco in August 1966 would be their last, they were optimistic about writing, recording, and other possible individual and group endeavors. It was the grueling White Album sessions, which began in May 1968 and lasted until October, that first exposed the fraying fissures of their musical partnership. Ringo Starr, producer George Martin, and engineer Geoff Emerick all quit while working on the album. While Starr and Martin did return to the fractious sessions, Emerick did not and wouldn't work with the Beatles again until the *Abbey Road* album.

For Emerick, the breaking point came during the "Ob-La-Di, Ob-La-Da" session on Tuesday, July 16. Paul's tune wasn't a favorite among the other Beatles, and the session was tense to say the least. As Emerick tells it in his autobiography, while working on the track, George Martin said, "Paul, can you try rephrasing the last line of each verse?" "If you think you can do it better, why don't you fucking come down here and sing it yourself?" Paul replied testily, which provoked an equally irritable response from the usually steady George Martin: "Then bloody sing it again!" Emerick said he'd never heard Martin raise his voice so loudly in a session. In recalling this episode in an interview with the author in 2006 Emerick stated, "It was such a horrible time for me, because you're seeing this great band disintegrate in front of you." When he returned to Abbey Road the following day, he told George Martin and then the Beatles that he was quitting. Ken Scott was his replacement.

Ringo's temporary departure occurred on August 22 during sessions for another McCartney track, "Back in the U.S.S.R." He would miss sessions on the 23rd, 26th, 27th, 28th, 29th, 30th, and September 3rd. In an oft-repeated story, Starr was sent a telegram by the other Beatles imploring him to return, saying: "You're the best rock 'n' roll drummer in the world. Come on home, we love you." He wouldn't return until the evening of September 4 to take part in the filming of the "Hey Jude" and "Revolution" promo clips, returning to Abbey Road Studios on September 5, where Harrison had draped flowers all over his drums as a welcome back. George Martin didn't so much quit during the White Album sessions, as he simply used the excuse of going on a belated extended summer holiday, departing on September 9 and returning on October 1. Martin had relegated production duties to Chris Thomas, who was 21 and only learned he was taking over as the de facto producer via a note

Martin left him. Thomas revealed the contents of the note in Mark Lewisohn's *Recording Sessions* book: "Chris, Hope you had a nice holiday; I'm off to mine now, Make yourself available to the Beatles. Neil and Mal know you're coming down."

Thomas would primarily be responsible for work on Paul's songs "Birthday," "Helter Skelter," and "I Will," John's songs "Cry Baby Cry," "Glass Onion," "Happiness Is a Warm Gun," and "What's the New Mary Jane," and George's "Piggies." His last date as producer was September 26. He would go on to work with Badfinger, Wings, and Paul McCartney, among the many other groups and artists he would produce through the years. Often either forgotten or not mentioned, McCartney had actually briefly quit way back during the *Revolver* sessions when the group was working on Lennon's "She Said, She Said."

The underlying tensions that existed in the group, exacerbated by the death of Brian Epstein and compounded by the nature of the weight of recording a double album, was the root cause of the difficult birth that was the White Album. Finishing recording the album didn't relieve the pressure, given how much postproduction work was needed to ready the album for release and how many other projects the group was involved in, including the launch of and activities surrounding Apple and their own burgeoning solo careers. In addition to the White Album, this period saw

The manager of the Beatles, Brian Epstein, died on August 27, 1967. Courtesy Photofest.

the release of John and Yoko's *Unfinished Music No. 1: Two Virgins*, Mary Hopkin's *Post Card*, produced by Paul, and Jackie Lomax's *Is this What You Want?*, produced by George. Leaping back so quickly into the *Get Back* project from the start may not have been such a great idea.

Lindsay-Hogg was a key player in the British television pop scene whose work on the seminal British television show *Ready Steady Go!*, which debuted on August 9, 1963, more than prepared him for working with the Beatles. Lindsay-Hogg first directed an episode of *Ready Steady Go!* on February 12, 1965, and continued directing episodes through the end of 1966. Although the show was broadcast to a hodgepodge of British television networks in varying timeslots and didn't always receive high ratings, it was considered by many to be most important and influential British pop music television show of the 1960s.

The show was Lindsay-Hogg's launching pad to working with the Beatles, beginning with the promotional films for "Paperback Writer" and "Rain" in 1966. He also worked with the Rolling Stones, directing the promotional films for "2,000 Light Years from Home," "Jumpin' Jack Flash," and "Child of the Moon," in addition to *The Rolling Stones Rock and Roll Circus*. The show was taped on December 11 and 12, 1968, on a circus-styled set, and featured a host of musical artists, including Marianne Faithfull, the Who, Eric Clapton, Jethro Tull, Taj Mahal, and a group called The Dirty Mac, consisting of John Lennon, Yoko Ono, Keith Richards, Lennon, Clapton, and drummer Mitch Mitchell of the Jimi Hendrix Experience. The Stones' unhappiness with their performance meant the film was not released until October 1996. Lindsay-Hogg would continue to have a long, fruitful run with the Rolling Stones, directing promotional films for 19 songs between 1973 and 1982. He also worked with McCartney, directing promotional films for four songs from Wings: "Helen Wheels," "Mull of Kintyre," "With a Little Luck," and "London Town." Lindsay-Hogg also continued to work directing long-form music projects, including concert films, the feature film *Two of Us* (a fictional account of an April 1976 meeting between John Lennon and Paul McCartney), along with other work in television (*Brideshead Revisited*), film (*Nasty Habits, Object of Beauty*), and theater (*Whose Life Is It Anyway, Agnes of God*). Lindsay-Hogg is also a painter and published a luminous memoir, *Luck and Circumstance*, that proved he is as adept at writing as he is at directing. Since the death of his father in 1999, he is the Fifth Baronet of Rotherfield Hall.

Lindsay-Hogg brought *Rock and Roll Circus* cinemaphotographer Anthony B. Richmond over to the *Get Back* project. His first film as cinematographer was *Only When I Larf*, adapted from the Len Deighton novel and directed by Basil Dearden in 1968, starring Richard Attenborough and David Hemmings. While working on the film, he met Lindsay-Hogg. The two shot the movie's main title sequence. Lindsay-Hogg then asked Richmond to work on two promotional clips he was going to shoot for the Rolling Stones, "Jumping Jack Flash" and "Child of the Moon." He worked on *One Plus One (1 +1)*, also known as *Sympathy for the Devil*, released in 1968. Richmond then reteamed with Lindsay-Hogg on another project related to the Rolling Stones, *Rock and Roll Circus*. Talking about the *Get Back* series, Richmond said: "I thought it was good generally. I thought it was much too long." He went on to say that *Let It Be* was dark and focused on the group breaking up, which was "less evident" in the *Get Back* series. Richmond is still waiting to do further work on *Let It Be*. He has done a restoration on the film but has never done a color correction.

One Plus One's (uncredited) camera operator Les Parrott was also part of the *Get Back* crew. In addition to the *Rock and Roll Circus*, he also worked on *Performance*, which costarred Mick Jagger. Parrott recalled his time on *One Plus One*, beginning with waiting for Jean-Luc Godard to show up: "France was in turmoil, strikes and all manner of other social unrest and as Godard was writing the yet unseen script, his arrival date in the UK was not known." Filming began at Olympic Studios in Barnes, which was formerly a cinema. Parrott described the shoot: "So we started to film the Stones recording 'Sympathy for the Devil.' There were no formal setups The camera would roll and Godard would point and nudge where it was to go." The cameraman explained one small part of the lyrics to the song changed dramatically one day: "The recording was going on a pace. Bongos were added and Nicky Hopkins did his magic on the piano. Keith Richard directed a backing track session of himself, Marianne Faithfull and his girlfriend Annette Pallenberg. During this time, Bobby Kennedy was shot, causing Mick Jagger to rerecord the lyric from Kennedy to the Kennedys." In keeping with the internal and external combustible forces of that time, a fire engulfed the studio, halting production, and with Godard fleeing back to France to attend the Cannes Film Festival.

Parrott talked about working on the original *Get Back/Let It Be* shoot and how impressed he was with what Peter Jackson did with the *Get Back* series: "I found the restoration quite mind blowing, we were after all shooting on standard 16 mm. The edit being so long was equally amazing, having the time to let a scene just roll on to a totally different conclusion was again so insightful. Another thing that was new for me was hearing everything they were all saying. On many occasions I would be shooting with a telephoto lens. I could see them fine but could I hear their words? Often no." He talked about being witness to the group beginning to break up: "In the intervening years I have been asked many times what was it like watching the Beatles breaking up. Well, they weren't; not while we were filming anyway, and again as the camera operator I was never party to all of the conversations for the reason mentioned."

Let It Be's original film credits list the Beatles and Neil Aspinall as producers of the film. Uncredited producers include Allen Klein, Mal Evans, and Saul Swimmer. Klein had previously produced three films by Italian film director Luigi Vanzi: *A Stranger in Town* (1967), *The Stranger Returns* (1967), and *The Silent Stranger*

(1968). He also produced two films directed by Saul Swimmer, *Without Each Other* (1962) and *Mrs. Brown, You've Got a Lovely Daughter* (1968), which starred Herman's Hermits. Swimmer directed the Apple Films production *Come Together*, an Italian Western, and is best known for directing *The Concert for Bangladesh* in 1971.

Let It Be's assistant director was Ray Freeborn, who simultaneously worked on *The Magic Christian*, uncredited, as second assistant director. The boom operator was Ken Reynolds, who also worked on *The Magic Christian*. He had also worked on another film starring Peter Sellers, *Never Let Go*, in 1960 and would go on to work on *Coronation Street*. Sound engineer Peter Sutton was also working on *The Magic Christian* and would work on Richard Lester's *The Bed Sitting Room* the same year. He would go on to have a long career in film and TV, working on *The Twelve Chairs*, *A Touch of Class*, two *Pink Panther* films, *The 39 Steps*, *Star Wars: Episode V: The Empire Strikes Back*, *The Great Muppet Caper*, Pink Floyd's *The Wall*, *Labyrinth*, and *A Handful of Dust*. Ray Mingaye was the other sound person. Graham Gilding was the film coeditor, who would go on to work on the Marc Bolan/T. Rex documentary *Born to Boogie*, produced by Ringo Starr. Tony Lenny, the other film editor, had worked in film since 1964 and would go on to work on *An American Werewolf in London*, *A Room with a View*, and *The Sheltering Sky*. Peter Hollywood was an uncredited assistant editor, who had worked on *Oh, What A Lovely War* and would go on to work on *Tam Lin*, *Blade Runner*, *The Adventures of Baron Munchausen*, and Richard Lester's *The Four Musketeers* and *Superman III*. The clapper/loader was Paul Bond, who would have a long career, working most recently on *Downton Abbey*. Mike Fox and Les Parrott were camera operators. Ronnie Fox Rogers, another camera operator, had worked on *Gonks Go Beat*, *Alfie*, and *Joanna* prior to *Let It Be* and later worked on *LeMans*, *The Rocky Horror Picture Show*, *Superman*, and *McVicar*. Jim Powell was the gaffer. Alf Pegley was the propman and was also working on *The Magic Christian*; he also worked on *The Pleasure Girls*, *Repulsion*, *Cul-de-sac*, and *Up the Junction*, among many other films. Also on the camera crew was Colin Corby, who worked on *Those Magnificent Men in Their Flying Machines*, *Privilege*, *A Dandy in Aspic*, and *One Plus One/Sympathy for the Devil* and would later work on the Who documentary *The Kids Are Alright*, *Young Sherlock Holmes*, *Labyrinth*, *Good Morning, Vietnam*, and many other films. Mike Malloy worked on *Performance*, *Walkabout*, *A Clockwork Orange*, and *Barry Lyndon*. Ray Andrew worked on *The Mouse on the Moon*, *Thunderball*, and *The Italian Job* before working on *Let It Be* and subsequently worked on *The Shining*, *An American Werewolf in London*, and *The Princess Bride* and served as a camera operator on the global Live Aid telecast. Mike Delaney also worked on *The Kids Are Alright*. Terry Winfield worked on *Primitive London*. Others credited as camera operators included Nigel Cousins, John Holland, and Roger Boyle.

The initial cameras used were two 16-mm BL outfits. When the *Let It Be* film came out, it would come out in 35 mm, which was Klein's idea. Sound was recorded by Nagra tape recorders from the first day, as soon as one of the Beatles showed up (in some cases even sooner) and ran until the last Beatle left for the day. The Swiss-made, portable, battery-powered Nagra tape recorder was launched in 1951; the cinema model launched in 1958, and for the next 20 years became the go-to audio recording machine for Hollywood movies. In 1965, a miniature version of the machine was used by the US intelligence agencies. Nagra IV-L was the most advanced model available at the time *Let It Be* was filmed was not only used by the Beatles but was also onboard the *Apollo 11* spacecraft that went to the moon in 1969. The use of these Nagra audiotape recorders was one of the reasons that the *Get Back/Let It Be* musical period of the Beatles was so heavily bootlegged, a topic that will be covered in greater detail in this section.

Two Nagra tape recorders were in use during the Twickenham filming. The tape recorders used reels of tape that lasted about 15 minutes, the use of two recorders (one each attached to the two cameras), meaning no audio would be lost due to the need to change reels. Everything was recorded in mono, with this model of the Nagra tape recorder equipped with an audio limiter. The rooftop concert was the exception because there were six tape recorders attached to six cameras; two on the roof, one in the lobby, and the three in the street, capturing street noise and interviews.

George Martin was not initially involved in his usual role as record producer while the group was rehearsing at Twickenham, with Glyn Johns on hand instead. Johns started out as a musician and recorded a handful of singles between 1962 and 1965. But he had quickly abandoned being an artist to get behind the board in 1964, as an engineer and mixer and then got his first producer credit as a coproducer of the Pretty Things album *Get The Picture?* in 1965. He then worked on 10 albums with the Rolling Stones, as an engineer and mixer, and had also worked with the bands the Small Faces, the Move, Spooky Tooth, Procol Harum, the Easybeats, Traffic, and Led Zeppelin, along with Joe Cocker, Bob Dylan, Billy Preston, and Leon Russell, as well as producing albums by Family, Humble Pie, and three albums for the San Francisco–based Steve Miller Band. In fact, he was scheduled to head to America to continue to work with the group at Sound Recorders in Los Angeles when the *Get Back/Let It Be* sessions were to wrap in January 1969 and, like Ringo Starr, was on a deadline. The Steve Miller Band released two albums in 1969, *Brave New World* in June and *Your Saving Grace* in November, with the former coproduced by Johns and Steve Miller and the latter produced by Johns. Sessions for the album had also been recorded at Olympic, and Paul McCartney, credited as Paul Ramon, sang backing vocals on "Celebration Song" and provided backing vocals, bass, guitar, and drums on the album's final track "My Dark Hour." When the Beatles moved to Apple and proceedings became more like a conventional recording session, Alan Parsons served as tape operator, along with recording engineer Neil Richmond. Parsons began working at Abbey Road in October 1967. His work on *Let It Be* was uncredited, with his first credited work being for the *Abbey Road* album as engineer. Coincidentally enough, Johns first worked with the Beatles on April 19, 1964, under almost equally odd circumstances as *Get Back/Let It Be*. The Beatles were to be appearing on the independent British ITV's Redifussion television special *Around the Beatles*. They had decided not to perform live due to their unhappiness with live television sound. Prior to filming (which occurred on April 28) they went into IBC Studios in London and recorded eight songs (including one medley of five original songs). While not quite as meticulously recorded as what they would do at Abbey Road Studios, the recordings were haphazard and poorly edited for broadcast, but four of the songs appeared on *Anthology 1*. The engineer for the session was Terry Johnson and the second engineer/tape operator was Glyn Johns.

"I had been retained originally as an engineer and was quite happy with that, even when I realized that George Martin was not producing," Johns said in his autobiography *Sound Man*. "At the outset I was quite embarrassed when I realized he was not going to be involved. By the time we moved to Savile Row, George, realizing I was in an awkward position, was kind enough to take me to lunch in order to put my mind at rest, saying I was doing a great job, everything was fine, and I was not stepping on his toes in any way. What a gentleman he is." Johns, like Lindsay-Hogg, Richmond, Parrott, and Ethan Russell, one of the photographers on the *Get Back/Let It Be* project, had worked on *The Rolling Stones Rock and Roll Circus*.

There were several instruments that became the basis of the *Get Back/Let It Be* sessions. In the spirit of the more stripped-down, live nature of the project, unlike on say *Sgt Pepper*, there wasn't a wide variety of instruments used. John's Epiphone Casino-ES-230TD was still very much his go-to electric guitar, and after the paint was stripped off after returning from India, the instrument was still very much the same. He also had a Martin D-28 acoustic guitar. Lennon's most bravura instrumental performance during the sessions was his lap steel guitar work on "For You Blue." The instrument was a Hofner Hawaiian standard available in the UK through Selmer. Paul continued to play his iconic Hofner bass, with the setlist from the last show in 1966 still taped to it. Also, at some point during the *Get Back/Let It Be* sessions, he took the Bassman sticker from his amp and placed it on the instrument. He did have his Rickenbacker 4001S bass but didn't use it much. Paul made good use of the 1960 Bluthner Concert Grand Model 1 piano. It's been repeated through the years how McCartney modified the piano. In *The Beatles Recording Reference Manual, Volume 5, Let It Be through Abbey Road (1969–1970)* by Jerry Hammack, Hammack indicated that Paul Hicks, who was one of the engineers on *Let It Be . . . Naked*, said "McCartney put pieces of paper in the piano strings," an "experiment" that yielded a "unique piano sound." Harrison had his Gibson Les Paul, which was given to him by Eric Clapton and which George named "Lucy." George also had a rosewood Telecaster, which he had Fender custom-make for him. He also played a Gibson J-200 acoustic guitar that John also played. Ringo had a new Ludwig Hollywood five-piece drum set with a maple finish. He swapped out the new snare with his old wooden Ludwig oyster black pearl Jazz Festival snare drum. There were other instruments used during the period including a Fender VI, six-string bass, that George or John would play when bass was needed and Paul was at the piano. There was a Lowrey DSO heritage deluxe organ augmented by a Leslie speaker cabinet 147RV.

While the Beatles were at Twickenham, they had been asking Johns to bring in a mixing board and multitrack tape recorder so they could have the ability to have proper playbacks of the new songs they were working out. Johns set up a basic rig for this purpose, but the use of the equipment would be short-lived because they would move to their basement studio at Apple by mid-month.

This first day, January 2, saw the debut of John's "Don't Let Me Down," "On the Road to Marrakesh," (which eventually became "Jealous Guy"), Paul's "Two of Us" (originally titled "On Our Way Home" and later covered by Apple publishing act Mortimer but not released until 2017 on RPM Records as part of the album *On Our Way Home*), and the joint composition "I've Got a Feeling." Some of the cover jams included versions of "Johnny Be Good" and "Quinn the Eskimo." Such jams were throughout the sessions, reflecting the group's broad musical tastes and offering a humorous insight into their interpersonal relationships and individual personalities.

The short workweek concluded on Friday, January 3. There is an impression one would conclude on the second day at Twickenham that George Harrison may be more of a voice within the group than his mythical moniker of the quiet one would suggest. He talks about how he has mostly slow songs to introduce to the group for possible inclusion on the upcoming album or to be performed at the still-unresolved concert. But focusing on how they are slow songs, he almost reluctantly admits that they are perhaps not the best kind of tunes to be performed live by the group. He then goes on to talk about his friend Eric Clapton and, obviously in an expansive mood, goes on to talk about other musicians he admires. He says the best jazz band he ever saw was the Ray Charles Band. He focuses in on how Billy Preston steals the show when the Ray Charles Band performs and how Charles lets Preston play organ because he feels he's so much better at playing the instrument. This could be just Harrison riffing on the talents of other musicians, or he was already angling to get Preston to play with the group at some point.

Further work is done on "Don't Let Me Down" and John's composition "The One after 909" is debuted. As for solo music that wouldn't be part of the *Let It Be* album, John's "Gimmie Some Truth" and George's "All Things Must Pass" are debuted. George played a little snippet of "Every Little Thing" from *Beatles for Sale*, and "I'm So Tired," sung by Paul, is played. The group jams on a bunch of old songs together, including "Thinking of Linking" and "Midnight Special."

After no doubt having spent most of the weekend off thinking about it, on Monday, January 6, Lindsay-Hogg gets into a lengthy discussion about how the live show is going to play out. George Harrison's eight-track equipment is delivered to Twickenham from his home in Esher so the group can hear playbacks of the new songs they are working on. In discussing the ways the songs would be structured, the group concludes that a keyboard player could be helpful, and Nicky Hopkins's name is mentioned. It's obvious that not just Harrison but some of the others also think a fifth member would be helpful because they will need another person for the live concert and won't have the luxury of overdubbing. There's a sense of tension among the Beatles this day, most obviously seen in the infamous verbal exchange between McCartney and Harrison, with Harrison finally telling his bandmate, "I don't mind. I'll play, you know, whatever you want me to play, or I won't play at all if you don't want me to play. Whatever it is that will please you, I'll do it. But I don't think you really know what that one is." In the *Anthology* book, McCartney reflected on how his behavior could have been misinterpreted back then: "Looking back at the film now, I can see it could be easily construed as someone coming on a bit too heavy, particularly as I was just a member of the band and not a producer or director. But I think it led to a couple of barney's, and in one of them George said 'Right, I'm not having this!' I think I was probably suggesting what he might play, which is always a tricky one in a band."

Over the weekend, George wrote "Hear Me Lord," which would appear on his *All Things Must Pass* album.

On Tuesday, January 7, Lindsay-Hogg again brings up the live concert, with the idea of the group performing in Tripoli. Paul counters by saying he likes the idea of playing somewhere they shouldn't be and being taken away by the police. Lindsay-Hogg also suggests other possibilities, like playing at a hospital or orphanage. The obvious tensions from the previous day find the group openly talking about how they have been in a slump, with George offering: "The Beatles have been in the doldrums for at least a year. Ever since Mr. Epstein passed away, it's never been the same." There's also this exchange:

GEORGE: I think we should have a divorce.

PAUL: Well, I said that at the last meeting. But it's getting near it, you know?

JOHN: Who'd have the children?

PAUL: Dick James.

While the exchange is troubling and shows they're not hiding their differences, their sense of humor remains intact.

Peter Jackson's *Get Back* series uses a clip of the Beatles performing "Rock 'n' Roll Music" from their 1966 tour from Japan simultaneously with them playing the same song at Twickenham. Paul's "Maxwell's Silver Hammer," which would ultimately end up on *Abbey Road*, is debuted.

On Wednesday, January 8, George spends time talking about the shows he watched the night before on the BBC that inspired him to write "I Me Mine"; in the Peter Jackson series, this conversation is interspersed with clips from the television shows, including one episode titled "Immortality Inc." of a science-fiction program called *Out of the Unknown* on the rich buying immortality. The other show he watched was *Europa: The Titled and the Unentitled*, on the 1969 New Year's Honours List and what the British people think of such Honours, along with the previous summer's investiture of the Prince of Wales, and it is where there was an Austrian band playing a Strauss waltz that inspired him, initially, musically by the waltz music, to write "I Me Mine." In Harrison's memoir, *I Me Mine*, which is named for the song, he explains simply that the song is "About the ego: the eternal problem." The longer explanation is how taking LSD was an experience that triggered some of these feeling for George about the ego.

Paul asks John if he has any new songs, with John clearly at a loss for new material. George says legalize pot and John responds, "Queen says no to pot smoking FBI agents," taken from a newspaper headline. This line will make its way into the *Let It Be* album. Different ideas for set designs are discussed. Returning back to the discord and overall lethargy of the group, Ringo says "We've been grumpy for 18 months," which if he's being accurate, dates back to before they began working on the *Magical Mystery Tour* film and even before Brian died. Some of the group's current code names came up, with Ringo being "Russia" and George "France." Further work is done on "Two of Us," "Don't Let Me Down," "I've Got a Feeling," and "Maxwell's Silver Hammer." One of the more prominent covers the group jammed on this day was "You Win Again."

Thursday, January 9, would mark one of the more controversial moments in the sessions, when Paul starts improvising lyrics during the evolution of the song "Get Back." The lyrics, which on the surface sounded racist, were actually a parody of the news in England of the far right, particularly Conservative politician Enoch Powell and the anti-immigration stance that was not uncommon in England and had been particularly virulent since 1968. Later in the day McCartney touched on the same issues, this time in a song with a blues feel; these improvisational fragments have been referred to as "Commonwealth" and "Enoch Powell." In the *Get Back* series the songs are interspersed with press coverage and news footage on the anti-immigrant debate in the British news.

Paul's "The Long and Winding Road" and George's "For You Blue" are debuted. "Let It Be" comes in for further work. A number of songs that would show up on future albums are debuted, including three songs by Paul that would show up on *Abbey Road*: "Golden Slumbers," "Carry That Weight," (which Paul wrote for Ringo to sing on the album in progress), and "She Came in through the Bathroom Window." Paul's "Another Day" is debuted; it would be released as a solo single in February 1971. John's song "Suzy Parker," sometimes called "Suzy's Parlour," is debuted, a 1950s-style rocker seemingly about an American model named Suzy Parker. This song has never appeared on any subsequent releases from the Beatles. There were some wonderful cover jams of "Honey Hush," "House of the Rising Sun," and "Mama You've Been on My Mind."

The week ended on January 10 with what seemed to be the completion of a makeshift control room by Glyn Johns. Given that the tape recorder is Harrison's, it's odd that on a day where good progress seems to be made, George casually announces he's leaving the group, suggesting the group put an ad in the *NME* for a replacement in a discussion with John and Mal. The filming is stopped, and although it wasn't captured by the cameras, Harrison apparently then says: "See you round the clubs." One wonders if Harrison's seemingly abrupt departure was premeditated because he was scheduled to attend a recording session for the Apple group Trash that evening at Trident Studios. The group was working on a song called "King of Fuh," and John Barham's string parts were being recorded at this session. Barham recalled the session as being lighthearted; "There was a lot of laughs when they played the tape in the studio," he told author Stefan Granados in *Those Were the Days: The Beatles and Apple*. The day's events also inspired Harrison to write the song "Wah Wah" when he returned home; it later appeared on *All Things Must Pass*.

Much else happened at Esher that was part of a personal drama playing out for George. A French model named Charlotte Martin had broken up with Eric Clapton. Pattie was friends with the girl, and Pattie said she could come and live with her and George after Clapton broke up with her. While Martin was living with the Harrisons, she and George began having an affair. The affair prompted Pattie to go and live with Belinda (née Watson) and Jean-Claude Volpeliere-Pierrot, a fashion photographer, whose sister was the model Marie-Lise Volpeliere-Pierrot, one of Pattie's closest friends during her modeling years. Jean-Claude's wife Belinda was a model and fashion stylist. They had two sons (one of whom Ben, became lead singer of the 1980s British pop band Curiosity Killed the Cat). That night when George came home and Pattie wasn't there, he supposedly asked Martin to leave and then rang Pattie at Jean-Claude and Belinda's wanting to get back together. Harrison also had dinner at some point in the evening with Klaus Voormann and his wife Christine, most likely after leaving Esher and before he worked in the studio with the group Trash. Harrison was clearly at wit's end, not only with the Beatles but also with his personal love life. He was obviously seeking some kind of comfort and solace and also went and visited his parents at their home in the country and went to Liverpool.

While Harrison seemed tense and troubled during the Twickenham filming, one wouldn't think he was at such a crossroads.

Further filling in this momentous day after Harrison left, back at Twickenham, John, Paul, and Ringo decided to carry on without George, with Lennon saying: "If he doesn't come back by Tuesday, we'll get Clapton." Further work is done on" Get Back," "Two of Us," "I've Got a Feeling," "Don't Let Me Down," and "Maxwell's Silver Hammer." In the evening, the three met with Harrison to convince him to rejoin the group. They held a meeting at Ringo's house, attended by the four Beatles and Yoko and Linda. From all accounts, the meeting did not go well. In another odd coincidence, the *Wonderwall* film, featuring Harrison's soundtrack music, opened in Italy. This is where episode 1 of the *Get Back* series ends.

On Monday, January 13, the US version of the *Yellow Submarine* soundtrack is released. Meanwhile, at Twickenham, various members of the band and crew sit in a tight semicircle on director's chairs and, depending on who you're looking at or listening to, seem depressed, tired, hungover, concerned, helpless, or nervously amused. Those in attendance include Ringo, director of photography Anthony Richmond, Mal Evans, Michael Lindsay-Hogg, Paul and Linda, roadie Kevin Harrington, Glyn Johns, and Neil Aspinall.

Ringo talked about how the meeting with George started out well but then fell apart at the end. Paul jokes about how in 50 years' time people will say the Beatles broke up "because Yoko sat on an amp." He doesn't appear to be disparaging Yoko, instead feeling that if John wants her around, that's fine with him and it's not the reason why there are such simmering animosities percolating within the group, although George Harrison might disagree.

The *Get Back* series also doesn't quite add to the notion that Ono is a problem. Yet Yoko's presence may be contributing to George's unhappiness with John; one reason the meeting at Ringo's house ended badly is George felt Yoko was speaking for John. Oddly, viewing Jackson's series, Yoko barely utters a word throughout the entire eight hours, hardly seeming like someone speaking for John.

One scene that offered a candid insight into John and Paul's relationship and their feelings about the interpersonal tension in the group was an audio conversation captured by a microphone that had been hidden in a flower pot in the cafeteria, where the two met to have their discussion. John seems quite lucid, and the two seem to be honest with each other, although McCartney is clearly mad, unsettled, feeling a little guilty about things but also simultaneously a bit exasperated. Later, the three remaining Beatles rehearse the song "Get Back," and even though it's only the three of them, it's clear progress has been made on the song. A decision to move the live show date ahead a full week is agreed upon.

On the ninth day of the sessions, January 14, there's a wonderful moment when Paul Bond, a member of the film crew, gets to watch Paul at the piano, playing and talking about songwriting. The young man is clearly tickled to be having this moment with McCartney. Paul talks about and plays a little of "Woman," a song he wrote that was recorded by Peter and Gordon.

Other activity on this day includes a van delivering pieces for the set of *The Magic Christian* that will be put on another stage. What follows is one of the more amusing yet revealing moments from Twickenham when Peter Sellers stops by to say hello. Sellers seemed bemused by the whole thing and has some cryptic exchanges with John. John's ramblings are amusing, but he's clearly not himself and doesn't seem to be hiding the fact that the previous evening he'd been indulging in unnamed substances. In fact, on this day, he and Yoko are interviewed by CBC, Canadian television. Lennon looks washed out and jittery. He eventually admits he's feeling sick, the interview is temporarily halted, and Lennon obviously goes and gets sick in the bathroom or something. Whether he was still high from the night before, or wasn't but needed a fix, is hard to tell. Surprisingly, after being sick, Lennon returns and continues to be interviewed and seems more with it. Ringo also seems worse for wear, tired and most likely hungover, and at one point even falls asleep. With the situation with George still unresolved, rehearsals for the next day are canceled. It is agreed that John, Paul, and Ringo will meet again with George.

John's "Mean Mr. Mustard," which would appear on *Abbey Road*, was debuted as was Paul's "Back Seat of My Car," which would be the closing track on his *Ram* album. Matt Busby, the manager of Manchester United football club, announced his retirement after managing the club since 1945; he would later be name-checked by John in "Dig It." He was awarded the CBE in 1958, knighted in 1968, and became Knight Commander in 1972. He died in 1994.

A meeting is held on January 15, bringing some resolutions to the group's stalled situation. There will be no TV special, and the group will move to Apple's studio to record, demands made by Harrison that were conditions for his remaining with the group. January 16 is the last day of filming at Twickenham, with Paul spending time demoing "Oh Darling!"

Johns and George Harrison head to Apple to see how things are progressing with the studio. They discover that the mixing desk Alex Madras has built is unsatisfactory and when used has distortion and hiss. This prompts Johns to contact George Martin and get some equipment sent over from EMI.

On January 17, the UK *Yellow Submarine* soundtrack album is released.

Over the weekend of January 18 and 19, EMI engineers Dave Harries and Keith Slaughter scramble to get the Apple studio up and running. They get two four-track desks (REDD.37 and REDD.51), an eight-track tape machine, and microphones from EMI.

NOT SO SWEET APPLE TRAX

The Beatles would be recording at their Apple studios for the first time. Their chris-
tening of the studio boded well for the space, because long after the group broke up
it would become a successful studio, albeit for a short time. The original location for
Apple was on Baker Street, which the Beatles' Apple company and boutique moved
into in December 1967. They left Baker Street for Wigmore Street on January 22,
1968, then moved to 3 Savile Row in June of that year. In the *Anthology* book, Ringo
talked about moving from Twickenham to Apple: "The days were long, and it could
get boring, and Twickenham just wasn't really conducive to any great atmosphere. It
was just a big barn. Then we moved to the new studios in the basement of Apple to
carry on. The facilities at Apple were great. It was so comfortable, and it was ours,
like home."

On January 20, the group held what turned out to be a productive rehearsal at
Apple, though no cameras were allowed. Outside of Apple offices in the street Tony
Richmond interviewed two Apple scruffs. This is currently the date these activities
are portrayed, but in Doug Sulpy's research, he indicates it probably was January 26.

Plans for the sessions continue to be modified on January 21. The Beatles will
record but still plan to do no overdubbing. Filming will also continue. The live show
is back on, though no details have been worked out. Glyn Johns feverishly works on
the recording equipment, but it still needs tweaking. An article by Michael Housego
in *The Daily Sketch* titled, "The End of a Beautiful Friendship?" is one of the big topics of conversation. The article details the general acrimony and the crossroads the
Beatles career appears to be at, focusing on Harrison's brief departure and suggests
that Harrison and Lennon came to blows. Lennon asks Derek Taylor if they can sue,
and Taylor laughs it off and says "no," seemingly unconcerned with the piece. *The
Daily Sketch*, which went through various incarnations since its founding in 1909,
was conservative in its political viewpoint throughout its history and was no fan of
long-haired rock stars. By 1971 it would fold.

Lindsay-Hogg tells John he just saw a rough cut of *Rock and Roll Circus* and
broaches the idea of Lennon doing some kind of introduction. Harrison has a bunch
of vinyl records from One Stop Records with him in a bag on this day, including a
Smokey Robinson and the Miracles Greatest Hits album. The shop had two locations
in London, as well as Surrey and Manchester, and specialized in imported American
Records. Also around the studio that day was a copy of the Rolling Stones 1968 *Beg-
gar's Banquet* album. The Beatles just can't seem to let the Housego article go, and
Paul reads parts of the article in a mock monotone, newsreader voice, while the others play music that only makes the whole experience even more unnerving between
the article details the troubles within the group. One line seems to catch everyone's
attention, that the group's current state of affairs revolves around problems with

"Drugs, divorce and a slipping image." Doug Sulpy and Ray Schweighardt took the phrase for the title of their detailed account of the fraught *Get Back/Let It Be* sessions: *Drugs, Divorce and a Slipping Image: The Complete, Unauthorized Story of The Beatles' 'Get Back' Sessions*, when it was first released in in 1994, by Sulpy's The 910 Magazine and retitled *Get Back: The Unauthorized Chronicle of the Beatles' Let It Be Disaster*, when it was published in 1997 by St. Martin's Press.

Regardless of the Housego article, the group quickly and somewhat successfully worked on a lot of songs this day, and everyone seemed happy with the sound. Once again, the need for a piano player comes up, and once again Nicky Hopkins is mentioned. In due course, a Fender Rhodes electric piano arrives at the studio. John's "Dig a Pony" (also referred to as "All I Want Is You") is debuted and further work is done on" I've Got a Feeling" and "Don't Let Me Down." Cover jams include "You Are My Sunshine," "Milk Cow Blues," and "Blue Suede Shoes." Also, on this day Ringo is interviewed by journalist David Wigg. This would be the first of many interviews throughout 1969 and 1970 when Wigg would interview all four Beatles (and Yoko Ono). Wigg was a British journalist, and the series of interviews began with the intention that they would be heard on the BBC program *Scene and Heard*. After receiving an official release by Polydor Records on vinyl in 1978, the oft-bootlegged interviews are the most extensive interviews with all the members of the group beginning with and during the *Get Back* sessions and lasting through to the breakup of the group and through to the postbreakup solo years until 1973. The original double album and cassette releases in the UK, US, Australia, and Japan includes music of the Beatles interpreted by the Martyn Ford Orchestra. It would be released on CD in the US in 1990, in Japan in 1998, and on Grey Scale, the gray market reissue label in Europe in 2016.

January 22 would prove to be one of the better days of the sessions. Lennon seemed to be having a wonderful time, playfully announcing prior to a take, "And now your hosts for the evening—the Rolling Stones." It is on this day that photographer Ethan Russell starts taking pictures. Russell had worked on the concert film hosted by the Rolling Stones, *The Rock and Roll Circus*, as a photographer. Michael Lindsay-Hogg and Anthony Richmond also all worked on that film, and Russell was friends with all three. The three reteamed for the *Get Back/Let It Be* project. Russell's photos ultimately were used for the *Let It Be* album, including the cover, along with the *Get Back* book, that was included in most, non-US editions of the album upon release. In 2009, Russell spoke to the author about the project. When asked was *Let It Be* as horrible as everyone made it out to be, he said: "'Horrible' doesn't seem like an appropriate word, in fact inappropriate. There was tension. But I didn't have a basis of comparison not being in other Beatle sessions. The thing I still find remarkable is that the biggest group in the world had such a solid work ethic that they would show up at 9 AM—which really means they had to be up at 6 or 7 to get there—as it was out in Twickenham. Imagine trying to find a group—especially a successful one—to do that today."

Any possibility that the group would perform live at London's Primrose Hill area were off. Billy Preston dropped in to say hello because he was in London doing two television shows. Preston quickly joined in the sessions, and his work on the song "Get Back" was acknowledged when the track was released as a single, the first time ever another musician was credited on a Beatles single, "The Beatles with Billy Preston."

"It was great honor," said Preston about the unique billing in an interview with the author. "I was really very grateful because I didn't know it until the record came out. That was quite a surprise." Why Preston became the only musician ever to become so much a part of the group is a question he finds hard to answer. "It's a blessing. It's hard to explain," he stated. "I guess the spirit of the music and the gift that God has given me and the joy I get playing warmed their hearts, which encouraged me to play." When looking back on his time with the Beatles and at Apple, he said "It was a good experience. When I first got there, we reminisced and jammed and had a great time. As time went on, I would be with them in the office at Apple and certain things started coming up that they were discouraged about. So, I was there when they kind of decided to stop. It was unfortunate."

"I've Got a Feeling" became the first song the group worked on with Preston, and it went quite well. Further talk about the live concert centers on the idea it could be performed half indoors/half outdoors. It's also quite clear at this point that although there will be no television show, there will be a movie, and John mentions that the film would be the third film the group still owes to UA. Peter Brown dropped in and mentioned to John about scheduling a meeting with Allen Klein on Friday. John suggested it be a dinner meeting. It was Derek Taylor who suggested to Peter Brown that the Beatles get in touch with Klein.

Allen Klein's place in the pantheon of people who got mixed up in the business affairs of the Beatles stands alone. To go into the details of how Klein wormed his way into running Apple and being in charge of their business affairs, the effect he would have on the group, and the people who were part of the group's inner circle before, during, and after their breakup would require a book. One of the most curious aspects of Klein eventually managing the Beatles was exactly what Mick Jagger said to the group and at what time to either say Klein would be good for them or warn them off. Klein renegotiated a more lucrative deal for the Stones with Decca. In an investigative article in the London-based, *Sunday Times* from April 13, 1969, titled "The Toughest Wheeler-Dealer in the Pop Jungle," which detailed various lawsuits, and that without informing the Stones, he registered the name Nanker Phlege, which was the Stones company in the UK and US and received all the group's royalties from the US on all their London Recordings. ABKCO still owns the Rolling Stones London recordings, which is all of the music they recorded until the last album before their debut album on Rolling Stones Records and distributed by Atlantic Records in 1971, *Sticky Fingers*. Klein said he set up the US-based company to reduce the group's heavy tax burden in England. Reportedly, Jagger had an opportunity to make all of the Beatles aware of this and other problems they had with Klein but either never did, did it half-heartedly, or did it too late. Much of this situation with Jagger, Klein, and the Beatles has never been fully explained by any of the parties involved, and most likely never will. The timing and acrimony of their breakup might have been different if Klein never entered the picture. As things would unfold over the next several months, Klein's place in the world of the Beatles would greatly impact the *Let It Be* album and film. Just before his death in 2004, Alistair Taylor answered questions about his time with NEMS, the Beatles, and Apple. Known as Mr. Fix-It, he started working for the Beatles in winter 1967 after Brian Epstein's death. Prior to that he worked for NEMS, first as Brian's personal assistant and then as general manager from November 1964. He was with Epstein the day Epstein first went to see the Beatles perform at the Cavern. He began talking about what it was like working at Apple compared to NEMS: "Times there were not pleasant. Imagine the difference between working in a library and an abattoir. NEMS was order and organization, ultra-professional. It was Brian. At Apple, work was a four-letter word. Nothing got done." Taylor felt there were too many people living off the Beatles. He talked about Alex Madras, who was supposed to be building a studio in the basement of Apple. "Alexis decided to turn the basement into a studio. The building almost collapsed when he began knocking down a supporting wall. Sheer and utter chaos." He spoke affectionately and had fond memories of George Harrison:

> George was the most rounded personality and truly wonderful person to be around. He tried to teach me the sitar and I imported the very first Moog Synthesizer into the UK for him. My favorite memory of George involves Mary Hopkin. She was recording and during a break George whispered something to Mal Evans who immediately went off on some errand or other. Fifteen minutes later he strode into the studio and presented her with a Martinez acoustic guitar, one of the finest guitars in the world. "This is from George."

Taylor was also close to Paul, but in the end he said he

> didn't socialize much with the boys during the Apple days. They became almost nocturnal. It was a rarity to see them together and during the filming of *Let It Be*. I kept well out of the way as friction scorched the film set and heaven help anyone who got in the way. I can't watch *Let It Be*. It's too painful. To see these people breaking up before my eyes. It's all too much. I've described the album as the sound of a group breaking up. It has some great music but I never liked what Spector did.

As for the Beatles, the Apple period was when the group truly started to break up. "The cracks in the relationships appeared and they soon became chasms."

Further work was done on "I've Got a Feeling," "Don't Let Me Down," and "Dig a Pony," with the version of the latter song on *Let It Be . . . Naked* taken from this day. There's a nice snippet of the group performing "Going up the Country."

January 23 features one song the group works on that doesn't seem so much a song as it is avant-garde chaos, featuring Paul on drums, John on guitar, and Yoko wailing into a microphone. It is decided the new date for the show will be the following Thursday. Harrison suggests "Get Back" sounds like "I'll Be There" from the Four Tops. Later, he also suggests releasing "Get Back" as a single. Further work was done on "Get Back" and "Oh, Darling!"

On January 24, there is a discussion about doing a book on the filming/sessions. John said he would talk to designer John Kosh, and they would use Ethan Russell's pictures. Billy Preston is working on Lulu's television show that day. John suggests Preston should join the group, and Paul says it's hard enough with four people in the band. The group runs through a long list of songs. Paul tries his Rickenbacker bass because Johns is not happy with the sound of Paul's Hofner bass, but the Ricken-

Phil Spector's work on the *Let It Be* album contributed to Paul McCartney wanting to end the Beatles. Courtesy Photofest.

backer also doesn't quite seem to be cutting it. Paul picks up an acoustic guitar, and with John, they turn "Two of Us" into an acoustic number with an Everly Brothers vibe; work on the song from this day would later appear on the *Let It Be . . . Naked* album. John's "Dig It" would be debuted, along with a cover of "Maggie Mae," with work on the song from this day appearing on the *Let It Be* album. "Polythene Pam" and "Her Majesty" are debuted and will eventually appear on *Abbey Road*. Further work is done on "On the Road to Marrakesh." Paul's "Teddy Boy," which would appear on his debut solo album, is debuted. Some of the cover jams from this day include "School Days" and "Stand By Me," along with an unrecorded Lennon and McCartney song "Fancy Me Chances with You."

The group works on Saturday, January 25, and Paul talks affectionately about the home movie footage he had been viewing of their time in India; in the *Get Back* series, some of that footage is interspersed while Paul is talking. George is seen playing his famous psychedelic "Rocky" Fender Stratocaster guitar. Alan Parsons starts work as tape operator. There's a wonderful run through of "For You Blue," with Lennon playing brilliant Hawaiian lap steel guitar, with work from this day appearing on both the *Let It Be* and *Let It Be . . . Naked* albums. The Primrose Hill concert idea is officially out, yet again. Lindsay-Hogg and Johns suggest to Paul that the concert be held on the roof of the building, and several people go up on the roof to inspect things. Further work is done on "Two of Us" and "Let It Be." A cover of "Bye, Bye Love" was performed. This is the point where episode 2 of the *Get Back* series concludes.

On Sunday, January 26, various members of the group continue to bring new songs to the sessions. Ringo plays what he has so far on "Octopus's Garden," and George Harrison helps him flesh it out. Heather McCartney truly steals the show on this day. The daughter of Linda and her first husband Joseph Melville See Jr., who Linda divorced after 18 months of marriage, the adorable six-year-old was singing, playing drums, and doted on by Paul, Ringo, John, Glyn, and Mal. At the end of the day, while listening to a playback of "The Long and Winding Road," Harrison asks McCartney if the track will have strings, and Paul says "I dunno," although work on the song from this day would appear on the *Let It Be* album. Further work would be done on "Let It Be." A cover of "Twist and Shout," followed by "Dig It" is performed, with work on "Dig It" from this day appearing on the *Let It Be* album. A cover jams included "Blue Suede Shoes"/"Shake Rattle and Roll."

On January 27, George Harrison plays "Old Brown Shoe" at the piano and says he wrote the song the night before, explaining that as he was writing it, he was thinking how John would say to finish a song as much as you can once you start working on it. Paul talks about "The Long and Winding Road" and says he doesn't know what to do with it. While John is playing, Yoko gives him a big kiss, and John announces to everyone that Yoko's divorce just came through, adding, "Free at last!" Paul does a bit of "Strawberry Fields Forever." John asks if they will be using a helicopter as part of the rooftop filming.

At one point, there's a rather historic shot in the control room, where Glyn, George Martin, and Alan Parsons are all gathered together. Between the three of them, they collectively produced at least 50 percent of the best British rock albums of the 1960s and 1970s. There's another playback of some of the songs, which is like a big party attended by the Beatles, the film crew, and the producers and engineers. It seems everyone is invited, and it's all rather cozy and intimate. Further work is done on "Let it Be," "The Long and Winding Road," "Don't Let Me Down," and "I've Got A Feeling." Work on "Get Back" from this day would appear on the *Let It Be* and *Let It Be . . . Naked* albums. Further work would be done on "Oh, Darling!" Cover jams include versions of a medley of "Shake, Rattle and Roll"/"Miss Ann"/"Blue Suede Shoes." In the evening John and Yoko meet with Allen Klein at the Dorchester hotel. One of the things that Klein suggests, to help ease the problems with Apple, is to dump the "Liverpool crowd," meaning people like Neil Aspinall, Mal Evans, Derek Taylor, Peter Brown, Alistair Taylor, and Tony Bramwell.

On the 28th, George Harrison introduces "Something" to the *Get Back/Let It Be* sessions. He says he's been working on it for like six months, with the song originally unveiled back on September 19, 1968, during the White Album sessions and again John helps him figure out how to complete the words.

A Fleetwood Mac single is lying on a piano. It's most likely "Albatross," which had been released at the end of November and was the only UK number 1 of the Peter Green–era Fleetwood Mac. Paul leaves for a meeting. Lennon talks about meeting with Allen Klein. Yoko says that Klein owns half of MGM, although it's not clear if she's talking about the film studio or the record label. There a couple of shots of fans peering through a window at the sessions. There seems to be a lot of wine drinking going on this day. Further work is done on "I've Got a Feeling." Work from this day on "Don't Let Me Down" appeared on the B side of the "Get Back" single. Further work is done on "Old Brown Shoe." "I Want You," which would appear on *Abbey Road*, debuted. A snippet of "Love Me Do" is played. In the evening, at around 9 p.m., all of the Beatles meet with Allen Klein at Apple.

On January 29, the day before the rooftop concert, the discussion about Klein continues. While John is effusive in his praise for Klein, some of the others are not, to which John says, "We're all hustlers." "And a con man who is on our side for a change," adds Ringo, presumably in reference to Klein. There is a big discussion, mostly between John and Paul, with Paul hedging about the rooftop concert. It's not so much that he doesn't want to do it, as that he thinks they could do more than just performing a short set without a real audience—maybe even still do the television show. The others chime in, and although George doesn't really want to do it, John and Ringo do. They also discuss the setlist and then, while musically riffing on "Dig

It," John sings the setlists. George talks about wanting to do an album of his own songs instead of giving them away for others to cover, and by having that outlet, it would also help preserve the Beatles; John and Yoko encourage him to go through with it. A version of "I Want You" is performed, but instead of singing "I want you" with help from Billy Preston, they sing "I had a dream." John and Paul sing "Two of Us" through clenched teeth like some kind of demented ventriloquist act. "Besame Mucho," a cover the Beatles had performed in the past, was dusted off. Further work was done on "All Things Must Pass" and George's "Let It Down," which would also be on the *All Things Must Pass* album. Further work was also done on Paul's "Teddy Boy." Some of the oldies performed on this day include Buddy Holly's "Mailman Bring Me No More Blues" and yet another oldies medley, which was a staple of the entire Twickenham and Apple sessions that consisted of another Buddy Holly song "Not Fade Away," "Bo Diddley" by of course Bo Diddley, "Cannonball," a Duane Eddy instrumental, and "Hey Little Girl," which was recorded by Dee Clark and written by Otis Blackwell and Bobby Stevenson.

For several days before the rooftop concert, considerable work was done on the roof and throughout the Apple building. This was done, along with an engineer, hired by Mal Evans, actually coming to the building to inspect the roof and ensure the safety of the endeavor. What amounted to a makeshift stage was assembled on the roof for the group. Also, considerable safety measures were implemented on the roof and within the building. On the roof, a barrier was constructed along the edge Inside the building, support scaffolding was constructed to make sure the weight of all the equipment and people could be supported.

UP ON THE ROOF

In the history of the Beatles, few days are more historic than January 30, the day of the "Rooftop Concert," as it came to be known. And for good reason; the 42 minutes of the group playing together would constitute the last time the four played together in public. Yet it was by no means certain that the event would happen; at the end of the previous day, they'd still been discussing whether it would go, with Ringo and John all for it, Paul still hedging, and George remaining silent. It was also fitting that a lunchtime concert would be their last because the lunchtime shows at the Cavern in Liverpool were where they solidified their stardom.

To get the equipment up on to the roof required not only some effort but also a little ingenuity, especially in dealing with Paul's bass cabinet and Billy Preston's 1969 sparkle-top Fender Rhodes 73 suitcase electric piano bottom. Mal Evans and roadie Keith Harrington had difficulty getting the equipment up to the roof due to the stair banisters and low ceiling. Mal Evans's suggestion of using the skylight was also initially stymied; there still wasn't enough room. Finally, the skylight frame was removed, and both bass cabinet and keyboard bottom were successfully hoisted through.

On the morning of January 30, while the film and sound crews were making final preparations, the Beatles were meeting in a downstairs office. Were they still deciding whether to perform or not? Or were they just simply going over what songs they'd perform, discussing last-minute technical details, and dealing with emotional housekeeping? On the roof above, five cameras were ready to capture the Beatles playing their first public concert since August 1966. There were also three cameras down on the street, one camera on the roof of a building across the street, and one hidden camera in the lobby's reception area. Director Michael Lindsay-Hogg, cinematographer Anthony Richmond, and photographer Ethan Russell were ready to capture the visual side of the event. George Martin and Glyn Johns were in the basement recording sound and monitoring the action on the roof via a closed-circuit television feed. The sound crew on the roof consisted of tape operator Alan Parsons and technical engineers Dave Harries and Keith Slaughter. Mal Evans and Kevin Harrington were the "road crew" for the day. Harries talked about the chaotic nature of the project: "That album involved a great deal of work for myself and Keith Slaughter the other Technical Engineer on those sessions, particularly in preparing at very short notice suitable facilities on the roof of the building. Despite our limited P.A. equipment, I was so pleased to discover that people could hear the music in Piccadilly Circus." Harries was able to once again, relive the experience through Peter Jackson's *Get Back* series. "With regard to the *Get Back* film, it accurately showed just how good the Beatles really were. Their songwriting skills are very apparent." I also asked him if he remembers that filming going on past January: "The sessions did run into February and Ethan Russell did take pictures but I can't remember details." Later on, around the time of *Let It Be . . . Naked*, plans to release the *Let It Be* film did come up: "Yes, I visited the people at Apple and discussed the film and following that I was interviewed on camera. Maybe one day they will publish those interviews. Also, I've met people like Glyn Johns several times since to do with my work."

Apple staffers who witnessed the occasion included Apple executive Peter Brown; Ron Kass, the first head of Apple Records, and his wife Anita; Jack Oliver, who held many positions at Apple and eventually succeeded Kass as the head of Apple Records; Ken Mansfield, the former Capitol Records employee who became the US head of Apple Records; and Chris O'Dell, who worked for Derek Taylor. Derek Taylor, the head of press for Apple, chose to stay in his office, no doubt anticipating press inquiries. Tony Bramwell, who handled Apple promotion, also stayed in his office. Receptionist Debbie Wellum and doorman Jimmy Clarke were both situated in the lobby. Peter Asher, head of A&R for Apple, was in Los Angeles on business, and Neil Aspinall, managing director of Apple, was, surprisingly, having his tonsils out.

Interestingly, George Harrison would have his tonsils removed at London's University College Hospital the following month on February 9. While in the hospital, he apparently played a cassette tape of mixes from the January sessions.

As could be expected of a late January day in London, the weather was cold and gray.

Once Paul emerged from below and alighted onto the roof, it became clear the show would go on. Dressed in a dark suit, striped-white shirt, and brown shoes, he seemed a little apprehensive but unaffected by the cold. Ringo was next, dressed in a red raincoat (or as it's called in England, a mac), with Maureen; they were all smiles. Billy was the next to emerge, dressed in a dark leather coat, and then John, dressed in his brown fur jacket, dark jeans, and white tennis sneakers, and finally George, wearing black low-rise Converse sneakers, green pants, and a heavy black fur jacket that looked like it was made from a shag rug. John seemed upbeat and relaxed, and George was his stoic self. Yoko was also on the roof. Linda Eastman would be seen later in the control room, but Pattie Harrison was nowhere in sight. Eastman was roughly two months pregnant with her and Paul's daughter, Mary, who would be born on August 28. Her condition may have been the reason she didn't join Yoko and Maureen on the roof.

The Beatles started off by playing a little snippet of "Get Back." Then they did a complete version of the song. It sounded good, but Lennon's lead notes are occasionally out of tune. Given how Harrison normally was the group's lead guitarist and Lennon himself has always denigrated his playing, it's curious why Harrison wasn't playing the lead. They did one more version, and it's somehow both looser *and* tighter, with all four seeming relaxed and in a good groove, a reminder of just how good a live band they could be. "Don't Let Me Down" was next, and the three-part vocal harmonies in the beginning sounded really good. John forgot part of the lyric and everyone found it funny, although Paul did look a little concerned.

This is the point when the police show up at Apple's front door, coming from West End Central Police Station, just down the road at 27 Savile Row. Meanwhile, the Beatles did an inspired version of "I've Got a Feeling," which will appear on the *Let It Be* album. After the song, Ringo stepped out from behind his kit and looked out over the roof to see the crowds below. George also had a look. This seemed to make them both happy. They next do a rockin' version of "One after 909." This performance will also be on the *Let It Be* album. It takes a little time to get set to play "Dig a Pony," with Kevin Harington kneeling and holding a clipboard with the lyrics for John. This is yet another performance that will make its way on to the *Let It Be* album. A little bit of "God Save the Queen" is played, and then the group performed "Don't Let Me Down" again.

Now the bobbies, police constable (PC) Ray Shayler and PC Ray Dagg, both first seen in the Apple lobby and since joined by PC Peter Craddock, are on the roof and come close to derailing the rest of the show. Shayler and Dagg had informed Mal Evans that the police were receiving lots of noise complaints, and the Beatles needed to turn the music off. But without missing a beat, the group didn't pause after "Don't Let Me Down" and instead went right into "Get Back" again; George defiantly turning his amp back on. Paul's ad-libs about getting arrested are a nice cheeky touch, and John's line after they finish the song—"I'd like to say thank you on behalf of the group and ourselves and I hope we've passed the audition"—provided a fitting end to the concert and the live performing career of the Beatles. Everyone departed back down the stairs to the Apple offices; John was the last one of the group to depart, perhaps sensing the gravity of the occasion and wanting to linger a little and soak up the atmosphere. Chris O'Dell, who worked in the A&R department at Apple for Peter Asher, recalled to the author, her memory of the rooftop concert and seeing the recent *Get Back* series:

> The roof has been a very strong memory for me, however, sometimes I wonder if I've underplayed it in my mind or in my memory. Of course, at the time you never thought that that concert would live on so long or be seen so many times. My memory of the temperature, the coldness, outside is extremely strong, but seeing the documentary really reminded me of what it was like that day to be sitting on the roof. I must admit I definitely today feel like one of the lucky people. I also have to say that the Beatles sounded really good that day.

When everyone listened to the playbacks later, they seemed happy with the results, although when John's flubbed lines comes up on "Don't Let Me Down," he seemed to not want to acknowledge it and a bit embarrassed. Everyone agreed to move forward filming and recording the more acoustic new songs they have worked on right away, but that won't happen until the next day because all the group's gear needed to be retrieved from the roof and brought down and returned to the basement.

A close listen to the entire rooftop concert, it should be noted, yields brief moments of other songs, including Lennon's "I Want You," "Danny Boy," "A Pretty Girl Is Like a Melody," composed in 1919 by Irving Berlin and which became the official theme song of the Ziegfeld Follies and then a jazz standard, "Ooh, My Soul!" from Little Richard, and "Rainy Day Woman 12 and 35," from Bob Dylan's *Blonde on Blonde* album.

In the evening, Glyn Johns went to Olympic Studios and made stereo mixes of the music recorded during the sessions. These mixes were cut to acetates for the Beatles.

January 31 was the last day of filming, the once brightly lit basement studio was now darkened to set the mood for the more acoustic-based numbers to be filmed. There's a brief jam with a little snippet of John's "Run for Your Life" from *Rubber Soul*. Then the group performed Paul's "The Long and Winding Road" "Two of Us," and "Let It Be"; versions of the latter two songs will end up on the *Let It Be* album.

"Let It Be" does have some rock muscle and might have also made for a good rooftop performance. But the dark setting and more somber songs make for a bit of letdown after the joyous rooftop concert.

When the filming and sessions were completed, the group performed what would be considered 18 oldies during January 1969 that would eventually come out on the two BBC releases *Live at the BBC* and *On Air—Live at the BBC Volume 2* of recordings from 1963 through 1966.

Afterward, Michael Lindsay-Hogg immediately started editing the footage.

Ringo was fully ensconced in filming *The Magic Christian* from February 3 through May 2, with one day of filming outside of Twickenham on April 9 at the Barclays Rowing Club in Putney. Ray Freeborn, Ken Reynolds, Peter Sutton, and Alf Pegley, who had all been part of the *Get Back/Let It Be* crew, also went on to work on *The Magic Christian*. Jeremy Lloyd, who appeared in *A Hard Day's Night* and *Help!*, and Patrick Cargill, who appeared in *Help!*, were both in the film. Ken Thorne, who was involved in the music score for *Help!* was also on board. The film was directed by Joe McGrath, who cowrote the script with Terry Southern. McGrath had worked with the Beatles on *A Hard Day's Night* and *Help!* and directed the promotional clips for "Help!," "Ticket to Ride," "I Feel Fine," "Day Tripper," and "We Can Work It Out." The Beatles had never previously worked with Terry Southern, but it was inevitable the cowriter of *The Magic Christian* and many other screenplays that matched the cutting wit of the Beatles would someday work with at least one of them. Also, Southern was one of the people depicted on the cover of the *Sgt. Pepper* album, was one of the 12 writers depicted, and was the youngest. Others involved with the film who had previously crossed paths with the Beatles or, would in the future, included Spike Milligan of the Goons and John Cleese and Graham Chapman from the Monty Python troupe. Peter Sellers, the film's star, had become close to the Beatles over the years, especially Starr; it was Sellers's yacht that Starr had escaped to when he quit the Beatles during the summer 1968 during the White Album sessions. It was there that Ringo wrote "Octopus's Garden."

On February 5, at Apple studios, Alan Parsons worked on stereo mixes of the songs done on the roof on January 30: "I've Got a Feeling," "Don't Let Me Down," "Get Back," "One after 909," and "Dig a Pony." Also on this date, *Goodbye*, the final album from Cream, is released. The album, half live performances and half studio recordings, contains the song Badge, cowritten by George Harrison and Eric Clapton. Along with Clapton and his Cream bandmates Jack Bruce and Ginger Baker, the album's producer Felix Pappalardi also plays piano and mellotron. Also on rhythm guitar is George Harrison using the alias L'Angelo Misterioso.

With all of this activity going on, it also marked the beginning, of what would be a long, protracted period of the Beatles untangling and attempting to secure their various business and management problems. The cast of characters and organizations involved would take up a great deal of the Beatles' time. It's amazing how much work they accomplished in this period, particularly producing the superb *Abbey Road* album. While some of these behind-the-scenes business dramas will be touched on, a full accounting of all the machinations would take up several books and obscure their music in this period, other activities, and finally seeing the release of the *Let It Be* album and film. *Apple to the Core*, by Peter McCabe and Robert D. Schonfeld from 1976, although being the first book on the business of the Beatles and is an important read, does contain some information, particularly related to the group's music, that has been better chronicled in many other books. More recent books that delve into some of the same territory but offer unimpeachable musical context include *You Never Give Me Your Money: The Beatles after the Breakup* by Peter Doggett, published in 2011; *Northern Songs: The True Story of the Beatles' Song Publishing Empire* by Brian Southall, published in 2007; and *Those Were The Days: The Beatles and Apple* by Stefan Granados, that was updated in 2020.

On February 20, Ringo Starr attended the UK film premiere of the film *Candy* at the Odeon Cinema in London, which features his first film role outside of his work with the Beatles.

It wasn't long before the four Beatles reconvened to record, with Glyn Johns and Billy Preston also in attendance, although for which project is unclear. With Apple Studio still under further construction, the musicians spent the weekend of February 22 and 23 at one of their favorite studios, Trident Studios to work on "I Want You." On his birthday, February 25, George worked on solo versions of "Old Brown Shoe," "Something," and "All Things Must Pass," at Abbey Road Studios, without the other Beatles or George Martin.

Paul married Linda at the Old Marylebone Town Hall Register Office in London on March 12, attended by his brother Michael and Mal Evans. The marriage was then consecrated at St John's Wood Church by Reverend Noel Perry-Gore. That evening, a reception was held at the Ritz Hotel.

On March 20, John and Yoko were married in Gibraltar. They celebrated their honeymoon with a "bed-in" for peace at the Hilton Hotel in Amsterdam, bunking down in room 902 from March 25 to 31.

An acetate of a mono mix of "Get Back" (prepared by Jeff Jarratt at Abbey Road Studios) was played on the radio April 6, Easter Sunday, by DJ John Peel and DJ Alan Freeman. Paul didn't like what he heard, so the track was remixed again, this time by Glyn Johns and Jerry Boys at Olympic. It was released in the UK on April 11, backed with "Don't Let Me Down" on the B side. A stereo mix made at the same session by Johns and Boys became the American single release. It would be different from the mix used in the film and different from the one that would appear on the *Let It Be* album.

"The Ballad of John and Yoko" was released as a single on May 30 in mono, even though the previous single, "Get Back," was released in stereo. The song, about the soap opera that the couple's lives had become, was very much a duo recording featuring just Lennon and McCartney but nonetheless credited to the Beatles. Recorded on April 14 with George Martin and Geoff Emerick back in the fold at Abbey Road Studios, this was the beginning of Lennon's broadside song releases, quickly recorded news chronicles of his life and the world around him, harkening back to the folk protest songs of Bob Dylan and Phil Ochs, with the lyrics more personal than political at first. Though the lyric "Christ, you know it ain't easy" made the song receive less airplay in the US than it might ordinarily have received, it still topped the charts in the UK.

It could be argued that the sessions for *Abbey Road* began two days later, on April 16, although on February 22 and 23 the Beatles worked on "I Want You" at Trident Studios. Along with work on "Old Brown Shoe," earmarked as the B side of "The Ballad of John and Yoko," the group worked on George Harrison's "Something."

Songs that would eventually be released on the *Abbey Road* album were started as far back as the White Album sessions, with the introduction of Lennon's "Mean Mr. Mustard" and "Polythene Pam." During the *Get Back/Let It Be* sessions "Sun King," "Carry

George Martin produced almost all of the music created by the Beatles; with his work on the *Abbey Road* album, he sent the group out in style. Courtesy Photofest.

That Weight," "Maxwell's Silver Hammer," "Oh Darling!," "Octopus's Garden," "I Want You," "She Came in through the Bathroom Window," "Golden Slumbers," and "Her Majesty" were all debuted. The only songs to appear on the *Abbey Road* album that were not debuted by the end of January were "Come Together," "Here Comes the Sun," "Because," "You Never Give Me Your Money," and "The End." Lennon actually wanted "I Want You" to close the *Abbey Road* album, and it was his idea to have the song end abruptly, an effect achieved by the tape having been cut.

While the Beatles were working on *Abbey Road*, Glyn Johns was attempting to prepare *Get Back* for release. The album he assembled included "Get Back," "Dig a Pony," "The One after 909," "I've Got a Feeling," "For You Blue," "Let It Be," "Two of Us," "Dig It," and "Maggie Mae," which would all appear in some form on the official *Let It Be* album when released in May 1970. The songs on Johns's version that would not be found on *Let It Be* were "Don't Let Me Down," "Teddy Boy," and the oldies medley "Rocker" (which is a snippet of "I'm Ready" from Fats Domino) and "Save the Last Dance For Me." He also did not include "Across the Universe" and "I Me Mine" on the first version of the *Get Back* album that he prepared. He did include studio chatter.

A cover shot was prepared for the album, featuring the Beatles, with long hair and dressed in their hippie finery, in the same pose and location where the cover shot of *Please Please Me* had been taken—an outdoor balcony at EMI's Manchester Square headquarters in London. The group even used the same photographer who had taken the previous shot, Angus McBean, though the new photo was slightly altered because the exact construction of the balcony had been changed since 1963. The proposed back cover art also replicated the look of the original album, with liner notes by Tony Barrow, who'd written the original back cover copy for *Please Please Me*. The new album title mirrored the full title of their debut album; *Please Please Me with Love Me Do and 12 Other Songs* replaced by *Get Back with Don't Let Me Down and 9 Other Songs* (subsequently and then being replaced with *Get Back with Don't Let Me Down and 12 Other Songs*). The new McBean photo that would not be used would eventually be used for the 1973 double album compilation *1967–1970*, referred to as the *Blue Album*, and the original McBean photo would adorn the double album compilation *1962–1966*, referred to as the *Red Album*. Late in July the Beatles saw a cut of the film, which was nearly three hours.

The release date for the album continuously changed, and by summer, the Beatles were fully committed to making the *Abbey Road* album with George Martin at Abbey Road Studios. It would be the first album the group would record entirely with eight-track and, when recording at Studio 2, using the new TG12345 console, the first such machine at Abbey Road Studios to not use valves and instead use transistors. The first date they used the new console was April 19, with work on "I Want You." Oddly enough, the album ceremoniously named after the road where EMI

Studios was located would also be recorded at other studios (Trident and Olympic); Billy Preston would also play on the *Abbey Road* album.

On May 5, Lew Grade's ATV company became the owner of the Lennon and Mc-Cartney song catalog through its acquisition of Northern Songs. Three days later, on May 8, Allen Klein became the manager of the Beatles. On May 26, both *Unfinished Music No. 2: Life with the Lions* by John and Yoko and *Electronic Sound* by George Harrison are released on Zapple; both had previously been released in the UK on May 9. Zapple was intended to be an Apple imprint that handled avant-garde music and spoken-word releases but only released these two albums.

From May 26 to June 2, the Lennons held another bed-in for peace, this time at the Queen Elizabeth Hotel in Montreal. On Sunday, May 31, "Give Peace a Chance" was recorded live in John and Yoko's hotel room. It features John on acoustic guitar and vocals; Yoko on vocals, handclaps, and tambourine; percussion supplied by André Perry, who also produced the recording; Tommy Smothers playing acoustic guitar; and the combined voices of the many others who happened to be there when this spontaneous, everlasting, and timeless anthem of peace was recorded. "Give Peace a Chance" was released on July 7 in the US, reached number 14, and on July 4 in the UK, reaching number 2. It was the debut single of the Plastic Ono Band and the first solo single from a Beatle. The B side featured Yoko's "Remember Love." Although credited to Lennon and McCartney, Paul had no participation in the writing of the song, and it has been said that Lennon gifted his songwriting partner with the credit for helping him record "The Ballad of John and Yoko." Although created as another one of Lennon's topical broadsides, the song has remained one of the most popular songs ever written advocating peace.

It was sometime in June when all the Beatles returned from separate holidays that the idea to do a proper studio album with George Martin at Abbey Road Studios became the group's official plan.

On July 7, Blind Faith, comprised of Steve Winwood, Eric Clapton, Ginger Baker, and Ric Grech, plays Hyde Park in London.

In June 1969, Brian Jones was fired from the Rolling Stones. On July 3, 1969, he died.

July 20 was the day that Neil Armstrong walked on the moon.

On August 8, Iain Macmillan took the photos of the Beatles walking across the zebra-striped road crossing in front of Abbey Road Studios that would grace the cover of the *Abbey Road* album. It's interesting that the last concert performed by the group on the roof at Apple, the last album cover photo shoot outside of Abbey Road Studios, and the last photos of them taken as a group at John's house all occurred so close to home, so to speak. Their fame had truly made them prisoners, and they couldn't even venture beyond their recording studio base, business office, and one of their homes to perform, be filmed, or be photographed for the last time.

At Abbey Road Studios on August 11, John Lennon would add backing vocals to "Oh Darling," marking his last musical contribution to music of the Beatles before they broke up.

The Woodstock Music and Art Fair took place on a dairy farm in upstate New York on August 15–18. Like Monterey Pop, none of the Beatles would participate. Although highly unlikely, there was the possibility the group would perform but only if Lennon's Plastic Ono Band could also perform. This was also highly unlikely, as at the time Lennon could not enter the US because of his drug busts.

At Abbey Road Studios, on August 20, the Beatles worked on "I Want You" and finalized the master tape for *Abbey Road*. It would be the last time all four would be at Abbey Road Studios.

On August 22, the Beatles held a photo shoot at Lennon's estate in Ascot with photographer Ethan Russell, who was present for the *Get Back* filming. It would be their last-ever group photo session. Monte Fresco of *The Daily Mail* was also present.

The Isle of Wight Festival was held August 29–31.

On September 13, at Varsity Stadium at the University of Toronto, the Plastic Ono Band made their debut at the Toronto Rock 'n' Roll Revival Festival and consisted on this occasion of Lennon, Ono, Eric Clapton on guitar, Klaus Voormann on bass, and drummer Alan White. Lennon initially wanted Harrison to join the group, asking Clapton, after Harrison passed. White had played around the British music scene, most notably with the Alan Price Set. He would go on to play on "Instant Karma," "Imagine," the *Some Time in New York City* album, and George Harrison's *All Things Must Pass* album. White also made appearances on recordings of other Apple acts, including the Radha Krishna Temple, Billy Preston, and Doris Troy. He would also play with future Wings member Denny Laine. White would later play extensively with Yes, recording nearly 20 albums with the group from 1973 until 2021. He died on May 26, 2022. The Plastic Ono Band would feature various musicians, and Lennon would release five studio albums, one live album, and one compilation album under the moniker. Yoko would initially release two albums in the 1970s under the moniker and then revive the name in 2009, releasing an EP and album, with one more album in 2013 and a collaboration with the Flaming Lips in 2011

The Plastic Ono Band had joined the bill at the last minute to help the promoter sell tickets, even though this oldies revival show not only boasted such rock 'n' roll pioneers as Chuck Berry, Little Richard, Jerry Lee Lewis, Fats Domino, Bo Diddley, and Gene Vincent but also current bands such as Chicago, the Doors, and Alice Cooper. The Plastic Ono Band rehearsed on the way over to the concert during their plane ride. As for their performance, oldies covers of "Blue Suede Shoes," "Money (That's What I Want)," and "Dizzy, Miss Lizzy" were interspersed with original numbers: "Yer Blues" from the White Album (which Lennon and Clapton had played at the Rock and Roll Circus); "Cold Turkey," about Lennon's experience withdrawing from heroin; and "Give Peace a Chance." There were also two numbers by Yoko, "Don't Worry Kyoko (Mummy's Only Looking for Her Hand in the Snow)" and an epic, nearly 13-minute "John John (Let's Hope for Peace)." A live album of the set would be released as *Live Peace in Toronto 1969* in December. Lennon actually wanted the Beatles to record "Cold Turkey" and make it their next single, but they all nixed the idea.

By the time of the Toronto concert, work on *Abbey Road* had been completed. It certainly appeared as if the group intended it as their swan song, but given all the material left over from the *Get Back* sessions, it's hard to tell. But on September 20, when John, Paul, and Ringo (George was in Liverpool, attending to his mother, who was ill) gathered at Apple to sign a contract with Capitol that Allen Klein had renegotiated, John unexpectedly announced that he would be leaving the group. This was not presented to them with animosity or acrimony, and everyone agreed to keep it quiet for the sake of the new music. *Abbey Road* was released just days later, September 26 in the UK and October 1 in the US. The single "Something"/"Come Together" was released on October 1 in the US and October 31 in the UK.

On November 6, Ringo began recording his debut solo album at Wessex Studios in London. He and his family moved to Highgate, North London, in December.

John and Yoko's *Wedding Album* is released on October 20 in the US and November 7 in the UK.

On December 1, George, Ringo, and their wives attended a show by Delaney and Bonnie and Friends at the Royal Albert Hall in London and saw them perform at a concert after-party at the Speakeasy Club. Either Eric Clapton, who was playing with the group, or Delaney Bramlett, or both, convinced Harrison to join the tour and play with the group. Clapton hitched his ride with Delaney and Bonnie, after having them onboard Blind Faith's summer tour of America for nine dates in 1969. Like he did after discovering the music of the Band and quitting Cream, Clapton's discovery of Delaney and Bonnie brought about the demise of Blind Faith. Poor Ginger Baker! George, in particular, loved the show and ended up joining the band on tour, playing gigs with the group on December 2, 3, 5, 6, and 7 in the UK and December 10 to 12 in Copenhagen. The four-disc, box-set reissue of *Delaney and Bonnie and Friends on Tour with Eric Clapton*, features Harrison on discs two through four from the Colston Hall, Bristol show on the 2nd, and Fairfield Halls in Croydon shows on the 7th.

Ringo Starr and his family moved to Highgate, in North London on December 5.

On December 6, the Rolling Stones play at the Altamont Speedway.

The first version of "Across the Universe" is released on the album *No One's Gonna Change Our World* on December 12.

On December 15, Glyn Johns picked up work again on preparing *Get Back* for release. Elsewhere, John and Yoko performed at a "Peace for Christmas" concert at

London's Lyceum Ballroom, joined by George Harrison, among others. Two performances from the show, "Cold Turkey" and "Don't Worry Kyoko," would eventually appear on the *Some Time in New York City* double album in 1972 even though the performances were obviously not recorded in New York. The album was credited to John and Yoko/Plastic Ono Band, with another side featuring four performances from the Fillmore East in Manhattan from June 1971 of John, Yoko, Klaus Voormann, Frank Zappa, and members of the Mothers of Invention, including Howard Kaylan, Mark Volman, and Aynsley Dunbar.

With only days left in the decade that changed the modern world, on December 19, in Missisauga, Ontario, Canada, John Lennon met Marshall McLuhan, the Canadian linguistics professor-turned-father of mass media theory. The event drew little interest in books on the Beatles, but this moment, where Lennon met McLuhan, is a true meeting of the minds. Lennon, along with Andy Warhol, were artists in the 1960s, who, although sometimes perceived as a little wacky by the mainstream media and many people, were two individuals who early on understood "media" in all its shapes and forms. McLuhan and Lennon hit it off, and the older professor (he was 57), embraced Lennon's approach to using the media. Their filmed meeting is basically McLuhan interviewing John and Yoko.

Paul, George, Ringo, and their wives closed out the year, and the decade, at Ringo's new home for a New Year's Eve Party on December 31.

The year 1969 had turned out to be another extraordinary one for pop music, now more referred to as rock music. The album continued to be the dominant mode of recorded musical expression, but the live, rock-concert experience was becoming even bigger, with more large outdoor festivals such as the Isle of Wight festivals of 1968, 1969, and 1970; the Glastonbury Festival, which began in 1970; and, of course, the first Woodstock festival in 1969. The biggest album event of the year was perhaps the release of the Who's rock opera *Tommy*. Other notable British rock albums included *Let It Bleed* from the Rolling Stones; Led Zeppelin *I* and *II*; the one and only album from Blind Faith, which was self-titled, *In the Court of the Crimson King*; the debut album from King Crimson; and *Arthur* from the Kinks. American music was spearheaded by the self-titled debut album from Crosby, Stills, and Nash; *Everybody Knows This Is Nowhere* from Neil Young and Crazy Horse; *Volunteers* from the Jefferson Airplane; *Happy Trails* from the Quicksilver Messenger Service; *Clouds* from Joni Mitchell; *Nashville Skyline* from Bob Dylan; no less than three albums from Creedence Clearwater Revival; and the self-titled debut album from the Stooges, featuring Iggy Pop, a portent of punk, several light-years away.

The lavish book that was planned to be released as part of the *Get Back* package was causing further delays in the album's release. John Kosh, known to all simply as Kosh, had worked with John and Yoko on the design for the *Life with the Lions* and *The Wedding Album*, along with the sleeve design for the "Ballad of John and Yoko,"

"Cold Turkey," and "Give Peace a Chance" singles. He also worked on the iconic design for *Abbey Road*. He described the process to the author:

> After Iain MacMillan shot *Abbey Road*, the chromes arrived by courier from the lab and were laid out on my light box. Iain and I poured over the film strip and marked the frames. One stood out, even though Paul was out of step. Of course, that along with other clues led to the rumors of Paul's demise. These rumors were flouted. Derek Taylor issued an edict that, if challenged, we should mumble that, "well it looks like him." The cover was hastily produced to fit the schedule of the postponed *Let It Be* release—at that point still titled *Get Back*. I was paid £750 for my part in *Abbey Road*—happily the most parodied cover ever. To pay my rent, I had to cash the Beatles & Co. cheque. It was signed by John and Paul. What an idiot.

Kosh also talked about his concept for what would become the *Let It Be* album package: "The *Let It Be (Get Back)* cover was my answer to the White Album—a funereal package as a tribute to the Fab's swan song. But *Abbey Road* interceded so the transition is no longer apparent." The decision over which cover idea to use—the one that aped *Please Please Me* or Kosh's "funereal" design—was finally made by Paul. "I mocked up both the *Let It Be* and *Get Back* covers with Jack Oliver for Paul while he wavered on the title," says Kosh. "John wanted to *Get Back* to their roots whereas Paul wanted to *Let It Be*. I had prepared final art for both as the deadline was looming." Kosh also talked about the book, titled *Get Back*, that came with the album in many countries but not the US and his work on it, when the title of the album changed from *Get Back* to *Let it Be*:

> I flew to New York to arrange the manufacture in the states, but it was hampered by the negotiations with United Artists. It seemed they wanted the movie but not the album, and certainly not the book, so we were stymied. I worked very closely with Ethan Russell, choosing the pictures. Jonathan Cott handed me the text, which was promptly censored by EMI after receiving complaints from the printer, Garrod & Lofthouse. George Harrison aptly renamed them Garage & Shithouse. It was all about George's dialogue. The censors changed "fucking" to "fooking." Hence George's epithet. The book was scheduled, printed, and sloppily bound well ahead of the album. It was impossible to change the title and reprint what amounted to hundreds of thousands of copies. Both Neil and Mal were genial and helpful in dealing with the creative mayhem swirling around us. I could use Neil's large office to spread out the huge, untrimmed press sheets on his floor. The only Beatle to take a peek was George, back from the states.

The final package with the book was only issued that way in the UK, Canada, Australia, New Zealand, and Southeast Asia. The perfect-bound color book included Russell's photos, censored dialogue from the film, and text by *Rolling Stone* magazine writers Jonathan Cott and David Dalton. As for the actual record jacket and label, the usually honest, somewhat cryptic, but occasionally florid Derek Taylor wrote of the album's music on the back cover: "This is a new phase Beatles album . . . essential to the content of the film, *Let It Be* was that they performed live for many of the tracks: in come the warmth and the freshness of a live performance; as reproduced for disc by Phil Spector." In the US, the label boasted a red Apple label, with the Apple on the back of the album cover also in red.

Kosh verified that he was interviewed for the Peter Jackson *Get Back* project, not for the series itself but no doubt for extras to appear in some kind of home DVD/Blu-ray release. He most likely wasn't the only one, and like the interviews done in 2003 around the time of the *Let It Be . . . Naked* project, the interview material remains unreleased, with no plans, as of this writing, for any kind of release.

AND IN THE END

The 1960s were technically over on January 1, 1970. But that doesn't mean the music, ideas, and changing cultural attitudes of that decade were finished. The 1960s would be resurrected many times after the first day of 1970.

The Beatles, or at least three of them—Paul, George, and Ringo—worked at Abbey Road Studios in the early part of the month. Footage of the group working on Harrison's "I Me Mine" was now included in the *Let It Be* film, meaning a final version of the song was needed for the soundtrack, with overdubs for the song done on January 3. There would also be overdubs done on McCartney's "Let It Be" on January 4, and on the 4th and 5th, George Martin and Paul McCartney added brass and cello to "Let It Be."

John did not attend these January sessions. He and Yoko were in Aalborg, Denmark, with Yoko's ex-husband, Anthony Cox, his second wife Melinda, and Yoko and Anthony's child, Kyoko; the Lennons would not return to England until January 25. Despite the rancor within the group due to their business differences, these final Beatles sessions nonetheless contained some humor. As heard on *Anthology 3*, before a take of "I Me Mine" from the 3rd, Harrison says: "You all will have read that Dave Dee is no longer with us. But Mickey and Tich and I would just like to carry on the good work that's always gone down in Number Two." Harrison was referring to Studio 2 of Abbey Road, where most of the Beatles recordings were done. The "Mickey and Tich" reference was to British group Dave Dee, Dozy, Beaky, Mick, and Tich, and Dee's departure from the band in September 1969.

Primarily on the 5th, but also on the 8th, Glyn Johns completed work again on what he thought would be the finished *Get Back* album. And once again, the Beatles couldn't all agree on this latest mix of the album.

While George and John had been busy recording and performing outside of the Beatles, and Ringo had been working on his film career and was now recording his debut solo album, Paul had been relatively quiet about solo plans of his own. But just before the end of 1969, he bought a Studer tape recorder and, with just the use of the machine and a mic, began demoing what would become his first solo album. At some point, he also began recording at Morgan Studios in Willesden in northwest London, where groups such as the Bonzo Dog Doo-Dah Band, Led Zeppelin, Jethro Tull, Blind Faith, and Supertramp had all recorded. He also booked sessions at Abbey Road on February 21, 22, 24, and 25. At both studios, he booked sessions under the pseudonym "Billy Martin" (no, baseball fans, not that Billy Martin).

Badfinger's *Magic Christian Music* was released on January 9 on Apple. On February 11, the original soundtrack album for *The Magic Christian* was released on Commonwealth United Records. Commonwealth United Entertainment was involved in film, music, and publishing for a short period of time before being sold. From 1968 through 1970, the company produced 10 films, including *The Ballad of Tam Lin* in 1970, which was its last film production, two Jess Franco-directed films, and *That Cold Day in the Park*, Robert Altman's third film. Three tracks from *Magic Christian Music*—"Come and Get It," "Carry on to Tomorrow," and "Rock of Ages"—are also on the soundtrack album. The soundtrack album also includes incidental music from Ken Thorne, "Something in the Air" from Thunderclap Newman, and Noel Coward's "Mad about the Boy," performed by Miriam Karlin, uncredited, and "Lilli Marlene" performed by Ringo and Peter Sellers. *The Magic Christian* had its American premiere on January 29 in Los Angeles. Ringo and Maureen attended.

The *Hey Jude* album was released in the US on Capitol Records on February 26. Other than George's blue jeans and red tie, Paul's white shirt, and Ringo's colorful tie, the Beatles are all dressed in dark clothes, and there is a pall that seems to be hanging over them in this cover shot taken by Ethan Russell at John's home in Ascot, their last-ever group photo session. It's clearly a long way from the fresh-faced, smiling exuberance of the four on the cover of *Please Please Me*. The *Hey Jude* album was initiated by Allen Klein, who wanted to get an album out quickly to cash in on the group's new royalty rate that he'd negotiated with EMI. Klein tasked Allan Steckler of ABCKO as the main point person there to manage Apple to come up with the tracks that would be used on the album. The idea for the album was to create a compilation album of tracks that Capitol had yet to release in the US on an album.

The album unintentionally bears some relation to the official *Let It Be* album, although that was not the intention, drawing from the period that kicked off *Get Back/Let It Be* through its inclusion of the "Hey Jude"/"Revolution" and "The Ballad of John and Yoko"/"Old Brown Shoe" singles as well as "Don't Let Me Down," the B side of the "Get Back" single. The remaining tracks are the "Paperback Writer"/"Rain" single, the US "A Hard Day's Night"/"I Should Have Known Better"

And in the end, the final photo shoot of the Beatles at John Lennon's home, Titttenhurst Park, in Ascot, England, on August 22, 1969, with Linda McCartney and Yoko Ono. Courtesy Photofest.

single, and "Lady Madonna. "Don't Let Me Down" is the only track out of chronological order in the track listing.

The next time when nonalbum tracks from the *Get Back/Let It Be* period would see release was on the double album *1967–1970* (known among fans as the "Blue Album"), which featured the single versions of "Get Back" and "Let It Be." The *Past Masters Volume 2* CD, released in 1988, included "You Know My Name (Look up the Number)," the B side of the "Let It Be" single, in mono. Then, more than 25 years after the *Get Back/Let It Be* period and the first bootlegs of the sessions, Beatles fans were treated to a treasure trove of previously unreleased material from the *Get Back/Let It Be* period on the 1996 *Anthology 3* release. Of the 23 tracks on the second CD of the set, 12 are rarities from Apple Studios or the Apple rooftop. These include: a demo of "Old Brown Shoe"; an alternate take of "I Me Mine"; "Dig a Pony" from January 22, 1969; "I've Got a Feeling" from January 23; "Two of Us" from January 24; and "For You Blue" and "Let It Be" from January 25. Also included is the master track of "The Long and Winding Road" from January 26 with the Phil Spector postproduction embellishments removed, marking it the first stab at a release like that on *Let It Be . . . Naked*. There is also a medley of "Rip It Up"/"Shake, Rattle and Roll"/"Blue Suede Shoes" from January 26 and "Mailman, Bring Me No More Blues" from January 29, 1969. There's only one rooftop performance of "Get Back." From the Apple studio sessions are performances of songs that would later appear on *Abbey Road*, "She Came in through the Bathroom Window" from January 22 and "Oh! Darling" from January 27. Finally, there's a performance of "Teddy Boy," taken from performances from January 24 and 28; the song would later appear on the *McCartney* album.

On March 6, the "Let It Be"/"You Know My Name, Look up the Number" single, produced by George Martin, was released. What was odd about the single is that "Let It Be" was released in stereo, and "You Know My Name, Look up the Number" was released in mono. The B side, one of the silliest released songs in the Beatles canon began in 1967. Lennon, taking the title from words he saw on a London telephone directory, may have written the song as light comic relief after all the heaviness of making the *Sgt. Pepper* album. It wouldn't have been out of place on a Bonzo Dog Doo-Dah Band album, with its boozy, leering cocktail-jazz-on-acid feel. The first recording of the song took place at Abbey Road Studios on May 17, with further work done on June 7, 8 (including sax by Brian Jones), and 9. They wouldn't come back to the song until April 30, 1969, finally finishing it on November 26. Like "The Ballad of John and Yoko," someone in the group's inner circle would get name-checked; this time it was Denis O'Dell.

On March 12, Pattie and George Harrison moved into Friar Park in Henley on Thames in Oxfordshire.

McCartney continued work on his solo album, returning to Morgan on March 5, and Abbey Road on March 16, finally completing work at the latter studio on March 23. That same day, Phil Spector would begin his work on producing the final and official version of *Let It Be* that would be released in May. He would spend just seven days at the studio, wrapping up his work on April 2—presumably, on the eighth day he must have rested.

When Spector began his work on March 23, the last time the *Get Back/Let It Be* material had been worked on was on February 28 at EMI, when Malcolm Davies was the producer, Pete Bown was the balance engineer, and Richard Langham was the tape operator and worked on remixing of "For You Blue."

On January 27, John, at George's suggestion, had chosen to work with Spector on "Instant Karma," which was released on February 6 in the UK. Lennon thought he had written a good song, but he felt that the track was not coming together in the studio. After listening to it, Spector quickly came up with the right production to make Lennon happy and propel the song to number 3. The song was another case of Lennon borrowing from one of his favorite records of the early 1960s, in this case, the opening piano chords of "Some Other Guy" by Richie Barrett from 1962, which Lennon used for the opening of "Instant Karma." The Beatles performed "Some Other Guy" often at the Cavern, and their performance of it at The Playhouse Theatre in London from June 1963 appears on the first *Live at the BBC* release from the Beatles, which was released in 1994. There's also the famous Cavern Club performance of August 22, 1962, of the song by the Beatles on film, with excellent sound, and one of the first live performances of the group captured on film. I asked Klaus Voormann to recall working on the session. Previously, I had spoken to him about that historic session and asked him if he could provide any new insights. He offered me what he wrote about the session from his German autobiography, which has never been translated into English. Voormann was given no time to prepare for the historic "Instant Karma" session. "'Klaus, come over to the studio right away. We want to record a song I wrote this morning,'" was the call he received from Lennon. He talked about what happened when he first got to the studio:

> On arrival at EMI Studios I was greeted by a beaming Mal Evans, who had been the Beatles road manager for years. During recording sessions, Mal was usually present to assist each member of the band as needed. "Hey, what's going on here," I asked Mal as a group of people moved large pieces of equipment and speakers on either side of us. "I don't know myself," Mal replied. "This has been going on all morning. Some American guy has organized the whole thing." I greeted Alan White, who was already busy testing his drum kit.

And then John and Yoko entered the room.

> They said neither "hello" or "how are you." Instead, they simply headed straight to the piano to play us the new song. Their excitement was obvious. I could sense how important this song was to John. No cup of tea, no small talk. The two of them got right down to business as if to say "This is the song and we want to get started right away." John wanted to get the song out of his system as soon as he could, which could only be achieved by getting it recorded as fast as possible. We understood the message without another word having to be spoken. We took up our positions, put the headphones on and began to play along with John, who remained at the piano. The backing track came together very quickly. We understood what John expected. It was at this point that the mood in the studio changed. Then he stood up suddenly. "Stop, hold on!" John's behavior was actually quite impossible. He made no effort to create a pleasant mood or interact with any of us. He just wanted to record this song, without having to hear another sound or see anything else. At that moment nothing else mattered."

It was at this point that Voormann and White were aware of other people involved in the session.

> John dashed up to the control room. Yoko scurried along behind him. It was difficult to figure out what was going on in the dimly lit room. Only a few vague figures could be discerned. John was engaged in an animated discussion with a short person who wore sunglasses. A few minutes later he stormed back over to the piano with Yoko close behind. "Okay, one more time." Without looking at us, he counted in. The structure of the song was simple so that we were quickly back in the chord progression. We played

the song through several times, until a thin reedy voice sounded from the control room. "Hold it"

It was at this point that Phil Spector made his appearance.

The door to the recording studio opened and a short man approached us, "Who the hell is this?" Alan and I exchanged glances expressing that thought. He reminded me of a mouse. In order to appear taller than he really was, he wore high-heeled Beatle boots. He wore a smart, bright, properly ironed white shirt. The breast pocket was embroidered with the initials "P.S." I still couldn't figure out who this person was, nor did I have any idea about his actual function. Phil had them gather around a microphone. He let the tape run a few times before recording began. I think it took two takes at most. A few hand claps by everyone there were added, and then Phil was satisfied.

Voormann explained how quickly the song went from the studio to the world. "The next step was the final mix. With all of the equipment necessary available at the EMI studio, the song was immediately cut to vinyl. This was the first time in music history that a song had been recorded, mixed and cut all in one day."

It has been said that Spector's work on "Instant Karma" was a kind of "audition" to fix *Let It Be*, but it would seem it was really more of a case of Lennon desperate to fix "Instant Karma." But it does seem that it was Allen Klein who may have set the wheels in motion for the Beatles working with Spector.

Spector's importance on the evolution of recorded pop music and elevating rock 'n' roll beyond its primitive beginnings cannot be overstated, and countless articles and books have been written about his exalted place in the history of popular music. His accomplishments were overshadowed by his erratic behavior over the years, outsized ego, retirement and seclusion from the business, and murder of actress Lana Clarkson for which he was sent to prison in 2009 and died there in 2021.

The producer was at a crossroads when he arrived in London in 1970. The single he produced for Ike and Tina Turner in 1966, "River Deep, Mountain High" had flopped in the US, only reaching number 88. As a result, the album named after the song was only released on London Records in the UK, where the single had reached number 3. A&M Records finally released the album in the US in 1969, with a hype sticker affixed to the shrink wrap that declared "River Deep, Mountain High" 'is a perfect record from start to finish—You couldn't improve on it,'" signed by George Harrison. About all Spector had done since the commercial failure of "River Deep, Mountain High" was make a handful of recordings with the American R&B group the Checkmates.

Spector had come to London with his bodyguard George Brand. With Brand installed in one room and Spector in another at the Inn on the Park in Central London, Klein was able to keep an eye on the erratic and down-on-his heels producer by having Spector room with Klein's ABKCO promotion man Pete Bennett. It's still hard to believe that on Spector's first day at Abbey Road working on the *Get Back* tapes, Paul McCartney was in the same building, and their paths didn't cross; one wonders what would have happened if they did connect. Spector worked that day mixing several tracks, including two different versions of "I've Got a Feeling," along with "One after 909" and the rooftop version of "Dig a Pony." He created an extended mix of "I Me Mine," and became another in a long line of people taking a crack at mixing "Across the Universe."

On March 25, Spector did mixes for "Two of Us," "For You Blue," and "Teddy Boy." It's interesting that there was no contact between McCartney and anyone on the production side in regard to the use of this song. Had McCartney ever communicated to Glyn Johns that he would be including "Teddy Boy" on his debut solo album?

The next day, March 26, was also a busy day. Spector mixed "Let It Be," "Get Back," "Maggie Mae," and "The Long and Winding Road with Abbey Road engineers Peter Bown and Roger Ferris." Work was done on "Dig It" on March 27, with Ferris returning, but Bown had left and was replaced by Mike Sheady and "For You Blue" on March 30. Spector then moved out of the cramped Room 4 and took over the large Studio 1 on April 1, but the day would be no April Fool's joke. With a 35-piece orchestra, a 14-member choir, and Ringo present to overdub drums (and be the last Beatle to ever attend a recording session of any kind for any of the group's recordings), "Across the Universe," "The Long and Winding Road," and "I Me Mine" were embellished, with the assistance of arrangements by Richard Hewson on "The Long and Winding Road" and "I Me Mine," arrangements by Brian Rogers on "Across the Universe,' and additional help with the orchestral score by John Barham on "Across the Universe" and "The Long and Winding Road." The orchestra and choir were used on both "Across the Universe" and "The Long and Winding Road," but only strings were used on "I Me Mine." Rather than add any echo in postproduction, as keeping with his style, he began right away adding echo to any new instruments he was recording. Although Spector was producing the session, the conducting of the orchestra was left to the arrangers. Spector's dictatorial production style emerged in full this day, enraging most of the people present, with engineer Pete Bown walking out and being coaxed back over the phone by Spector, who apparently apologized to the Abbey Road Studios veteran.

Spector finished his work on April 2, with stereo mixing of "The Long and Winding Road," "I Me Mine," and "Across the Universe."

In the midst of all the chaos and rancor surrounding Allen Klein's involvement with the Beatles, Phil Spector's postproduction work on *Let It Be*, and conflicts over its release date vis-à-vis the release date of Paul's solo album, Paul decided he would not be doing any press. Instead, he answered questions provided by Apple press officer Derek Taylor and Apple's managing director Peter Brown for a Q&A insert provided with press copies of the album, along with a track-by-track analysis of the songs. While Taylor was involved, it does seem that Brown was the one who drew up the questions. Did Paul have any input into these questions? Probably not. Did Taylor or Brown realize they were supplying some rather loaded questions? Through the years, Brown and Taylor seemed certain McCartney knew what he was doing. McCartney has addressed these issues in the *Anthology* book and in *Many Years from Now*. He indicated that the press thought the Q&A sheet was going to be included in every album, and not just for the press, in lieu of interviews. Paul seemed to think his answers didn't state the Beatles were breaking up, but he also didn't seem to fear it would be interpreted that way, by saying in *Many Years from Now*, about some of the loaded questions that were written by Brown: "if that's what he wants to know, I'll tell him. I felt I'd never be able to start a new life until I told people."

There were four questions in a row that ultimately were at the crux of McCartney, in effect, saying the Beatles were over as far as he was concerned, although hedging ever so slightly but closing the door completely on writing anymore with Lennon:

Q: Are you planning a new album or single with the Beatles?

A: No.

Q: Is your break with the Beatles temporary or permanent, due to personal differences or musical ones?

A: Personal differences, business differences, musical differences, but most of all because I have a better time with my family. Temporary or permanent? I don't really know.

Q: Do you foresee a time when Lennon-McCartney becomes an active songwriting partnership again?

A: No.

The reaction to the questionnaire was swift, with most people assuming the Beatles had broken up, particularly the *Daily Mirror*. A writer for the publication on seeing the questionnaire, interpreted McCartney's remarks, as proof of what had been hinted at for some time, that the Beatles had broken up. The *Daily Mirror* headline, screamed in bold type: "PAUL QUITS THE BEATLES." Oddly, John Lennon was glad McCartney finally admitted they were done, but angry because when he'd told everyone he was leaving in September 1969, he was asked to keep it quiet, so Klein could conclude his negotiations with EMI. Ever the press agent, and a man who could eloquently coax the sun out of a cloud, Derek Taylor issued one of his most famous statements on April 10 in response to the press reports that McCartney was quitting the Beatles: "Spring is here and Leeds play Chelsea tomorrow and Ringo and John and George and Paul are alive and well and full of hope. The world is still spinning and so are we and so are you. When the spinning stops—that'll be the time to worry. Not before. Until then, The Beatles are alive and well and the Beat goes on, the Beat goes on." *McCartney* was released on April 17.

Acetates of *Let It Be* were sent to the group sometime in the first week of April. Paul's copy came with a note from Allen Klein indicating changes had to be made to the final album. On April 14, Paul sent a letter to Klein about addressing those changes:

Dear Sir,

In [the] future, no one will be allowed to add to or subtract from a recording of one of my songs without my permission.

I had considered orchestrating "The Long and Winding Road" but I had decided against it. I, therefore, want it altered to these specifications:

1. Strings, horns, voices and all added noises to be reduced in volume.
2. Vocal and Beatle instrumentation to be brought up in volume.
3. Harp to be removed completely at the end of the song and original piano notes to be substituted.
4. Don't ever do it again.

Signed

Paul McCartney
c.c. Phil Spector
John Eastman

There is much confusion over whether Paul heard the final Spector mix. Ringo, in an interview with *Melody Maker*, said he did but was apparently not going to do anything about it. It has also been said that his letter indicates that he did and wanted changes made, but either Klein didn't tell Spector, or he did and Spector did nothing. It has also been said that Paul's objections came too late and no changes could be made.

Originally, John, George, and Ringo asked Paul to delay his album release from April 17 until June to avoid releasing it so close to the *Let It Be* album, which was scheduled for April 24. Ringo went to Paul's home to discuss the matter, which led to an argument and McCartney telling Starr to get out. Realizing the issue was important for Paul, Ringo persuaded the others to change *Let It Be*'s release date to May 8 in the UK and May 18 in the US. The phrase "Phil + Ronnie" was etched in the deadwax (the run out groove) of the album.

On the same day that *Let It Be* was released in the UK, Allen Klein officially became the business manager of the Beatles. John had first given Klein authority to look after his affairs on February 3, with Harrison and Starr soon following suit.

What is interesting about all the subterfuge over the release of *Let It Be* are the credits; the album is unusually described as being "reproduced for disc by Phil Spector," and Glyn Johns and George Martin are given a thank-you. While Martin's presence was admittedly nebulous at best, Johns should have been given a more respectful and accurate credit. In his memoir *Sound Man*, Johns said of the Spectorized *Let It Be*, "John [Lennon] gave the tapes to Phil Spector, who puked all over them, turning the album into the most syrupy load of bullshit I have ever heard."

On May 11, the single "The Long and Winding Road"/"For You Blue" was released. It would be the group's last single while they were still together.

The *Let It Be* film opened in the UK on May 20 at the same location as their previous three films, the London Pavilion. Unlike those other premieres, none of the Beatles were present. However, there was a considerable contingent of musicians, celebrities, and those with a connection to the Beatles who attended, including John Lennon's ex-wife Cynthia and Paul's former girlfriend Jane Asher, as well as director Richard Lester. Others in attendance included Apple recording artist Mary Hopkin; Sir Joseph Lockwood, the Chairman of EMI; Spike Milligan from the Goons; Lulu; folk singer Julie Felix; and various members of the Rolling Stones and Fleetwood Mac. The film's US release had been scheduled for May 13 in New York; it was pushed back to May 28.

There are two postscripts to the musical side of the *Get Back/Let It Be* project. Regardless of what Spector did with *Let It Be*, he would go on to work extensively with both George Harrison and especially John Lennon, along with producing Yoko Ono's 1981 album *Season of Glass*, her first work after John died. And despite the bad blood between Harrison and Lennon since Yoko became a part of John's life, Harrison would play on the "Instant Karma" single and Lennon's best remembered album, *Imagine*. Harrison even wrote and recorded the song "It's Johnny's Birthday" for Lennon's 30th birthday; it appeared on Harrison's *All Things Must Pass* album and had been recorded on October 7, 1970, two days before Lennon's birthday, at Abbey Road Studios.

Few movie soundtrack albums have caused so much stress and turmoil and took so long to come out. Lost in all this album drama is the fact that the long-delayed movie was finally released. It was very much seen through the prism of the breakup of the Beatles, and the movie became to many people, the chronicling of their dissolution, regardless of the fact that when they finished filming, they went on to make what is regarded as one of their best albums, *Abbey Road*. But given that *Let It Be* was released months after *Abbey Road*, most people who saw the film had no idea of the true sequence of events, let alone the behind-the-scenes dramas.

To say the film was not met with acclaim is an understatement. The critics were not kind; even those who could discern the luster of the Beatles in the movie still fell back on shorthand cliches about the film. In the *New York Times* on May 29, 1970,

Howard Thompson wrote: "The very helter-skelter, unstudied nature of the picture provides a revealing close-up of the world's most famous quartet, playing, relaxing and chatting. Their faces have changed, naturally, and all of them now show more assurance and ease, especially the spectacled John Lennon, with his ascetic features enshrouded in flowing hair. Paul McCartney's is a kind face with more character, lighting up when he fondles a little blonde cherub (his wife's daughter). Ringo Starr leans back more soulfully than ever on the drums, while George Harrison remains the quiet enigma of the four." In *Time* on June 8, 1970, a rather perfunctory review of the film said: "Rock scholars and Beatles fans will be enthralled with the film. Others may find it only a kind of mildly enjoyable documentary newsreel," concluding by saying: "*Let It Be* may not be much of a movie, but it's a fine concert." In *Time Out's Film Guide* from 2006, Phil Hardy said retrospectively that the film: "survives as a fascinating record of both the Beatles collapse and their unending power over their audience (us). After an hour in which one watches the Fab Four bickering and disintegrating before our eyes, almost magically they reform and take us back to happier times with their impromptu concert on the Apple rooftop."

While mainstream film reviewers could forgive some of the weaknesses of the film, not wanting to appear out of touch with the pop music scene, the rock press, firmly established but still in its infancy in 1970, was not going to be so forgiving of the *Let It Be* album. The *NME*, in an oft-repeated quote from a review by Alan Smith from May 9, mournfully stated, "If the new Beatles soundtrack is to be their last then it will stand as a cheapskate epitaph, a cardboard tombstone, a sad and tatty end to a musical fusion which wiped clean and drew again the face of pop." The British press had no problem cutting the Beatles down to size, and Smith's sometime bitter review was not unusual. John Mendelsohn, in *Rolling Stone* on June 11, was a little more forgiving, laying the blame for the album's shortcomings on Spector's overproduction, saying Spector, "proceeded to turn several of the rough gems on the best Beatle album in ages into costume jewelry." After suggesting listeners seek out the raw bootlegs of the session, he concluded, "Musically, boys, you passed the audition. In terms of having the judgment to avoid either over-producing yourselves or casting the fate of your get-back statement to the most notorious of all over-producers, you didn't. Which somehow doesn't seem to matter much anymore anyway."

On March 16, 1971, the soundtrack album would win the Grammy for Best Original Score Written for a Motion Picture or a Television Special. The ceremony was held at the Hollywood Palladium in Los Angeles, and the award was accepted by Paul and Linda from John Wayne. The song "Let It Be," was nominated for Song of the Year and Record of the Year but lost in both categories to Simon and Garfunkel's "Bridge over Troubled Water." At the Oscars on April 15, the Beatles won the award for Best Original Song Score; Quincy Jones accepted the award on their behalf because none of the Beatles attended the ceremony.

Like the Beatles' other films through the years, *Let It Be* received the occasional screening at art house cinemas, colleges, and at midnight movie showings. The film was released on VHS, Betamax, and laser disc in 1981 and on video disc in 1982. And that is where the home video release of *Let It Be* ends; the film has never subsequently been on DVD, Blu-ray, or available on streaming platforms. The original footage would be used for the 2021 Peter Jackson *Get Back* series, but even as of this writing, there are no plans to release *Let It Be* in any format.

Although *Let It Be* would have no future on home video, bootlegged tapes of the *Get Back* project would proceed beyond its humble beginning in 1969. This was also true of the music. Cassette and vinyl copies of the Glyn Johns acetates circulated widely, and bootleg sets of music grew more expansive over the years, with improved sound quality and housed in lavish packages. These bootleggers came up with imaginative names for their releases, which became sought after and delivered an extraordinary product. These included *Sweet Apple Trax*, *Jamming with Heather*, *Celluloid Rock*, *Rockin' Movie Stars*, and *Posters, Incense and Strobe Candles*.

Unless you picked up one of the official *Let It Be* film reissues early in the 1980s, you had to wait until 1995 to be able to sit at home and see officially released footage, when excerpts of the film were included in the *Anthology* TV series.

Apple had initially planned to reissue *Let It Be* at the time *Let It Be . . . Naked* was released on November 17, 2003, and had filmed interviews for bonus material. But the final consensus was that Paul, Ringo, and others involved with the project didn't want to revisit the negative intergroup dynamics and offer them up for public consumption. But we still had *Let It Be . . . Naked*, a package that included two discs in the CD set (a vinyl version was also available in the UK only). The first disc featured a new mix of the original *Let It Be* album, eliminating Spector's heavy-handed production and between-song chatter; the album was resequenced, "Dig It" and "Maggie Mae" were dropped, and "Don't Let Me Down" was added. Digital correction was done on "Two of Us" and "I Dig a Pony," and speed/pitch alterations were made to "Across the Universe," giving the album a focused, cleaner sound. It is more of an album than an audio document masquerading as a soundtrack. Some might say that it lacks the charm of the original album and prefer Spector's heavily orchestrated production.

The second disc, named *Fly on the Wall*, featured slightly less than 22 minutes of jams, music, and miscellaneous conversation. It was a disappointing offering for many because there were not complete versions of songs, nor, as had been hoped by fans for years, the complete rooftop concert.

Paul Hicks, Allan Rouse, and Guy Massey coproduced and mixed the album. Massey spoke with the author about his work on the album. "*Let It Be . . . Naked*, was definitely a team effort. Paul and I, I think, dipped into a hat to choose the tracks we mixed, so we effectively split the album in half and mixed half each. Once again, when we were at a stage to play the mixes to each other, we all made our comments and adjusted accordingly. When the three of us were happy, we had playbacks for those at Apple for their input and made changes accordingly." He commented on any direction he and the team received about Spector's work on the album. "Yeah, the remit was to 'de-Spectorize' the album, so that's what we did, removing any of the overdubs that were recorded during the Spector sessions and stripping it back to the more band-oriented arrangements. We had scope to re-edit if we felt we could improve performances individually and were given the green light to re-sequence and such."

He talked further about the overall concept: "The concept was to have it almost back to the early days I guess, the four—five with Billy Preston—of them playing with little embellishment, and of course the rooftop performances were used and were as live as live could be. Paul and Ringo, and Olivia and Yoko, were all involved towards the end to help tie it all into as coherent a version as we could possibly make." The Nagra tapes from the filming were not used but were worked on: "I believe we digitized all the multi-tracks from all the sessions and researched outtakes, etc., for any additional parts/edits we needed to achieve. I think all the Nagras from the film were archived too." He talked about the experience of listening to the original tapes of the rooftop concert. "Yeah, it's such an iconic performance. Paul Hicks and I had worked on a fair bit of it for the *Anthology* project, so we were aware of it and how great it was. The tapes, as all of the master tapes are, were in impeccable order and it was a blast being able to listen to them and the elements therein to scrutinize, etc. It was great fun!"

The years went by and still no *Let It Be* film was reissued. Beatles fans even started online petitions to get the film rereleased. Then, on January 30, 2019, it was announced that Peter Jackson, the New Zealand–based director who made *The Lord of the Rings* trilogy, would use newly restored original footage from 1969 to create an entirely new film. It was also confirmed that the original *Let It Be* film would also be rereleased at some point. On March 11, 2020, just as the world was about to go into lockdown related to the COVID-19 pandemic, Disney announced that they had acquired the rights to release the film theatrically, with a premiere date set for September 4, 2020. But just a few months later, on June 12, Disney announced the premiere was being pushed back to August 27, 2021, due to the pandemic. To help tide fans over, Jackson offered a sneak peak of the film online on December 20, 2020. The following year, with the pandemic now prematurely ebbing, it was announced on June 17, 2021, that *Get Back* would now be a three-part series and not released theatrically but instead stream in three parts on Disney+ over Thanksgiving weekend, November 25, 26, and 27.

At the end of summer 2021, Paul McCartney held a private screening of a 100-minute cut of *The Beatles: Get Back* for family, friends, and the famous at his

Long Island home. Some of the people who attended included musicians Jimmy Buffett, Jon Bon Jovi, and Steve Van Zandt, along with Alec Baldwin, Jerry Seinfeld, Julianne Moore, Angelica Houston, and former New York City mayor Michael Bloomberg, many of whom also had summer homes on the east end of Long Island.

A theatrical premiere of the 100-minute cut was held on November 17 at Cineworld Empire in London, with Paul, his daughter Mary, George Harrison's son Dhani, Ringo's son Zak, Glyn Johns, Giles Martin, and Pattie Boyd and her husband Ron Weston in attendance, along with Noel Gallagher, Mick Hucknall, Martin Freeman, Elvis Costello and his wife Diana Krall, and Gary Kemp. On November 19, a US premiere was held at El Capitan Theater in Hollywood. There were children of the Beatles at this premiere also, including Julian Lennon, Sean Lennon, and Stella McCartney. Others in attendance included Peter Asher, and Bob Iger, the chairperson of Disney, introduced the film.

Before the series aired on Disney+, there were several related projects. The first was the reissue of the *Let It Be* album on October 15. Peter Jackson's participation in the *Get Back* project began in 2017, at a time when Apple was already thinking about the album's 50th anniversary and still in the process of finding missing audio material from the period.

The new *Let It Be* album music reissue series was released in various configurations: a single CD, a double CD, a single standard vinyl album, an LP vinyl picture disc, a five CD/Blu-ray box set, and a four-LP/12-inch EP vinyl box set.

The four-LP/12-inch EP vinyl set was cut from hi-res digital files, mastered at half-speed at Abbey Road Studios, and pressed on 180-gram vinyl. The Glyn Johns disc and the first two songs on the EP were remastered from archive stereo tapes.

The two box sets are beautifully packaged and, like its three Apple reissue predecessors—*Sgt. Pepper's Lonely Hearts Club Band* (2017), *The Beatles* (the White Album) (2018), and *Abbey Road* (2019)—there is little or no quibbling about the presentation. This time around, the deluxe vinyl version came with a hardcover book.

The first album of the box is the original, 12-track album with the new stereo mix produced and mixed by Giles Martin, engineered and mixed by Sam Okell, and mastered by Miles Showell, all at Abbey Road Studios. Albums 2 and 3, presented as a gorgeous, two-LP gatefold package, consist of *Get Back—Apple Sessions* on one album and *Get Back – Rehearsals and Apple Jams* on the other album, totaling 27 tracks. Album number 4, *Get Back LP—1969 Glyn Johns Mix*, features 14 tracks. The *Let It Be* EP is a 12-inch, four-song disc and includes "Across the Universe," mixed by Glyn Johns in 1970 of the February 1968 recording; "I Me Mine," the last track recorded by the Beatles on January 3, 1970 (excluding John Lennon who was on holiday in Denmark), also mixed by Johns in 1970; "Don't Let Me Down," recorded live at Apple on January 28, 1970, with a new mix by Giles Martin; and the "Let It Be" single with a new mix by Giles Martin.

Once again, Martin and his team have done an excellent job coming up with a new mix of an album from the Beatles. It provides a rich, detailed sound that clears up some of the muddiness and sloppiness of the original *Let It Be* album mix, yet retains the charm that was completely lost on the *Let It Be . . . Naked* remix. As on recent remixes of albums from the Beatles and solo albums from John Lennon and George Harrison, lead vocals are brought closer to the fore and figure more prominently.

The *Sessions* album consists almost entirely of songs that, in one form or another, would show up on the *Let It Be* album or related singles. The two exceptions are a snippet of "Please Please Me" and a snippet of "Wake up Little Susie," made popular by the Everly Brothers, whose influence informs the lovely harmony interplay between John and Paul on "Two of Us."

On the *Rehearsals* and *Apple Jams* albums, there are tracks that show up in one form or another on *Let it Be*, including "I Me Mine," "Get Back," and "Let It Be." Several other tracks would appear on *Abbey Road*: "She Came in through the Bathroom Window," "Polythene Pam," "Octopus's Garden," "Oh Darling!," and "Something." There is also a version of "All Things Must Pass," as well as a version of "Gimmie Some Truth," that appear on John Lennon's 1971 *Imagine* album. Also of interest are a snippet of a cover of "The Walk," a hit in 1958 for Jimmy McCracklin, and the gorgeous "Without a Song," featuring Billy Preston, with support from John Lennon and Ringo Starr. A finished studio version of that song was on Preston's 1971 album *I Wrote a Simple Song*, which was his debut album for A&M.

The *Glyn Johns 1969 Mix* album is probably the most anticipated disc of this set. It is beautifully packaged with an update of the group's debut album cover shot at EMI's Manchester offices by photographer Angus McBean. This mix and running order more faithfully reflect the original roots approach the Beatles envisioned for the *Get Back* project. The album contains a running order different from *Let It Be*. It includes the cover "Save the Last Dance for Me," a hit for the Drifters in 1960. It does not include "Across the Universe" and "I Me Mine," which appeared on the original *Let It Be* album. This disc has come under some scrutiny. Mike Carrera, writing in the *Daily Beatle* on October 22, 2021, indicated that the disc released throughout the world except in Japan, is actually not the 1969 mix from Johns but a selection of his mixes from both 1969 and 1970. The only way to get the entire 1969 mix is to buy the superdeluxe CD SHM box from Japan. Carrera stated that although the Japan box is a rarity, the sound quality of the 1969/1970 mixes in the rest of the world are superior, and it would appear that is why they were selected. It is also important to note that sometime during his involvement with the project, Johns did a stereo mix of the rooftop concert. According to the notes by Kevin Howlett in the book that comes with the deluxe sets that tape is missing. The involvement of Johns in this project was quite unique, in that George Martin had for the most part been the group's sole record producer throughout the group's entire career. Add to that Phil Spector's coming aboard in the 11th hour to resurrect the shelved project, and essentially, you have three producers involved. If one would like to go even one step further, budding engineer and future super producer Alan Parsons was also present for the *Get Back/Let It Be* project as tape operator. It's this variety of production contributors that has both made the album be perceived as muddled and left the door open for it to be reimagined twice officially and through the seemingly infinite bootlegs that have surfaced for more than 50 years. It appears that the source of the bootleg was the acetate Johns prepared, with Lennon's copy inadvertently the culprit. An acetate that Johns brought to America at the request of Harrison for Denny Cordell to hear and to be used in a production he might do for Joe Cocker is also a possibility.

Ryan White, who directed the 2013 documentary *Good Ol' Freda*, about Beatles fan club secretary Freda Kelly, told the author about why he chose to work on the film and provided insight on what it's like being the director of a film related to the Beatles: "I like Cinderella stories. They usually make great premises for documentaries because they have all of the dramatic elements of a great story. I felt like Freda encapsulated the quintessential Cinderella story—from shy schoolgirl to 11 years working for the Beatles." He talked about the biggest challenge working on a Beatles-related film: "Clearing the music rights was definitely a gargantuan task for *Good Ol' Freda*. Not only were we trying to license Beatles music but also legendary acts like Buddy Holly, the Isley Brothers, the Marvelettes, and Little Richard—all on a shoestring budget. Ultimately, it was a testament to Freda herself that all of the record labels (especially Apple) were willing to work within our very limited budget."

When *Get Back* finally streamed on Disney+ over Thanksgiving weekend, the majority of Beatles fans who watched gave the series a big thumbs-up. While the series, according to Nielsen, was the seventh-most-streamed original program that week, the focus in the press was on viewership demographics, zeroing in on the fact that 54 percent of viewers were older than 55 years of age. The age-group was far from Disney's usual young demographic, but reading between the lines, it was almost perceived as bad for some reason that people who are this old were the primary group of people who watched it.

Peter Jackson had several key collaborators that he worked with on the film. Emma Montanet, the production manager, had worked on other Beatles -related documentaries, including the Beatles *Anthology* and *The Beatles in Help!* Other music-related films she worked on include *Hendrix: Band of Gypsys* and *The Who: The Making of Tommy*. Dean Watkins, credited as general manager, worked with Jackson on *The Hobbit* trilogy, among many other films. The person who was Jackson's primary collaborator on the film was editor Jabez Olssen. He also worked on the *Hobbit* trilogy and *They Shall Not Grow Old*, the 2018 documentary on World War I that Jackson had been working on when the *Get Back* film was first considered. Clare Olssen, a producer on the film, was the c-producer of *They Shall Not Grow Old*.

On the Apple side, there were numerous primary producers, starting with Paul, Ringo, Yoko, and Olivia. Jeff Jones is the CEO of Apple Corps. Jonathan Clyde, has worked on many Beatles-related film projects, including *Sgt. Pepper's Musical Revolution* with Howard Goodall; *The Beatles: Eight Days a Week—The Touring Years*, directed by Ron Howard; *The Beatles: 1*, *The Beatles on Record*; *All Together Now*, about the making of *LOVE* show in Las Vegas; *The Beatles in 'Help!'* documentary; the *Concert for Bangladesh Revisited with George Harrison and Friends*; and *The Making of the Beatles First US Visit*. Martin R. Smith, along with working on the *Sgt. Pepper's Musical Revolution* and *The Beatles: 1*, has a long list of music documentary credits. Ken Kamis of Key Creatives also worked on *They Shall Not Grow Old* and the *Hobbit* trilogy.

Though clocking in at nearly eight hours, the series is riveting for the most part. The series is broken up into three episodes. Episode 1 primarily covers the beginning of the *Get Back* filming, which takes place at Twickenham. Episode 2 primarily covers the group's time after they left Twickenham and settled in at their own studios in the basement of their Apple headquarters. The third episode takes place almost entirely at Apple, climaxing with the group's historic rooftop concert on January 30, 1969.

One aspect of the series that's different from the original film is that Jackson adds context through a short introduction about the Beatles that gives a potted history of the group, subtitles, and the use of newspaper articles that fill in some of the historic background of the time. Episode 1 at times is admittedly a bit tedious because the band works in fits and starts at the dark, bare, cavernous Twickenham film soundstage, which is not the most ideal location for any kind of drama or storytelling. Conversely, Apple Studios was an intimate space with white walls that was well lit and was where the Beatles seemed to be more comfortable and relaxed. It was during this second episode that Billy Preston shows up, his warm personality and intuitive musicianship brightening the mood considerably. The third episode is the most enjoyable because the songs the Beatles are working on are in a more complete state and the best part of the whole series being the concluding rooftop concert.

As the credits for the series roll, footage from the final day of shooting, January 31, is shown: the Beatles performing versions of "Two of Us," "The Long and Winding Road," and 'Let it Be," songs deemed too acoustic for the rooftop performance. In the *Let It Be* film, these performances were presented in their entirety. Jackson most likely didn't want to repeat that; maybe when an expanded DVD/Blu-ray of the series is released, these performances will be shown uncut, without credits scrolling on-screen.

In an advance review of the film, Kenneth Womack, in *Salon* on November 25 said: "Peter Jackson's 'The Beatles: Get Back' is a mesmerizing feast for the eyes, a veritable time machine that transports viewers back to the Beatles' heyday in January 1969. New fans and diehards alike will revel in the carefully restored images of the Fab Four as they bring such classic tunes as 'Get Back,' 'Don't Let Me Down,' and 'Let It Be' to life in the studio, culminating in the famous Rooftop Concert." In *The Atlantic*, James Parker's review was headlined "Like Watching Six Different Marriages Fall Apart." He made the astute observation that *The Beatles: Get Back* "is a film about the Beatles, but it's also a film about a film," which is something that is very much part of its appeal. It's so meta, it's already spawned another project, *The Beatles: Get Back—The Rooftop Concert in the IMAX Experience* using proprietary IMAX digital remastering (DMR) technology. Initially slated to only be shown on January 30, 2022, the 60-minute theatrical film presents the entire rooftop concert. The screenings on the 30th also included a live satellite Q&A featuring Peter Jackson. At midnight on January 30, the complete performance debuted on streaming services in stereo and Atmos, remixed by Giles Martin and Sam Okell, followed by a broadcast the same day on Sirius XM. The rooftop concert audio is now available on most streaming services, though there is, as yet, no plan to release it on vinyl or CD.

Jackson has been interviewed extensively about the *Get Back* series. The most far-reaching and informed interview that Jackson gave was for the *Things We Said Today* YouTube videocast, which aired on November 21, 2021. The show is hosted by Ken Michaels, of Ken Michaels radio, who also is the host of the radio show *Every Little Thing*. He was joined by his regular cohosts, veteran New York radio personality Darren DeVivo of WFUV in New York and Alan Kozinn, longtime former reporter for the *New York Times*, author, and current reporter for the *Wall Street Journal*. The three interviewed Jackson for nearly four hours. The interview ran prior to the *Get Back* series debut airing on Disney+, so the marathon session was more a preview of the series. Jackson talked about how much more revealing the series was compared to listening to the endless bootlegs of the *Get Back/Let It Be* project: "When you add the pictures it changes it so much. There's so much more information that just comes at you when you actually put the pictures with the sound." Jackson felt the series really changed when the Beatles left Twickenham for their studio at Apple. "They're way more motivated and focused when they are actually making an album." Early on, Jackson connected with Michael Lindsay-Hogg and it's clear from interviews with both of them, that they have tremendous affection and respect for each other. "I talked to him for four years," said Jackson. "I had to get Michael's OK." Jackson loved how Lindsay-Hogg used a little audio tape machine during the making of *Let It Be* and how he had the foresight to put a hidden microphone bug in the flowerpot of the cafeteria at Twickenham, that fortuitously captured a key conversation between Paul McCartney and John Lennon. Jackson felt that Lindsay-Hogg was under many challenges in making the movie and how unlike things were for Jackson with the *Get Back* series, the *Let It Be* director had to eventually take into consideration the soundtrack album and that "the album and the film had to speak to each other." As opposed to *Let It Be*, for the rooftop concert segment in *Get Back*, Jackson "used all the rooftop footage." Jackson wanted to use as much of the original footage that was shot as possible because "that stuff is going to go back into the vaults for 50 years. It's great stuff. I'm not going to have that on my conscience that I've seen it and no one else can." Jackson digitized lots of footage and all the Nagra reels and found more Nagra audio in the process. He said he would love to help Apple go through all their archives. One of the most fascinating revelations in the interview was photos Jackson found that shows that filming continued at Apple after January 31, 1969. The pictures seem to date the filming in February because Paul's beard is gone, John's hair is long, and an upright piano is present. The proceedings were definitely filmed, and even though Ringo Starr was supposed to be filming *The Magic Christian*, he is there.

A DVD and Blu-ray release of the series was set for February 8, 2022, in the States and February 28 in Europe. It was then delayed until May 27, then to December 31 (an odd date to release anything), and then to January 2023. Various reports have indicated that ether the 5.1 or stereo mix was not working. The Beatles official store indicated the set would ship in July 2022, yet the Beatles Twitter feed has stated: "Hello All—We had a technical and supply chain issue with our 'The Beatles: Get Back' Blu-ray & DVD. We're sorry for the delay. We look forward to sharing a new release date soon." Any copies that were available from the few that had leaked out were going for as high as $1,000. Some fans and Beatle pundits have suggested there are no technical problems with the set, but that Disney has reconsidered how to package it. The original set planned for release had no bonus material, aside from four collector's cards. On May 17, the news was that the DVD and Blu-ray of the *Get Back* series, would be released on July 12. On July 13, 2022, the Emmy Awards were announced. The *Get Back* series received five nominations for Outstanding Documentary or Nonfiction Series, Outstanding Directing for a Documentary/Nonfiction Program, Outstanding Picture Editing for a Nonfiction Program, Outstanding Sound Mixing for a Nonfiction or Reality Program (Single or Multi-Camera), and Outstanding Sound Mixing for a Nonfiction or Reality Program (Single or Multi-Camera). But, for home viewers, or even as a theatrical release, the *Let It Be* film is still not available.

Michael Lindsay-Hogg told the author about interaction he had with Peter Jackson while he was making *Get Back*:

> Over the long editing period, he'd occasionally ask a question like, "Do you have any idea what was happening on Day 5? I can't figure it out," and sometimes I'd get an enthusiastic link, showing me a bit which he thought worked well or when he'd found

an extra implement in his tool box to solve a technical problem. I had a picture of him in my imagination, barefooted—favorite shoes are no shoes—with wires coming out of a large machine connected to wires coming out of his head. He developed something I wish we'd had in 1969. Our recording system was pretty primitive, but in 2021 he found a way to separate the vocal part of a recording from the ambient noise or guitar playing underneath.

Lindsay-Hogg talked about the famous scene in the cafeteria where we hear John and Paul talking: "I bugged the flower pot at lunch that day. I thought, correctly, that George might quit, but when I played the tape back after, all I got was muffled Beatles but plenty of the scraping of cutlery and murmuring ambient conversation and laughter from the pub in the next room. But, with what Peter came up with, he was able to create that wonderful scene in *Get Back* with Paul and John talking clearly about how they'd treated George over the years, with just images of the flower vase on the table." Hogg had nothing but praise for Jackson:

> There were a couple of things I couldn't or didn't put in *Let It Be*, which Peter was able to use in *Get Back*. I thought he told a long and complicated story with diligence and insight and kindness to all. From the moment I met Peter in January 2020 in Los Angeles, I really straight out liked him. He's good humored with an enthusiastic brain which works at a rapid pace. He asked me to tell him the "story" of *Let It Be*, and, as I got to the end, which was about The Beatles having broken up just before its release and how I was dealing myself with United Artists, since no one else was, he said, "So except for you, *Let It Be* was really an orphan." It was but I'd never heard that particular word applied to it before, and I knew then that Peter had another quality—empathy.

Beginning March 18, 2022, and running through March 2023, the Rock & Roll Hall of Fame would run an immersive exhibit related to *The Beatles: Get Back* that included high-definition film clips, audio, original musical instruments (including John Lennon's 1965 Epiphone Casino guitar), handwritten lyrics, and clothing worn by the Beatles, supplied by Paul McCartney, Ringo Starr, and the estates of George Harrison and John Lennon.

The music of the Beatles would continue to have an enormous influence long after they broke up. Whether it would be the solo albums the group released or how other groups and artists continued to be influenced by the innovative music of the group or the rich and peerless compositional legacy of Lennon and McCartney and also ultimately, George Harrison.

For several years, the center of the youth culture and groundbreaking moviemaking had been drifting back from England to America. While England and America would both contribute equally to pop and rock music at varying times, America would have a film renaissance in the 1970s that has yet to be eclipsed and may stand as the last golden era of film. Some movies continued to use pop and rock music in new ways while other films contained themes and settings that reflected youth culture and the spirit of the 1960s that imbued American film directors with a sense of rebellion, anarchy, and looking at moviemaking and art from an entirely new perspective. Oddly enough, some of those same influences that shaped 1960s film-making—European films, television, and the auteur theory—also continued. The pop music movie reached its full maturation in the 1970s. Some of the American film directors who would dominate the 1970s and reflect the aforementioned char-acteristics may not have first emerged in the 1970s, but their most acclaimed works did. Those directors include Martin Scorsese, Robert Altman, Francis Ford Coppola, Woody Allen, Hal Ashby, Peter Bogdanovich, Paul Mazursky, Brian DePalma, Alan J. Pakula, Mike Nichols, John Cassavetes, Stanley Kubrick, Sidney Lumet, Roman Polanski, Michael Cimino, George Lucas, Stephen Spielberg, and others.

Some of these directors would use pop and rock music as a key element in their films or even make music movies, including Brian DePalma with *Phantom of the Paradise* in 1974, Australian Jim Sharman with *The Rocky Horror Picture Show* in 1975, Brit Ken Russell with a film adaptation of The Who's *Tommy* in 1975, Robert Altman with *Nashville* in 1975, John Badham with *Saturday Night Fever* in 1977, Martin Scorsese with *The Last Waltz* in 1978, Brit Franc Roddam with the Who's *Quadrophenia* in 1979, Brit Allan Parker with *The Wall* in 1982, Hal Ashby with *Let's Spend the Night Together* in 1983, Jonathan Demme with *Stop Making Sense* in 1984, and Peter Bogdanovich with *Runnin' Down a Dream* in 2007.

Pop and rock musicians would also get involved in films. David Bowie would go on to star in *The Man Who Fell to Earth* in 1976 and continue to work as an actor for decades. Kris Kristofferson's film career, for a short time, eclipsed his music career.

Ringo Starr would have a substantial film career that would include *Candy, The Magic Christian, 200 Motels, Blindman, Born to Boogie, That'll Be the Day, Son of Dracula, Lisztomania, Sextette*, and *Caveman*. Unfortunately, *Caveman* in 1981, al-though a commercial success, had mostly bad or mixed reviews and seemed to stall Starr's acting career other than the odd cameo. However, he did find some lauded work on television, particularly his work for the beloved *Thomas & Friends*, UK children's series between 1984 and 1986.

George Harrison would go on to have a stellar film production career. *The Concert for Bangladesh* film, released in 1972, that chronicled the August 1971 concert at Madison Square Garden to raise funds for refugees, still stands today as a one of the best concert films in rock history. He cofounded Handmade Films in 1978 and the company made such acclaimed and successful films as *Monty Python's Life of Brian, The Long Good Friday, Time Bandits, Mona Lisa*, and *Withnail and I*.

Paul McCartney continued to effectively use promotional films, even longer-form projects. In 1984, the feature film *Give My Regards to Broad Street*, with a screenplay by and starring Paul was released. Linda, Ringo, George Martin, Geoff Emerick,

Barbara Bach, and a host of musicians and A-list actors also appeared in the film. He also reteamed with Richard Lester for the 1991 *Get Back* concert film of McCartney's 1989–1990 world tour. It was announced on July 20, 2022, that the film would be reissued on Blu-ray on August 17. Through the years there would be more concert films along with children's and animated films.

John Lennon would continue on making films, mostly more underground and political films but may have pursued the medium more once he emerged from his "lost weekend" period, had he lived longer.

Denis O'Dell would continue on in films after leaving Apple. Other than the film *The Offense* in 1973, directed by Sidney Lumet, he made five films with Richard Lester. In an interesting note, his last film was the ill-fated *Heaven's Gate* from 1980, directed by Michael Cimino. For many, the film was the critical end of the golden era of American cinema of the 1970s.

The films of the Beatles and, to some degree, the promotional films they were part of would also have an enormous impact in the 1980s on music videos and MTV, but in the near term, those films would have subtle influences on cinema. Beyond how the Beatles affected the pop music film and youth films in general, their contribution to cult films (*Magical Mystery Tour*), adult feature animation (*Yellow Submarine*), and music documentaries (*Let It Be*), almost, but not quite, overshadowed the enormous influence of *A Hard Day's Night*. There would continue to be films and televised projects from the individual Beatles, and the critical and commercial success of the *Anthology* series in 1995 and *Get Back* series in 2021 proved the continued interest in the group's music and how indelible their iconic imagery resonates for new old fans and new generations alike.

A few days before the final submission of this manuscript, on July 20, Peter Jackson told Mike Fleming Jr., co-editor-in-chief, film, of *Deadline* magazine: "I'm talking to the Beatles about another project, something very, very different than *Get Back*. We're seeing what the possibilities are, but it's another project with them. It's not really a documentary . . . and that's all I can really say."

It would appear the long and winding road of the *Get Back/Let It Be* project, and ultimately, the complete end of the Beatles is still nowhere in sight.

Sⴄⴄⴄⴄⴄⴄ Bibⴄⴄⴄⴄⴄⴄⴄⴄ

Sⴄⴄⴄⴄⴄⴄ Bibⴄⴄⴄⴄⴄⴄⴄⴄ

The following selected bibliography includes the primary sources used in the research for this book. Some of these books were the foundation of the text and others were useful in varying degrees or helpful in the background understanding of various subtopics. The bibliography in no way constitutes all of the book-related background research used for this project. Articles from a variety of media, interviews and personal and professional conversations over the years and specifically during the research and writing of this book, were also helpful. A wide variety of visual and aural materials, specifically related to the music and films covered and other ancillary media, also were very helpful. Except for a couple of books, all of the books listed in the bibliography are from the author's personal library.

BEATLES MOVIES

Axelrod, Mitch. *Beatletoons: The Real Story Behind the Cartoon Beatles.* South Carolina: Pickens, 1999.

Barrow, Tony. *The Making of the Beatles' Magical Mystery Tour.* New York: Omnibus, 1999.

———. *John, Paul, George, Ringo & Me: The Real Beatles Story.* New York: Thunder's Mouth Press, 2005.

Brodax, Al. *Up Periscope Yellow: The Making of the Beatles' Yellow Submarine.* New York: Limelight Editions, 2004.

Bron, Eleanor. *The Pillow Book of Eleanor Bron.* London: Metheun, 1985.

Carr, Roy. *Beatles at the Movies: Stories and Photographs from Behind the Scenes at All Five Films.* New York: HarperPerennial, 1996.

Di Franco, J. Phillip. *A Hard Day's Night.* New York: Chelsea House Publishers, 1977.

Glynn, Stephen. *A Hard Day's Night.* New York: I. B. Tauris, 2005.

Gross, Edward. *Fab Films of the Beatles*. Las Vegas: Pioneer Books, 1990.

Harry. Bill. *Beatlemania: The History of the Beatles on Film, Vol. 4 (Beatles Series)*. London: Virgin Books, 1984.

Hieronimus, Robert R. *Inside the Yellow Submarine: The Making of the Beatles' Animated Classic*. Iola, WI: Krause, 2002.

Hieronimus, Robert R., and Laura E. Cortner. *It's All in the Mind: Inside the Beatles' Yellow Submarine, Vol. 2*. Owings Mills, MD: Hieronimus and Co., Inc., 2021.

Lari, Emilio. *The Beatles Photographs from the Set of* Help! New York: Rizzoli, 2015.

Lewisohn, Mark. *The Beatles* A Hard Day's Night*: A Private Archive*. New York: Phaidon Press, 2016.

Morton, Ray. A Hard Day's Night *(Music on Film)*. Montclair, NJ: Limelight Editions, 2011.

Neaverson. Bob. *The Beatles Movies*. London: Cassell, 1997.

O'Dell, Denis. *At the Apple's Core: The Beatles from the Inside*. London: Peter Owens, 2002.

Reiter, Roland. *The Beatles on Film*. New Brunswick, NJ Transcript, 2008.

Rolston, Lorraine, and Andy Murray. A Hard Day's Night*: The Ultimate Film Guide*. London: York, 2001.

Skellett, Paul, Simon Weitzman, and Simon Well. *Eight Arms to Hold You (50 Years of* Help!*)*. Woolbridge, Suffolk: ACC Editions, 2017.

Spinetti, Victor. *Up Front: His Strictly Confidential Autobiography*. London: Robson, 2006.

Yule, Andrew. *The Man Who Framed the Beatles*. New York: Donald I. Fine, 1994.

MOVIES

Austen, James. *TV A Go Go*. Chicago: Chicago Review Press. 2005.

Balio, Tino. *United Artists: The Company that Changed the Film Industry*. Madison: University of Wisconsin Press,. 1987.

Betrock, Alan. *I Was a Teenage Juvenile Delinquent Rock 'n' Roll Horror Beach Party Movie Book: A Complete Guide to the Teen Exploitation Film: 1954–1969*. New York: St. Martin's Press, 1986.

Bramley, Gareth, Geoff Leonard, and Pete Walker. *John Barry: A Life in Music*. Bristol: Sansom and Company, 1998.

Brode, Douglas. *The Films of the Sixties*. Secaucus, NJ: Citadel, 1980.

Brunsdon, Charlotte. *London in Cinema*. London: BFI, 2007.

Burlingame, Jon. *The Music of James Bond*. New York: Oxford University Press, 2012.

Cardullo, Bert, ed. *Michelangelo Antonioni Interviews*. Jackson: University Press of Mississippi, 2008.

Chapman, Seymour and Paul Duncan, eds. *Michelangelo Antonioni The Complete Films*. Los Angeles: Taschen, 2008.

Crenshaw, Marshall. *Hollywood Rock*. New York: HarperPerennial, 1994.

Donnelly K. J. *Pop Music in British Cinema*. London: BFI Publishing, 2001.

Glynn, Stephen. *The British Pop Music Film*. London: Palgrave/Macmillan, 2013.

Halliwell's Filmgoer's and Video Viewer's Companion, 9th ed. New York: Charles Scribner's Sons, 1988.

James, David E. *Rock 'n' Film*. New York: Oxford University Press, 2016.

Jastfelder, Frank, and Stefan Kassel. *The Album Cover Art of Soundtracks*. New York: Little Brown, 1997.

Kael, Pauline. *Going Steady*. New York: Marion Boyars, 2009.

Kubernik, Harvey. *Docs That Rock, Music That Matters*. Los Angeles: Otherworld Cottage Industries, 2020.

Murphy, Robert. *Sixties British Cinema*. London: BFI/Palgrave, 1992.

Nourmand, Tony, and Graham Marsh. *Film Posters of the 60s: The Essential Movies of the Decade*. New York: Overlook, 1997.

Romney, Jonathan, and Adrian Wooton, eds. *Celluloid Jukebox*. London: British Film Institute, 1995.

Sandahl, Linda J. *Rock Films*. New York: Facts on File, 1987.

Sikov, Ed. *Mr. Strangelove*. New York: Hyperion, 2002.

Soderbergh, Steven. *Getting Away with It*. London: Faber & Faber, 1999.

Spencer, Kristopher. *Film and Television Scores, 1950–1979*. Jefferson, NC: McFarland and Company, 2008.

Strong, Martin C., and Brendon Griffin. *Lights, Camera, Soundtracks*. Edinburgh: Canongate, 2008.

Walker, Alexander. *Hollywood, England*. London: Harrap, 1974.

GET BACK/LET IT BE

Barrell, Tony. *The Beatles on the Roof*. New York: Omnibus, 2017.

Doggett, Peter. *Abbey Road/Let It Be (Classic Rock Albums)*. New York: Schirmer, 1998.

Get Back. New York: Callaway, 2021.

Goodman, Fred. *Allen Klein*. Boston: Mariner, 2015.

Heylin, Clinton. *Bootleg: The Secret History of the Other Recording History*. New York: St. Martin's Press, 1994.

Lindsay-Hogg, Michael. *Luck and Circumstance*. New York: Knopf, 2011.

Mansfield, Ken. *The Roof*. Nashville: Post Hill Press, 2018.

McNab, Ken. *And in the End*. New York: Thomas Dunne Books, 2019.

Spizer, Bruce. *The Beatles Finally Let It Be*. New Orleans: 498 Productions, 2020.

Sulpy, Doug. *Get Back*. New York: St. Martin's Press, 1997.

BEATLES DISCOGRAPHY

Belmer, Scott "Belmo". *The Beatles Artifacts*. Ft. Mitchell, KY: Belmo Publishing, 2004.

———. *The Beatles Discovered*. Ft. Mitchell, KY, Belmo Publishing, 2005.

Castleman, Harry, and Walter J. Podrazik. *All Together Now: The First Complete Beatles Discography, 1961–1975*. New York: Ballantine, 1975.

Donnelly, Stephen E. *The Beatles Discography*. Denver: Outskirts Press, 2017.

Dowlding William J. *Beatlesongs*. New York: Fireside, 1989.

Howlett, Kevin. *The Beatles at the Beeb*. London: BBC, 1982.

———. *The Beatles: The BBC Archives: 1962–1970*. New York: Harper Design, 2013.

Iscove, Charles. *The Lost Lennon Tapes Project*. Essential Records: 2009.

Russell, Jeff. *The Beatles: Album File and Complete Discography*. London: Blandford, 1989.

Southall, Brian. *The Beatles Album by Album*. London: Welbeck, 2020.

Spizer, Bruce. *The Beatles Are Coming*. New Orleans: 498 Productions, 2003.

——. *The* Beatles for Sale *on Parlophone Records*. New Orleans: 498 Productions, 2011.

——. *The Beatles on Apple Records*. New Orleans: 498 Productions, 2003.

——. *The Beatles Solo on Apple Records*. New Orleans: 498 Productions, 2005.

——. *The Beatles' Story on Capitol Records*. New Orleans: 498 Productions, 2000.

——. *The Beatles' Story on Capitol Records, Part Two*. New Orleans: 498 Productions, 2000.

——. *Magical Mystery Tour and Yellow Submarine*. New Orleans: 498 Productions, 2021.

Stannard, Neville. *The Long and Winding Road: The History of the Beatles on Record*. New York: Avon, 1984.

Unterberger, Richie. *The Unreleased Beatles*. San Francisco: Backbeat, 2006.

Wallgren, Mark. *The Beatles on Record*. New York: Fireside, 1982.

Wiener Allen J. *The Beatles—The Ultimate Recording Guide*. New York: Facts on File, 1992.

MUSIC OF THE BEATLES

Everett, Walter. *The Beatles as Musicians: The Quarry Men through Rubber Soul*. Oxford: Oxford University Press, 2001.

——. *The Beatles as Musicians:* Revolver *through the* Anthology. Oxford: Oxford University Press, 1999.

McInnerney, Mike, Bill DeMain, and Gillian G. Gaar. *Sgt. Pepper at Fifty*. New York: Sterling, 2017.

Mellers, Wilfrid. *Twilight of the Gods the Music of the Beatles*. New York: Schirmer, 1973.

Skellett, Paul, and Simon Weitzman. *All You Need Is Love*. London: Flood Gallery, 2019.

LYRICS/SONGS OF THE BEATLES

Davies, Hunter. *The Beatles Lyrics*. New York: Little Brown, 2014.

McCartney Paul. *The Lyrics: 1956 to the Present*. New York: Liveright, 2021.

Turner, Steve. *A Hard Day's Write*. New York: Harper Perennial, 1994.

BEATLES GEOGRAPHY

Bacon, David, and Norman Maslov. *The Beatles England*. San Francisco: 910 Press, 1982.

Bedford, David. *Liddypool*. Deerfield, IL: Dalton Watson Fine Books, 2009.

Broadbent, Tony. *The Beatles in Liverpool, Hamburg, London: People, Venues, and Events That Shaped Their Music*. Vallejo, CA: Plain Sight Press, 2018.

Leigh, Spencer. *The Beatles in Liverpool*. Chicago: Chicago Review Press, 2012.

Porter, Richard, David Bedford, and Susan Ryan. *The Beatles Fab Four Cities*. Woolridge, Suffolk: ACC, 2021.

Schreuders Piet, Mark Lewisohn, and Adam Smith. *The Beatles London*, 2nd ed. Northampton, MA: Interlink: 2008.

BEATLES TIMELINE

Carr, Roy, and Tyler, Tony. *The Beatles Illustrated Record*. New York: Harmony Books, 1978.

Frame, Pete. *The Beatles and Some Other Guys*. New York: Omnibus, 1997.

Hill, Tim. *John, Paul, George & Ringo: The Definitive Illustrated Chronicle of the Beatles, 1960–1970—Rare Photographs, Ephemera, and Day-By-Day Timeline*. New York: Metro-Books, 2008.

Lewisohn, Mark. *The Beatles Day by Day*. New York: Harmony, 1990.

———. *The Complete Beatles Chronicle*. New York: Harmony, 1992.

Schultheiss, Tom. *The Beatles: A Day in the Life*. New York: Perigee, 1981.

Wells, Simon. *The Beatles 365 Days*. New York: Harry N. Abrams, 2005.

Winn, John C. *That Magic Feeling*. New York: Three Rivers Press, 2009.

———. *Way Beyond Compare*. New York: Three Rivers Press, 2008.

BEATLES BIOGRAPHY

The Beatles Anthology. San Francisco: Chronicle, 2000.

Braun, Michael. *Love Me Do*. Los Angeles: Graymalkin Media, 1964.

Brown, Craig. *150 Glimpses of the Beatles*. New York: FSG, 2020.

Davies, Hunter. *The Beatles*, 2nd rev. ed. New York: McGraw-Hill, 1985.

Hertsgaard, Mark. *A Day in the Life*. New York: Delacorte Press, 1995.

Kozinn, Allan. *The Beatles*. London: Phaidon, 1995.

Norman, Philip. *Shout! The Beatles in Their Generation*. New York: Fireside, 1981.

Womack, Kenneth. *Long and Winding Road*. New York: Continuum, 2007.

BEATLES ENCYCLOPEDIA/REFERENCE

Badman, Keith. *The Beatles after the Break-up 1970–2000. A Day-by-Day Diary*. New York: Omnibus, 1999.

Harry, Bill. *The Ultimate Beatles Encyclopedia*. New York: Hyperion, 1992.

———. *The Encyclopedia of Beatles People*. London: Blandford, 1997.

Grein, Paul. *Capitol Records Fiftieth Anniversary 1942–1992*. Hollywood: Capitol Records, 1992.

Knight, Judson. *Abbey Road to Zapple Records*. Dallas: Taylor, 1999.

Rodriquez, Robert. *Fab Four FAQ 2.0 The Beatles Solo Years, 1979–1980*. New York: Backbeat, 2010.

Rodriquez, Robert, and Stuart Shea. *Fab Four FAQ*. New York: Hal Leonard, 2007.

WRITINGS ON THE BEATLES

Evans, Mike, ed. *The Beatles. Paperback Writer*. London: Plexus, 2012.

Harry, Bill. *Volume 3: The Beatles: Paperback Writers*. New York: Avon, 1984.

Skinner, Julie. *Read the Beatles*. New York: Penguin, 2006.

Thomson, Elizabeth, and David Gutman, eds. *The Lennon Companion*. New York: Schirmer, 1987.

Womack, Kenneth, and Todd F. Davis, eds. *Reading the Beatles*. Albany: State University of New York Press, 2006.

BEATLES ART/PHOTOGRAPHY

Aldridge, Alan. *The Man with Kaleidoscope Eyes: The Art of Alan Aldridge*. New York: Harry N. Abrams, 2009.

———. *The Beatles Illustrated Lyrics*. Boston: Houghton Mifflin/Seymour Lawrence, 1971.

Babiuk, Andy. *Beatles Gear*. San Francisco: Backbeat, 2001.

Benson, Harry. *The Beatles Now and Then*. New York: Universe, 1998.

———. *Fifty Years in Pictures*. New York: Harry N. Abrams 2001.

———. *Once There Was a Way*. New York: Harry N. Abrams, 2003.

Bonis, Bob. *The Lost Beatles Photographs*. New York: It Books, 2011.

Davis, Andy. *The Beatles Files*. New York: CLB, 1998.

Evans, Mike. *The Art of the Beatles*. New York: Beech Tree Books, 1984.

Freeman, Robert. *Beatles: A Private View*. New York: Big Tent Entertainment, 2003.

———. *Yesterday: The Beatles 1963–1965*. New York: Thunder's Mouth Press, 1983.

Henke, James. *Lennon Legend*. San Francisco: Chronicle Books, 2003.

Hoffman, Dezo. *The Faces of John Lennon*. New York: McGraw-Hill, 1986.

———. *With the Beatles*. New York: Omnibus, 1982.

Russell, Ethan. *Dear Mr. Fantasy*. Boston: Houghton Mifflin, 1985.

Ryal, A. J. S., and Curt Gunther. *Beatles 64: A Hard Day's Night in America*. New York: Doubleday, 1989.

Spencer, Terence. *It Was Twenty Years Ago Today*. New York: Henry Holt and Company, 1994.

Whitaker, Bob. *The Unseen Beatles*. San Francisco: CollinsPublishers, 1991.

BEATLES INTERVIEWS

Badman, Keith. *The Beatles off the Record*. New York: Omnibus Press, 2000.

Iscove, Charles. *The Lost Lennon Tapes Project*. Self-published, 2009.

Muni, Scott, Denny Somach, Kathleen Somach, and Kevin Gunn. *Ticket to Ride*. New York: William Morrow and Company, 1989.

Peebles, Andy. *The Last Lennon Tapes*. New York: Dell, 1981.

The Rolling Stone Interviews 1967–1980. New York: St. Martin's Press/Rolling Stone Press, 1981.

The Rolling Stone Interviews: The 80s. New York: St. Martin's Press/Rolling Stone Press, 1989.

Sheff, David. *The Playboy Interviews*. New York: Playboy Press, 1981.

Wenner, Jan S. *Lennon Remembers*. New York: Verso, 2000.

BEATLES INSIDERS

Asher, Peter. *The Beatles: From A to Zed*. New York: Henry Holt and Company, 2019.

Boyd, Pattie. *Wonderful Tonight!* New York: Harmony Books, 2007.

Bramwell, Tony. *Magical Mystery Tours*. New York: Thomas Dune Books, 2005.

Brown, Peter, and Steven Gaines. *The Love You Make*. New York: Signet, 1983.

DeLillo, Richard. *The Longest Cocktail Party*. New York: Playboy Press, 1972.

Ellis, Geoffrey. *I Should Have Known Better: A Life in Pop Management—The Beatles, Brian Epstein and Elton John*. London: Thorogood, 2005.

Kane, Larry. *Lennon Revealed*. Philadelphia: Running Pres, 2015.

———. *Ticket to Ride*. Philadelphia: Running Press, 2003.

———. *When They Were Boys*. Philadelphia: Running Press, 2013.

Miles, Barry. *The Beatles: A Diary*. New York: Omnibus, 2007.

———. *The British Invasion*. New York: Sterling, 2009.

O'Dell, Chris. *Miss O'Dell*. New York: Touchstone, 2009.

Taylor, Derek. *As Time Goes By*. New York: Fireside, 1987.

———. *It Was Twenty Years ago Today*. London: Faber & Faber, 2018.

RECORDING/RECORD LABELS

Abbott, Kingsley, ed. *Little Symphonies: A Phil Spector Reader*. London: Helter Skelter, 2011.

Brown, Mick. *Tearing Down the Wall of Sound*. New York: Alfred. A Knopf, 2007.

Emerick, Geoff. *Here, There and Everywhere*. New York: Gotham, 2006.

Johns, Glyn. *Sound Man*. New York: Blue Rider Press, 2014.

Granados, Stefan. *Those Were the Days: The Beatles and Apple 2.0*. London: Cherry Red, 2021.

Lawrence, Alistair. *Abbey Road: The Best Studio in the World*. New York: Bloomsbury, 2012.

Lewisohn, Mark. *The Complete Beatles Recording Sessions: The Official Story of the Abbey Road Years, 1962–1970*. New York: Harmony Books, 1988.

Martin. George. *All You Need Is Ears: The Inside Personal Story of the Genius Who Created the Beatles*. New York: St. Martin's Press, 1997.

Massey, Howard. *The Great British Recording Studios*. New York: Hal Leonard, 2015.

Miles, Barry. *The Zapple Diaries: The Rise and Fall of the Beatles Last Label*. New York: Abrams Image, 2016.

Ribowsky, Mark. *He's a Rebel*. New York: E. P. Dutton, 1989.

Scott, Ken. *Abbey Road to Ziggy Stardust*. Los Angeles: Alfred, 2012.

Southall, Brian. *The Rise and Fall of EMI Records*. New York: Omnibus, 2009.

Southall, Brian, Peter Vince, and Allan Rouse. *Abbey Road*. New York: Omnibus, 1997.

Thompson, Dave. *The Wall of Pain: The Life of Phil Spector*. London: Sanctuary Encore, 2005.

Williams, Richard. *Phil Spector: Out of His Head*. New York: Omnibus, 2003.

Womack, Kenneth. *Maximum Volume: The Life of Beatles Producer George Martin, The Early Years, 1926–1966*. Chicago: Chicago Review Press, 2017.

———. *Sound Pictures: The Life of Beatles Producer George Martin, The Later Years, 1966–2016*. Chicago: Chicago Review Press, 2018.

BRITISH INVASION

Blaney, John. *Beatles for Sale*. London: Jawbone, 2008.

Buttafav, Umberto, and Enzo Gentile, eds. *Here Come the Beatles: Stories of a Generation*. New York: Skira/Rizzoli, 2008.

Kramer, Billy J. *Do You Want to Know a Secret*. The Autobiography of Billy J. Kramer. Sheffield: Equinox, 2016.

McMillian, John. *Beatles vs. Stones*. New York: Simon & Schuster, 2013.

McAleer, David. *Fab British Rock 'n' Roll Invasion of 1964*. New York: St. Martin's Press, 1994.

Philo, Simon. *British Invasion: The Crosscurrents of Musical Influence*. New York: Rowman & Littlefield, 2015.

Schaffner, Nicholas. *Beatles Forever*. New York: McGraw-Hill, 1978.

———. *The British Invasion: From the First Wave to the New Wave*. New York: McGraw-Hill, 1983.

Viner, Harriet. *Groovy Bob: The Life and Times of Robert Fraser*. London: Faber & Faber, 2001.

LONDON/ENGLAND

Bacon, Tony. *London Live*. San Francisco: Miller Freeman Books, 1999.

Davies, Hunter. *The New London Spy*. New York: David White, 1966.

Du Noyer, Paul. *In the City*. UK: Virgin, 2010.

Frame, Pete. *Rockin' around Britain*. New York: Omnibus, 1999.

Levin, Bernard. *Run It Down the Flagpole*. New York: Atheneum, 1971.

Levy, Shawn. *Ready, Steady, Go!* New York: Doubleday, 2002.

Melly, George. *Revolt into Style: The Pop Arts in Britain*. New York: Penguin, 1972.

Miles, Barry. *London Calling*. London: Atlantic, 2010.

Neill, Andy. *Ready, Steady, Go!* New York: BMG, 2020.

Neville, Richard. *Hippie Hippie Shake*. London: Bloomsbury, 1995.

Sandbrook, Dominic. *Never Had It So Good: A History of Britain from Suez to the Beatles 1956–63*. London: Abacus, 2005.

Sinclair, Andrew. *In Love and Anger*. London: Sinclair-Stevenson, 1994.

Tow, Stephen. *London, Reign over Me*. Lanham, MD: Rowman & Littlefield, 2020.

Whitcomb, Ian. *Rock Odyssey: A Musicians Chronicle of the Sixties*. Garden City, NY: Doubleday, 1983.

Woolridge, Max. *Rock 'n' Roll London*. New York: St. Martin's Press, 2002.

Worden, Mark, and Alfredo Marziano. *Swinging London*. Gloucestershire: Ambereley, 2021.

PSYCHEDELIA

Babbs, Ken, and Paul Perry. *On the Bus*. New York: Thunder's Mouth Press, 1990.

Bisbort, Alan, and Parke Puterbaugh. *Rhino's Psychedelic Trip*. San Francisco: Miller Freeman, 2000.

Green, Jonathan. *Days in the Life*. London: Pimlico, 1998.

Greenfield, Robert. *Timothy Leary*. New York: Harcourt, 2006.

Henke, James, Charles Perry, and Barry Miles. *I Want to Take You Higher: The Psychedelic Era, 1965–1969 (Rock & Roll Hall of Fame & Museum)*. San Francisco: Chronicle, 1997.

Jack, Richard Morton. *Psychedelia*. New York: Sterling, 2017.

Leary, Timothy, Ralph Metzner, and Richard Alpert. *The Psychedelic Experience*. New York: Citadel, 1995.

Miles, Barry. *Hippie*. New York: Sterling, 2004.

Roberts, Andy. *Divine Rascal*. London: Strange Attractor Press, 2019.

FICTION

Burke, John. *A Hard Day's Night* (novelization). New York: Dell, 1964.

Fabian, Jenny and Johnny Byrne. *Groupie*. New York: Omnibus, 1997.

Hine, Al. *Help!* (novelization). New York: Dell, 1965.

Norman, Philip. *Everyone's Gone to the Moon*. New York: Random House, 1995.

Orton, Joe. *Up Against It*. New York: Grove Press, 1979.

Wilk, Max. *The Beatles Yellow Submarine* (novelization). New York: New American Library, 1968.

Index